I0797932

PHILIP JENKINS

KINGDOMS *OF THIS* WORLD

HOW EMPIRES HAVE MADE AND REMADE RELIGIONS

BAYLOR UNIVERSITY PRESS

Waco, Texas 76798

Cover and book design by Ely Encarnación
Cover image: Cover art: (Map) J. C. R. (John Charles Ready) Colomb, "Imperial Federation, map of the world showing the extent of the British Empire in 1886" (London: MacClure & Co., 1886), housed at the Norman B. Leventhal Map & Education Center at the Boston Public Library, https://collections.leventhalmap.org/search/commonwealth:x633f896s. (Background) Pexels/Dan Cristian Pădureț.

Library of Congress Cataloging-in-Publication Data

Names: Jenkins, Philip, 1952- author.
Title: Kingdoms of this world : how empires have made and remade religions / Philip Jenkins.
Description: Waco : Baylor University Press, 2024. | Includes bibliographical references and index. | Summary: "Provides an extensive historical and sociological analysis of the interactions between religions and empires from the ancient world to the present"-- Provided by publisher.
Identifiers: LCCN 2023050023 (print) | LCCN 2023050024 (ebook) | ISBN 9781481319935 (hardcover) | ISBN 9781481319966 (adobe pdf) | ISBN 9781481319959 (epub)
Subjects: LCSH: Religion and state. | Imperialism--Religious aspects.
Classification: LCC BL65.S8 J455 2024 (print) | LCC BL65.S8 (ebook) | DDC 322/.1--dc23/eng/20240404
LC record available at https://lccn.loc.gov/2023050023
LC ebook record available at https://lccn.loc.gov/2023050024

To Leila and Diana

Contents

Acknowledgments

Major thanks to Timothy Larsen for support and encouragement. Thanks also to Kathryn Hume for valuable early advice on the structure of this project and for reading the final manuscript.

Not for the first time, I offer my warm thanks to the supportive editors and staff at Baylor University Press, who have been such a pleasure to work with.

Note on Dates and Places

I have throughout used the familiar BC/AD dating system. The problem with this is that, of course, it is a Christian-derived framework that relies on the supposed dating of the birth of Christ, and Anno Domini is "the Year of the Lord." Many writers prefer to avoid this usage by deploying the more neutral CE and BCE, which refers to the Common Era, and I have regularly used that myself. The problem with "CE" is that the Common Era is identical with the Christian pattern and equally depends on the same (probably inaccurate) dating for Jesus' birth.

In any kind of global or transnational study, place names are considerably more difficult, and potentially controversial. Using a modern national name gives the reader an excellent sense of the setting of a particular story, but it can be very anachronistic, and on occasion, it can even support undesirable nationalist ideologies or contested territorial claims. When describing the area around Java and Borneo in ancient or medieval times, we should be careful about using a term such as "Indonesia," which was not invented until the nineteenth century, for a state that was not created until 1949. Generally in such cases, I will use a phrase such as "the regions that we today would call" Indonesia, or Ukraine, or whichever example might arise; but I might slip.

Introduction

> The Papacy is no other than the ghost of the deceased Roman Empire, sitting crowned upon the grave thereof: for so did the Papacy start up on a sudden out of the ruins of that heathen power.
>
> ***Thomas Hobbes***

When Thomas Hobbes analyzed the roots of the Roman Catholic Church in 1651, he was making a polemical point designed to expose the non- and indeed anti-Christian nature of that institution, but in fact, he made an excellent case for historical continuity. The Papacy had indeed inherited many of the symbols and titles of the old pagan empire. Moreover, Hobbes continued, "the language also which they use, both in the churches and in their public acts, being Latin, which is not commonly used by any nation now in the world, what is it but the ghost of the old Roman language?"[1] His comment points to an enduring truth in the rise and spread of great religions, and by no means only of the branches of Christianity. Repeatedly through history, we find a close linkage between world faiths and successive empires. The world's religious history can scarcely be understood except in reference to those imperial realities and their stubborn survivals.

A map of Christian populations today indicates the persistence of multiple imperial ghosts. The great centers owe their origins to various Christian empires over the past half millennium: the Spanish, Portuguese, French, Belgian, British, and others. Within those empires, many people moved voluntarily, as settlers and colonists. Others were conquered or enslaved, and (at least initially) had new religious systems imposed upon them, although over time, those conquered peoples made the religion their own. Crudely, this is the story of how a religion that in 1500 was overwhelmingly Europe-centered became by the end of the millennium a vast transcontinental enterprise. The world's largest Roman Catholic communities today are found in Brazil, Mexico, and the Philippines, recalling the influence of the long-defunct empires of Spain and Portugal. Soon, the Democratic Republic of Congo, the old Belgian Congo, will be counted among that elite of Catholic nations. The Anglican Communion likewise, with some ninety million believers worldwide, retains the unmistakable imprint of the old British Empire. In each case, such survivals go beyond the mere fact of geographical presence and are evident in the political traditions and structures of the respective religions, in their languages and forms of communication.[2]

Although the papal analogies are not exact, the ecumenical patriarch of Constantinople is still first among equals in the hierarchy of the Orthodox Christian world. He is based in a city that has not had a significant Christian population since the 1950s but still retains the aura of the New Rome founded by the Roman emperor Constantine in the fourth century. The present incumbent is the 270th to hold the see. Other later realms have left their mark on Orthodox Christianity. Even today, after so much turmoil and persecution, the lands of the former Russian Empire still account for some 75 percent of the world's Orthodox believers.[3]

But such continuities are in no sense new and can in various ways be traced through the centuries. The Persian Empire left its spectral inheritance, as did various Islamic caliphates and the Ottoman realm, and so did several once-powerful empires in South and Southeast Asia. A map of the lands swiftly conquered by the Arab caliphate during its first century or so of existence—say, by 750 AD—gives an excellent (if not perfect) idea of the heartlands of Islam in the modern world, from Morocco to Pakistan, from the Caucasus to Yemen. Christianity, Islam, Buddhism, and Hinduism alike all reflect successive imperial encounters.

In some cases, the empires favored and promoted religious communities, while in others, populations and faiths were conditioned by reactions against intruding foreign powers, by what we might term "empire shock." Much of modern Islamic history can be written in terms of the response to European imperial advances across Asia and Africa. By 1914, indeed, the overwhelming majority of the world's Muslims lived under the rule of one or other of the European empires, and the destruction of the Ottoman Empire during the First World War threatened to reduce that independence still further. Modern political Islamism grew out of attempts to reconstruct the faith to respond to those successive traumas. Judaism, too, has been reshaped by encounters with successive imperial frameworks, whether benevolent or hostile.[4]

Empires are an inescapable component in the making, remaking, and rethinking of the world's faiths. To varying degrees, all those religions exist in what we might call a postimperial environment. A global history of the world faiths is of necessity an imperial history.

How Empires Remake Religions

The reasons for those imperial connections are more complex than they might at first appear. In some cases, empires demanded that their subjects conform to an official faith, or at least they strongly favored churches or institutions, for instance, by supporting missionary endeavors. But such preferential treatment goes only some way to explaining the religious maps. In some cases, religions grew and spread despite the militant opposition of the imperial regimes that exercised political control over given territories: Christianity in the ancient Roman world is the obvious example. Time and again, we witness the unintended consequences of imperial decisions and edicts.

What mattered was less the official attitude of any particular empire than the conditions those entities created to maintain their rule. These would include efficient means of communication by land and sea; new trade routes, and the cities that grew from them, which became entrepôts for commodities and ideas; the widespread military establishments that defended imperial frontiers; the maintenance of public order; and the suppression of threats to travel and trade. Of their nature, empires brought together different peoples and ethnic groups who otherwise would have remained ignorant of each other's existence: empires do an excellent job of moving subjects, often against their will. To use a concept now popular in political analysis, empires turned many communities of locally rooted Somewheres into highly mobile Anywheres, with all that implied for values and ideology. Crucially, the new imperial orders promoted common languages of communication, and often some degree of literacy and written communication. In 1896, the Hindu reformer Swami Vivekananda declared, appreciatively, "This British Empire with all its drawbacks is the greatest machine that ever existed for the dissemination of ideas." Beyond extending the boundaries of faiths, that imperial context transformed the ideas that were, and are, communicated, as religions restructured their messages for a new and larger world, and for citizens of that world—"cosmopolitans." Hobbes' remarks on the Papacy point to by no means the only example of a religious institution appropriating imperial ideology and iconography. Such continuities are frequently reflected in the visual arts.[5]

Whatever the wishes of any given regime, it was this "empire-ness" that allowed the rise and circulation of religious traditions and beliefs. As in the case of Rome, many of those features persisted after the formal regimes were destroyed, leaving behind only phantoms, but very potent ones. Imperial memories die hard, often astonishingly so. However often, and however rightly, we denounce the evils associated with empires—their links to racism and slavery, exploitation and colonialism—those realms are an essential part of the move toward transcontinental and globalized religious structures.[6]

To be clear, I do not mean that religious developments happened to occur at the time that a particular empire existed (or was rising or falling), nor did they result from globalization or from cross-cultural contacts broadly defined. Rather, the trends or movements that I will discuss happened in the way that they did because of the characteristics of empires and the resulting dynamics. They were products or outcomes of the nature of empire. Understanding empires—what they are, how they operate, and their broad commonalities—is essential to advancing our knowledge of religions, and of religion in general. That imperial dimension affects how religions grow or shrink over time, the opportunities and constraints open to them, and even how they are defined as religions.

Empires in History

Historically, empires have been commonplace, to the point of being, for large parts of the human experience, a standard and normal form of political organization. Understanding those quite diverse structures is fundamental to any attempt at writing global or transnational history.[7]

When we think today of empires, the images that come most readily to mind stem from a classic age between, say, the sixteenth century and the mid-twentieth, the time of the great European overseas ventures. In popular memory, the British Empire is by far the most significant, which is reasonable in terms of its immense geographical sweep: at its height, it ruled roughly a quarter of the planetary surface, and a quarter of its people. But other factors also apply. Because of the prevalence of the English language, that empire and its history are easily accessible to readers and researchers in the Western world. The British imperial story has become a standard feature of modern-day cinema, television, and literature, from *Gunga Din* and *Gandhi* to adaptations of E. M. Forster and Paul Scott. Few histories of empire resist the temptation to quote the poems and stories of Rudyard Kipling or the novels of Joseph Conrad, and the present work will be no exception. Even the musical *Hamilton* concerns a colonial revolt against that same British dominion and the creation of a postimperial successor state. At least among nonspecialists, that British emphasis often conditions perceptions of empire and its implications.[8]

Far less familiar than the British are the experiences of other key nations, such as the French, Dutch, Spanish, and Portuguese, although in those cases too, notable imperial-focused novels, films, and works of art abound. Portugal pioneered the European expansion in the late fifteenth century, and the country's national epic is the *Lusiads* of Luís Vaz de Camões (1572), which mythologizes that country's encounter with India and the East. In the past century, that mythology was given physical form in the huge sculptures of Lisbon's Monument to the Discoveries, one of the country's most spectacular tourist sites. The Netherlands created an empire that at various points extended its power into North and South America and the Caribbean, as well as Africa and South Asia, and especially the East Indies. It was this last region that gave the setting for the searing denunciation of imperial exploitation in the novel *Max Havelaar* (1860), the greatest work of Dutch fiction.[9] In his classic study, *Orientalism*, the scholar Edward Said showed how frequently such imperial-derived images of non-European cultures and peoples appeared in literature and music of many Western lands, especially in the nineteenth century. Westerners saw the East through a "colonial gaze." Even that most English of genres, the country-house whodunit, traces its origins to Wilkie Collins' *The Moonstone* (1868), which is saturated in themes of imperial war and plunder, and wild Orientalist stereotypes.[10]

That picture of the "age of empire" requires some qualification. Modern images of empire usually emphasize European and racial supremacy, of white nations governing nonwhites, however we define those malleable terms. The classic vision imagines a pith-helmeted European being carried in a litter by faithful African or Asian natives. But some of the greatest empires did not span the oceans in anything like the British or French sense and rather ruled over extensive neighboring territories, yet they still very much held that imperial character. These were land empires. The Austro-Hungarian Empire ruled by the Habsburg dynasty until 1918 was one teeming and diverse example, although, in our modern sense, it represented the rule of white elites over other white European populations. Language, ethnicity, and religion all played a role in delineating power and privilege, but nothing like what we would call "race." (I will for present purposes set aside any discussion of the term "whiteness"). Imperial encounters and multicultural complexities are essential to writings of such towering figures of European literature as Joseph Roth. Germany offers another example. When in 1871 the Prussian king extended his power over most of later Germany, he was proclaimed the *Kaiser* (caesar) of a new empire, the Second Reich, which was as thoroughly white and European as the Habsburg realm before it. Only in later decades did that German Empire expand its power into Africa, Asia, and Oceania.[11]

The Russian Empire likewise projected its power (mainly) over land rather than sea, subjugating vast swathes of land dominated by non-Slavic and non-Christian peoples and fighting countless border conflicts and colonial wars across Central Asia and the Caucasus. It was Russia, indeed, that undertook the most successful expansion by any European power in the nineteenth century, acquiring some 1.5 million square miles of new territory. Of the ten largest cities in the Russian Empire in 1900, all but Moscow and St. Petersburg were located in territories that had been conquered since the mid-eighteenth century, which today we call Poland, Ukraine, Georgia, and the Baltic states. Those struggles, and the imperial dreams they represented, fascinated the country's writers and cultural figures, some of whom had participated personally in these military ventures. The Caucasus occupied a role in Russian culture comparable to the western and southwestern borderlands in US thought or to India's northwest frontier for the British. This was the setting for novels by such venerated figures as Alexander Pushkin and Mikhail Lermontov. The literary career of Leo Tolstoy began and ended with works arising from his own experiences on the turbulent borderlands of empire, in Russia's "Wild South," most famously in his novella *Hadji Murat*. Yet the Russian experience so rarely counts in the Western popular consciousness alongside those other European imperial projects.[12]

That age of empires was by no means only a European affair. If we just look at the early modern period, China was a mighty realm, indeed, the world's most powerful and, at times, the wealthiest, and other far-flung realms included the Mughal and Ottoman Empires. There were also plenty of regional examples such as Ethiopia, Vietnam, and the enormous Sokoto Caliphate of nineteenth-century West Africa. In most cases, the expanding European empires were invading and annexing those other preexisting empires, Aztec, Mughal, Ottoman, Vietnamese, and others. For most of their subjects, the coming of the Europeans did not mean accepting an unprecedented foreign yoke but rather shifting allegiance to new masters. The older overlords, meanwhile, who now found themselves reduced to subject status, commonly suffered deep social and cultural traumas, which sparked movements for fundamental reconstruction. I will often return to the religious consequences of what I have termed those moments of empire shock.

Nor of course were empires any novelty in that era. In ancient and medieval times, we think of Alexander's Greek Empire and its sprawling successor states, as well as Rome, Sasanian Persia, the Islamic caliphate, and the Mongol realm. In terms of their territorial extent, some of the very largest empires in history were the Eurasian realms of the nomadic Scythians, Xiongnu, Uighurs, the Turkic Khaganate, and others that remain quite unknown to nonspecialists.[13]

Children of Empire

Beyond making our world, the imperial experience wrote our family histories. If we just focus on the "high imperial noon" of European empires in the nineteenth century, we understand how thoroughly the structures and deeds of those states shaped the experience of virtually all Africans and most Asians, and their modern descendants. Perforce, that would include the great majority of the world's Hindus and Muslims. But if we shift the chronology somewhat, the same is true of North Americans or Europeans. Whatever one's ethnic or racial identity, whatever passport one carries, our ancestors belonged to some empire or other, whether as rulers or ruled, or successively one and then the other. In some cases, these were distant ancestors, and in others, we are speaking of our parents.

That is obviously true of residents of such countries as Britain or France, but we might take an American example. The ancestors of many millions of modern white Americans arrived during the surging wave of immigration between 1880 and 1924. Most of them had formerly been subjects of one of the great continental land empires, the Russian, German, or Austro-Hungarian: that was certainly the case with most of the country's Jewish migrants. Irish immigrants arrived from a vital but deeply resentful corner of the British Empire. Italians who arrived in the 1890s stood only a generation away from the liberation war that had detached the country from Habsburg rule, and at a time when the new Italy was seeking to build its own empire in north and east Africa. The Chinese who arrived in nineteenth-century California were subjects of the imperial Qing dynasty. Most Black Americans are descended from an enslaved population imported in their millions on the ships of multiple European empires, by no means only the British.

In countless surprising details, bygone empires still shape our maps of the world. It was the political and economic needs of multiple European empires that created the labels by which we classify so many different regions, which now seem so inevitable, for instance, such classifications as the Middle East, Black Africa, the Maghreb, "the Indies" (East and West), and arguably, even "Asia" itself. Commonly, those invented labels were accepted and internalized by the peoples of those regions themselves.[14]

Also strictly contemporary are the economic reverberations. In 1973, the world's dominant economies organized as the G7, the Group of Seven: the United States, Japan, Germany, France, Britain, Italy, and Canada. With the exception of the last, that represents a list of the world's most ambitious imperial powers as they existed in 1914, while Canada itself was a recent imperial possession. Although the global economic balance has shifted since that era, that older world is not quite extinct. Since 2000, experts have identified various rising and emerging economies that promise to match or overtake the familiar Euro-American leaders by 2050 or so. Alongside the traditional developed world are now a series of rising nations, grouped under catchy acronyms. The original list named the BRICs (Brazil, Russia, India, China and, later, South Africa) but other (overlapping) contenders include the MINTS (Malaysia, Indonesia, Nigeria, Turkey, South Africa), and the KIMs (South Korea, Indonesia, Mexico). Besides the obvious rich nations of the Global North, the current roster of G20 nations includes a dozen or so of these "inbetweener" names as rising global contenders. None of those nations can be understood historically without a firm grounding in the history of empire and empires. Some of those states were themselves great empires in their own right—Russia, China, and Turkey are the obvious examples—or else they formed part of one or other of the mighty imperial systems. Others owe their national existence and identity to the intervention of foreign empires. In other cases still, their political orders are defined by the elites that emerged in the struggle against empire. Each of these powers is shaped by its historical memories. If the British have forgotten the Opium Wars of the 1840s, the Chinese emphatically have not. We are all postcolonial or postimperial, even if not all of us acknowledge it.[15]

Why the History of Empires Matters

Imperial dimensions feature prominently in contemporary historical research and writing. Any study of ancient Western history must centrally address the Roman world system, and scholars of Asia cannot avoid studying the successive empires and dynasties of China, India, and Central Asia. But such approaches are essential to much more modern periods. The study of empires is a booming academic field in Britain and such former Commonwealth nations as Canada and Australia and is well represented in Continental European scholarship. Courses on empires and imperialism, on comparative empires, and on colonialism, proliferate in major universities around the world. So do areas of emphasis in research and teaching in history departments. US historians are increasingly aware of their own country's record as an aggressive and successful imperial power, which projected its power into the Pacific and the Caribbean. Those insights permeate literary scholarship.[16]

The impact of such intense concern is evident in many diverse eras and topics. In his book *Blood and Ruins*, Richard Overy analyzes the Second World War as the Great Imperial War of 1931–1945, an era of clashing imperial visions and aspirations (and nightmares). In consequence, Overy is almost literally describing a different planet from what we find in most other current books on this conflict, with their North Atlantic and European obsessions.[17]

The role of empires is now recognized as pivotal in many scholarly disciplines and fields of study. Modern studies of the history of science recount how transcontinental discoveries and observations demanded a total rethinking of natural history and classification. Similar statements can be made about the history of medicine.[18] In many eras, imperial administrators sought to define, map, and quantify the resources of their possessions, and in the process they revolutionized the scientific methods they were applying, while simultaneously creating new social and geographical realities in those territories. Mapping, counting, and drawing borders have often created divisions and conflicts where none existed before. Empires are no less central to the burgeoning field of the history of climate and environment. Often, changing climatic circumstances have conditioned the rise and fall to empires. Empires in turn have had a prodigious role in reshaping the environment, through their decisions on land use, food production, forest clearance, land reclamation, and the use of waterways. Through moving people, and the diseases they carry, empires have shaped global demographic patterns. For present purposes, as we will often see, when those people travel, they carry their gods with them.[19]

Repeatedly, human empires have promoted global conquests by other species. Such biological consequences can be hard to recognize precisely because they have been so thoroughly absorbed into new societies, and so acclimatized. Just to take a seemingly trivial example, we are well used to the near-universal presence of the domestic cat, but that animal has a distinctly imperial history. Domesticated cats spread from the Levant to Italy in the mid-first millennium BC, and their farther expansion across Europe correlates excellently with the later growth of the Roman Empire. The later Spanish and Portuguese Empires supplied the means for cats to reach the Americas, along with horses. That was only part of a larger story of biological conquest. In the case of Britain, the Romans introduced some fifty species of fruits and vegetables, as well as such familiar animals as rabbits: all became an integral part of the rural landscape.[20]

Later empires spread many other species across their possessions, and in the process they utterly transformed economies, cultures, and environments. Mesoamerican societies pioneered the use of rubber, which successive empires developed as a highly lucrative cash crop, as production spread to South and Southeast Asia and Central Africa. Our food worlds are also imperial legacies. From their new American conquests, the Spanish brought such later staples of the European diet as the potato and tomato. Likewise from the New World were chili peppers, which Portuguese traders then carried to Asia, making possible the spicy cuisines of Korea and India. A comparable traffic ran from the Old World to the New, as European empires sought fertile new areas in which to plant desired crops. Both the Dutch and French introduced and cultivated coffee in their respective possessions in Java and the Caribbean. Although tea was available across much of eastern Asia, with a strong Chinese focus, it was the nineteenth century British Empire that created the very profitable tea industry in its South Asian possessions, in Assam, Darjeeling, and Sri Lanka. When the British sent a fleet of convicts to create a new Australian colony in 1788, the ships carried vines for planting, and wine production boomed both in Australia and New Zealand. Empires set our tables.[21]

Mixed Realities

So rich is contemporary scholarship on empire, and so diverse, that it is difficult to highlight particular motifs, but some examples should be stressed, as they will feature so frequently in the present book. Traditionally, the literature on empire tended to assume a binary opposition between rulers and ruled, colonizers and colonized, which was sometimes framed in simplistic terms of light and darkness, day and night: empires shed light in heathen or Oriental darkness. Such visions shaded readily into racial dichotomies of white and black.

For some decades now, such interactions have rather been understood in nuanced terms of hybridity and complex interchange, and very much as a two-way process that transforms both sides of the equation. Concepts such as creole, mestizo, and "half breed" complicate simple assumptions and challenge ideas of purity. Sizable hybrid populations find themselves in an ambiguous position between rulers and subjects. Of their nature, empires create hierarchical societies marked by subtle but unavoidable gradations of power and status. People viewed with contempt by elites might have privileges that set them above those at the bottom of the social or racial ladder. No less influential have been studies of empire from the standpoint of those below, the colonized or oppressed. Empires succeed or fail depending on how effectively they mobilize marginal and middling local populations to their cause, to persuade them of the advantages of that political order. Modern historical writing often speaks of subalterns (borrowing a term of military origin), those who maintained their distance from attempts at integration. The thriving field of subaltern studies foregrounds the role of the colonized, and more particularly, their agency, which went far beyond merely reacting to changes forced upon them. That was especially apparent in religious terms.[22]

If the colonized did indeed accept what imperial rulers offered them, they transformed those legacies to suit their own needs and purposes. That idea underlies so much of the modern history of religion worldwide. Empires spread religions to distant corners of the world, but those religions are transformed in the process. Empires propose, but their subjects dispose.

The Empires Come Home

Beyond acknowledging the realities of empire, current scholarship constantly stresses the imperial impact on metropolitan homelands. Empire, in this view, was never something that merely happened "over there," and for better or worse, empires and their ideas tended to come home. Remarkably often, it is the armies and navies that supply the means of transmitting objects or ideas. Put another way, much that we think of as European history did not actually occur on European soil. However often the novels written in nineteenth-century England, say, depict highly localized and self-contained village or small-town worlds, modern scholars stress how the fortunes of those characters were absolutely grounded in imperial contexts, in prosperity derived from the exploitation of Africa and South Asia. As I have suggested, such interactions shaped the range of foods that we regard as such basic commodities as the tea and sugar that were so essential for the characters of Jane Austen or Charles Dickens, not to mention such drugs as opium. Surprisingly often in domestic fiction, we find incidental references to characters wandering in distant corners of the empire, where they have either acquired wealth or suffered dreadful fates. The same was true for French realist fiction.[23]

Many studies look to the effects of empire to explain the prosperity of Western nations and the industrial and financial leaps that have given them hegemony over the rest of the globe. That kind of analysis has become standard in recent years as scholars have shown how grounded many Western enterprises were in slavery and the slave trade. According to some interpretations, it was the capital derived from this human commerce that made possible the British Industrial Revolution and its European successors. That heritage is evident in such famous ports as Liverpool or Bristol. Even where industrial growth was designed for military customers, it was usually to build warships and equip armies that were primarily intended to defend and expand empires, often with the goal of advancing slave systems. Britain's main adversary was France, where such slaving ports as Nantes and Bordeaux played a comparable role in national prosperity. For much of the history of the institution, slavery was indissoluble from empire. Modern historians sometimes understate that in the British case, because in the first half of the nineteenth century, that empire not only abolished slavery in its own domains but struggled hard to end it in a global scale. But that represented a vast departure from earlier precedent.[24]

While not denying the connections with slavery, in a sense this sort of analysis does not go far enough in emphasizing the imperial foundations of the prosperity of leading Western nations. Notably, it takes no account of the profits from imperial trade in India or the East Indies, which was assuredly based on exploitation but by no means always on actual unfree labor. Nor does it acknowledge such settler colonies as Australia, Canada, and South Africa. All those factors gained a new importance from the 1830s, when slavery was legally forbidden in the British Empire, and after the French followed suit in 1848. It was the profits of empire in this wider global sense that generated the wealth that made some British magnates and aristocrats richer than European monarchs. That same prosperity allowed them to build the sumptuous country houses that have so often featured as location settings for all those nostalgic television series recreating Victorian or Edwardian life. As the British, French, and Dutch economies globalized during the nineteenth century, their efforts were mainly concentrated within their respective areas of imperial control, both formal and informal. London, Paris, and Amsterdam all flourished as capitals of global empire, just as Venice, Seville, and Lisbon had in earlier centuries. Lesser cities such as Marseille prospered mightily from imperial commerce, which was quite separate from any involvement in the slave trade. Urban history is often a subset of imperial history. So also is Europe's corporate and business history.[25]

Empires transformed the life of the homelands in multiple ways, not least in forms of government. Nations needed to restructure their forms of government and bureaucracy to rule their vast new worlds, with all that implied for the creation of social statistics and quantification. Forms of social control and policing originally developed on distant frontiers were imported to the homeland. Just to take one example, many US states have state police systems that ultimately derive from the model pioneered in Pennsylvania in 1905. That paramilitary force was a direct imitation of the Philippine Constabulary, which the United States had formed to control its restive new Pacific colony following the Spanish-American War of 1898. Its Pennsylvania advocates believed it was an appropriate means for controlling unrest among the diverse ethnic groups of the state's industrial areas, which were portrayed almost as a turbulent internal colony. The distinctive hats still worn by such forces represent the height of military fashion in the era of Theodore Roosevelt.[26]

To maintain their visions of supremacy, those same imperial nations rethought attitudes to race, gender, and sexuality, in the process creating ideas that survived long after the formal empires themselves had crumbled. The rhetoric of whiteness is inseparable from empire. The need to maintain racial standards inspired new racial and eugenic theories, which placed a special burden on women as the safeguards of the race, with all that implied for physical health and sexual purity.[27]

An Age of Apology

Contemporary concerns about racism and social justice have stimulated a reconsideration of imperial histories, with a central emphasis on the violence and ruthless exploitation involved in such ventures. Much current research focuses on those who defied and resisted imperial power, particularly during the latter years of empire, when guerrilla wars were raging widely. The British have undertaken the painful reexamination of atrocities committed during fighting in Kenya, Malaya, and elsewhere.[28]

It is little comfort for the British to recall that the worst imperial atrocities were associated not with the British but with other European nations: the German record in southwest Africa was actively genocidal, while the Belgian rule in the Congo inflicted horrific carnage on Native peoples. In 2020, the Dutch king apologized for "excessive violence" committed in the country's former East India possessions. More sweepingly, the Dutch government expressed regret for the Netherlands' deep involvement in slavery and the slave trade. Apart from such obvious sins, historians have denounced multiple empires for leaving former possessions in situations that inevitably produced violence, misery, and ethnic conflict.[29]

Issues concerning the memories of empire are fiercely debated in several European nations, focusing on public monuments and statuary and on representations in museums. At the end of the nineteenth century, Cecil Rhodes personified both imperial expansion and the predatory violence that accompanied it, yet even so he was widely celebrated both in Southern Africa and Great Britain. The name Rhodesia was given to a vast expanse of south-central Africa, the lands we now know as Zambia and Zimbabwe. In recent years, a movement to remove all such images and commemorations uses the simple slogan, "Rhodes must fall!" Conversely, there have been efforts to remember those who fought against empire, such as the fiery religious activist John Chilembwe, who led a revolt against British rule in Central Africa in 1915. In 2022, his statue appeared on the plinth adjacent to Nelson's Column in Trafalgar Square, alongside older figures of Victorian imperial warriors. Many European institutions are debating the restoration of artistic treasures secured during imperial wars in Africa and Asia, which are increasingly characterized as *loot*: that word is an English appropriation from the Hindi term for "booty."[30]

What in the United States has been a struggle for racial justice has manifested in Europe as a continuing campaign for decolonization, to exorcize the ghosts of empire.[31]

Writing Religion into Empire

As imperial encounters had such a transformative impact on societies, on everything including food and architecture, medicine and policing, transportation and urban growth, it is inevitable that they should affect religious life. Gods and churches travel quite as widely in imperial baggage as do cats and tomatoes.

Religious themes do indeed feature in the literatures on empires, ancient and modern. We cannot tell the story of Europe's nineteenth-century empires except in terms of Christian political rule over non-Christians, whether those were Muslims, Hindus, or followers of traditional or tribal faiths. The stories of mission and conversion are no less inseparable from the imperial context. The stunning global expansion of Catholic Christianity in the early modern period—one of the most important moments in the whole Christian story—depended on the Iberian empires that supported and sponsored those enterprises. In later eras, a distinguished literature places the history of Protestant missions and global Christian expansion in the context of empires, especially in the British and Anglophone world. More broadly, such an approach is fundamental to the work of such fine historians as David Hempton, Mark Noll, and Brian Stanley. To use a military analogy, empires created the theaters in which missionaries were able to advance their cause, and to varying degrees, the missionaries extended imperial interests. All too easily, imperial missions generated missionary imperialists. If Christian mission is not wholly a subset of imperial history, it is incomprehensible except when considered from that perspective. Of course, the linkage between imperial aggression and Christian expansion has produced much cynical commentary through the centuries and considerable soul searching among later believers.[32]

Countless imperial studies at least touch on religious themes, including the role of empires in promoting faiths and how religion serves as a vehicle for anti-imperial resistance. In American history, an imperial lens is increasingly applied to many aspects of religious change in the colonial and early national periods, including the topic of revivalism. Plenty of writings consider the imperial relationship with non-Western and traditional faiths as they came into contact with hegemonic Christianity.[33]

Yet for all this outstanding scholarly work, it is not easy to find broad surveys that relate religious developments to the workings and realities of empires as such, as they have existed in various times and places, from Babylon and Rome to Madrid, London, and Moscow. There are some provocative essays, including a characteristically brilliant piece by Lord Bryce, "Religion as a Factor in the History of Empires," published in 1915, which spanned the centuries from Roman times through later Spanish, Russian, and British examples. As he observed, when we study any empire, in any era, we must ask, "What are the circumstances and conditions which enable the ruling nation to rule and dispose the subject nations to submit? Of these circumstances and conditions religion must evidently be one, and one of such importance as to deserve careful examination." Bryce also paid due attention to religion as a force disposing subjects not to submit but rather to rebel. Amira Bennison offers an excellent survey on empire and religion in the *Oxford World History of Empire*, while John Gascoigne presents an equally wide-ranging historiographical view. Each essay in its way examines the spectrum of possible official responses to religion, the sponsorship of official variants of faith, and the degrees of toleration for dissidents. Each examines the role of faith as an ideological justification for imperial authority and, at the same time, discusses the manifold uses of religion as a recurrent focus of opposition to those empires.[34]

Kingdoms of This World

Acknowledging these distinguished precedents, we can still say that a systematic history of the relationship between religion and empire remains to be written. This book provides a foundation for that global story, of how earthly kingdoms contributed to making the great religions, those far-flung kingdoms not of this world.

It is divided into two halves. The first half, in chapters 1–5, discusses empires and the making of world faiths. I show how imperial actions and precedents shaped the world religions that we know today, and how those faiths acquired their geographical frameworks. Chapter 1 defines the essential terms and concepts that we will find throughout this book, ideas such as empire and colony, core and periphery. It summarizes the common features of empire in multiple cultures, what I have termed their "empire-ness." I place special weight on the part played by imperial memories in conditioning the behavior of later states and of faiths. Chapter 2 shows how those factors and forces contributed to making the Bible, with the events and beliefs portrayed there, and chapter 3 places the growth of Christianity in the context of great empires, both Roman and Persian. Chapter 4 describes the remarkable parallels between Eastern and Western experiences, in showing how empires first propelled the rapid growth of Buddhism as a world religion and then constrained that process, at least in South Asia, to the benefit of Hinduism. Chapter 5 shows how the political/religious empires of Islam conditioned the geographical and cultural spread of that faith.

The book's second part, in chapters 6–10, addresses worldwide empires and their unintended consequences, focusing on the great age of European empires, from the fifteenth century onward, when those mighty dominions created a globalized world. Chapter 6 describes the efforts and limitations of deliberate missionary enterprise, in seeking to spread the faith of the conquerors across the globe. Yet many of the most significant religious developments occurred despite such efforts, rather than because of them. Chapter 7 portrays the immense and usually unforeseen religious outcomes of imperial-driven movements of populations, whether as slaves, deportees, or voluntary labor. The consequences for the distribution of faiths are evident in global maps of ethnic and religious minorities. Chapter 8 describes how imperial policies actively stimulated the growth of anti-imperial movements, usually of a religious character. That was especially apparent in the reconstruction of Islam during this era. In chapter 9, we see how encounters with the dominant imperial faith sparked the reconstruction and revival of other traditions, often in the direction of greater fundamentalist rigor and a return to real or supposed ancient roots. Global contacts transformed the religions of metropolitan nations, in ways that older elites found uncomfortable. Such impacts on the homeland were actually all the greater following the formal ending of empires, as we see in chapter 10.

A concluding chapter suggests that the religious impact of empires has indeed ended, but only because virtually all the changes they drove and inspired have been so fully integrated into the processes of globalization. Empires made the religious world we know.

Of necessity, any broad account of "empires" must offer a definition of that often controversial term and specify what distinguishes them from other kinds of political arrangements. As we will see, the structural factors that marked those empires as so distinctive also made them ideal vehicles for the making and transmission of religions.

PART ONE

Empires and the Making of World Faiths

The whole expanse of the inhabited part of the world is not large enough to have two kings.

Timur, founder of the Timurid Empire

1
What Is an Empire?

Tu regere imperio populos, Romane, memento
(hae tibi erunt artes), pacique imponere morem,
parcere subiectis et debellare superbos.

(But, Rome, 't is thine alone, with awful sway,
To rule mankind, and make the world obey,
Disposing peace and war by thy own majestic way;
To tame the proud, the fetter'd slave to free:
These are imperial arts, and worthy thee.)

***Virgil's* Aeneid *4:851–853, translation by John Dryden*[1]**

Modern debates over the virtues and vices of empire have a long pedigree. Written late in the first century BC, Virgil's paean to empire in the *Aeneid* offers an idealized vision of what became known as the Roman Peace, Pax Romana. As such, it reflected the justifications of many conquerors and empire builders through the ages, but it should be considered alongside another passage written more than a century later, which might have been intended as a riposte. In 98 AD, the Roman historian Tacitus wrote a biography of his father-in-law, the distinguished general Agricola. Tacitus recounts a historic victory that Agricola won against the natives of Scotland, and in a famous set piece, he reports a magnificent speech allegedly delivered by the enemy Celtic chieftain Calgacus. The speech constitutes one of the most blistering condemnations ever uttered against empires, culminating in the declaration that "to ravage, to slaughter, to usurp under false titles, they call empire; and where they make a desert, they call it Peace" (auferre, trucidare, rapere, falsis nominibus imperium; atque, ubi solitudinem faciunt, pacem appellant). Whether the native leader actually spoke such words, the prominent place that Tacitus gives them shows that not even all Romans uncritically accepted the imperial ideal.[2]

Few would dispute the fairness of Calgacus' charges against empire, against its systematic greed and violence and its quest to subjugate whole peoples and cultures. Just to take one celebrated example that both Virgil and Tacitus knew very well, Caesar's conquest of Gaul in the 50s BC reportedly involved the death or enslavement of millions of the native inhabitants. Calgacus' protest finds many echoes in modern writings on the topic, which are equally suspicious of claims of a Pax Britannica or its various later equivalents. But even if we take the grimmest interpretation of the foundation of empires, and the intentions of their founders, we should never underestimate their impact on the societies they acquired, how fundamentally they would change them. The ensuing imperial order, and ultimately, even the vaunted "Peace," was by no means mythical, and it completely changed the environments in which cultures and religions would develop.[3]

Varieties of Empire

In different periods, the term "empire" has been applied to very diverse types of entity, operating in quite different ways, and they vary greatly in their geographical scope. Having said this, the term can properly be applied in a way that distinguishes it from other concepts such as the nation-state or kingdom. In 1915, Lord Bryce defined empire simply as "any wide dominion in which one nation rules other bodies of men, peoples or tribes, of diverse blood, speech and habits." The key elements here are those of one society extending its power over others, diversity of populations and territories, and geographical scope (while granting that "wide," like "large," is a relative concept). In modern times, Amira Bennison similarly writes of "a political structure which covers a large geographic area inhabited by a diverse assortment of peoples with different languages, cultures, and belief systems." Stephen Howe remarks that the imperial entity is made up of multiple territories or regions, "usually created by conquest, and divided between a dominant center and subordinate peripheries." One nation or people rules several or many others, which originally had some kind of independent existence, even if they were not actually states in the modern sense.[4]

Beyond those crucial elements, it is by no means easy to identify common themes that unite empires through history. As we have seen, race was not necessarily a factor. Nor must an empire have an emperor or *Kaiser*, or a monarch of any kind. Empires have varied enormously in their political arrangements and the degree of honor paid to a single sovereign. To take the most famous instance of all, from the third century BC onward, Rome extended its power over much of the Mediterranean world, which it thoroughly dominated by (say) the 50s BC. By any criterion we might reasonably apply, this was indisputably an empire, and on a very substantial scale. Yet in Roman history, that was the time of the republic, and generals and armies were fighting not for an individual sovereign but for the Senate and People of Rome, Senatus Populusque Romanus. The Roman *Empire*, strictly defined, began only in 27 BC, when Octavian became the first emperor—the imperator, or "the one who commands"—under the name of Augustus. Yet we can scarcely avoid the language of empire for that sprawling and ethnically diverse parcel of possessions that Rome controlled long before that date.[5]

Other empires were equally diverse ideologically. At the start of the twentieth century, the French Empire dominated huge swathes of Africa and Oceania, as well as Indo-China. Yet like early Rome, that hegemonic France itself was a constitutional republic, subject to the whims of its electorate. After the Russian Revolution of 1917, that country's new Communist rulers inherited one of the world's largest empires, with its immense diversity of ethnic and religious groups. In 1883, the great British scholar of empire, Sir John Seeley, had written of "the great conglomeration of Slavs, Germans, Turcomans and Armenians, of Greek Christians, Catholics, Protestants, Mussulmans and Buddhists, which we call Russia." Not only did the new Soviet Union continue to rule these territories, which by any reasonable standard constituted an empire, but the country's leaders made anti-imperialism a fundamental part of their political ideology, with no obvious embarrassment about the situation prevailing within its own borders. That anomaly endured until 1991. That Russian situation finds a close analogy in modern China, where the equally anti-imperialist Communist state happily exercises authority over territories, cultures, and populations annexed by its overtly imperial predecessor in earlier centuries.[6]

How Empires Evolve and (Sometimes) Vanish

Tacitus' account of a savage war of conquest waged by an "advanced" nation against a "barbarian" counterpart represents a well-known and quite authentic aspect of the story of empire, but it is only one aspect. Following those initial encounters, interactions between rulers and ruled can change very substantially, so much so as to challenge any familiar definitions of empire. If we look back far enough in the past, then most nation-states too began with acts of conquest and violence, although those origins are usually forgotten. It remains open to debate whether such a bygone history of itself invalidates the legitimacy of nation-states any more than empires.

Empires evolve over time, and in some cases so substantially that they lose what had previously been their essential imperial qualities. Even something as basic as the concept of center (or core) and peripheries is more fluid than it might appear. Surely, we might think, the Roman or Persian or British Empires involved rule by a dominant society, by Rome or Persia or Britain. But as empires expand, so does the definition of that core people or territory that originally ruled so many strangers. The former strangers become part of the imperial mainstream.[7]

Subjects and subalterns—or their descendants—can become citizens. In the early phases of the Roman Empire, Romans, broadly defined, ruled over other peoples, but over time, regional elites came to share a common sense of identity. In 87 BC, Rome extended its citizenship to subject peoples in the Italian peninsula, and in 212 AD, the emperor Caracalla further extended that privilege to all free men in the empire. In that sense, if you lived in (say) Egypt or the Rhineland, you were not the foreign subject of a colonial empire based in Rome. Rather, as a citizen, you were an integral part of that empire and its ruling elite. Three centuries after the time of Julius Caesar, the Gaul that had provided the setting for his appalling massacres was a heavily Romanized land, with the appropriate network of cities and villas, and (now) of contented Roman citizens. By that point too, the city of Rome itself had forfeited much of its older status as the unquestioned capital of empire, which was rather to be found in whichever of several great provincial cities where the emperor himself had taken residence. By the fourth century, a New Rome, Constantinople, challenged the glories of the old. Over the following centuries, the emperors and ruling elites of that eastern-based Roman Empire were drawn from many ethnic groups, including Greeks, Slavs, Syrians, and Armenians, although virtually never Italians. That empire spoke the "Roman" language, which at that point was Greek. Concepts of core and periphery shift, often substantially.[8]

Repeatedly, empires have ended not in the sense of formal conquest and destruction by a barbarian enemy but because different populations come to share a common loyalty and identity. Great Britain was originally a sequence of empires within the main island of Britain before becoming the united nation that went on to establish its new possessions overseas. The kingdom of Wessex ruled subordinate peoples, who ultimately merged to form the kingdom of England. That kingdom in turn ruled the other nations of the archipelago, before they were eventually consolidated into Great Britain, with a new British identity. The kingdom that began its colonial expansion in the 1580s already had several centuries of experience ruling conquered lands within the British Isles themselves, most notoriously in Ireland. That British state already fulfilled most of the criteria for imperial status in its home territories long before its subjects first ventured into the tropical unknown. Something very similar was true of the French or Germans who set out to build their colonial empires during the nineteenth century. In earlier decades, many of those peoples had been part of independent or marginal territories that were reluctantly brought under the sway of a new nation-state, and only gradually did they accept the new national identities that were offered to them. In such instances, empires gradually evolved into nations, to the point that they forgot their imperial origins.[9]

Throughout this book, I will often have cause to mention the role of historical memory in shaping empires and imperial ideologies, but in this case, we observe the reverse process, of historical amnesia. As older peripheral populations come to accept their place in those new nations and emerging great powers, so they come to see such a process as natural and inevitable and write their history accordingly. Regions and peoples forget that they too were once the restive and grudging subjects of empire.

Colonies and Settlers

Empires differ in how they view subject lands and peoples, and those distinctions can be enormous. The fact of being part of a given empire can cover a very wide range of types of status and of degrees of exploitation.

In common parlance, imperialism and colonialism are often presented as close to synonymous, which they are not. Certainly, colonialism grows out of imperial rule, but empires have existed without colonialism, which means not just occupying a territory but settling it, usually with the people of the imperial motherland. The terminology dates back to the Roman practice of establishing settlements, or *coloniae*, of military veterans in conquered lands, which reduced the need to pay those soldiers in cash. At the same time, *coloniae* projected Roman culture and order onto the new land, opening the way to wider settlement not directly associated with those specific centers. Conversely, many empires have been content to extract tribute or taxes from an occupied territory, or to exploit its economic resources, without making any attempt to establish a presence of the dominant imperial race. In some instances, they merely establish a strategic military presence, to seize positions but not possessions. In that sense, British rule in India had nothing to do with colonialism: there was never any deliberate policy to build up British communities or towns, as opposed to having bureaucrats, soldiers, or merchants who happened to live there. At the time of the Indian Mutiny in 1857, the British population of India—military and civilian combined—was scarcely forty thousand, out of a total of two hundred million. In the vital imperial city of Calcutta, a census in 1837 found only three thousand British out of a total of more than four hundred thousand. Much the same point about settlement was true of the Dutch in the East Indies. Even at the height of its splendor as the capital of French Indo-China, the white population of Hanoi never rose above 5 percent of the whole. Inevitably, imperial officials, soldiers, and traders had children with local women, and those mixed-race populations came to be quite numerous, but that is quite distinct from any attempt to create settler colonies.[10]

Empires that did use intensive colonial settlement were likely to endure and to become assimilated to the imperial norm, as occurred in the case of Canada or Australia. Ideally, such settlements illustrate the observation of the French statesman Turgot, in 1775: "Colonies are like fruits which cling to the tree only till they ripen." Settler colonies were particularly successful when they represented geographical extensions of the original imperial core, and over time they came to be seen as natural and even providential extensions of an expanding nation, rather than aspects of empire.[11]

Manifest Destiny

This was the case with nineteenth-century US expansion to the West and Southwest, into such regions as Texas and Oregon and Minnesota, which in retrospect we tend to see as the natural fulfillment of a nation's historic destiny, as examples of successful nation building. At the time, such an action was quite as "imperial" as British or French advances into their spheres of influence in Africa or Asia. No less recognizable from the long experience of other empires was the US practice of relocating Native and subject populations to areas where they could not challenge imperial rule. At the time, Americans themselves acknowledged that reality, notably in such much-reproduced cultural products as the famous 1861 painting entitled *Westward the Course of Empire Takes Its Way*. If the United States under Andrew Jackson and James Polk was not an aggressive imperial power, engaged in extensive colonial settlement, then the whole concept of "empire" has no meaning. In the later nineteenth century, those expansionist impulses segued easily into the acquisition of formal imperial possessions overseas. The US territorial homeland—what became the "Lower Forty-Eight"—was an empire even before any formal outreach beyond the seas.[12]

The descendants of these settlers might object to such terminology, arguing in effect, "It's not an empire; we were just building our natural homeland." We see a similar process, and justification, with the Russian Empire as it expanded from the seventeenth century onward, seizing territories that it soon came to regard as integral to the homeland. One such was the Swedish imperial border fortress of Nyenschantz, which the rising Russian state captured in 1703. The Russians promptly replaced it with what became the mighty city of St. Petersburg, the political capital of their own emerging empire and its heart of culture and intellectual life over the next two centuries. Meanwhile, the Russians were absorbing huge territories in Central Asia, Siberia, and the Caucasus, as well as eastern Europe. As in the American case, Russia's expansion must be seen as a colonial and imperial project, although retroactively, that was presented as a kind of manifest national destiny, a logical extension of the national heartland. Who could doubt that St. Petersburg was always destined to be Russian, just as San Francisco was intended to be American? In both instances, Russian and American, the definitions of the "core" territories of the imperial power changed quite dramatically over time.[13]

In contrast, territories that were ruled but not colonized were more difficult to maintain in the long term and were far more difficult to absorb into some new national identity. In few places in Africa, for instance, did European rulers actually plant the deep roots that would allow them to establish white or white-ruled societies. A ferociously hot climate deterred Europeans, and those climates were very hospitable to insects that spread devastating diseases. Sober statistical evidence fully justified the description of West Africa as the "white man's grave." In most of Africa, the end of empires did not involve combatting or uprooting European settlers, with the exceptions of Algeria and South Africa and a smaller-scale conflict in Kenya. To adapt Kipling's phrase, the end of empire in much of Africa and Asia just meant that the captains and the kings departed, without the need to uproot whole cities full of terrified white settlers. Physically adjacent and contiguous colonies became integral territories of emerging nations; remote territories did not and were remembered as components of empire.[14]

Informal Empires

Other factors decided how heavily the burden of empire fell on given regions. Maps of empires as they existed at given moments in time are often misleading because they both over- and under-claim. In the Roman case, for instance, the area credited to that empire often includes territories subject to very different degrees of control, from wholly owned lands incorporated into the empire to the domains of subject kings, which were far more loosely affiliated. In the European Middle Ages, cities like Venice and Genoa created sizable de facto empires through their trading and commercial ventures, which were reinforced by navies and networks of bases, fortresses, and merchant settlements.[15]

In modern times, we encounter the phenomenon of formal and informal empire. In 1883, the historian J. R. Seeley famously wrote that the British Empire seemed to have been acquired "in a fit of absence of mind," and by no means all of those lands were formally annexed or incorporated under British political control as part of some imagined grand design. Until 1858, British hegemony in the Indian subcontinent technically was quite separate from the British state and was rather exercised through a private corporation, the East India Company. In an earlier era, a similar situation prevailed in the Dutch-controlled regions of South Asia and the East Indies, where the parallel interest was the VOC, the Vereenigde Oostindische Compagnie, the world's first multinational corporation. There were other less noticed but still deeply impressive concerns, such as the English Hudson's Bay Company or the Dutch West India Company.[16]

Nor was it easy to draw the precise bounds of imperial authority. Well into the twentieth century, it was commonly acknowledged that such important territories as Argentina and Uruguay were effectively part of the British world and its economic system, imperial possessions in all but name. But as they never moved to political incorporation, they never appeared on maps daubed with the distinctive British shade of pink. The British never contemplated any kind of colonial settlement of such loosely affiliated lands, although in practice, commercial ties promoted a considerable degree of migration. The United States, meanwhile, regularly invaded and occupied many small states in the Caribbean and Central America and in practice exercised full-fledged rule, although never formally incorporating, such regions as Cuba, Haiti, and Nicaragua into its imperial orbit. There were degrees, gradations, of empire.[17]

What Empires Have in Common

Such a list of caveats and distinctions can be extended considerably, not least in terms of the technological resources available to different empires in various eras. Having said that, we can legitimately point to commonalities that must strike us over time. For all those differences, empires have followed similar patterns in their behavior and attitudes, and those common characteristics have often shaped religious responses. Although the following list of seven crucial features is not exhaustive, and in no sense constitutes a corpus of predetermined historical laws, it is widely applicable.

i. Communications

Of their nature, empires need to maintain rule over territories that are geographically large, and indeed might be transcontinental or global. That places a high premium on building and maintaining systems of communication, which might mean roads or sea routes, with all the institutions that implies. Empires serve a vanguard role in developing and exploiting new technologies of communication. No less important, those means of communication must be safeguarded effectively from multiple threats, including piracy and brigandage. Only thus can the imperial court or capital ensure firm authority over distant lands, while maintaining the ability to send military reinforcements. Accelerated and extended forms of communication connect territories that previously had little or no contact. Perceptions of the known world expand, often spectacularly, and those larger visions become normalized.[18]

ii. Cities

Improved systems of communication generate new economic arrangements, as well as new social systems and hierarchies. Trade builds empires, and empires build trade. Empires breed merchants as well as proconsuls.

Such new connections promote urbanization in the form of seats of government, garrison towns, and trading cities or entrepôts. Cities commonly become theaters of imperial power, where great public works and monuments are displayed. Urban growth also occurs in the metropolitan heartland, both in imperial capitals and in major provincial cities heavily oriented toward imperial trade and commerce. Those metropolitan centers play an important intermediary role in transmitting people, ideas, goods, and cultures from the metropolis to the periphery and vice versa.[19]

iii. Government and Military

Empires need institutions of rule, which at the minimum demand mechanisms for the collection of taxes and tribute. Some empires are content to rely largely on local middlemen, but most develop more elaborate and intrusive systems of domination. Depending on the situation, such rule involves spreading bureaucratic systems, with the literacy that involves, as well as the language of the dominant power.[20]

Empires depend on military strength, with all that implies about the role of the military in societies, the status of military elites, and the scale of resources they receive from the state. That military theme can transform the metropolitan society by giving power to new elites and on occasion, by promoting violent and authoritarian values. Military service, often on a very wide geographical scale, profoundly affects the life experience of ordinary people and their geographical and cultural perceptions.

Imperial military forces reflect the broad composition of the larger empire, usually with a generous representation of peoples from the empire's more remote areas and its borderlands. Those peoples often follow distinctive religious and cultural patterns, which they transmit widely. Such military service disseminates the language and lifeways of the larger empire to those peripheral regions.[21]

iv. Language

Even if empires do not demand the use of their own language or some common lingua franca, their operations do result in such a linguistic spread, which may have lasting consequences. Imperial languages develop an aura of prestige and an association with power and high culture. The longer the empire endures, the more likely it is that older local languages will be consigned to a marginal status, or indeed driven out of use entirely.

Intentionally or otherwise, empires promote the use of lingua francas that may well have originated among subject populations but achieve very wide circulation and commonly survive the empires that permitted their existence. The world's modern linguistic map is in large measure an imperial legacy.[22]

v. Governors and Governed

The fact of empire generally involves a cultural disparity or inequality between the ruler and the ruled, the core and the periphery. Depending on the scale of that gap, the effects on local societies might be enormous. Deliberately or not, empires foster harmonization across the whole of the territories they rule, in terms of language, institutions, and social and economic arrangements. In some extreme examples, the new order might represent a revolutionary transformation, introducing urbanization, commerce, and even literacy itself.

Except in the immediate phase of conquest, empires must form a working relationship with local subordinate populations. Some govern through traditional elites. Some recruit local people as soldiers or administrators and commonly use local groups or peoples as allied or surrogate forces. Some empires offer local people means of participating in empire, and even of joining the ruling elite. Other regimes maintain a strict and rigid segregation between rulers and ruled.

Conquered or annexed communities face a familiar range of decisions and dilemmas in responding to empires, with a well-known spectrum of types of accommodation or resistance. The exact course of action depends on the cultural resources available to the conquered and occupied, and this often finds expression in religious terms. That experience—whether of accommodation or resistance—often forms new identities and new consciousness, and it can create new senses of nationality, or of religion.[23]

vi. Population Movements

Empires are associated with the spread of new populations. These might be confined to administrators and soldiers, but some create whole new worlds of settlers and colonists across territories they rule. Empires take symbolic possession of the lands they rule through acts of naming and renaming, mapping and remapping. Those settler/colonial centers serve as hubs to spread new values, customs, and languages.

Empires undertake significant population movements that are involuntary or that include some degree of compulsion or servitude. Such movements include episodes of enslavement or deportation, which are common and even inevitable parts of early warfare. Furthermore, military needs provoke the relocation of hostile or restive populations to other regions of empire. All such activities result in cultural diffusion and new forms of contact between different populations and different regions. Such relocations enhance ethnic diversity in occupied or colonized territories as different groups interbreed.[24]

vii. Frontiers and Borderlands

Empires create borders where, usually, none had existed before, and the fact of those borders constitutes a powerful cultural reality. Beyond fortifications, borders demand towns or trading centers, where influences from inside and outside the empire meet and interact and spread much farther afield. The extensive Roman

> frontier, the *limes*, is recalled through the modern English word "liminal," and imperial borders are often liminal in terms of culture and religion, besides their economic functions. Borders might be marked by land or sea.[25]
>
> Especially where they stood on the borderlands between rival empires, such diverse borderlands became "shatter zones" that offer refuge from groups at odds with the major empires, those who flee wars and slave trading, and they can become centers of resistance. These regions are subject of intense if sporadic conflict and frequent changes of political control. This further contributes to instability and to cultures of lawlessness. Such peripheries of the periphery are commonly the setting of vital cultural interactions and religious innovation.[26]

These diverse impacts reflect the pragmatic needs of the empire and its agents, rather than any sense of altruistic concern for subjects, and building the various cities and roads can involve great human suffering. Calgacus' (imagined) speech enumerated the horrors of Roman conquest, of destruction, enslavement, and family separation, of the creation of a "desert." But the long-term effects can be truly transformative, and often surprisingly positive. However embarrassed academic historians might be to admit the fact, one of the best statements of the potential consequences of empire comes from the comedy film *Monty Python's Life of Brian* (1979), in which a revolutionary nationalist leader asks his followers, rhetorically, what have the Romans ever done for us occupied people? He soon receives a lengthy roster of embarrassingly specific answers, until in exasperation, he is forced to conclude, "All right, but apart from the sanitation, the medicine, education, wine, public order, irrigation, roads, a fresh water system, and public health, what have the Romans ever done for us?" The final Roman contribution to be mentioned is, "Brought peace." Although the revolutionary scoffs, the absence of endemic warfare is a vital prerequisite for the expansion of commerce and the development of culture.[27]

Repeatedly through history, even regimes that began in conditions of extreme bloodshed, such as the Romans or the notorious Mongol conquerors, benefited their (surviving) subjects by establishing peace, order, and superb communications. The Pax Mongolica even included an efficient postal service. Empires spark social revolutions.[28]

Religious Dimensions

Many of the common features that I outline here have powerful religious implications, as much in the disruption of older societies as in the innovations introduced by the conquerors. But surprisingly, perhaps, such a list of commonalities does not include ideological themes or religious elements. In fact, empires vary greatly in their explicit affiliation with a religious or spiritual identity. Some empires ground themselves absolutely in religion, others do not, any more than all empires can be assumed to have autocratic monarchs.

Many empires—by no means all—have used religious rhetoric, which might imply giving a sacred or even divine role to the emperor, with an imperial cult followed throughout the realm. In a text possibly from the third century AD, the Persian emperor Ardashir instructed his successors, "Know that kingship and religion are twin brothers, there is no strength to either without its companion, because religion is the foundation and support of kingship, and kingship is henceforth the guardian of religion." In some instances, an emperor might be central to the cosmology of a given society, so that the harmony and even survival of the world was intimately connected to his fortunes. Famously, that was the case in imperial China, where a flawed or evil emperor forfeited the Mandate of Heaven, and the whole society suffered accordingly through invasions, plagues, or natural calamities. Traditional Chinese religion imagined the heavenly hierarchy as a direct copy of its earthly imperial counterpart, under the Jade Emperor, with his extensive court. Just as in the material world, ritual specialists understood the need to bribe minor divine officials to win access to higher levels of that hierarchy.[29]

In other cases, imperial authorities claim a direct blessing to assure divine protection. Through the ages, virtually all religious traditions have been called upon to provide justifications for imperial power, including Christianity, Islam, Buddhism, Hinduism, and Shinto, and all have complied to a greater or lesser extent. Christian churches run by the state, or closely affiliated with it, have regularly served this supportive function through the rituals of coronation or of invoking divine aid in times of war or crisis. In turn, empires have adopted the rhetoric and iconography of faiths, usually appropriating its most vigorous and conspicuous forms available in particular eras. In many early Asian empires, that usually meant variants of Mahayana Buddhism; from the thirteenth century, Islamic conquerors maintained a close alliance with the Sufi orders, which then stood at their spiritual and intellectual apex. Such a religious orientation proved crucial in early modern times, when the Spanish and Portuguese empires grounded themselves absolutely in Catholic belief and doctrine in its most grandiose Tridentine manifestation and aggressively expanded that faith throughout their dominions. In more modern times too, many empires deployed religious justifications for their power, and in many cases, the elite figures making such statements probably believed them quite sincerely. Boasts of divine right were by no means cynical.[30]

Religion has often justified imperial wars and conquests, most famously in the case of Islam. At least in terms of its official ideology, the Islamic caliphate that prevailed from the seventh century through the thirteenth was primarily a religious enterprise, in which the caliph was the successor, *khalifa*, of the Prophet Muhammad and enjoyed both temporal and spiritual authority. Legal scholars created doctrines that consecrated imperial expansion, drawing a sharp division between different worlds, of *dar al-Islam*, where the faith and religious law prevailed, and the hostile world of war, *dar al-Harb*, which was open to conquest and annexation by a legitimate Muslim sovereign. Such claims were maintained by the Ottoman Empire, until the abolition of the caliphate in 1924.[31]

But other faiths were just as ready to sanctify imperial warriors. At least from the fifth century AD, the Roman Empire framed its wars in strongly religious terms, as struggles for official Christianity against the rival powers of Zoroastrian Persia, and later the caliphate. Such claims to God's favor on the battlefield persisted remarkably late. During the First World War, several of the major participants were Christian empires, and all made extensive use of religious rhetoric and propaganda. Those Christian states, indeed, presented their military claims in religious terminology at least as forthright as did the Ottoman Empire, and sometimes even more starkly. As late as the 1930s, Catholic Italy used an aggressive rhetoric of holy war to justify its invasion of (equally Christian) Ethiopia, while militarist Japan invoked State Shinto as the basis of its newly won Pacific empire. At least among major powers, they appear to represent the last use of such explicitly religious groundings for imperial war, although, as I will suggest, modern-day Russia offers some parallels.[32]

The Limits of Imperial Faith

But by no means all empires grounded themselves in religion, and such justifications can change with surprising speed. When Napoleon III was empire-building aggressively in the 1850s and 1860s, he presented himself as the faithful champion of Catholic Christendom, destined to protect Christian missionaries and minorities around the world. By the end of that century, the French Empire was still basking in a continuing era of imperial expansion and settlement, but by this point, the government was not only militantly secular but aggressively anti-clerical, to the point that a religious civil war seemed possible.[33]

Similarly, the Russian Empire firmly proclaimed its Orthodox Christian identity as the rationale for its existence and expansion, and that remained true until in 1917, when the regime was overthrown by violently anti-religious Communists. Nevertheless, as we have seen, the older empire retained its broad outline and general patterns of domination under atheist Soviet rule. Well into the 1930s the Soviets fought to suppress Muslim anti-colonial insurgencies just as brutally as their czarist predecessors. During the Second World War, the Soviets precisely followed the precedent set by czarist governments when they undertook the mass deportations of Muslim populations from Crimea and the Caucasus, with hideous loss of life. Under a thin façade, that imperial system continued until that Soviet conglomerate was dismantled in its turn in 1991. Even today, the nation of Russia counts at least 170 nationalities and many religious groups, very few of whom had ever petitioned voluntarily for the right to submit to that hegemony. Again in very recent times, this reduced Russia, this empire in miniature, has rooted itself in Orthodox ideology, to proclaim an intimate alliance between state and church. Ideologies and religions change, but empires persist.[34]

Toleration and Persecution

Nor have empires pursued any predictable or consistent policies in terms of the religious believers over whom they rule. Some empires have been broadly tolerant, while others have rigidly enforced strict conformity, with others representing stages in between such extremes. Most ancient empires had little interest in imposing a religious system, beyond acquiescence to a cult of the emperor or perhaps formal acknowledgment of a preferred official deity. Provided subject peoples observed such signs of loyalty, their own religious practices were of little concern. Commonly, Roman officials would ask local people the names of their gods, decide how closely they corresponded to particular deities that they knew, and immediately initiate a cult of Jupiter or Hercules or Diana, coupled with the name of that local god. Chinese emperors visibly and enthusiastically supported and participated in local religious life and its rituals. When episodes of persecution did occur, they arose because some religion was viewed as potentially seditious; it rejected imperial claims and titles; and it was associated with extreme or degrading practices, including perverse sexuality. In the Roman context, Christianity suffered in all three categories. Alternatively, religions were suspect because they were associated with hostile foreign influences. If such evil features were lacking, there was no reason for official intervention.[35]

In contrast, Christianity represented a serious departure from those older and more tolerant precedents. Partly for theological reasons, the converted Roman Empire adopted very harsh policies not just toward pagans but also toward dissident Christian believers. The more aggressively Christian the Roman Empire became, the more severe the persecutions that the Zoroastrian Persians launched against their own Christian minorities, who could be seen as agents of this foreign power. In later times, Catholic realms like the Spanish and Portuguese ferociously enforced their own distinctive creeds. Empires could aspire to destroy rival faiths, and on occasion, they succeeded.[36]

Religious ties or allegiances, then, have characterized some empires but not others, and no overarching statements can be made about such orientations. Outcomes are likewise diverse. The Spanish conquered Mexico, and the religious system they imposed sank deep roots, albeit with local adaptations, and persisted for centuries. The French conquered Algeria, but their religious system was easily uprooted once direct political control ended. This does not mean that official creeds or ideology were irrelevant to the fate of religions. Empires have often striven to promote their particular versions of faith, and those efforts have been spectacularly reflected in architecture and art. Patronage mattered enormously. Conversely, a religion could suffer dreadfully when an empire withdrew its support and patronage and redirected its favor to other beneficiaries. In extreme cases, such as Bolshevik Russia, the resulting persecutions were horrendous. But such official attitudes were only one element among many and had to be considered alongside the other factors associated with empires. Catholic missions, for instance, actually flourished under the anti-clerical French Empire. Nor did the official Anglicanism of the British Empire prevent the dramatic success of various unapproved faiths, not least Roman Catholicism. Empires opened more doors than they could effectively police. Imperial ideologies did matter, but rarely could empires simply decree a new faith and expect universal obedience.[37]

From Frontier to Frontier

Some other features are very common to the imperial experience, if they are neither essential nor universal. To illustrate several of these points, I will cite a story that is not necessarily of great significance in its own right, but it does highlight several of these motifs and continuities in empires as they have existed in many times and places.

In New Mexico we find the community known as the Genízaros, people of mixed Native American heritage who followed the Hispanic lifestyle. Genízaros, or their parents, had been captured or traded, and they occupied a curious status of semi-slavery. They could rise socially through military careers, joining special militia units to fight Indian tribes, and they led Spanish colonization of new areas. The word Genízaro is actually borrowed from the Turkish janissary (*yeni-cheri*, "new soldiers"), mediated through the Italian form *giannizzero*. "Janissary" was one of the most feared terms in early modern Christian Europe. From the fifteenth century, the Ottoman Empire levied a tribute of its conquered Christian peoples, who were forced to supply young sons to state service. Those sons were converted to Islam, and they received a strict military training. As adults, the janissaries represented the most fanatical and skilled imperial soldiers, although they remained slaves. They led the Ottoman advances against Europe's Christian powers, against the Habsburg states of Spain and the Holy Roman Empire, which regularly cooperated in fighting the Turkish foe.[38]

When, around 1700, the Spanish found themselves on yet another remote frontier, fighting such ferocious enemies as the Apache and Comanche, they interpreted the situation in familiar terms. Whatever they called themselves, however different their technologies, those enemies of Christian truth were essentially identical to the traditional foe that Christians knew from the Mediterranean world, the Turks. To fight Indians, then, the Spaniards resorted to tried and true methods from the European battlefield, which meant using slave-soldiers—American janissaries, or Genízaros.[39]

The Genízaro story illustrates several of the major themes that we noted above, including the role of military forces in spreading imperial ideas, above all on the borderlands. But it particularly illustrates the imperial tendency to spread ideas, institutions, and memes across territories ruled, not necessarily as a part of any conscious top-down policy. On occasion, empires deliberately promote conformity to metropolitan standards and beliefs, sometimes sparking social revolutions in the process; but they also provide a setting for more casual and accidental kinds of transmission. That is natural enough in societies where armies range widely through imperial lands and beyond. Imperial servants or officials might encounter an idea or institution or technology in one part of the realm and take it with them when they are transferred far afield or even halfway across the world. Some of those transplants remain isolated curiosities, while others sink deep roots in their new settings. Empires have institutional memories, so that experiences from the distant past can linger on to affect later generations. Imperial powers carry their long memories across the world.[40]

Such cultural transmission has a special relevance to understanding how religious motifs are carried and, on occasion, how whole religions might travel. In the last centuries BC, Roman armies in the eastern provinces encountered the Persian-derived cult of the hero Mithras, who was worshipped in ceremonies confined to initiates. That cult spread wherever the Roman armies marched, and inscriptions are preserved as far away as northern Britain and Algeria, commonly in military settings. In this instance, the religious system would perish within centuries, but other religions encountered on the frontier had a far more lasting impact, including the world faiths that we know today. Throughout this book, we will repeatedly note instances of such encounters, and their far-reaching effects. On the frontiers of empire, Buddhists discovered artistic styles that would exercise a lasting influence on their material representations of the Buddha and other holy figures. Arising from their missionary ventures into distant corners of the European empires, Christians faced debates and insights that they brought home to the metropolis.[41]

A Traffic in Myths

It should be said that the ideas or motifs acquired in those distant imperial settings were not necessarily accurate or properly understood. One hugely influential figure in sixteenth-century Europe was the English magician Dr. John Dee, who was a welcome guest at several royal courts. Among his other achievements, he actually coined a term to describe England's growing colonial possessions—namely, "the British Empire." He claimed to receive mystical visions by using an obsidian spirit mirror, which was in fact an Aztec product that priests had originally deployed for similar visionary purposes. It was sacred to the god Tezcatlipoca, "Smoking Mirror." Presumably, the object was a Spanish war prize, which somehow found its way to Dee, who in turn used it without the slightest inkling of its original spiritual or mythological context.[42]

Religious encounters on the frontiers led to the importation of themes that were not only poorly understood but that were actually crude stereotypes or prejudices concerning races or religions. False ideas then permeated the larger imperial society, where they inflicted lasting harm. This is the subject of a very large literature on the theme of "Orientalism," and it has a particular relevance for impressions of other religions. Whatever the Spanish thought, the religious systems of Apaches had nothing to do with Islam, and still less were either of those faiths connected to diabolism. Other religious borrowings were equally tainted. When modern media denounce violent criminals with the racially charged term "thug," they are using a word that emerged during a panic over ritual murders allegedly carried out by a secret Hindu/Muslim *thuggee* network in the British-controlled India of the 1830s. Such nightmarish images easily spilled over into stereotypes of South Asian religion in general. With its depiction of evil and violent *thuggee* cult leaders commanding cohorts of slavish devotees, the 1939 film *Gunga Din* remains invaluable for understanding such imperial-derived stereotypes. If empires carry their gods with them, they also bring their demons.[43]

But such demonization was neither new nor confined to the West. Other empires too have viewed foreign-derived religions through curious stereotypes and treated them accordingly. At various points, the Roman Empire had encountered religious sects that practiced behaviors they considered intolerably deviant, including cannibalism and human sacrifice and orgiastic sexuality. When Romans had to make sense of the emerging Christian sect, they understood it through those older and, in fact, quite irrelevant precedents, which were derived from utterly different cultural and geographical settings. As with Orientalism, the essence of such anti-primitivist stereotyping is its tendency to merge images of very different cultures, to paint all with one broad brush.

In later eras, imperial societies exercised their imaginations quite extravagantly in stereotyping cultures they encountered, using atrocity tales to dehumanize them and borrowing from the accumulated myths of multiple empires through the centuries. Commonly, such speculations focused on the sinister religions of the alien society and their supposed practices of (once again) cannibalism and mass human sacrifice, practices that served to read a culture outside the acceptable spectrum of human behavior. Painting a religious system in these bloody colors justified a wholesale assault on the society that tolerated it and showed the necessity for conversion to the approved imperial religion. In the European context, the vision of an African "heart of darkness" proved a powerful stimulus both for conquest and for missionary campaigns.[44]

Ideas of racial and ethnic superiority are an invaluable justification for imperial rule, and once established, they provide a lens for understanding so many other aspects of newly encountered cultures, including their religious features. To return to the analogy of Dr. Dee, imperial ventures supply visions of other faiths, but they are often distorted through poorly understood mirrors.

Memories of Empire

One other critical theme, one imperial commonality, must be discussed at greater length, and that is the role of memory. Writers have long used the contemplation of the ruins of fallen empires as object lessons in the transience of human achievement. In a famous poem written in 1818, Percy Bysshe Shelley imagined an ancient statue of the long-dead Pharaoh Ozymandias, king of kings, whose power now lay in ruins. Its condition taught a harsh lesson for later rulers, including the mighty despots of Shelley's own day: "Look on my works, ye Mighty, and despair!" The poet made a fair point about how oblivion overcame once-great conquerors: even their names were lost, as "Ozymandias" is properly known as Ramses II. But if individual rulers were forgotten, the realms they founded exercised a long and even astonishing influence, which commonly expressed itself in religious forms. Empires remember motifs and words, as in the case of the janissaries, but the fundamental fact of empire is also difficult to eradicate.[45]

Even when a great imperial realm fades or vanishes, it leaves an aura of prestige, which persists in part through material remains such as buildings, monuments, and roads. Although they are by no means the most important vehicles of memory, coins well illustrate this process. During the first millennium BC, a number of states began issuing coins in gold and silver, a practice that soon became a trademark of empires, Persian, Greek and Roman. In Rome, it was Julius Caesar who pioneered the practice of including on coins the portrait of a living being, namely himself. Through the centuries, imperial coins circulated far and wide beyond the frontiers, and the wealthiest and strongest regimes produced the purest and most reliable money. With their depictions of rulers in their majesty, those coins in turn inspired warlords and would-be monarchs to imitate them, often crudely, and in the process those original coins spread imperial iconography and visual rhetoric across much of the known world. They became, in fact, one of the most effective forms of propaganda. When empires adopted new religious forms, the accompanying symbols appeared on new generations of coins, which were noted and copied throughout those same distant regions—again, not necessarily comprehended in full. The coins served as an advance guard of the human emissaries of the rising religion.

Even if empires begin in massacre and enslavement, by creating a desert, they succeed in portraying themselves as the most ambitious expressions of political power. As such, they are commonly treated as singularly glorious and auspicious. The admiration and envy that they inspire is manifested in imitation, both by contemporaries and by later generations. Empires have often borrowed from each other, in terms of iconography, titles, and rhetoric: over time, for instance, Roman emperors acquired titles and pageantry characteristic of their Persian rivals. Smaller states copied their magnificent neighbors, to the point of seeking to become empires in their own right. Later entities aspire to reproduce those original glories, appropriating older symbolism and rhetoric, usually to lay claim to ancient roots and the legitimacy that goes with them. To that extent, empires are a cumulative phenomenon. As Thomas Hobbes observed, religious institutions, too, draw on that treasure trove of imperial memories and resonances.

Remembering the First Empire

The role of such memories, and specifically in religious contexts, is evident from the earliest times. Imperial memories underlie the very oldest religious texts and stories that we possess.

When nineteenth-century European archaeologists investigated the cultures of the ancient Near East, biblical and classical authors alike taught them about the existence of the great Babylonian and Assyrian empires, which supplied a framework for their understanding. Even today, the study of ancient eras in these regions is known as Assyriology. Only gradually did scholars realize that both empires were the successors and imitators of a still older realm, which had carried a charisma comparable to that of Rome in later millennia.[46] The first true empire builder we can know about with any confidence—and in large part, from his own recorded words—was Sargon, the first Semitic ruler of the older Sumerian world. About 2300 BC, he conquered much of Mesopotamia and Syria, which he ruled from his (still unidentified) capital of Akkad. Akkadian forces ranged widely, from Arabia and the Persian Gulf into Anatolia, and trading relations extended to India. A climate-driven catastrophe caused the collapse of that realm in the twenty-second century BC, but Akkadian memories proved lasting and set the expectations for the Babylonian and Assyrian successor realms that ruled the area over the next 1,500 years, including the custom of self-deification, of kings proclaiming themselves divine. Neo-Assyrian kings of the eighth and seventh century BC quoted Sargon's advice about the proper means of governing an empire.[47]

Both Babylonians and Assyrians venerated Sargon and his era, attributing many writings to him and to members of his family, with varying degrees of plausibility. His daughter Enheduanna was the first person ever to be identified as a writer of religious texts, including hymns and myths that were still in use centuries after her time. As a quasi-divine figure, Sargon himself was often remembered in songs, myths, and legends, some of which are echoed in the Bible. Reputedly, Sargon was the son of a priestess who preserved his life by hiding him in a basket in the rushes, much like Moses long after him.[48]

The enduring legacy of Sargon's empire was evident in its Akkadian language, which foreshadows the very long afterlife of Latin following the fall of the Roman Empire in the West and its evolution into Europe's Romance languages. A thousand years before Sargon's time, the Sumerians had developed a writing system called cuneiform, which worked well with their own language. In an epochal move, Sargon appropriated this already ancient system for his own extremely different East Semitic tongue of Akkadian. Written in cuneiform, Akkadian survived for a millennium and a half as the standard language for those later empires. Both Assyrian and Babylonian languages began as dialect variants of that original Akkadian, such as the Old Babylonian in which Hammurabi delivered his famous law code about 1750 BC or the Middle Babylonian in which the *Epic of Gilgamesh* was written some centuries afterward. Middle Babylonian was the language of diplomacy across the Middle Eastern world, while Middle Assyrian became a lingua franca throughout the region. To speak Akkadian was to speak power, to speak empire. Not until the eighth century BC was Akkadian gradually replaced by another Semitic language, Old Aramaic. Like other languages once associated with imperial splendor, Akkadian found its last strongholds in priestly circles, at the turn of the Common Era.[49]

The Endless Restorations of Rome

In the Western tradition, Rome represents the summit of imperial aspiration, to be emulated by later rulers much as the Akkadians had been long before them. After the Western branch of that empire ended in the fifth century AD, a proudly Roman continuation survived in Constantinople, New Rome, over the following millennium. In the West, Charlemagne was proclaimed emperor, *imperator Romanorum*, in 800, and with some interruptions, the Holy Roman Empire persisted until 1806. In the ninth and tenth centuries, Germanic Christian emperors frequently used a phrase on their coins and documents that became almost a manifesto of their power: *renovatio imperii Romanorum* (renewal of the empire of the Romans). A millennium later, Napoleon Bonaparte drew on Roman traditions when he was crowned as emperor in 1804: he had previously held the Roman-derived rank of first consul.[50]

Such attempts at Roman revivalism are well known in the history of Western and Latin Europe, but they were deeply influential in the East, where caesars likewise proliferated. When the remnants of the Byzantine Empire fell to the Ottoman Turks in 1453, the new Islamic ruler, Mehmed, claimed the title of *qayser-i Rûm*, emperor of Rome. Christian states likewise appropriated the Roman titles, with imperial caesars or tsars in Bulgaria, and later in Russia. The Russians claimed that their own realm constituted a Third Rome. In the nineteenth century, that historical obsession was further reflected in the neo-Byzantine architectural styles adopted by Russian authorities throughout their ever-swelling territories. In terms of practical politics, the dream of restoring Orthodox Christian control over Constantinople was a driving force in Russian foreign policy well into the twentieth century. Nor was Russia alone in such fantasies. When Greece won its independence from the Ottomans in the nineteenth century, nationalists formed their intoxicating "Great Idea" of a Byzantine restoration that would unite all Greeks around the wider Aegean world under a new regime based, of course, in Constantinople. All these schemes involved at least some explicitly religious content, but it was not a necessary component of Roman revivalism: the Napoleonic tradition was far more secular.[51]

Empires of varying degrees of plausibility and duration proliferated during the nineteenth century, whether they drew directly on Roman precedent or were mediated through Napoleonic memories. France again became an empire in 1852, Germany in 1871, and transient empires surfaced sporadically in Mexico, Haiti, and Brazil. The German phenomenon declared itself a Second Reich, a successor of the empire founded by Charlemagne, and in 1933, Hitler vaunted his new National Socialist regime as a Third Reich. Italian revolutionary nationalists such as Giuseppe Mazzini used the concept of a restored Roman Empire, in the democratic form of a "Rome of the people." Even so, Mazzini assumed that this new liberal Italy had a natural duty to conquer a Mediterranean empire in Tunisia and farther afield. In the 1920s, the Italian Fascist regime made abundant use of Roman rhetoric and iconography in its attempt to build and expand their Mediterranean empire, under the headship of a Roman-styled leader, or *dux*, a *duce*. Italians used as their symbol the Roman symbol of the fasces, the bundle of rods that connoted unbreakable unity, hence Fascism.[52]

Other empires likewise drew heavily on Roman terminology, not least in the word "colony," and some formally appropriated Roman titles and offices. In 1876, Britain proclaimed its Indian Empire, celebrating the event with spectacular *durbar* ceremonies appropriated from the practice of India's older Mughal Empire. But even there, Roman memories were present. Until 1948, British coins gave the reigning monarch his proper title under the abbreviated form of IND. IMP, *Indiae imperator*—emperor of India—and in appropriately prestigious Latin. More generally, imperial officials of many nations were popularly characterized with such Roman terms as proconsul or legate. In the 1950s, some intellectual French officers fighting in the Algerian independence struggle imagined themselves as latter-day Roman warriors holding the frontiers against the barbarians. Two influential novels of the era bear the titles *The Centurions* and *The Praetorians*. It is scarcely possible for Euro-Americans to conceive of empire without referring back to Rome.[53]

Reclaiming Empire

Such attempts to reclaim an imperial inheritance are by no means confined to the West, or to memories of Rome. Warring Chinese kingdoms each struggled to restore the glories of past dynasties, and we will often see such efforts in a South Asian context. The Aztecs presented themselves as the true heirs and continuers of the splendid Toltec Empire that had perished some centuries before their rise to power. In each case, the later regime tried to graft itself onto its predecessor in as convincing a fashion as can be achieved.[54]

All such imperial restorations rely on a degree of myth-making, and of showmanship, but some are less plausible than others. As recently as 1971, the shah of Iran invested lavishly in pageantry that would commemorate the 2,500th anniversary of the Persian Empire, of which he claimed to be the heir and living representative. He adopted several of the magnificent titles that had been held by those ancient Persian monarchs. In reality, that particular shah was a parvenu, the son of a warlord who had seized power in the 1920s, and his imperial circus was intended to secure legitimacy for a fragile regime. In this instance, the celebration not only failed; it accelerated the decline of the regime, which collapsed in 1979. In other cases too, what is claimed as a continuation or a revival is in fact at best an aspiration, an appeal to ancient imperial memories. When Britain's African empire began to crumble in the 1950s, the first independent Black nation took the name of Ghana, commemorating an ancient African empire that in reality was located far from that particular territory. No less anxious to grasp at ancient splendors was the Islamist terrorist group ISIS, based in Iraq and Syria, which in 2014 claimed to restore the caliphate. It thereby staked a claim to the legacy of the vast political and religious empire that had once ruled much of the medieval world.[55]

Beyond the Frontiers

The aura of majesty and power that empires project can be immensely attractive, and that symbolic power lingers in surprising ways. I have already noted how ideas circulate on the frontiers, but in many cases, they can become remarkably effective bearers and transmitters of imperial ideology, crucial reminders of imperial glories.

I have mentioned one story from a Native American context in the case of the Genízaros, but another North American instance illustrates this point. After Native forces defeated the US cavalry at the Battle of the Little Big Horn in 1876, they fled across the border into Canada, under the leadership of the Lakota chieftain Sitting Bull. Canadian authorities were naturally alarmed by these warlike new arrivals, but Sitting Bull was anxious to present himself as a grateful guest. He showed his hosts the medals that his ancestors had received from earlier generations of British agents and soldiers, presumably during the War of 1812, when the Lakota had sided with the British against the Americans. Those earlier officials had told the Native chiefs that if ever they needed assistance, they should turn to the British once more, and now, sixty years later and several hundred miles away, they were claiming the imperial promise. They sought the protection of the venerated grandmother, Queen Victoria, and her red-coated soldiers. Unlike Dr. Dee's mirror, these objects were not just exotic curiosities, regarded with superstitious awe. Rather, they were palpable symbols of a real empire, association with which could carry serious political advantages.[56]

However improbable the story might appear, it finds many echoes through the centuries on the frontiers of various empires, in the territories that were all too often classified as savage or barbarous. An empire projected its reputation, its soft power, through such material trappings, through coins, medals, and other symbols of the monarch and the imperial family. The idea of handing such objects to a friendly warrior chieftain on the imperial periphery would have made wonderful sense to agents and administrators through the centuries, whether Chinese, Roman, or Persian. Those predecessors would have thoroughly appreciated the effort to win the support of such a border people against a rival empire. Of their nature, such objects can survive for centuries, passing on the memories of empire to later generations. Through such contacts, surrounding societies acquired pretensions of their own, becoming kingdoms and even empires and adopting the culture that they associated with those glories. Such cultural diffusion supplies a splendid entrée to the major religion associated with the great empire in question, whether it be Buddhism or Christianity or Islam, and it encourages the neighboring state to adopt that faith as part of the "imperial" package.

Empires leave stubborn and enduring ghosts, and religious institutions have often evoked them, sometimes with stunning success.

2
The Kingdoms of God

> And Babylon, the glory of kingdoms, the beauty of the Chaldees' excellency, shall be as when God overthrew Sodom and Gomorrah. It shall never be inhabited, neither shall it be dwelt in from generation to generation.
>
> ***Isaiah 13:19–20, KJV***

The history of the ancient people of Israel famously involves twelve tribes who claimed descent from the sons of the patriarch known as Jacob, or Israel. Ten of those tribes subsequently vanished from the historical record, provoking generations of historical speculation about where their modern descendants might be located, with many strange corners of the world cited as possible candidates. The circumstances of their "disappearance" in fact pose little mystery. In the eighth century BC, the tribes constituted the Northern Kingdom of Israel, with its capital at Samaria, which existed alongside the Southern Kingdom of Judah, centered on Jerusalem. During a war between the two states, northern and southern, the king of Judah sought help from the aggressive Assyrian Empire, which defeated Israel (732 BC) and deported some of its people to Mesopotamia. The rump state of Israel survived for another decade, until its king plotted to seek Egyptian help against Assyria. An enraged Assyrian king invaded once more, and in the words of the conqueror, "Samaria I looked at, I captured; 27,280 men who dwelt in it I carried away" into Assyria: the king in question bore the auspicious name of Sargon II. The ten tribes ceased to exist as identifiable political or social realities. The Samaritans, who still survive in greatly shrunken numbers, claim descent from survivors of those groups who escaped deportation. If the removals had not happened, the whole later history of Israel would have been very different and presumably would have had a less exclusive focus on Jerusalem.[1]

The details of this wrenching conflict are described at length in the Bible, which, as in so many other instances, describes the workings of empires in considerable detail. In so doing, it illustrates many of the broad themes that we encountered in the previous chapter, in this instance the forced relocations of populations. Also described are the religious consequences of these imperial clashes. Whether they realize it or not, every Christian or Jew who has ever studied the Bible becomes immersed in the history of empires, and countless sermons and lessons through the years have recounted those connections. In particular, those later generations view the experience of empire from the standpoint of a borderland society regularly caught up in the schemes and ambitions of great powers, frequently (if reluctantly) absorbing their cultures. Almost unconsciously, we learn not just the practices and terminology of empire but the rhetoric and methods of the deadly opponents of such regimes. Neatly encapsulating that dichotomy is the ancient metropolis of Babylon itself, which has a whole biblical history, both as a literal imperial center and as a rhetorical symbol of dreadful evil.[2]

Beyond forming the context for the history of the Hebrew people, those encounters profoundly affected the religion of Judaism and later the earliest phases of Christianity. In both cases, that applies to the earliest and most formative phases of the faiths, as is powerfully reflected in their most basic scriptures and their core theological assumptions. Repeatedly, we see how critical doctrines arose through the interplay with great empires, often in reaction against those mighty states and their policies. Like other subject peoples in so many other eras, Jews debated the impact on their culture and faith, the choice between collaboration and resistance. As in other contexts, exposure to a wider world encouraged greater universalist approaches among some believers, while driving others to nativist and exclusivist responses. The Bible, both Old and New Testaments, is a priceless textbook on the subject of religion and empire.

Israel and the Empires

The history of Israel involved a series of encounters with several great empires, from pharaonic Egypt through the Assyrian and Babylonian domains, to the Hellenistic Greeks and the Romans. These successive interactions were both positive and negative, involving acts both of subjugation and liberation. Both strands are inescapable in the scriptural tradition.

For the Hebrew people, the two critical events in their early history were the exodus from Egypt, probably around 1200 BC, and the exile to Babylon in the 580s BC, followed by the return to the Holy Land some sixty years later. Historians have challenged the literal truth of that Exodus, and the actual numbers cited by Scripture are impossible to credit, but some kind of flight from the fearsome pharaonic empire almost certainly did occur. The founding of the nation thus involved an act of resistance against empire, a mass defection. Moses himself bears an Egyptian name, and so do the Levites, who feature so often in that story. It has plausibly been suggested that the Hebrews asserted their new freedom with a daring act of anti-imperial appropriation. At least, the sacred ark of the covenant described in the Old Testament bears an uncanny resemblance to the imperial tent of the Pharaoh Ramses II, who probably ruled at the time of the Exodus.[3]

In later times, that new Israel was a buffer state, a contested borderland between the empires that were the great powers of their time. Besides Egypt, the eastern counterpart based in Mesopotamia and Syria was either the Neo-Assyrian Empire, which prevailed from 911 to 609 BC, or its neo-Babylonian successor, from 626 through 539 BC. Those territories were in their turn absorbed into the Persian Empire. For long stretches of Israelite history, the nation was either subject to one of those empires or else it was never allowed to forget the looming presence of those overweening neighbors. When the prophetic tradition first comes into view from the ninth century BC onward, those writings offer frequent commentary on other empires. The prophets struggled to understand the role of the various imperial powers in the greater divine plan, presumably as scourges to chasten a sinful and rebellious people. In the canonical Old Testament, as it is known to Jews and to Protestant Christians, the words "Assyria," "Babylon," and their cognates feature some 430 times, and that does not include individual rulers of those nations. "Egypt" occurs 640 times, and again, that does not count such related terms as "pharaoh" (240 occurrences) or particular settlements or geographical features.[4]

Apart from physical conquest, those empires were beacons of science and high culture of a kind that fascinated the thinkers of a marginal state such as Israel. Assyrians and Babylonians alike were heirs to the common Akkadian tradition and to the Sumerians before them. When nineteenth-century Europeans translated the texts of that older Akkadian-derived world, many were shocked to find how many parallels they found to the Old Testament, which hitherto had been viewed as a unique divine gift to the Hebrew people. Such basic ideas as the creation narrative, as well as the global flood and the story of Noah, found echoes in Babylonian texts written during the second millennium BC. Israelite thinkers could easily have absorbed these at any point during the Neo-Assyrian supremacy, and they evidently had a transformative effect on the thought-world that we find in the Bible. Even so, the Hebrews were not content simply to mimic those imperial originals. The famous creation mythology of the Near Eastern world at that time was the Babylonian *Enuma Elish*, which gave a pivotal role to the city of Babylon as the center of the universe. The biblical book of Genesis gives this tale a subversive twist, as that city's majestic role is grotesquely parodied in the tale of the Tower of Babel.[5]

Empire and Monotheism

Those imperial neighbors exercised enormous and even decisive cultural influence, and on the most basic assumptions of life. That included something so basic as the uncompromising monotheism that is such an obvious feature of the Hebrew Bible as we have it. But that emphasis was not always so central.[6] In its earlier phases, from the twelfth through the eighth century BC, Israelite religion closely resembled that of other Semitic societies, with a variety of deities both male and female and a multiplicity of sacred places and shrines. Although that society gave its main devotion to one presiding deity, to YHWH, that did not necessarily imply that other gods were thought not to exist. In technical terms, this was not monotheism but henotheism, the following of one paramount deity among a group. Remnants of that belief in plural gods are scattered through the biblical texts as they survive, often quite incongruously: in Genesis, God even declares, "Let us make Man in our own image."[7]

Matters changed decisively from the later eighth century onward, when the nation faced an existential threat from the Assyrians, who conquered and eliminated the Northern Kingdom of Israel in 720 BC and who would obviously soon be posing a like threat to Judah. A massive siege of Jerusalem followed in 701, when only a sudden onslaught of plague (probably) saved the city. The Southern Kingdom barely survived. Meanwhile, the Assyrians went on to ever greater glories, and the annexation of Egypt in 671 BC gave them hegemony over the whole Middle East.[8]

These events provided the backdrop to a sweeping religious revolution among the Hebrew people, a radical and indeed quite unprecedented reform program. To appease God's obvious wrath and to urge his favor on the desperately threatened state, Hebrew thinkers now preached strict and uncompromising monotheism, removing any survivals of older deities and devotions. Only by such a reformation, they believed, would God allow the survival of a purified and strengthened nation. That movement led to far-reaching iconoclasm against once-cherished Hebrew sites and objects that were now denounced as idolatrous, profoundly reshaping both religious thought and popular practice. The two key figureheads were the kings Hezekiah (716–687 BC) and Josiah (640–609), both of whom were regarded very highly indeed in later Jewish and Christian tradition. Clerical elites now wrote and rewrote scriptural texts to claim not just that God demanded exclusive worship and belief but that he had always done so. The historical reconstruction found a focus in the book of Deuteronomy, which was probably composed in the mid-seventh century and presented as a rediscovered ancient text. The monotheistic revolution is well known to biblical scholars, but at every stage, it can be understood only as a response to the imminent threat of imperial conquest, with the mass deportations and cultural annihilation that would ensue.[9]

Exile and Return

That all-embracing reform policy seemed to be justified when, in 612, the Assyrians were decisively defeated, a momentous collapse that King Josiah just lived long enough to witness. But the new imperial victors, the Babylonians, were scarcely less intimidating. In the 580s, they ended the existence of the Southern Kingdom of Judah: they destroyed the Jewish Temple and deported large sections of the population to their metropolitan homeland. In doing this, the conquerors were following a policy that would be quite standard for many empires, but in the Hebrew case, the experience powerfully accelerated the ongoing revolution in religious life. The prophets gave the exile a cosmic significance, emphasizing the theory of the righteous remnant of God's chosen people, who would be preserved even after the larger mass of the community had fallen away into sin and idolatry. The process of editing and rewriting older scriptures to reflect newer perceptions continued apace.[10]

When eventually the Persian king Cyrus freed the Hebrews and allowed their return, those thinkers developed daring new theologies about the nature and unity of God, and his willingness to work through people of any nation. As expressed in the very influential words of the prophet known as Second Isaiah, this new universalism was a product of that imperial contact. Prophetic texts applied to Cyrus laid a foundation for messianic expectations and are still regularly read (and sung) as such in Christian churches.[11]

Some of those prophetic utterances acquired an amazing afterlife. Probably in the late eighth century, the prophet we know as First Isaiah proclaimed the doom of Babylon and its king, who at that point was the

Assyrian Sargon II, whom we have already encountered as the destroyer of the Northern Kingdom of Israel. Appropriating a royal title, the prophet spoke of the king as the Morning Star (or Light-Bringer, or Son of the Morning), who had aspired to sit enthroned in heaven but was brought down in ruin. Over the centuries, that passage gave rise to a belief in a powerful angelic being who had launched a failed rebellion against the deity and was accordingly cast down into the pit. In the Latin Christian translation, the "son of the morning" was rendered as Lucifer. A short passage of strictly contemporary relevance—a polemical denunciation of an overambitious emperor—laid the scriptural foundation for the whole theology of Satan as it would later appear in early Judaism, and more elaborately in both Christianity and Islam. While the Persian Cyrus became a first draft for the Messiah, Assyria's Sargon offered a prototype for Satan himself.[12]

The Old Testament religion that is so familiar, and the religion of Judaism founded on it, even in matters as foundational as monotheism itself, was a response to imperial threats, pressures, and demands.

After Alexander

That imperial context not only continued after the return from Babylon; it intensified. We tend to miss that fact because the standard Jewish Bible (which is the Protestant Old Testament) does not explicitly portray events that occurred after the fifth century BC. There are indeed references to such developments between the fourth and second centuries, but they are thinly disguised as prophecy, notably in the book of Daniel. Other Christian traditions such as the Catholic and Orthodox do indeed include several books covering this later era, such as the books of Maccabees.[13]

The obvious biblical denunciations of empire in certain eras conceal the fact that the Hebrews actually spent long periods living fairly contentedly under the authority of various foreign realms, absorbing their influences and taking advantage of the opportunities they presented. As we read few accounts of heroic resisters against those empires, or prophetic attacks on their evil deeds, we easily forget just how natural such imperial contexts came to appear. In reality, from the sixth century BC through the fourth, Israel was an acquiescent component of the vast and very cosmopolitan Persian Empire. In the mid-fifth century, it was reportedly the Persian emperor Artaxerxes who sent the Jewish priest and scribe Ezra to restore his community in Jerusalem and to rebuild the temple. According to the work that bears his name, the imperial agent undertook a racial purification of the people, forcibly separating Jewish men from their foreign-born wives and families and drawing razor-sharp boundaries beyond which any thoughts of universalism were not permitted.[14]

Like most empires, the Persians drew borders and divisions that profoundly affected the ways in which subjects defined themselves, and in the process, they created "Jews." The Hebrew residents of the old kingdom of Judah belonged to the "province of Judah," Yehud Medinata, and increasingly the term "Judah/Judea" marked the territory both of a religion and an ethnic group. This was a world well used to the idea of particular nations or peoples with their characteristic customs and their known homeland. In anything like its modern sense, the word "Jew" appears as an ethnic or religious term in the fifth and fourth centuries BC, and the Greek word Ioudaios could mean either Jew or Judean.[15]

Although this is controversial, some scholars suggest that the Hebrews borrowed heavily from the Persian religious system, the Zoroastrian faith, with its dualistic vision of cosmic struggle between the forces of light and darkness and its strong belief in angels. Such an account is open to debate, because it is not clear whether in fact Zoroastrians themselves held those particular beliefs as explicitly as they would in later centuries. Many of the developments once attributed to Zoroastrian influence might actually have arisen internally, from the Jewish tradition. Even so, it would have been natural for the Hebrews to have appropriated at least some ideas from yet another set of foreign rulers.[16]

When that Persian realm was in its turn overthrown by Alexander the Great, the land of Palestine was contested between two of the dominions founded by his successors, the empires of Ptolemy and Seleucus: the Ptolemies prevailed in the third century BC, the Seleucids in the second. Stretching as they did from Greece and Egypt to what we would call Pakistan and the "-stans" of Central Asia, the twin empires brought together a bewilderingly broad range of cultures and religious traditions, and spread ideas and practices over this enormous area. They exercised a profound and lasting influence on the culture and thought of the Eurasian civilizations of the day, including those of the Jews.[17]

The proliferation of cities bearing Greek imperial names suggests the scope of the emerging transcontinental world and its far-flung communications. We see the dozens of cities called Alexandria (or Philippi, or Antioch, or Seleucia) from Europe through the Middle East and deep into Central Asia: each commemorated an emperor or a member of his family. Seleucus made (Syrian) Antioch his capital, the Ptolemies based themselves at (Egyptian) Alexandria. Both cities became energetic centers of thought and learning, and were among the world's largest urban centers. So was Seleucia-Ctesiphon, which stood near ancient Babylon and eventually became the metropolis of a new Parthian (and later Persian) empire. From such capitals, Greek language and culture spread throughout these realms. We might usefully imagine a "Hellenistic triangle" formed by imaginary lines joining those three imperial capitals of Antioch, Alexandria, and Seleucia-Ctesiphon, and that triangle retained its pivotal role for a full millennium, until after the rise of Islam.[18]

This imperial geography shaped the Jewish world as it developed during this era. Although Jews had traveled and migrated long before Alexander's time, the new systems made travel far easier, as the diaspora became a fundamental part of Jewish life (the word "diaspora" itself is Hellenistic Greek for "dispersal"). Empires make diasporas possible. Sizable Jewish communities existed in each of those key "triangle" centers, which would be so critical for early Christianity. In fact, Egypt became home to a flourishing alternative temple that operated independently of the institution in Jerusalem itself. When the Talmud was compiled in the early centuries of the Common Era, the rabbinic sages involved worked both in Palestine and in the other Jewish homeland of the time, Babylonia. Jews living far from Jerusalem and its temple had to develop creative ways of preserving their faith, which they did through the new institution of the synagogue. The concept began in Ptolemaic Egypt and spread throughout the diaspora.[19]

Living in an *Oikoumenē*

The religious implications were no less far-reaching, during a pioneering era of globalization. Many peoples once separated from each other thought and wrote in the Greek language and applied Greek categories to every aspect of culture and religion. It was in these years that both Egyptian and Babylonian authors wrote histories of their traditional societies and beliefs, in the Greek that would be required to reach an audience across the then-known inhabited world, the *oikoumenē*. This is the term that gave rise to the English "ecumenical."[20]

In the third century BC, Jews took the historic step of translating their scriptures into that language, in the so-called Septuagint. Much of that work was done in Alexandria, under Ptolemaic rulers, and it remained the standard version of the Bible that was used for centuries by Jews and Christians alike. Although this translation helped explain the religion to non-Jews around the civilized world, it was principally intended to serve the needs of the ever-larger number of Jews who were far more comfortable communicating in the imperial language. The linguistic inheritance of the Greek translation is incalculable. It is from the Septuagint that we derive fundamental words that supply the vocabulary of religion and faith in most Western languages. A selective list of such borrowings in English would include "angel," "demon," "blasphemy," "idol," "paradise," "holocaust," and "proselyte." The Septuagint Greek word *diabolos* gave us "devil." The concept of the Lord's anointed, *moschiach*, or "messiah," entered Greek as *Christos*. The Septuagint also popularized the word *Ioudaios*. In the mid-second century BC, the second book of Maccabees coined the word *Ioudaismos*, "Judaism," to describe a package of religious customs and beliefs in a sense we can recognize today.[21]

The whole collection of translated scriptures was *ta Biblia*, which either implied "the books," or more grandly, "The Book," and that became Bible. Individual books within that collection received such Greek titles as Genesis and Exodus, and the first five became the Pentateuch. When early Christians commented on the Scriptures, thereby creating the theology of the new faith, they were wrestling with the Septuagint version, and with the many quirks and emphases that the translators had incorporated into the text.

Beyond vocabulary, the new imperial context raised challenging issues of assimilation and resistance. Jews were quite accustomed to living peacefully under foreign empires, and they had no critique of the notion of empire as such. Traditions of earlier Jewish monarchies not only credited David and Solomon with sizable imperial dominions of their own but certainly exaggerated the span of their power. But quite unintentionally, the Greek empires threatened to subvert prized religious assumptions and (once again) caused revolutionary changes within the Hebrew tradition—within what was now known as Judaism.

Ptolemaic and Seleucid rulers encouraged what they saw as an amiable syncretism, a merger of different deities and worship cults, some focused on divine rulers. Jewish elites were generally content to accept such policies as part of a wide-ranging policy of Hellenization. In the 160s BC, however, such changes inspired an explosive reaction when the Seleucid emperor Antiochus IV Epiphanes seized temple treasures and sought to place his own image in the temple, while seeking to forbid circumcision. Led by the Maccabee family, a militant faction of Jews rebelled against the Seleucids, and in the process they created a new sense of national identity, together with whole new structures of religious belief. Above all, that meant the apocalyptic worldview, with its rich attendant literature. The monstrous figure of evil portrayed in the book of Daniel, who is usually taken as a first draft of the antichrist, is modeled directly on Antiochus himself. Yet despite that successful war of secession, Greek influences remained. The accounts of the great Maccabee revolt were written in Greek and used the Seleucid dating system, commonly known as "the year of the Greeks." As new Jewish kingdoms emerged, they modeled themselves entirely on the Seleucid rulers, adopting their symbols of power.[22]

A Roman World

During the first century BC, the ascendant Roman Empire took Palestine and Syria into its sphere of influence, through cooperation with local sovereigns. That Roman power continued some of the advantages offered by the older Hellenistic states, by expanding communications and secure travel and trade. The diaspora stretched even farther, particularly into Europe. But the Roman presence revived all the older issues of collaboration and co-optation, and a potent new nationalism, explicitly grounded in religious belief, inspired militant sects such as the Zealots.

Such themes were evident in the writings of the sectarian community that emerged at Qumran, probably during the turbulent decade of the 160s BC. Ideas of empire, and resistance to it, were central to the worldview of the Qumran sectaries, who were presumably those Essenes who are described in many writings of the time. In the Dead Sea Scrolls, we see a whole theology founded on an end-times confrontation with the evil forces of the "Kittim," a term that originally meant the Hellenistic Greeks but which now segued readily to cover the Romans. The sectaries looked to a messianic liberation led by a new manifestation of the greatest Jewish imperial leader, David. In the meantime, faithful believers must separate absolutely from the polluted world with all its temptations. This radical approach, with its messianic and apocalyptic views, its vision of a cosmic struggle between light and darkness, profoundly influenced the emergent Jesus movement. It left a legacy for other later dualist sects, including the Manichean tradition, which came close to becoming another world religion in its own right, alongside the Abrahamic faiths.[23]

Relations with Rome dominated Jewish political and religious thought until the calamitous anti-imperial uprising of 66 AD, which culminated in the sack of Jerusalem in 70 AD and the fall of the Second Temple. A new revolt in the 130s resulted in the Roman decision to expel Jews from the land: Jerusalem ceased to exist under that name, becoming a Roman imperial city with the thoroughly Latin name of Aelia Capitolina. Other massacres and conflicts arising from these revolts devastated the Jewish communities of many great cities, including Alexandria.

Making Judaism

These calamities began the long Jewish exile from the Holy Land, but they also inspired a redefinition of Judaism scarcely less significant than that of the earlier monotheistic revolution. In the centuries after 70 AD, Jewish thinkers undertook a thorough reconstruction of the faith that is expressed in the writings of the Talmud, which records countless rabbinic discussions over every aspect of life and practice. But the new rabbinic Judaism closed many other avenues of discussion that had hitherto been commonplace in the Jewish world but were now discredited following their association with recent disasters. This meant discarding and forbidding most of the older apocalyptic beliefs of Essenes and other groups, together with overt messianic nationalism. The rabbis earnestly wished to discourage any such outbreaks in future, while removing openly subversive writings.[24]

The new formulation of Judaism suppressed many once-influential bodies of scripture and speculation that had hitherto been extremely influential, such as the writings associated with the mysterious patriarch Enoch and many apocalyptic manifestos. Many of those alternative scriptures vanished from circulation for centuries to come, and a good number were wholly lost. The Hebrew Bible, as it would be defined over the following two millennia, was much more limited in its concept of scripture and canon than it would once have been. Moreover, in an apt symbol of the new approaches, the rabbis who defined the canon rejected a number of books that had apparently been written in Greek and had no basis in the Hebrew, which was now the required gold standard of authenticity. This was a significant reaction against the "ecumenical" world that had created the Septuagint.[25]

The "normal" Judaism that emerged from the defeat by imperial Rome in fact represented a significant break from previous precedent, although it presented itself as being far more rooted in antiquity than it actually was.

Jesus, the Empire, and the Kingdom

That lengthy Jewish struggle against empire is well known to anyone who has ever studied the times of Jesus of Nazareth and Christian origins. The Roman presence pervades the accounts we find in the Gospels. Even Jesus' birth story, as recorded in Luke, begins by recording that "a decree went out from Caesar Augustus that the whole world should be enrolled." Jesus' life ends when he is executed by Roman authorities, with Roman soldiers in attendance, and by the Roman method of crucifixion. A board placed on his cross describes his crime in Hebrew and in the two imperial languages of Greek and Latin. Even today, billions of Christians regularly recite a creed that commemorates the Roman official who presided over his trial, Pontius Pilate.[26]

Besides such famous facts, we might easily miss the everyday penetrations of empire into the story reported in the New Testament, so many key events of which occur in places named for emperors or members of their families, whether Roman dynasts or Hellenistic Greeks before them. The list includes, at a minimum, Caesarea Maritima, Caesarea Philippi, and both Antiochs mentioned in Acts, not to mention Seleucia, Ptolemais, Philippi, and Thessaloniki (Thessalonike was a half sister of the great Alexander). Also in this category was the Sea or Lake of Tiberias, the name that the Romans had given to the Sea of Galilee a very short time before the events portrayed in the Gospels. The Palestine of Jesus' day was a palimpsest of empires, past and present. In the seven churches of the book of Revelation, that category of imperial namesakes includes both the cities of Laodicea and Philadelphia. All seven cities, moreover, were connected through efficient and well-known networks of Roman roads. The earliest Christians were literally walking in an imperial landscape, passing through imperial streets and highways.

Illustrations of this imperial context abound. Several stories in the English translations of the Gospels indicate the dreadful reputation attached to "publicans," a word commonly conjoined with "and sinners" (or pagans, or harlots). The Greek word signifies a tax collector or tax farmer, someone who subcontracted the collection work for Roman authority, making a sizable personal profit through exorbitant transactions. The English term "publican" derives from a Latin translation that roots the term even more firmly in Roman bureaucratic practice.[27]

Modern scholars differ as to how centrally anti-imperial policies featured in the initial Christian message. Frequently in the Gospels, Jesus refers to the central theme of his teaching as the kingdom of God, in Greek, the *basileia tou Theou*, and *basileia* is exactly the word that in its time would have been applied to the empire of the Romans.[28] The original Greek text knows nothing of the distinction that so naturally emerges in English translations between the (Roman) empire and the kingdom preached by Jesus. We might just as properly translate Jesus' aspiration as "God's empire." Given the other resonances of the thought-world of Qumran, we might legitimately ask whether that Jesus and his first followers were preaching the overthrow of the existing Roman imperial order, supplanting one kingdom/empire with another.

Almost certainly, the surviving documents as we have them deliberately underplay that explicit anti-Roman theme. The first written Gospel that we possess, that of Mark, was created in the immediate aftermath of the sack of Jerusalem, and that event has left a powerful imprint in the text. Exactly like the rabbis who were reconstructing Judaism at this very time, Mark and the other Gospel writers were keenly anxious to present their movement in a way that would discourage imperial persecutions. As we are told, Jesus deftly avoids the trap presented to him when he is asked whether it is right to pay taxes to the empire. Taking a Roman coin, he replies that one should give to Caesar that which is Caesar's, and give God what is God's. It was rhetorically essential to have Jesus declare that his kingdom (empire) was an inner spiritual reality, and assuredly not "of this world."[29]

Even so, some suggestive passages do remain to suggest an original anti-Roman bent. When Jesus exorcizes demons, they identify themselves by the Roman military name "Legion." Quite explicit in its hatred of Rome is the book of Revelation, which probably dates from the 90s AD, and which offers a phantasmagoric vision of evil and satanic beings who challenge God and his saints. Chief among them is a dreadful harlot mounted on a seven-headed beast, the notorious whore of Babylon, recalling the early empire that had been Israel's nemesis. But as the text makes clear, Babylon is a paper-thin disguise for Rome, which is the city actually intended here. As we are told, with geographical precision, "The seven heads are seven hills on which the woman sits." A list of kings supplied here can refer only to the Roman emperors, with special condemnation reserved for Nero, who is represented as the great beast whose number is 666. This is a fiery and quite unabashed anti-imperial polemic.[30]

That early context highlights a real paradox in the history of religions. Christianity began with a political heritage very close to that of Judaism, with a healthy suspicion of gentile empires. That thought-world and its scriptural supports have been oft-cited throughout Christian history, as rebels and dissenters have struggled against those they imagined as pharaoh or as Babylon. But as Christianity grew away from Judaism, and itself became mainly gentile in composition, so it became ever more entangled in that gentile political world. It was that relationship with those empires that would ensure the survival of the new faith and lay the foundation for what would ultimately become the world's largest religion. The city with seven hills became a primary center of the new Christian world.

3
Making Christianity

> It was at Rome, on the 15th of October 1764, as I sat musing amidst the ruins of the Capitol, while the bare-footed friars were singing vespers in the temple of Jupiter, that the idea of writing the decline and fall of the city first started to my mind.
>
> ***Edward Gibbon***

In the heyday of British imperial power in the 1920s, Rudyard Kipling published his story "The Church That Was at Antioch," a fascinating exploration of the relationship between dominant imperial forces and the religions of the lands they occupy. The story depicts Roman soldiers encountering early Christians in a situation that at every stage resembles the British India of the twentieth century. Relations between Jews and Jewish Christians foreshadow later tensions between Hindus and Muslims, while the imperial officers grimly struggle to maintain order and peace. In ancient times as in modern, the subject peoples loathe each other even more than they hate the alien occupiers. Throughout, the story is told through the eyes of the imperial Roman occupiers. We need not accept Kipling's apologia for British racial supremacy to be impressed by the picture he gives of the everyday realities of an occupied society in a time of religious ferment and specifically, in the context of a key imperial city. Kipling was making valuable points about the nature of empire and of imperial rule, and its potential role in allowing or preventing religious innovation. Perhaps inevitably, what he misses is the very strong role that empire could play in inciting religious-based antagonism to their rule and in the process reshaping that creed.[1]

As Kipling knew, the early history of Christianity was profoundly affected by the actions or policies of empires, but the posthumous memories of such entities were scarcely less important. Religions are very good at remembering, even if the exact details of those accounts might well stray from objective truth. Even in the very early phases of that faith, we are not just dealing with the Roman Empire, but also with other powers of the time, and above all the Persian realm. Not just in a geographical sense, the contours of emerging Christianity trace the borders of past empires. As in so many instances in all the great religions, issues of common language were a major component of that imperial influence. So were the empires' frontiers and the borderland societies that lay beyond them.[2]

Acts and Empire

Whatever the ideological role empires played in the mindset of Jesus and his first followers, there is no doubt about the influence of the Roman Empire on the emergence of that faith. That impact was evident in the easy communication systems that the empire made possible, the maintenance of order, and urbanization. In the aftermath of the Jewish wars against Rome and the hideous carnage that followed, it might seem absurd to speak of a "Roman Peace": in this instance, the conquerors really did turn Palestine into a desert, before pronouncing that peace. But in the wider world, those imperial institutions proved fundamental to religious growth.

These factors are all evident in the book of Acts, which purports to record events that occurred between roughly 30 and 60 AD and which in its present form dates from the end of that first century. Characters travel freely by sea or road, usually basing themselves in the great cities of empire. It was in Antioch where followers of the Jesus Way first acquired the name of Christians, and Antioch remained a key center for missionary expansion.[3] Acts reports that the apostle Paul visited many cities, allowing us to reconstruct his routes. When he traveled from Philippi to Thessaloniki, he must have used the splendid Roman road called the Via Egnatia, which remained a principal artery for imperial communications well into the Byzantine era, and indeed through Ottoman times. The road ran for six hundred miles from Byzantium (later Constantinople) to Dyrrachium/Durrës on the Adriatic. It would be possible to write a history of that particular road alone in terms of the religious and mystical ideas that it conveyed, from the early Jesus movement to the Christian heresies of the High Middle Ages. Paul's journey to Rome also gives a glimpse of the thriving sea routes that bound the empire. He planned to visit Spain, but there is no clear evidence that he ever accomplished this goal.[4]

Acts shows how imperial rule made possible extensive travel and relocation, and with that the ideas that individuals bore with them. In every case, the pioneering Christians are following the route already pioneered by the Jewish diaspora, and they established themselves in those communities. We see one sequence of examples in the section of Acts that we now know as its eighteenth chapter (those chapter divisions are much later additions), which reports events of the early 50s AD. The story begins in Corinth, a city that, for better or worse, had been closely tied to imperial fortunes. In the Hellenistic era, Corinth had enjoyed some political visibility until the Romans annihilated it in 146 BC. Decades later, they restored the city as a significant regional capital within their empire and as a meeting place for Greeks, Romans, and Jews. Corinth was a pivotal Greek center of the imperial cult, with the appropriate temples. The city, as the apostles knew it, was a recent Roman invention. It was here that Paul met the couple Aquila and Priscilla, who become faithful allies. Aquila was from Pontus, in northern Anatolia, and lived in Rome until the Emperor Claudius decided to expel the city's Jews. At that point, the pair relocated to Corinth. They then accompanied Paul to Ephesus, another of the greatest cities of the imperial East. Here Aquila and Priscilla heard the powerful preaching of Apollos of Alexandria, who had himself traveled to Ephesus and planned to proceed to Corinth.[5]

Acts frequently reports Paul's encounters with Roman authority, which are presented in the favorable terms that Kipling adopts in his fiction. We need not take the Acts account as unvarnished truth, as the author was striving to make his story palatable to a respectable Roman audience. But it does reflect several common imperial themes, not least the official wish to preserve legality and order, with little or no concern about the specific religious opinions at issue. Paul's preaching in the Corinth synagogue stirred furious complaints about his heretical doctrines, as Jewish leaders protested to the Roman proconsul, Gallio, "This fellow persuadeth men to worship God contrary to the Law." Gallio responded much as countless imperial officials would have done, before or since. If, he said, the charge involved some kind of crime or sedition, he would investigate it immediately. But as it only involved "questions about words and names and your own Law—settle the matter yourselves. I will not be a judge of such things." The Jewish law, as opposed to the empire's law, was not his business. Such a dismissal was in effect a license to preach dissident doctrine, unless and until mainstream religious leaders could frame it as somehow seditious or disloyal. Kipling memorably borrowed this story for fictional purposes, in his poem "Gallio's Song":

Whether ye rise for the sake of a creed,
Or riot in hope of spoil,
Equally will I punish the deed,
Equally check the broil;
Nowise permitting injustice at all
From whatever doctrine it springs—
But—whether ye follow Priapus or Paul,
I care for none of these things![6]

The stories in Acts suggest the shades of authority involved in imperial rule, ranging from direct Roman control to a delicate interaction with local allies and puppet rulers, and the Christians cleverly negotiated such nuances to their own advantage. Again, these would be sensitive questions for many later imperial regimes, certainly including the British in India. Paul's Roman citizenship gave him a trump card in navigating these subtleties.

Cities

The imperial metropolis was fundamental to the growth of the religion, and the book of Acts follows the trajectory of Paul's career until his arrival in Rome, which is its natural culmination. Rome early became a very influential center of the emerging church and a magnet for Christian thinkers from around the empire. In the 130s AD, an interested seeker in Rome itself could easily hear the teachings of such prestigious figures as the Egyptian Valentinus or Marcion, from the same Pontic region that had earlier produced Aquila. Romans of this era did not have to wander far to seek out the wider Christian world: it came to them. All spiritual roads led there. And when one encountered new insights and ideas in the metropolis, individuals took them back to their home territory, which might be a thousand miles distant.[7]

Although the empire persecuted Christians, it created the foundations on which the new movement could build and plant deep roots in given regions. As in the first phases, particularly crucial were the cities and the trade networks on which their prosperity was founded. The geography of the earliest Christianity can be visualized from an admittedly incomplete map of the churches known to have been founded before 300 AD, that is, in the times of persecution. Several dense clusters clearly emerge, which indicate the greatest bulwarks of Christian strength and numbers. These include central Italy; North Africa, chiefly in modern Tunisia and the far eastern parts of Algeria; Egypt, in the Nile Delta; the Levant, mainly the coastal regions of Syria and Palestine; southern and western Asia Minor; and southern Spain. In every case except the last, the clusters are obviously centered on one of the empire's greatest cities, respectively, Rome, Carthage, Alexandria, Antioch, and Ephesus. Moreover, each hub stood at the center of a far-reaching network of fine roads. One great Asian road stretched from Jerusalem to Tyre and Antioch, on to Smyrna and Ephesus, and then connecting to the Via Egnatia for access to Europe. Each of the five cities was also a vital center of the empire's Mediterranean sea traffic. With very few exceptions, every piece of surviving Christian writing from the second and third centuries that we can plausibly locate comes from one of those five celebrated centers. The exceptions include Lyon, which was the effective capital of Roman Gaul, as well as Edessa (Mesopotamia) and probably Jerusalem.[8]

The other concentration of very early Christian activity repays closer examination. It surrounds the thriving city of Córdoba, which was the cultural capital of the Iberian Peninsula under Roman rule, much as it would be in the Islamic Middle Ages. It was the two competing empires of Carthage and Rome that brought Iberia into the larger world of Mediterranean civilization, and from the third century BC, the victorious Romans developed its cities and communications, settling it with their own people. Córdoba became a Roman *colonia* in the 160s BC, and it was refounded in the 40s BC. It was a key junction on the great Via Augusta, the Roman road that ran nine hundred miles from the port of Gades/Cadiz to Narbonne in Gaul. Córdoba became a Rome in miniature. It produced such celebrated Roman figures as the philosopher and dramatist Seneca the Younger, and his nephew, the poet Lucan, who recorded the internecine wars for control of the Roman state in the time of Julius Caesar. Seneca's brother was the administrator Gallio, whom we have already met and who found a place in the New Testament. The city inevitably attracted Jewish migrants. Christianity was thus expanding into a very recently created social and cultural landscape, which was wholly the product of imperial enterprise. Córdoba was unquestionably a key Christian center in this early period, although no written record of that history survives, and in the fourth century the city's bishop Hosius was the de facto head of the Christian church in the Latin West. He probably chaired the famous Council of Nicaea, in 325.[9]

In each of those centers—the well-known Big Five, plus Córdoba—we see a metropolis with some imperial pretensions or memories of its own, which was surrounded by a network of smaller cities that together constituted a local urban hierarchy. That was the vital geography of the Roman empire's political structure, its economic life, and also of emerging Christianity. When the empire accepted Christianity in the fourth century, those same great cities became fundamental to the new church hierarchy of great bishoprics and patriarchates. Many of the debates that shaped early Christianity—notably the christological wars from the fourth century onward—can be seen as struggles between Antioch and Alexandria. As the church furiously debated its doctrines over the following three centuries, they were the metropolitan centers that constantly fought for recognition and prestige. Alexandria, at least, continued to assert its ancient imperial privileges within the Christian framework. In the fourth century, the powerful kingdom of Ethiopia converted to Christianity, but for most of its history, the story of the Ethiopian church constitutes a battle between local control (the monastic leadership) and the *abunas*, the representatives of the Coptic patriarchs (or popes) in Alexandria. The patriarchs kept alive a distant memory of Ptolemaic power.[10]

The only significant change in this model was the addition of Constantine's New Rome, in Constantinople. Over the following centuries, Constantinople secured absolute political dominance within the empire and, of necessity, within the church, as its older Eastern rivals faded into ruin or irrelevance. Alexandria, Antioch, and Carthage all fell under Muslim rule and were moreover undermined by environmental change or the reorientation of trade routes: Ephesus likewise faded, and Córdoba fell into the hands first of heretical barbarians and later the Muslims. As the cities declined, so did their role as ecclesiastical centers. Although Rome retained its shadowy dignity as the seat of the apostle Peter, the city itself fell on very hard times. Constantinople, in contrast, was simply "the City," and its modern form, Istanbul, commemorates that usage: the name derives from the Greek "to the City." Its church, Hagia Sophia, was the world's largest and most magnificent, and it provided the essential setting for imperial pageantry. As the imperial heart, Constantinople was the undisputed center of Greek and Eastern Christian thought, and of the Orthodox Church that for so long remained the livelier part of the Christian world, spiritually and intellectually. Empire and church were indissoluble.[11]

Persecution

The Roman Empire provided an essential template for Christian growth, and this was drawn on a map substantially different from its Hellenistic predecessors. Roman power in the Latin West opened the way first to the further spread of the Jewish diaspora, and then of Christianity. This is reflected in the rapid growth of that faith in Italy, Spain, and North Africa, and later in Gaul.[12]

The empire's conversion to Christianity consolidated the faith's expansion and laid a foundation for further growth. Empires varied greatly in how militantly they enforce any particular creed or doctrine. In general, religions that were strongly monotheistic tended to be exclusive, rejecting other systems of worship as demonic, but that did not necessary imply persecution: the great Islamic empires granted considerable latitude to their subjects. In the Roman case, matters played out very differently. When the empirc first accepted Christianity as its official faith, it initially did not enforce adherence to the faith, but compulsion soon became explicit. In 381, the Emperor Theodosius demanded acceptance not just of Christianity but of that faith in its precise orthodox form, as practiced in the great churches of Rome and Alexandria. Those who rejected these ideas were adjudged "demented and insane," to be condemned accordingly: their meeting places were denied the name of churches. Pagan temples were closed or seized, and as an organized system, paganism disappeared. Roman officials now adopted policies that ran directly against Gallio's tolerant disdain: questions about "words and names," and the divine law, emphatically did fall within their purview, to be decided with whatever force might be necessary. In 385, the Romans carried out the first execution of a Christian heretic, the Spaniard Priscillian, although this was technically for his sorcery and immorality, rather than his deviant belief.[13]

At least in its official statements, the Roman Empire never wavered in its enforcement of stern orthodoxy, which remained consistent until the Ottoman Turks snuffed out the political power of that institution in the fifteenth century. In terms of enforcement, that compulsion enjoyed mixed success. For centuries after Rome's conversion, many rival and dissident religious views circulated fairly freely within the Empire and even achieved dominance in some areas, including those who held nonapproved christological views, the so-called Monophysites and Nestorians. Jewish communities did survive in practice, and also remarkably enduring were dissident sects that drew from long-condemned movements such as the Manicheans. Having said this, the Roman Empire was successful to the extent that its religious life remained definitively Christian and most disputes and types of dissent occurred within that larger framework. Roman attitudes were so important because of the heritage that most later Christian states claimed from the empire. Enforcement of

Christian belief, and in orthodox forms, became a fundamental component of what a Christian ruler was required to do. When Charlemagne ruled the Frankish Empire in the late eighth century, he proved his orthodox zeal by the suppression of paganism wherever he encountered it, with forced conversions, the destruction of sacred shrines, and the use of massacres to intimidate subject peoples.[14]

Meanwhile, the Roman Empire itself directly fostered the new faith by establishing Christian churches and institutions throughout its vast territory, from Britain to the Balkan frontiers, beginning the lengthy process of conversion. The ease by which culture and religion crossed official borders encouraged Christian growth in buffer states on the frontiers, as well as smaller tribes and ethnic groups that barely constituted states. Between 350 and 550, Christianity achieved its spiritual conquest of multiple Germanic barbarian peoples, not to mention the Irish, while the frontier kingdoms of Ethiopia, Nubia, Georgia, and Armenia all became fortresses of the faith. Over and above the simple fact of conversion, imperial structures allowed the westward diffusion of specific Eastern practices and institutions. Monasticism was an invention of Egypt and Syria, but in the fifth century it began its triumphant conquest of Gaul, Spain, and later Britain. A faith born in Semitic Palestine now reached the Atlantic and the North Sea and in Africa, pushed toward the equator.[15]

The Latin West

In retrospect, we know that western Europe would become the principal heartland of Christianity and the epicenter of all later growth. The imperial legacy was very strong in this region, especially through the common use of Latin. Although Greek long remained the principal language of Christian thought and devotion, Latin became a critical medium. Before the empire, the Mediterranean world had a great many languages and language families, most of which have vanished, in some cases leaving little trace. That includes, for instance, the Punic of North Africa and the Celtic languages of much of the Continental West. Under the Roman Empire, Latin spread far and fast and eclipsed those older languages, at least among elites. In some cases, the lack of a vernacular written tradition accelerated decline and disappearance. When the empire fell in the West and was replaced by barbarian kingdoms, the newcomers found a Latin-speaking world, and in many cases, they gradually adopted the language for their own use. The territory of Gaul was originally Celtic speaking, and in the fifth century it was transformed by major invasions by

Germanic-speaking peoples, but Latin ultimately triumphed as the basis for French and other Romance tongues. Already in the fourth and fifth centuries, the churches that were widespread across the West inevitably, and exclusively, thought and prayed in Latin.[16]

Even after imperial power had effectively collapsed in the West, it was inconceivable for churches to use anything other than Latin. As the religion spread in the post-Roman centuries, the language was part of a larger cultural package. Usually, vernacular languages borrowed heavily from the new conceptual world and its technical phrases. To take a well-known example, the Greek speakers of the earliest church identified an office of overseer, *episkopos*, which became Latin *episcopus*. The English mangled the word to "bishop," German *Bischof*. The hegemony of Latin was all the greater when Christian missionaries brought not only the faith but the literacy through which it was expressed. In lands without literate cultures, Christian monks rapidly became scribes, teachers, and administrators, with the Latin terminology and often the Roman memories it implied. Between the sixth century and the eleventh, this is what occurred across Germanic Europe and later Scandinavia.[17]

For a thousand years, Latin was the critical language of Christian life and thought in the West, with the Vulgate Bible as a primary vehicle. Of course, there was scholarly writing in vernacular languages—Irish, English, Icelandic, and others. But it was incidental to the larger religious story. Christianity spread Latin, and Latin spread Christianity. That picture did not change substantially until the Reformation of the sixteenth century.

After the Fall

The imperial conversion to Christianity had special implications for the church's hierarchy. In early times, the church of Rome enjoyed a prestigious role for believers, grounded in memories of the great apostles Peter and Paul, who had been martyred there in the mid-60s. At this stage, however, it is far from clear that there was a single bishop enjoying anything like what we might think of as papal power. In the fourth and fifth centuries, the emperors were increasingly likely to locate their courts in cities other than Rome, leaving that city's bishops to enjoy new power as the emperor's deputies. When Attila the Hun threatened Rome, it was famously the then Pope Leo who left the city to meet him and plead for mercy. That viceregal role became all the more obvious with the end of the separate Western Empire in 476.[18]

The popes enjoyed real secular power in Italy, as they inherited many titles and dignities that had previously belonged to emperors, most famously that of the great bridge builder, *pontifex maximus*, or pontiff. For centuries, the main papal residence was the Lateran Palace, which had formerly been used by the Emperor Constantine. In the churches of the Latin West, the popes claimed an authority little short of the old emperors. When St. Augustine summarized recent debates about the Pelagian heresy for the benefit of his African hearers, he reputedly offered a simple summary of the state of debate: "Rome has spoken; the matter is settled" (Roma locuta; causa finita est). Literally, this was the language of command, of imperium. In the eighth century, papal officials forged an influential document that purported to show Constantine formally transferring secular power in Italy to the Papacy, and that "Donation" remained the charter of the Papal States until the nineteenth century. Thomas Hobbes had ample reason for accusing the Papacy of his own days as being the ghost of that now-deceased empire.[19]

But such resemblances were by no means confined to Rome itself: both in the Eastern and Western churches, imperial memories and continuities were evident. The organizational structure of the churches closely followed old Roman administrative patterns, and the "dioceses" of the Latin church preserved the name of an older secular unit. The word itself preserves a blandly bureaucratic Greek term *dioikesis*, which literally means "administration" or "management." The later empire appropriated the term for very large units that comprised several provinces. In the ninth century, the antiquarian-minded Carolingian dynasty revived the word as part of their Roman aspirations and used it in the more limited sense it has held ever since, as the territory ruled by a single bishop. Presiding over groups of bishops is a metropolitan archbishop, whose territory is still known as a province.[20]

Other survivals abounded. Imperial administration was often carried out in special buildings that bore the Greek name *basilike stoa*, the "royal stoa" or colonnade. These distinctively royal structures provided a model for many churches of the Christian empire, which took the name "basilica." In the East, imperial power had been asserted through special portraits of the ruling family, which were treated as if they marked the presence of the living beings themselves, duly honored with incense. From the sixth century such images powerfully shaped representations of Christ and other holy figures, especially in the emerging tradition of icons. Major churches often included domes or apses portraying an awe-inspiring vision of Christ as Ruler of All, Pantocrator, a very imperial aspiration.[21]

For Catholic and Orthodox Christians alike, Roman imperial memories were precious, and unavoidable.

The Empire in the Mirror

The story of Christianity within the Roman Empire is well known, to the point that many writers through the years have claimed that Providence specifically ordained the existence of that empire to support that new religion. John Milton was one of countless Christian commentators to have claimed that Christ's birth occurred at a time of universal (Roman) peace, when "No war or battle's sound / Was heard the world around." But there was another great empire in these centuries, in fact, a deadly enemy of Rome, and there too we see a narrative strikingly similar to what I have just described. Although the Persian Empire likewise was at times deeply hostile to Christians, whom it actively sought to suppress or exterminate, the fact of that empire's existence provided an essential template for Christian expansion. Christian communities flourished in the empire's booming cities, which they made the seats of church organization. They likewise benefited from the stability and peace that the empire imposed and its vast network of communications. Ultimately, the Persian Empire faded and died, but the churches that formed in this matrix survived and flourished, outlasting the empire by many centuries.[22]

The ancient Persian Empire was destroyed by Alexander the Great and subsequently divided among his Greek successors. But native power was restored under the Parthian Empire, which ruled from 247 BC to 224 AD, and then by the Sasanian (or Sassanid) dynasty, which retained the throne until 651 AD. The empire followed the Zoroastrian faith, which held a dualist theology but with a powerful devotion to the true god of light. For much of its history, Persia exercised a wide-ranging tolerance of other faiths, but on occasion, this attitude could reverse, suddenly and bloodily. Under the Sasanians, the state became increasingly militant and intolerant in its religious adherence. In the 270s AD, a leading religious figure was the priest Kartir, who left some immodest inscriptions that vaunted his services to this faith and his empire. He boasted of his persecuting activities and how he had "smitten" various minority religions:

> The heresy of Ahriman [the Devil] and the demons departed and was routed from the empire. And Jews and Buddhists and Hindus

> and Nazarenes and Christians and Baptists [?] and Manicheans were smitten in the empire, and idols were destroyed, and the abodes of the demons disrupted and made into thrones and seats of the gods.

This declaration of itself suggests the very wide spectrum of belief in the empire. But Kartir was not alone in his detestation of alien faiths, and many Christian martyrdoms were recorded in the fourth century.[23]

Faith on the Borders

The exact identity of those Christians denounced by Kartir has intrigued scholars through the years, but the more basic question is perhaps how they had established themselves in the empire. In explaining that, we must focus on the western regions of the Parthian dominion, in regions that today we place in northern Iraq or eastern Turkey. Jewish Christians were also present, among the very substantial Jewish communities that were so entrenched in Babylonia. Crucial to this religious story were the several border kingdoms that existed between the two great empires and areas of contention of the kind that modern historians term shatter zones, or shatter belts. Sometimes Rome ruled all these lands, sometimes Persia prevailed, but most commonly, the empires shared the territory between them, while tolerating a network of buffer states. Their independence meant that they were prized as refuges by religious groups that elsewhere would be persecuted. In the event of any renewed violence or persecution, their geographical position made it easy to flee across nearby frontiers. Refugee faith is potentially an effective means of disseminating religion.[24]

As religious havens, these states became vibrant centers of activity for Christians and Jews alike, where texts could survive after they had been destroyed in one or both of the great empires. By the second century AD, the Christian faith was well established in border kingdoms such as Osrhoene (with its capital at Edessa), and Adiabene (Arbela). Osrhoene in fact became the first kingdom anywhere to establish Christianity as its official religion, and Edessa's Christian school was a pioneering intellectual center of the faith. At one stage, the royal house of Adiabene converted to Judaism, but the area later became more definitively Christian. In the third and fourth centuries, the border city of Nisibis was a thriving Christian center and a principal point of contact between the two empires: it changed hands on several occasions. As we will often see, to trace the imperial frontiers is to map the patterns of religious development.[25]

The Paradox of Victory

The religious presence in the borderlands gained a new importance as relationships between Rome and Persia became deeply hostile in Sasanian times and wars were savage and prolonged. These conflicts persisted almost through the whole history of the Sasanian line, from the 240s through the 620s. Those imperial collisions meant mass enslavement, deportation, and forced movement, which brought reluctant populations into new lands. Here, they introduced new faiths, often to the horror of their new masters.[26]

The Persians faced the paradox of victory, as the harder they fought against outside enemies, the more they found themselves, unwittingly and unwillingly, importing alien ideas. One triumphant hero of the Sasanian cause was the king Shapur I, whose wars against the Romans raged through the 240s and 250s, culminating in his sensational capture of the Roman emperor Valerian. Briefly, Shapur even occupied Antioch itself. Following the examples of generations of conquerors in the region, he deported many peoples, bringing them home to Persian soil. In the 260s, Shapur settled many Roman prisoners to create a new city bearing his name, Gundeshapur. The city flourished, and in the fifth and sixth centuries, it emerged as one of the greatest intellectual centers of the ancient world. Reputedly, it presaged later universities, with a focus on medicine. And it was, par excellence, a Christian center.[27]

The Roman acceptance of Christianity as its official religion in the fourth century had a powerful impact in the borderland regions, far beyond such older centers as Osrhoene. By associating Christianity with the aura of that empire, which moreover was enjoying a military resurgence, the decision encouraged the adoption of Christianity by neighboring states anxious to share some of the reflected glory. Christianity gained a critical foothold at a very early date in the Caucasus, in Armenia, Iberia, and Georgia. Farther south, in the lands we would call Syria, Jordan, and Iraq, we find the feuding Christian Arab border states, respectively, the Ghassanid kingdom; the "Sons of Ghassan," allied with Rome; and the pro-Persian Lakhmids. By the sixth century, those regions were a hothouse of spiritual ideas and speculations, drawing on Judaism and Christianity alike, which powerfully influenced nascent Islam. Border cities such as Sergiopolis (Resafa) and Bostra became entrepôts for all kinds of trade and exchange, spiritual and cultural no less than commercial.[28]

But the conversion had other consequences for the border states. The newly Christian Roman Empire increasingly persecuted those dissident Christians it designated as heretics or schismatics, driving new waves of refugees beyond its borders. Particularly sensitive were those who held dissident views in matters of Christology. After the 430s, Rome condemned what it described as the heresy of the Nestorians, although it is open to question how accurately that label was applied. Twenty years later, the Monophysites suffered a similar fate. The main "Nestorian" center was the Church of the East, based in Persian-ruled Mesopotamia. When Roman religious constraints became too much in the fifth century, the center of Eastern Christian faith and scholarship moved eastward across the then-border, from Edessa to Nisibis, which remained a spiritual and intellectual hub well into the Muslim period. Gundeshapur became a refuge for scholars fleeing religious oppression in the Roman world, and like Nisibis, the city became the seat of a metropolitan, a great prelate of the Church of the East.[29]

The Church of the East

Quite contrary to its wishes, the Persian Empire found itself ruling an abundance of Christians, drawn from a diverse range of theological flavors. The Church of the East operated ever more closely with this empire, despite its apparently hostile religious traditions. It established an ecclesiastical hierarchy modeled on that of the Persian Empire, just as the churches in the West imitated Roman precedent. By the seventh century, the Church of the East actually allied with the Sasanians against the Orthodox Christians of Roman Constantinople, and at times it seems almost like an imperial state church. The church was based in the imperial metropolis of Seleucia-Ctesiphon, which was among the world's largest and most thriving cities. But the primate who based his ecclesiastical seat there recalled precedents that long predated even the Persian era, as he took the title of "patriarch of Babylon."[30]

Persia's Christians exploited the booming trade routes that the empire patronized and protected. Most famous was the legendary Silk Road, although that term demands qualification. As it stands, it suggests a mighty superhighway uniting China and the Middle East, with subsidiary access roads to India and South Asia. The reality bore little resemblance to this image, and the whole concept of such a road is a modern concoction, first formulated by a German geographer in the 1870s. In reality, the "road" is better imagined as an interlinked complex of roads and tracks of very varying quality, which cast its influence far beyond any one supposedly continuous Central Asian "artery." But those connections proved immensely lucrative, and they supported the existence of prosperous cosmopolitan cities across Central Asia, chiefly in the territory of Khurasan, which lay within Persian imperial frontiers. Among the greatest was Merv, at the time a very populous polyglot city that became a major intellectual center for the Church of the East. So did Herat, in modern Afghanistan, which like Merv was the seat of a Christian metropolitan; so did Balkh and Nishapur. Through its presence in such cities, the Church of the East spread its faith across Central Asia, reaching the distant Turkic and Mongol tribes and creating a vibrant missionary presence in China. Perhaps all Roman roads really did lead to Rome, but from Seleucia-Ctesiphon, at least some roads led deep into Asia. (We will return to these regions, and their religious significance, in the next chapter.)[31]

Just as the Western church spoke Latin, so the Church of the East used Syriac. Unlike Latin, Syriac was not the official tongue of the dominant power, which was Persian, but its history was inextricably bound up with that imperial story. Syriac originated as a dialect of Aramaic, which was spoken around Edessa. From the third century AD, it became a vigorous language of intellectual discourse and of Christian expression—in fact, one of the great learned languages of the Christian tradition. Wars and persecutions forced Syriac speakers to scatter far from these borderlands. In its variant Western and Eastern versions, Syriac was the language of the Monophysite church of the Jacobites and of the Nestorian congregations of the Church of the East. During the fifth and sixth centuries, Syriac was the usual spoken language throughout Mesopotamia. Christian missionaries then carried the language as they progressed through Persian lands into Central Asia, bringing with them the scriptures and liturgy. When local peoples accepted Christianity, the missionaries translated their sacred texts directly from the Syriac. In describing themselves, those believers did not use the Greek term Christians but rather Nasrani, "Nazarenes," as in the earliest times of the Jewish-born apostles.[32]

Sons of Light

Over and above its role in Christian growth, the Persian Empire provided the essential foundation for another world religion. Because of its enormous geographic extent, the Persian realm was exposed to very diverse cultural influences, and in the third century AD, they were synthesized by the prophet Mani, who was eventually executed in 274. (The priest Kartir himself shares responsibility for the act.) Manichaeism is famous for the absolute and even simplistic distinction that it declared between the forces of light and darkness, but in fact, the faith represented a complex synthesis of multiple creeds, including Zoroastrianism, Buddhism, and Christianity (particularly Jewish Christianity and Gnosticism). Mani also drew on sectarian Jewish ideas that might have dated back to Qumran and the Essenes. The wildly cosmopolitan Persian Empire provided a crucible for the blending of such ideas and moreover supplied the framework of travel and communications that allowed the rapid diffusion of the new religion. It supported the linguistic framework: Mani wrote his weighty Seven Treatises in Syriac, in which language they became venerated scriptures.[33]

Most of the great states of the day condemned and persecuted Manichean beliefs, but that did not prevent them spreading west through the Roman Empire, securing as their most famous convert the young St. Augustine, then living in North Africa. But Manicheans won their greatest triumphs in the east, using Silk Road networks to advance across Central Asia and making converts among the same peoples then being reached by the Church of the East. Manichaeism reached China, where it flourished at least into the seventeenth century. Manicheans and Christians alike were easily found in cities like Merv and Herat, where, as we will see in chapter 4, they encountered Buddhists expanding from their homelands.

Eastern Ghosts

As in the West, empires created an environment in which religions could thrive and grow, and those religions outlived the empires that had originally hosted them. In the seventh century, the Persian Empire was conquered by the rising power of Arab Islam, which absorbed the region into its caliphate. The Church of the East remained loyal to the Persian dynasty until its final days, and with a certain irony, it was a Christian metropolitan of Merv who provided an honorable burial for the last Sasanian king. At least some of that king's descendants, who found their way to China, may themselves have been Christian.[34]

But that church accommodated easily to Muslim rule. When the Arabs moved their imperial capital from Seleucia-Ctesiphon to the new city of Baghdad in 800, the patriarch moved with them. He presided over a still-vast church with a structure of metropolitans that precisely recalled the structure of the Persian Empire, with its ancient cities and regions. For centuries, the Syriac-speaking Church of the East appeared little inferior to the Catholic and Orthodox Churches of Europe and the Middle East, and far excelled them in missionary reach. In retrospect, we know that the Christian presence in Asia would all but collapse during the following centuries, while Europe occupied an ever more central role in the faith, but at the time, such a prognosis was far from obvious. European travelers to southern India in the sixteenth century were baffled to find sizable Christian communities that knew nothing of a pope in Rome but instead followed "the Patriarch of Babylon, the universal pastor and head of the Catholic Church."[35]

If the Roman Papacy was the ghost of the Roman Empire, then its Eastern counterpart was the phantom of Persian times, and even of Hellenistic eras. That is evident from the church's chronological system and its dating of years. Through the end of the Middle Ages, many scholars in the Arab, Middle Eastern, and Central Asian worlds continued to date by "the year of the Greeks," which was the calendrical practice of the Syriac Christian churches rather than the Christian Anno Domini or the Muslim dating by years of the hegira. This "Greek" numbering system instead used the Seleucid era, which marked time from the conquest of Babylon in 312 BC by the Greek general Seleucus I. Although that specific act of conquest is now largely forgotten (and who remembers the foes from whom he conquered it?), the long shadow it cast well into the Middle Ages points to the lasting impact of older empires like the Seleucids—and it was the church that did the remembering.[36]

Consciously or not, churches channeled dead empires.

4
The Light of Asia

> I have had this Dhamma edict written so that my sons and great-grandsons may not consider making new conquests, or that if military conquests are made, that they be done with forbearance and light punishment, or better still, that they consider making conquest by Dhamma only, for that bears fruit in this world and the next. May all their intense devotion be given to this which has a result in this world and the next.
>
> ***Ashoka, emperor of India's Maurya dynasty, c. 260 BC*[1]**

During the first millennium of the Common Era, the religion of Buddhism spread very widely over Asia. This seemingly limitless expansion finds an overwhelming visual symbol in the incredible temple of Borobudur, in central Java, which was likely built in the later eighth and early ninth centuries AD, around the time that Charlemagne dreamed of reviving the Roman Empire in the West. The name of the Java edifice probably signifies "City of Buddha." As pilgrims explore its elaborate complexities, they ascend symbolically through three realms that intimately reflect the Buddhist view of the universe, rising from the region of desire to that of forms, and ultimately to formlessness. It is perhaps the greatest nonverbal scripture ever produced within the Buddhist faith. Superlatives fail in describing Borobudur, which is simply the world's largest Buddhist temple, and arguably the most awe inspiring.[2]

Tourists who visit Borobudur must at some point wonder why this stupendous site is here, so very far from what we naturally think of as the heart of the Buddhist world—or indeed, why it lies so far beyond the frontiers of that world as we know it today. In fact, Borobudur was the work of the extravagantly wealthy Shailendra dynasty, which controlled the now largely forgotten seagoing empire of Srivijaya. That imperial connection goes far toward explaining both the temple's presence and its isolation from the larger Buddhist universe as we know it. Very much like Christianity in the contemporary West, the map of Buddhism was shaped by the fate of various empires. But in the Asian case, the great empires—or at least, some of them—withdrew their support, leaving the new faith to wither. They turned to other gods.[3]

Two Faiths

The analogies between Buddhism and Christianity are remarkably strong, and a historical sketch of one could apply equally to the other. Born in one region (in which it is now all but extinct) it spread into many societies far from its original home. During that diffusion, it encountered some highly literate and educated societies, where it had to frame its claims accordingly. Elsewhere, it actively introduced ideas of literacy and learning, profoundly affecting those societies and often incorporating older deities and customs into the new faith, in lightly disguised ways. The religion's followers built great institutions of communal living and also of teaching. Some of these schools became full-fledged universities. Monastic institutions had a vast impact on their surroundings, engaging in transformative agricultural and economic practices. Those communities were vital to developing the arts and sciences. The works of art that we recall from these eras virtually always have religious themes, and artists received patronage either from religious houses or from rulers seeking their favor. Rulers found ideological support from the religious institutions, which thereby became critical to the formation of states and the consolidation of empires.[4]

Each religion was highly cosmopolitan, encouraging its faithful to wander freely between institutions in many different societies, to observe and learn from them. Among other things, these transactions spread artistic styles and cultural motifs. In this process of travel and communication, pilgrimage to sacred sites served as a powerful stimulus. Whatever its founders intended, it was in effect a religion of holy figures, of shrines and pilgrimages. Cultivating those things gave additional power to the mighty monastic houses. And at every stage, religious evolution was utterly shaped by the attitudes of secular regimes, above all of successive great empires. That is the story of Buddhism, and of Christianity. If the Christian Church channels the spirits of dead empires, so does the Buddhist Sangha.

Buddhism and Bygone Empires

If the Western Christian Churches remembered the Latin of Rome, Buddhists too had their recollections of glorious times gone by, of their own imperial ghosts. The ancient canon of Buddhist scriptures is in the language of Pali, which is the language of the Theravada branch of the faith. In ancient times, Pali was known as Māgadha-bhāsā, and that led Buddhists to claim that it was the same language spoken in the famous kingdom of Magadha (roughly modern Bihar, India). That claim is probably not correct literally, but in a symbolic sense, it is potent. Just as Catholics trace Latin back to Roman times, so Buddhists stake their claim to continuity from another realm of enduring power and prestige.[5]

Magadha was central to a series of successive empires based in the region, namely the Nanda, Maurya, Shunga, and Gupta Empires, who together held power for close to a millennium. The Nandas established themselves in the fourth century BC, although their power was short lived. The Mauryas then dominated much of India from 322 BC to the 180s BC, to be followed by the Shungas over the following century. The Guptas prevailed from 240 AD through 550. One early Magadha ruler founded the city of Pataliputra, near modern Patna, which became the capital of all four realms in their turn, and of others later. Under the Maurya Empire, Pataliputra was one of the most important cities on the planet, with a population of four hundred thousand, perhaps more. Its only real competitors on the global stage were Alexandria and Carthage. Somewhat later, the Mediterranean had imperial Rome; India had imperial Pataliputra. The analogies between the two cities are not exact, but the religious analogies are strong. Rome became the metropolis for Christianity; Pataliputra for Buddhism.[6]

Buddhism originated with the career of the historical Gautama Buddha in the sixth or fifth century BC, developing alongside a number of other influential spiritual movements, such as Jainism. Jains and Buddhists alike received some support from secular rulers and empires, especially the Mauryas. This dynasty was founded by Chandragupta Maurya, who had fought against Alexander the Great and his Seleucid successors and who had a strong appreciation of Greek ideas and practices. He actually married a daughter of Seleucus I. That openness to things Greek extended to the structures of empire as established by Alexander. After defeating the Nandas and taking Pataliputra, the Mauryas were the first dynasty ever to unite the whole subcontinent under a single power.[7]

Chandragupta himself converted to the extreme asceticism of the Jains and reputedly fasted to death. But Buddhism also flourished, and it made its most important advances under Ashoka (304–232 BC), who was probably Chandragupta's grandson, born in Pataliputra. He became one of India's most esteemed rulers. Through a series of triumphant and bloody campaigns, he united much of the subcontinent under his rule, but the ghastly carnage of the wars appalled him and forced him to seek a new spiritual direction. As he wrote of himself, he had

> conquered the Kalingas eight years after his coronation. One hundred and fifty thousand were deported, one hundred thousand were killed and many more died (from other causes). After the Kalingas had been conquered, Beloved-of-the-Gods came to feel a strong inclination towards the Dhamma, a love for the Dhamma and for instruction in Dhamma. Now Beloved-of-the-Gods feels deep remorse for having conquered the Kalingas.

Probably around 260 BC, he made Buddhism the state religion and applied its moral and ethical principles to worldly government. In effect, he was seeking to build a spiritual empire. Anxious to exalt both themselves and the dynasty, Buddhist writers claimed that the early Mauryas were a branch of the Shakya line, which had produced the Buddha himself.[8]

Ashoka did much to create the map of Buddhism that we would know in later centuries. He sent monks and missionaries to Sri Lanka and Central Asia and built temples and stupas across India, initiating what we might term the Buddhist Millennium. Buddhist envoys traveled to Greece, Egypt, and the Hellenistic realms and into Southeast Asia. His career naturally reminds Westerners of Constantine, who led the conversion of the Roman Empire to Christianity. Coincidentally, both men adopted faiths that already had some three centuries of existence behind them, permitting them to spread even more widely and into very diverse cultural settings. But by common consent, Ashoka was a far superior figure, morally and spiritually. His symbol, the Buddhist wheel of dharma, appears on the flag of modern India.[9]

Although the Maurya Empire failed in the 180s BC, other successive empires held comparable power, and over the following eight centuries, they strongly supported Buddhism, which enjoyed a dazzling golden age in India itself. At this stage of Buddhist history, the Indian emphasis was very marked, and so was the connection with Indian empires. If we list the places associated with the Buddha's life and early Buddhist history—Bodh

Gaya, Lumbini, Sarnath, and Kushinagar—then we are drawing a map of modern-day northeast Indian states like Bihar and Uttar Pradesh, the plain of the Ganges, and southern Nepal. The very name Bihar comes from the Pali word *vihara*, an early monastic settlement, which recalls the Buddhist monasteries that once so proliferated in the area.[10]

The Great Vehicle

In the first two centuries AD, Buddhism experienced the immensely important movement called Mahayana, the "Great Vehicle," with its emphasis on mighty spiritual beings called bodhisattvas. Probably, those figures originated as local deities in northern India, before achieving still greater glories. This Mahayana form of the faith led Buddhist expansion into Central and Eastern Asia. Essential to that spread was the Kushan Empire based in northwest India, Pakistan, Afghanistan, and Bactria from the first century AD through the third, which pushed its authority as far east as Pataliputra and the Ganges Delta. Its most celebrated ruler was the emperor Kanishka the Great, who reigned from c. 120 to 144 AD, and who was termed a second Ashoka. Having said that, his coins suggest broader loyalties, commemorating as they do Vedic and Zoroastrian deities: the Kushans were rich enough to disperse their patronage lavishly. The Kushan Empire had close ties both with other empires in the Mediterranean sphere and in China. Its vital center was Gandhara in present-day Pakistan, around Peshawar, and Gandhara was a primary base for Buddhist missionary expansion and for artistic production.[11]

Crucially for later religious developments, the Kushan Empire's political geography connected it to the Silk Road, which opened doors for Buddhism across Central and Eastern Asia. Between the second and fourth centuries AD, Mahayana Buddhism established itself in China, Korea, and Vietnam. The penetration of China was critical, given that empire's position as the political and cultural heart of the region, the standard that other powers sought to emulate. Once established, moreover, the faith blossomed extravagantly, as China became a new spiritual center, rivaling India before it. The particular forms of Buddhism that now flourished so widely, and their artistic forms, reflected the cultural ferment of India's northwest border country, where Indian influences mixed with Greek and Central Asian traditions.[12] Kanishka's empire initiated a pivotal development in Buddhist history in the translation of sacred texts into the most prestigious language of culture and civilization in East Asia, namely

Chinese. The pioneer in this process was the Gandharan monk Lokaksema, who worked around 180 AD. Once available in Chinese, these texts were read by educated elites among the neighboring lands within the Chinese orbit—initially in Chinese itself and later in local translations. Buddhist wisdom became available in Japanese, Korean, Vietnamese, Uighur, and Tibetan.[13]

Buddhism remained strongly entrenched in India and in its empires. Buddhists had an excellent relationship with the great Gupta Empire that ruled India between the fourth and sixth centuries AD, although the Guptas also patronized traditional Hindu causes. (I will return to the quite complex definition of the term "Hindu.") Not well known in the West, the Gupta age was one of the greatest and most innovative in human history, certainly comparable to the Athenian golden age. To cite another Western analogy, this was the time of the Sanskrit playwright Kalidasa, who is often compared with Shakespeare.[14]

That same golden age imagery applies to Buddhism. From the fifth century AD, a great Buddhist university operated at Nalanda, some fifty miles from the Gupta seat of Pataliputra: in its day, Nalanda might have been the greatest center of learning in the world. When the far-traveled Chinese monk Faxian wandered through Buddhist India at its height, around 400 AD, his much-quoted accounts suggest an amazing profusion of monasteries, shrines, and stupas, with monks and nuns running into the countless thousands. Bodh Gaya, the site where the Buddha achieved enlightenment, had been a venerated shrine since the time of Ashoka, but most of the Mahabodhi temple structure that is visible today reflects the efforts of Gupta times. Also from this era we find the superb Buddhist paintings and rock sculptures of the Ajanta Caves in Maharashtra. Most were probably the work of the Vakataka dynasty, who ruled an empire that was the southern neighbor of the Guptas. Buddhist prestige in India itself enjoyed a last flowering with the northern realm ruled by Harsha in the early seventh century. He tolerated all religions, but particularly favored Buddhism, and built many shrines and stupas.[15]

The Silk Road and Beyond

The outpouring of patronage allowed the efflorescence of monasteries, with all the spectacular temples and shrines that proclaimed the paradoxical magnificence of this radically world-denying faith. Buddhism was a highly ambitious missionary faith, which benefited greatly from the peace and prosperity assured by those empires. The Guptas were legendary for their work in building fine roads and communication systems across northern India. Waterways were a special issue in everyday Indian life: Buddhist writings often frame spiritual dilemmas in terms of metaphors derived from crossing rivers, of bridges and ferries, suggesting the persistent role of such obstacles in India's material reality. Like their Christian counterparts half a world away, Buddhist monks took full advantage of the wider horizons created by empires and pushed enthusiastically across the frontiers, along the trade routes that those empires had made secure.

The most famous of these routes was the so-called Silk Road, or rather Silk Routes, which we have already encountered in the previous chapter and which ultimately connected China to Daqin, an amorphous term that could mean either Syria or the Roman Empire. The system included many ancillary roads and land routes, and it linked to vital maritime networks around the coasts of India and Southeast Asia, where spices were the most prized commodities. Whether by land or sea, these trading highways depended on the maintenance of order by the great empires of the day, such as the Sasanians or the Kushans. In later centuries, the well-trained armies of China's Tang dynasty (618–907 AD) used these routes to project their power far to the west. Indian empires served a comparable role, both by land and sea. The Gupta dynasty, in fact, was the first Indian realm for which we have documented evidence of a seagoing branch of the armed forces—an imperial navy. If empires did not actually create the Silk Routes, the success of those regimes strongly promoted their continued flourishing.[16]

Stability encouraged trade and generated wealth on an intoxicating scale, and it opened the way to spreading Buddhism. Buddhist remains and writings survive in profusion from the western Chinese oasis of Dunhuang, and monks roamed far through Central and Northern Asia. Monasteries and temples were well established much farther west along the "Silk Road," especially in Khurasan. At Merv in modern-day Turkmenistan, Buddhists rubbed shoulders with Zoroastrians, Muslims, and Christians. At Balkh, Buddhists may have predominated until the Arab conquest, and even beyond. Across the region, the phenomenal wealth derived from transcontinental trade is suggested by the lavish investment of patronage in Buddhist temples and shrines.[17]

The dissemination of Buddhist schools of thought is suggested by the legend of Bodhidharma, the first patriarch of the mystical school that the Chinese called Chan, a word that the Japanese adapted to Zen. Probably based on a historical original, Bodhidharma attracted an enormous body of legendary lore, and he is often depicted in art as a fierce and intimidating figure living a life of rigid asceticism in a cave. Physically, Bodhidharma is marked by his hairy eyebrows and bulging eyes, which reflect his alien ethnicity. (Reputedly, he cut off his eyelids to keep from falling asleep during meditation.) According to those stories, Bodhidharma brought his mystical wisdom from "the West"—either southern India or conceivably Persian Central Asia—in the early sixth century, suggesting the cultural doors opened by the Silk Routes. A famous tale recounts his meeting with a bemused Chinese emperor, to whom he described the core teaching of Buddhism as "vast emptiness, nothing holy!" which is in fact an excellent credal statement for the Mahayana tradition.[18] Even today, "Old Fish Eyes" remains a lively figure in Buddhist practice: Zen masters regularly draw out their pupils with the unanswerable question, "Why did the patriarch come from the west?" From China, Zen spread widely within the Chinese sphere of cultural influence, to Japan, of course, but also to Vietnam. Whether Bodhidharma ever existed or said the things attributed to him, he had plenty of identifiable historical counterparts. For historians, the question is not so much why he came from the west, but just how he succeeded in doing so: they marvel at the world of interlocking empires that allowed him to make the journey.

Another monument to this transnational traffic of ideas is the Heart Sutra, one of the most influential (and explosively radical) scriptures of that faith. Like Bodhidharma, the sutra teaches the emptiness of all forms and apparent realities, in the sense that they have only a contingent reality. It then goes on, shockingly, to apply this critique to the most sacred Buddhist teachings and assumptions themselves: they too are equally empty and as remote from true reality. The sutra was probably created in India in the fifth or sixth century, but the earliest written evidence for its existence is all Chinese, from the seventh.[19]

Kings, Monks, And Rice

Religions benefited immensely from the existence of friendly empires, but both sides, emperors and monks alike, stood to gain from their relationship. Beyond doubt, many of the rulers who poured forth their largesse on monks and stupas did so because they personally believed the Buddhist message and wished to symbolize its glories through great works of human ingenuity, adorned with superb treasures. This was certainly true of Ashoka and Kanishka and many other less famous counterparts. But regardless of a ruler's personal piety, Buddhism offered practical advantages that made it eminently worth cultivating. In part, the appeal was ideological. Because the faith so evidently stood at the cutting edge of culture and science, no less than spirituality, it carried an aura of progressive modernity, of prestige, and of cosmopolitanism.

Just as occurred with Christianity in the contemporary West, Buddhist monks supplied a whole literate class to operate government and to record the deeds of kings. As in the Christian world, monks and hermits acquired a formidable reputation for miraculous powers and healings, renown that persisted after their deaths and remained attached to their relics and shrines. Meanwhile, the monasteries that claimed the legacy of holy individuals took the lead in economic development. Historians of Asia often note a kind of historical triad that was fundamental to the formation of states and empires: kings, monks, and rice. Buddhism grew alongside royal power and new forms of agriculture based on mass irrigation. New forms of cultivation allowed a surge in population growth, with all that implied for the number of subjects to pay taxes and to donate to the monasteries.[20]

Monarchs enjoyed the reflected splendor that they received from patronizing temples and artwork, which redounded to the prestige of upstart dynasties that might have received their power only in recent years. As the monasteries were eager to report, the dynasty was powerful and auspicious precisely because it advanced the Buddha's cause. Such legitimacy was valuable for a realm like that of the Kushans, who derived from India's far western border country, so far from the traditional centers of imperial power in the country's heartland. Like other secular rulers, the Kushans readily realized just how broadly this faith was established and how fast it was progressing throughout what was to them the whole known world. To support Buddhism was evidently to stake a claim for status in an emerging global civilization, alongside the world's existing powers. Further expanding the realms of dharma promised multiple blessings. When a new territory accepted Buddhism through the endeavors of a given empire, that represented a gain both for Buddhism as a faith and an institution and for the empire with which it was aligned. At least in the early decades of conversion, the new territory inevitably accepted aid and guidance from the clergy of that empire, which occupied a kind of parental position. Worldly and spiritual empires spread together.[21]

Across Asia

Between the end of the sixth century AD and the start of the tenth, Buddhism enjoyed an astonishing era of expansion. For Western historians, this recalls the growth of Christianity in the same era, as that faith finally conquered Europe's remaining pagan Germanic and Slavic peoples and made inroads into Scandinavia. The Asian experience, however, took place on a far larger geographical canvas, and affected a substantially larger share of the world's population at the time.

As we have seen, Buddhism was already well established in China by the second century, but it gained immense vigor when it won the support of several regimes that were struggling to establish their legitimacy during a long era of division, conflict, and mass ethnic movements. One was the Northern Wei dynasty, which controlled much of northern China between the fourth and the sixth century, but traditional-minded Chinese scorned them as invasive "plaited barbarians." Their original capital at Pingcheng boasted some six thousand Buddhist temples and tens of thousands of monks, and huge statues of the Buddha linked the glories of the faith to the emperor's legitimacy. When the dynasty moved its capital to Luoyang at the end of the fifth century, emperors invested massively in new Buddhist projects, including the Longmen Caves that would ultimately include tens of thousands of sacred statues. They favored the influential Shaolin Monastery, which counted Bodhidharma among its monks. In 581, the Sui dynasty finally united the long-separated Northern and Southern dynasties. Its founding emperor Wen proved a vigorous advocate of Buddhist causes, both to give legitimacy to his own upstart regime and to provide an ideological cement for his very diverse realm.[22]

More broadly, the spread of Buddhism was already quite advanced by the time Japan accepted that faith in the sixth century, extending as it did far across what we might call "Monsoon Asia." Thailand became Buddhist shortly afterward, and the Khmer Empire in Cambodia was open to Buddhist teaching. If we visualize a map of Asia in the eighth or ninth century, say around the year 800 AD, then we would see Buddhism well established in most of the regions we know today. Over and above that, Buddhist missions were spreading throughout what we call Indonesia and the Philippines and into the Pacific. Buddhism also remained vibrant in Central Asia. Around 800, it was scarcely too much to think of an Asia that was as thoroughly Buddhist as Europe would become Christian. Given the incredible wealth of South and East Asia at the time, and the region's very high populations, Buddhism stood every chance of becoming by far the most flourishing and influential religion that had ever existed, and the best endowed in terms of buildings, monuments, and sacred structures.[23]

Some key advances occurred in a number of potent rising states of the time, which accepted Buddhism in order to align with the world's most sophisticated societies, and especially China. As in the Christian world, empires connoted power and ancient majesty, which a rising neighbor could hope to share through adopting its religious system, and thus its civilization. In a sense, the religious conversion was a proclamation of political maturity, a coming of age. This process is commemorated by some of the great temples and shrines of this era, which today are recognized as among the leading material monuments of the Buddhist tradition. At Nara in Japan, the Todai-ji temple complex was formally opened in 752. Korea's Haeinsa, the Temple of the Ocean Mudra, dates from 802, exactly from the time of the building of Borobodur.[24]

The Southern Seas

Potentially one of the most significant of the new territories was the southern seas, the regions that we today would call Indonesia, Malaysia, and the South China Sea. No later than the fifth century AD, Indian ways and beliefs spread rapidly through the southern seas, marked by the use of Sanskrit, and the Brahmi script that became the basis of most of the region's later writing systems. The very name Indonesia is a modern geographical label for the "Indian Islands," those areas under profound cultural and political influence from the subcontinent. Naturally, then, the region was thoroughly exposed to Indian religions, both Hindu and Buddhist.[25]

From the seventh century AD, the key state there was Srivijaya, a mighty commercial merchant empire of the seas, a thalassocracy, which controlled the Strait of Malacca and dominated much of the larger region from the seventh century AD though the eleventh. The state was Buddhist, and kings from Srivijaya sent offerings to the Buddhist center of learning at Nalanda. Srivijaya left its religious impact in Cambodia, where Mahayana Buddhism coexisted with Hinduism. Srivijaya's role in the Spice Routes generated incalculable riches, as illustrated by the sensational discovery of dozens of shipwrecks from the region, some of which rank among the great archaeological finds of modern times. The Belitung shipwreck represented the remains of an Arab voyage between Tang China and the Arab Gulf about 830 AD, and it contained a dazzling collection of treasures, notably an invaluable trove of Tang Chinese ceramics. Among other cargo, the *Intan* vessel was carrying an impressive collection of Buddhist ritual objects.[26]

Like many other empires, Srivijaya left a powerful linguistic heritage, in the form of the Malay language, which today is very widely spoken in Indonesia and Malaysia. Ancient Malay probably originated in Borneo, and in the early centuries of the Christian era it evolved into Old Malay, before spreading rapidly through its association with Srivijaya. The trade and commerce that the empire practiced and encouraged spread Malay across what became its later territories: the oldest known inscription dates from 683 and specifically invokes "Great Srivijaya!" Old Malay was the lingua franca that allowed trade to proceed within the commercial and political realm, and it was likewise a vehicle for the empire's Buddhist faith. The Old Malay language shows many borrowings from both Hindu and Buddhist religious vocabulary. (In chapter 8, I will return to the language's later functions in the service of another faith, namely Islam).[27]

This was the religious and cultural ambience that encouraged the Shailendra dynasty to create their microcosm of the Buddhist cosmos at Borobodur. While we can never truly know the intention of the patrons and builders, its presence in one of the very newest territories of the faith was surely an assertion that this land too was now worthy to take its place among the leading Buddhist societies. As such, it was ready to draw countless thousands of pilgrims and visitors to acknowledge the splendors both of Buddha and of Great Srivijaya. Its function would be similar to that of the most splendid cathedrals that Christian Europeans would build in their High Middle Ages.

Tibet's Empire

In addition to Srivijaya, another far-reaching empire accepted the Buddhist religion in these same years, to the point of becoming immersed in that tradition. From about 620, the Tibetan ruler Songtsen Gampo began an imperial expansion that over the following two centuries would extend its power deep into what we think of as India and China, as well as Central Asia. That Greater Tibet even had a coastline, on the Bay of Bengal. By the 820s, Tibet was dealing with China's Tang dynasty on terms of fair equality.[28]

Buddhism certainly did not achieve an overnight conversion of the whole Tibetan people, and older religious forms remained active. But the imperial adoption of Buddhism created a robust framework for the faith's later development in Tibet and its expansion. That imperial context—the exalted aspirations and the international relationships—shaped the distinctive aspects of historical Buddhism in that land, and its sacred landscape. Songtsen Gampo was a fervent advocate of Buddhism, who translated key scriptures. He founded a sumptuous temple in his capital, the Jokhang, or House of the Lord, which Tibet's faithful have long viewed as a place of special sanctity and pilgrimage. In a treaty with China signed in 822, that sacred area was titled the "Place of Gods," or Lhasa. Reputedly, the Jokhang temple was built to house holy Buddhist images brought by his two royal brides, respectively from China and Nepal. Whatever the truth of that story, the religious affiliation did indeed place the burgeoning empire at the heart of a much larger diplomatic universe and gave it convincing legitimacy on the international stage. In the eighth and ninth centuries, Tibet encouraged the arrival of Buddhist monks and scholars, especially from India. One was Padmasambhava, the much-venerated founder of Tibet's Tantric traditions and of its mystical and esoteric Buddhist pathway known as the Vajrayana.

Losing India

In their own ways, Srivijaya and Tibet illustrate the breathtaking growth of Buddhism in this era, but the two case studies point to an important and troubling conclusion. Tibet, of course, still remains a thriving Buddhist heartland, a heartland of the faith. In contrast, the faith became all but extinct in the territories that we think of as Indonesia. Buddhist expansion triumphed in some regions but suffered disastrous withdrawals in others, to the point of obliteration. Although the reasons for this decline were varied and applied differently to each society, some common themes do emerge, and they reflect the actions and behaviors of political empires. In each case, the contrasts with the Christian experience in the West are apparent.

The most marked change occurred in India, the cradle of Buddhism, where the faith continued in unabated splendor through the middle of the first millennium. Buddhist states and empires continued to arise, notably the Pala empire in Bengal and Bihar, which firmly supported the shrines and universities. About 800, the Pala emperor created a new university at Vikramashila, to rival an already declining Nalanda. Even so, this activity was on a rather smaller and more geographically constrained scale than its predecessors, as most states had largely withdrawn their support. In retrospect, the death of the great Harsha in 647 AD marks a turning point to that story. When the valiant Chinese pilgrim Xuanzang reached Bihar around that date, he found Pataliputra in ruins, and its Buddhist monasteries and shrines in a sorely dilapidated condition. The Silk Route trade declined as Muslim forces pushed into Central Asia, where they clashed with Chinese forces. (Those routes would revive in later centuries.)[29]

The Palas themselves were the last of India's great Buddhist regimes, and their power went into steep decline during the mid-ninth century. This was a time of widespread crisis in many parts of the world, due in large measure to a climate-driven crisis that had far-reaching economic effects. Central Asia suffered a historic drought that devastated the area for an incredible seven decades, from 783 through 850, with harrowing effects on trade routes. The crisis proved an empire slayer, with profound effects on the religions that those various regimes espoused. Apart from the disasters faced by the Palas, the Tibetan Empire collapsed in the 840s, and as we will see, China's great Tang Empire itself suffered greatly during these same years.[30]

Hinduism Old and New

In India, the millennium-old Buddhist order lost ground especially to resurgent Hinduism and the various empires and kingdoms that supported it. These respective religious labels must be applied cautiously. In modern times, we easily draw distinctions between Hinduism and Buddhism, but those differences were not always plain. Hinduism has been a very dynamic tradition, which has changed greatly over time. In its origins, Buddhism began as a reform movement within the larger spectrum of Indic religions, and it distinguished itself from those older systems by its critique of caste and brahminic privilege, and its rejection of animal sacrifice. Nevertheless, many followers of Buddhism were happy to maintain their support of at least some older practices, together with their deities and cults. Over time, supporters of those traditional approaches organized a revival, in what would be a prolonged process. Especially under the Guptas, thinkers and religious leaders were busy reconstructing that Hindu faith on lines that proved immensely appealing to elites and to ordinary people alike.[31]

Many of the most successful innovations borrowed heavily from Buddhist practice and thought, which had achieved such wide popularity. To compete, Hindus evolved from their central emphasis on the Vedic gods and the brahminical order, to create a new religion that looked much like Buddhism itself. Between the third and the eighth centuries AD, those innovations included attractive new forms of devotional practice to the gods (*bhakti*), with a new focus on such beloved deities as Vishnu and Shiva and their families. This new practice was probably modeled on contemporary Buddhist devotion to the bodhisattvas. In the Hindu manifestations, Shaivism, Shiva's path, proved very successful. Legends about these gods were preserved in the rich tradition of storytelling and mythologies, in the Puranas, and the age from 650 through 1100 is known as that of Puranic Hinduism. Hindu philosophy, meanwhile, achieved splendid new heights under brilliant figures like Adi Shankara (probably late eighth century), who created the mystical school of Advaita Vedanta and urged the necessity of monasticism. So thoroughly did he plunder Mahayana teachings that his Hindu critics denounced him as a crypto-Buddhist. Of course, this revival was by no means the work of one individual, and many other thinkers were active, but the cumulative effects were obvious.[32]

The new synthesis, which we can now properly identify as Hinduism, gained renewed confidence and credibility. Most significant, it gained the solid support of the region's emerging empires. Particularly determined in their devotion to Puranic Hinduism were the Chalukyas of Central India, who built many splendid temples to Shiva. No less aggressively Hindu were the Cholas of South India, who surged to widespread influence in the ninth century. The Cholas indeed are credited with building some of the greatest Hindu temples, and the most widely influential. A cluster of spectacular examples survives in and around Thanjavur/Tanjore, which at the turn of the millennium was the Chola imperial capital. A few centuries before, the dynasty would have been equally enthusiastic partisans of Buddhism.[33]

The Buddhist Crisis

As Hinduism rose, so Buddhism suffered repeated blows to its foundations, material no less than spiritual. On occasion, Hindus persecuted Buddhists, and quite ferociously. In the sixth century, northwest India faced the onslaught of peoples related to the Huns who had earlier invaded Europe. One of their leaders, Mihirakula, left a reputation in India quite as monstrous as his counterpart Attila would in the West, and the invaders devastated the Buddhist religious houses of the region. The pivotal border city of Taxila, seat of a university as well as many religious houses, never recovered from these disasters. Beyond simple motives of plunder, Mihirakula acted through religious inspiration: as a fervent devotee of Shiva, he loathed Buddhism. In seventh-century Bengal, the Shaivite king Shashanka reputedly killed monks and wrecked monasteries and destroyed the sacred bodhi tree. In the following century, another king in India's far south reputedly killed or expelled thousands of monks, although the evidence for this is shakier.[34]

Such acts were not typical, and other kings were able to repair at last some of the damage. But the tide clearly was turning against Buddhism. Not overnight but over a period of centuries, Buddhist temples and shrines were increasingly appropriated by Hindu successors across the whole subcontinent, down to the deep south. The same fate befell the once very widespread Jain faith, which like Buddhism had grown out of that larger Indic matrix during the previous millennium. Only in quite modern times have archeologists realized just how many Hindu temples stood on such older foundations.[35]

This story of displacement and appropriation was reproduced throughout much of the Indosphere, through Cambodia, Malaysia, and Indonesia. As a seagoing empire, another thalassocracy, the Hindu Cholas extended their political and cultural reach deep into those regions, where local rulers envied and emulated them and adopted their Hindu faith. In the eleventh century, the Cholas allied with the Cambodian Khmers, who were then also Hindu, to inflict serious setbacks on Buddhist Srivijaya. As in India itself, Buddhism was widely displaced across southeast Asia, a religious shift now illustrated by several awe-inspiring temples. The greatest is the Khmer center of Angkor Wat, built in the early twelfth century as a temple to Vishnu—in fact, one of the largest Hindu temple complexes anywhere in the world. Another visual symbol in the Shaivite Hindu temple erected at Prambanan in Java during the mid-ninth century, one of the most imposing places of worship of that faith outside India itself. It was presumably erected as a deliberate riposte to the claims of the Shailendra dynasty and was intended to overshadow and replace Borobodur itself. Borobodur was abandoned and all but forgotten until its rediscovery by the British and Dutch in the nineteenth century. The "East Indies" largely became a land of Hindu culture, upon which Islam would later be superimposed, albeit with many compromises. Here at least, Buddhism all but vanished.[36]

A Christian comparison might be suggested here. Between roughly the fifth century and the fourteenth, every territory of Europe was gradually and sometimes bloodily converted to Christianity, but in no region was there any significant backsliding to pre- or non-Christian forms. That was because in its European strongholds, Christianity never had to deal with another competing religion of anything like the same nature. Judaism was never substantial enough to constitute such a rival, while Islam was seen as a deeply threatening military and political foe. In government, Christianity sought and received an absolute monopoly of power, spiritual and secular, suppressing any and all potential rivals. In contrast, South Asian states did in fact have continuing older faiths besides Buddhism, which were likewise marked by rich scriptural resources and extensive institutional networks. Over time, they were able to reassert themselves and to present themselves as attractive competitors to Buddhism, especially when that faith appeared too expensive economically or too aggressive politically.

To contemplate anything like the Asian reality in European circumstances, we would have to imagine a situation in which France accepted Christianity for several centuries but then around 800 or so decided to revert to a restored and organized Druidism, which had triumphantly incorporated key Christian doctrines and practices. We would further have to imagine that Frankish rulers such as Charlemagne abandoned the Christian faith for this reinvigorated neo-Druidism, into which they poured patronage and political support. Just to frame the idea hypothetically is to demonstrate its absurd distance from any plausible historical reality.

Forgetting Buddhism

The decline in India was so critical for the larger Buddhist world because that land's shrines, libraries, and colleges had always provided a symbolic center for the faith, to which courageous pilgrims ventured in search of manuscripts and relics to bring home. The situation would become still worse in later years. Facing the relentless advance of Hinduism, Indian Buddhism was already much weakened by the tenth century AD, when the country faced the new onslaught of Muslim invaders. The first great Muslim incursion had happened in the early eighth century, but invasions, wars, and religious conflicts became ever more common. Once Buddhists lost their political moorings in empires that explicitly shared their values, they could no longer hope to rebuild and restore what had been destroyed in such violent eras.

Muslim depredations ruined Buddhism across much of northwest India, although the full establishment of Islamic power was a lengthy process. The Muslims certainly wrought destruction, particularly at the hands of legendary conquerors and persecutors like Mahmud of Ghazni around 1000 AD. In many cases, the Muslims were conquering sites that Hindu rulers had already appropriated from Buddhists. One devastating episode occurred in 1193, when Muslim raiders conquered Bengal and Bihar, plundering the remaining monasteries and slaughtering many Buddhist monks. The invaders sacked the intellectual centers of Nalanda and Vikramashila: neither returned to anything like their ancient glory, and they were ultimately forgotten. Indian Buddhism faded into oblivion, from which it has only been rescued in very modern times. Such important sites as the Ajanta Caves were rediscovered only in the nineteenth century, around the same time as Borobodur.[37]

Chinese conditions were also strained, although the outcome there was nothing like as terminal, and again, shifting imperial policies were crucial.

Buddhism had enjoyed great success there for several centuries, and as in India, it coexisted with older patterns. These readily reasserted themselves when China's emperors became concerned about the excessive growth of the Buddhist faith and its clergy, who at their most successful looked uncomfortably like a state within the state, a rival power to the institutions of empire itself. The agonizing economic crisis of the ninth century proved uniquely stressful, and divisive, and forced the dynasty to seize whatever assets it could to buttress its own strength. The Tang had enjoyed immense wealth and power from the seventh century onward, but signs of trouble were accumulating by the 840s. Large areas were falling out of imperial control, as pirates and bandits became ever more daring. China's emperors sought a convenient scapegoat in the form of supposedly foreign creeds such as Buddhism and what they thought was the sectarian offshoot of that faith, Christianity. A ruinous persecution ensued in the early 840s, the Huichang era. Thousands of monasteries were destroyed, and hundreds of thousands of monks and nuns were secularized, as they resumed their vital social roles as members of families and loyal taxpayers. The dynasty shifted its favor and patronage to older rival faiths such as Daoism and to native Chinese cults.[38]

Of course, this Huichang persecution did not eradicate China's Buddhism. Buddhist beliefs and values remained vibrant in China until modern times and generated important spiritual movements, as well as superb artistic treasures. Rather, the experience set limits to the faith's power in that land and ensured that it would exist alongside other traditions. Chinese Buddhism thus never enjoyed the kind of hegemony of which it might once have dreamed. Nor (with a few brief exceptions) has it exercised anything like the established official role that we see in other countries.

These reversals in no sense destroyed Buddhism, which continued to occupy its central place in the cultural life of so many lands. In Korea, Japan, and Tibet, Buddhism was intimately bound up with state ideology, and as such, it received rich patronage. Not only did Tibetan Buddhism survive, but it served as a repository for many ideas and texts that originated in India and reflect the spiritual life of that land before its decline. Much of what modern generations think of as distinctively Tibetan Buddhism, with what seem like its peculiarities, is a remnant of what had been the mainstream faith of an older Buddhist India. As in earlier eras, moreover, the faith conquered whole new lands as emerging empires adopted it in order to assert their position in the larger civilized world. This is what occurred in the eleventh century with the Bagan/Pagan

Empire based in what would later become Burma/Myanmar. Pagan itself became a sprawling landscape of faith, with literally thousands of surviving temples and pagodas. After some decades of chaos, even Angkor Wat was converted into a center of Mahayana Buddhism. As before, everything depended on the attitudes and political alignments of particular empires and their sovereigns.[39]

Any narrative of Buddhist history has to pay full attention to the role of imperial policies and decisions, both in promoting that growth and, in some cases, in constraining and even reversing it. But quite apart from such top-down edicts, Buddhism spread through conditions made possible by empires, and above all through their impact on communications and commerce. That allowed the faith to spread and to sink roots, and in some cases—if not all—to outlive those political entities. Even when Buddhism faded to all but nothing in one region, it remained robust and even buoyant in others.

Empires gave, and empires took away.

5
Persuading to Faith

> And if your Lord had pleased, surely all those who are in the earth would have believed, all of them; will you then force men till they become believers?
>
> ***Qur'an 10.99***

When historians debate the effectiveness of religious persecution, they often cite the words of the third-century Roman Christian writer Tertullian, who famously declared, "The blood of martyrs is the seed of the church." The harsher the efforts to destroy a faith, it seems, the more determined the surviving believers are to uphold it at all costs. Tertullian was writing in Roman Africa, in the city of Carthage, which eventually fell to the forces of the Islamic caliphate in 698 AD. Within a couple of generations of that event, the church effectively vanished, not just in Carthage, which ceased to exist as a major city, but in the whole region, which became thoroughly Islamicized.[1]

Of their nature, empires rule over diverse populations, and commonly, religion is a crucial part of that diversity. Regimes vary greatly in how they view religions that contradict official creeds, but in some cases, they seek to weaken or even destroy rivals, with varying degrees of success. Although the story of early Christianity suggests how a religion could indeed thrive under hostile governments, religions have often stumbled in the face of repression, to the point of being eliminated. In some instances, Christians themselves ruthlessly eliminated Jewish and Muslim minorities, through massacre and expulsion, not to mention the destruction of rival Christian creeds and heresies. The vestiges of the Great Mosque of Córdoba, once one of the treasures of Islamic architecture, survive today within the Christian cathedral, and for centuries, no Muslims were to be found anywhere in the vicinity. (That situation is now changing rapidly.) Although a hopeful maxim holds that "you can't kill an idea," it does invite the riposte that one does not readily find genuine religious Manicheans in the modern world.[2]

But religious pressures need not be so overt or so violent. That is especially true when empires favor some strong rival system that competes effectively for popular loyalties and outperforms all possible rivals in exploiting its opportunities. I have described how at least in some of its once-thriving areas, Buddhism was eliminated, and this experience is not uncommon in the world's religious geography. Historically, Islam offers an excellent example of how empires can build up established religions in a way that severely constrains rivals. Such policies might involve actual persecution, but other subtler means of persuasion are at least as effective. In the long run, imperial decisions can create something like a monopoly, even in a cultural setting that officially proclaims tolerance. Imperial pressures and preferences account for the modern-day distribution of the world's Muslims, and specifically of the rival traditions of Sunni and Shia believers. Empires need shed little blood, or need create few martyrs, to redraw the religious map quite fundamentally.[3]

Empires of Islam

At first sight, the experience of Islam seems to illustrate the triumph of compulsion and persecution. Many of the most significant Islamic nations today are overwhelmingly Muslim by faith, and even exclusively so. That is true in some instances where the region in question had previously been the preserve of some other faith, or faiths, which have all but vanished. That success, to the point of exclusivity, has often been cited by critics of Islam, who denounce the fanatical intolerance that they claim is at the essential heart of the faith. That charge is too sweeping, and it is quite wrong to single out Islam as more intolerant than any of the other great faiths. Having said that, it is legitimate to remark that historically, Muslim regimes have been strikingly successful in displacing competitors.[4]

There were reasons to expect that Islam should, in theory, have been fiercely intolerant. The religion arose in a world dominated by Rome and Persia, neither of which had any qualms about enforcing religious obedience and conformity, and which in theory might have provided models for a new polity. Also, Islam from its beginnings was associated with governance. Both Christianity and Buddhism were faiths that began quite separate from political power, and only gradually over time did they obtain the blessing of empires and kingdoms to the point of achieving official status. On occasion, both faiths had to debate how to reconcile their world-denying principles with the practical needs of government. In contrast, from its earliest phases, Islam was very much a kingdom of this world, devoted to securing godly rule. The Islamic calendar dates from the Hijra of 622, which commemorates not the divine revelation to Muhammad but rather the creation of a Muslim-ruled polity in Medina. For the next millennium and beyond, the religion of Islam was inseparable from empires, including some of the very largest such entities in all history.[5]

The Islamic world was ruled by the successors of the Prophet, the caliphs, and as Muslim forces conquered new lands and peoples, they were added to their vast and very diverse realms. When Muhammad died in 632, Islamic power was mainly confined to Arabia. Already under the Umayyad Caliphate (661–750), the empire stretched from Spain to Pakistan, and it expanded still further under the Abbasids (755–1258). In 751, Abbasid forces advancing into Central Asia allied with the Tibetan Empire to defeat the armies of Tang China. At its height, the Abbasid Caliphate covered some five million square miles.[6]

Other Islamic empires proliferated. As the Abbasids soon found, control over such huge territories was difficult, and breakaway kingdoms and empires increasingly detached from the Caliph's authority, establishing autonomous dynasties, some of which were quite as substantial as the great empires of antiquity. When the Abbasids seized power from the Umayyad house, Umayyad refugees established their own rival caliphate in Spain and North Africa. In the eleventh century, the Fatimid Caliphate controlled North Africa, Egypt, and the Levant, and in the twelfth, the successor house of the Ayyubids extended their power over Syria, Egypt, and northern Mesopotamia. In the eleventh century, the warlord Mahmud of Ghazni founded a dynasty that controlled Persia, northwest India, and much of Central Asia. Mahmud never aspired to be Caliph, so he appropriated a term that meant, in effect, "strong man," *sultan*. The same title was borrowed by the Seljuk Turks, who ruled the Middle East from the Aegean to Afghanistan, and by many later claimants. Each in turn pushed forward the frontiers of Islam.[7]

Increasingly, the Abbasid sovereign in Baghdad was left as an honorary figurehead, acknowledged in prayers but usually ignored politically. In 1258, the Mongols sacked Baghdad, in one of the bloodiest massacres of the era, and killed the Caliph al-Mustansir Billah, the thirty-seventh of his line. Even so, the idea of the caliph's office retained its significance, in offering a vital justification for empire. That symbolic role, that ghost of religious authority, persuaded the Mamluk sultans of Egypt to maintain the surviving line of the Abbasid caliphs almost as symbolic trophies of their court, a shadowy and barely relevant role that those figures retained until the sixteenth century.

Islam and Compulsion

Despite the political fragmentation and the rise of the sultanates, the same could be said of those successor realms as of the Baghdad Caliphate itself: their political structures were wholly and resolutely Islamic, even though very large portions of their subject peoples followed other faiths. Over time, those peoples too became mainly Muslim.

The story of Islamization was a complex process. A hoary myth imagined the first followers of the Prophet Muhammad demanding mass conversions through armed terror, demanding that conquered peoples accept "al-Koran or the sword!" In that view, conversion was a necessary outcome of jihad warfare. But that crude picture is far from the truth. When the caliphate was established in the 630s, its religious doctrines explicitly ordained tolerance of Christianity and Judaism, which were seen as flawed early drafts of the full revelation brought by Muhammad. The Qur'an itself commands, "Let there be no compulsion in religion."[8] The generous protections offered to Christians are recorded in a letter of Muhammad himself to the monks of Saint Catherine's Monastery, the Ashtiname, or Treaty. Moreover, that tolerance carried powerful practical benefits for the conquerors. As People of the Book, Jews and Christians were "protected people" or dhimmis, but they had to pay for the privilege. Non-Muslims were subjected to special taxes, the *jizya*, which were lucrative for the Islamic rulers. In the first phase of conquest, in fact, conversion to Islam was not easy and involved a kind of fictive adoption into one of the Arab tribes. Meanwhile, Christians and Jews could enjoy many of the advantages of the new imperial system, which permitted widespread travel and communication. Again contrary to myth, most early Muslim conquerors did not destroy the sacred buildings of older faiths or burn sacred writings. (As we will see, there were some exceptions.)[9]

Over time, however, Islamic empires proved very successful in exploiting their advantages, which on occasion involved the exercise of brute force. While Western historians often cite the toleration that Muslims granted to Christians and Jews, they forget the persecutions inflicted on Zoroastrians, who had under the Persian Empire counted as one of the world's greatest religions. Muhammad himself regarded the Zoroastrians as pagan fire worshipers and strongly favored the Christian Roman

Empire in its war against these enemies of God. After the conquest, Zoroastrian institutions were progressively eliminated, to be replaced by Islam. Gradually, Zoroastrians lost the protected status of dhimmi for that of the far less desirable *kafir*, pagans or unbelievers. The process was not accomplished overnight, and fire temples could still be found in many parts of Persia well into the tenth century. But accumulating pressure drove remaining believers either to convert or to migrate to more congenial homes in India, where the older faith survived in exile: today, the descendants of those exiles amount to fewer than a hundred thousand members of the strict Parsi sect. Some Zoroastrian customs and practices survived the collapse, for instance, the celebration of the old Persian New Year, Nowruz. But in terms of religious practice and institutions, Islamic imperial policies destroyed the faith founded by Zarathustra.[10]

Christianity under Islamic rule suffered fewer such direct or immediate assaults, but in many regions, the long-term consequences were similar. We see this from a map of the huge expanse of the caliphate as it existed around 750, before the schism into rival kingdoms. Two points emerge powerfully from this image. The first is that much of this territory had very deep-rooted alternative faiths, besides the Zoroastrians, including Buddhists and Hindus in the eastern lands, as well as Jews, Manicheans, and others. There was an extremely strong Christian presence and a deep-rooted church establishment. Any history of the early church and the time of the church fathers would give a pivotal role to the Christian lands of Egypt, the Levant (Syria and Palestine), and North Africa. As we have seen, the Church of the East was making spectacular missionary strides from Mesopotamia deep into Central Asia.[11]

But that brings us to the second obvious point of that map, which is (as I have already noted) how thoroughly Muslim virtually all of those territories are in modern times. Spain, of course, was reclaimed by Christian Europe in later centuries, and substantial Christian minorities survived in several regions, especially Egypt. Even so, they were clearly small minorities within a heavily Muslim population, and that was true even before the massacres and population movements of the twentieth century. Even Christian minorities are hard to find in large swathes of that former imperial territory, in lands such as North Africa or Afghanistan or Pakistan. That caliphate territory was thoroughly and irrevocably Islamicized, so that today those former frontiers map the spiritual heart of the Muslim world. In establishing its own religious system and uprooting potential rivals, this empire succeeded quite as well as its Roman Christian predecessor.[12]

How Empires Made Muslim Societies

If the critics of Islam are wrong to see the religion simply being imposed by authoritarian fiat, they are correct to stress the significance of top-down government action, of policies enforced by empires. Despite their customary restraint, the Islamic empire did on occasion inflict persecutions on minorities, which could sometimes be severe. In the eighth and ninth centuries, local officials and even some caliphs proclaimed fearsome laws against minorities. Christians in Egypt, Syria, and elsewhere, especially monks and clergy, were threatened with brandings and blindings, and these edicts commanded the destruction of churches, or at least the removal of crosses. There were isolated incidents of martyrdom, notoriously in ninth-century Spain. Even so, such episodes were usually localized, temporary, and quickly reversed, and were not sufficient of themselves to explain the crushing of the older faiths. Although Christianity did collapse swiftly in a few regions, such as North Africa, that was because the faith had been a preserve of elites and had failed to establish itself among the rural masses: when those Christian elites fled before the Islamic invaders, their religion failed to survive.[13]

Far more significant in explaining conversions was the provision of a rival religious system that soon became more attractive and credible than the older creeds. When the Arab rulers opened the gates to new converts, Muslim ranks swelled rapidly. Islam took advantage of the opportunities offered by its very widespread imperial system, which spanned continents. Pilgrims and scholars wandered freely between different lands and continents. So did migrants from Arabia and neighboring lands, whether in search of military glory or simply new lands to settle. Those groups created flourishing new settlements in conquered lands, so that Muslims quickly grew as a share of the total population.[14]

Imperial cities, meanwhile, proclaimed the glory not just of the dynasties, officials, and generals who built them so lavishly, but also of the invincible force of Islam. All the greatest cities were centered on fine mosques, some on a stunning scale and usually paid for by the proceeds of repeated wars and conquests. The most impressive of all were directly associated with ruling dynasties and proclaimed the direct reliance of those rulers on the divine. Not incidentally, they showed how the new political power of Islam took no second place to the older Christian and Zoroastrian worlds. That assertiveness drove the creation of the Umayyad Mosque of Damascus in the early eighth century. Many of the greatest edifices stood on the site of older sacred buildings and actually incorporated their remains: the Damascus Mosque replaced a Christian structure, and some of Persia's new mosques were built over Zoroastrian temples. Such repurposing declared the obsolescence of the old order.[15]

As later dynasties and sultanates broke away from the caliphate, so each asserted its arrival by founding great cities with colossal building works, to demonstrate at once its political power and its cultural sophistication. Such for instance was Cairo's Ibn Tulun Mosque, one of the most impressive Islamic sites in that country: the patron was a warlord who had secured de facto independence from the Abbasid Caliphate and built a short-lived empire in Egypt and the Levant. The Great Mosque of Kairouan in Tunisia, which reached its height under the Aghlabid dynasty in the ninth century, covers an area of almost a hundred thousand square feet. The major expansion of the Great Mosque of Córdoba closely coincided with the creation of the breakaway Umayyad Caliphate in Spain. We need not believe the literal claim that Córdoba at this time had some three thousand lesser mosques, but such places were obviously abundant. The more frequently empires rose and fell, the more need there was for arrivistes to build ever-wealthier mosques to legitimize their authority. At the same time, the proliferation of these mosques announced the supremacy of the faith of Islam to any and all who visited those cities. Quite apart from such symbolic statements, they became deeply impressive centers of Islamic learning and religious experiment, which engaged in lively exchanges with other centers perhaps thousands of miles removed.[16]

Language was critical in diffusing Islam. Although Arabic was by no means the empire's only language—Persian flourished—linguistic unity encouraged a sense of the obvious advantages of the faith. Even resentful Christians in Spain or Egypt or Mesopotamia found it hard to resist the attractions of Arabic speech and the culture it carried. The use of older languages rapidly declined across the empire's territories. Greek was one early victim of the transition, and by 700 the Caliph Abd al-Malik decreed that it would be replaced by Arabic as the language of administration. Already by the ninth century, conservative Christians in Spain lamented the decline of Latin, while other Christians in that land proudly displayed their high skills in Arabic. Historians know the surviving Christian populations as Mozarabs, from the term *musta'rab*, Arabized. Mesopotamian Christians, meanwhile, found Arabic increasingly ascendant over Syriac. The standard language of Christian Egypt had been the tongue of ancient Aigyptos, which gave its name to Coptic and produced an extensive and really distinguished literature. But Coptic was steadily displaced by Arabic, which was spread so widely by immigrants and by Islamic authorities, and then through its use in religious life. In the tenth century, when the Coptic Christian bishop Severus wrote his invaluable *History* of the patriarchs of Alexandria, it had to be in Arabic, so that his fellow Egyptian Christians would understand it.[17]

The new Islamic ways acquired critical mass, and it became normal and natural to follow them. Just to take one symbol of such "normality," I have already mentioned the total dominance of Islamic structures in the cities, and the same point would apply to middling and smaller centers: Islam ruled the visual landscape. But it also utterly dominated the soundscape of every city and village through the frequent calls of the muezzin to prayer, while Muslim regimes sternly forbade any rival public sounds, such as the ringing of Christian bells. Every day, people heard multiple reminders that these territories were properly and incontestably Muslim, so that the determination to continue in a non-approved faith demanded something like heroic stubbornness.[18]

The Penalties of Resistance

Islamic faith and Arabic culture offered an enticing package. At the same time, the penalties and restrictions imposed on non-Muslims served as a strong incentive to conversion, especially when those factors operated over a lengthy period of time. Varying according to time and place, those limitations shaped such vital aspects of daily life as one's clothing and adornment, the permitted size and kind of dwelling place, and the type of animal one could ride (as noble beasts, horses were reserved for Muslims; Christians rode donkeys). Permissible forms of speech and greeting were strictly controlled. Like the Abbasids, the alternative successor empires maintained the same range of carrots and sticks to attract converts. Over a period of several centuries, even a slow and gradual attrition of numbers would inflict serious damage on a non-approved faith, driving it toward ever-shrinking minority status.

We observe what we might call a ratchet effect, using the name of the mechanical device that limits movement to only one direction. For nonbelievers under Muslim rule, the subordinate community could exist for decades or even centuries without the outbreak of major violence or persecution, even though petty restrictions and insults were commonplace. On occasion, though, virulent persecution erupted in response to some natural cataclysm, or to the rise of a particularly zealous regime, or even to the whims of one singularly vicious despot. Following such an event, the subordinate community would be reduced or scattered still further, and its survivors could then expect peace until the next cycle of intolerance began. The ratchet turned another notch, and the non-approved community moved closer to elimination or exile.[19]

Disasters played a role. Over that very long time span, regions were struck by successive calamities, whether inflicted by human agents in time of war or by natural disasters and climate-driven events, by famine, drought, flood, or earthquake. Following such events, the decisions of government were crucial, as imperial patronage soon restored and even improved the facilities of the approved religion, while extending no such generosity to unapproved creeds. Churches and monasteries became fewer and more dilapidated, and many were taken over by the dominant religion. This was less a matter of the harms that empires could perpetrate than of the good they could distribute and how selectively they exercised this power.

Dar al-Islam

But Islamic conversion was far more than a grudging acceptance of an unpalatable reality. Under the auspices of Islamic rule, extensive missionary work made the new faith appear genuinely attractive, and in the process those activists secured mass popular conversions. The most important groups were the Sufi orders, which from the twelfth century onward spread their influence as widely as Christians and Buddhists had in earlier centuries. Like those infidel predecessors, the Sufis owed much of their appeal to the miraculous and mystical powers associated with key holy figures, and they used that reputation as a basis for missionary endeavors. Once a Sufi presence was created in an area, it offered something to believers and inquirers of all degrees of sophistication, from the promise of mystical enlightenment to the routine everyday practices associated with shrines, pilgrimages, and the veneration of holy tombs. Depending on the tradition, it might offer the chance to seek the divine through music, dance, and the arts. The orders became the cultural and spiritual heart of Islamic life for centuries to come.[20]

As with Christians and Buddhists before them, Sufi organizational structure was ideally suited to a world of transcontinental empires. The Sufis were organized in various orders or lineages, the tariqa, each looking to a distinguished founder, and they might operate over a range of thousands of miles. Sufi orders pushed imperial boundaries forward into new lands in Central and Southeast Asia, often following paths blazed by faithful merchants. Wherever there were rich trading networks, there were booming commercial cities, which adopted Islam in emulation of the distant political powers they knew. Sufi orders turned them into bases for mission and strengthened that religious loyalty. Some of those centers became the foundation for stupendously wealthy empires in their own right. From the thirteenth century, the Mali and Songhai empires created a lasting Islamic presence in West Africa.[21]

Probably between the tenth and twelfth centuries, Muslims went from being a small minority in the territories ruled by Islamic states to being an active majority, and then quite rapidly an overwhelming one. Just how the balance had tipped was evident in the early fourteenth century, when sudden climate-related changes severely tested many Eurasian societies at the start of what in Europe would be known as the Little Ice Age. An age of hunger and disease naturally provoked paranoia and conspiracy theory, which in Egypt and Mesopotamia were directed against Christians. The by-now heavily Muslim crowds of cities called for the destruction of these hated minorities. Christian populations could maintain themselves in some regions, usually in less desirable lands safely removed from the great cities and the centers of imperial power, but it was a struggle to maintain their existence. Mounting pressures pushed many others to accept Islam.[22]

The Triumph of Time

In their origins, Islamic empires had no wish to command religious uniformity, and little realistic hope of doing so, but over the long centuries, the nature of empire inexorably drove that outcome. Ultimately, the most important factor in Islamicization was the sheer endurance of Muslim political rule. In the short run, perhaps for a couple of generations, subject peoples could avoid the temptations and pressures of the new faith in the hope that its political authority would soon be overthrown, and that was not unrealistic. Territories did change hands between faiths, and the Byzantine Empire succeeded in pushing its power into the borderlands of Syria and Mesopotamia. We also think of the gradual reconquest of Muslim Spain and the crusading venture in the Levant from the eleventh century onward. But outside those border territories, Islamic rule remained firmly in place. Already by the early thirteenth century, Muslim empires had prevailed in Mesopotamia or Egypt for six centuries, for more than twenty generations, far longer than the earlier period of Christian hegemony in those same regions. That created a sense of inevitability and even an eternal quality.

Christian minorities gained hope in the thirteenth century when many Islamic lands were absorbed into the Mongol Empire, which genuinely did exercise full religious tolerance over its subjects. Individual Mongol rulers and aristocrats might themselves be Mahayana Buddhists, or Christian followers of the Church of the East, or have such believers in their immediate family circle. In the following century, however, the great empires that grew out of those conquests accepted Islam, and increasingly, in the strictest and least tolerant form. The Church of the East, which had survived so many catastrophes, was now all but eliminated across many of its previous territories, as the ratchet of persecution turned several notches. A literal death blow came with the conqueror Timur, who built a vast Asian empire between 1370 and 1405. Timur offered no toleration to religious rivals or minorities, and his forces engaged in appalling massacres of unbelievers of all kinds. Beyond the horrific damage to Hindus and other groups, he uprooted Christian communities across much of the territories he ruled.[23]

It was hard for any impartial observer to doubt that historical momentum lay with Islam rather than Christianity. From the fourteenth century, the Ottoman Turks were expanding their power across southeastern Europe, and Christian powers did not even begin a reconquest until the 1680s. Even well-informed and widely connected Muslims had little reason to suspect a looming European imperial threat until the time of Napoleon's arrival in Egypt in 1798. Napoleon himself made no overt challenge to Islamic assumptions, and his propagandists referred to him only as the Great Sultan, without hinting at any Christian background. Nor, as will see, did those conditions change under the relatively brief supremacy of European Christian empires in Islamic lands.[24]

If Islam has succeeded in eliminating rivals, it is not because of any singular Muslim tendency to brutality but rather because it successfully remained in place for so many centuries. It outlived all competitors.

Islam in India

Similar themes emerged as Islam sunk roots outside its Middle Eastern heartlands. In modern times, the Indian subcontinent represents one of the greatest bastions of Islam, and some 30 percent of the world's two billion Muslims live in one of the three nations of India, Pakistan, or Bangladesh. But before the coming of Islam, all those lands had a very different religious coloring, whether Hindu or Buddhist, and in each case, the establishment of Muslim rule was achieved by conquerors who carved out empires for themselves: the pioneering "Sultan" Mahmud of Ghazni was an early example. Yet armed conquest alone did not necessarily imply forcible mass conversions or acts of direct compulsion. Some Muslim-ruled territories thoroughly accepted the new faith, while others conspicuously did not and vigorously retained older identities. At different points, Muslim regimes ruled virtually the whole subcontinent, including vast areas that still today are passionate in their Hindu or Sikh faith. Even today, in the subcontinent as a whole, Muslims constitute just a third of the total population, which invites a question. If Islam really is so determined to dominate societies so totally, why is that figure closer to 30 percent than to 90, or more? We need to account not only for Muslim successes but also their limitations.[25]

As in the Middle East, the process of conversion was intimately associated with given empires and the specific opportunities they created. This meant initially the Delhi and Deccan Sultanates that prevailed between the thirteenth and sixteenth centuries, but especially the Mughal dominion created in the 1520s. As in the Middle East, imperial authority did on occasion involve acts of mass terror and violence, which demonstrated the absolute superiority of the new religion. In the early fourteenth century, the sultan of Delhi under the Khalji dynasty was Alauddin, whose triumphant wars involved the looting of such unimaginably vast treasure that later legend remembered him as the Aladdin of the cave reported in the *Arabian Nights*. Most of that plunder came from Hindu temples and shrines. The historical Alauddin was notorious for his brutality toward conquered peoples and to any groups suspected of rebellion. Throughout these wars, slaves were taken in epic numbers, many of whom died as they were transported to Central Asia for sale: children and young people were especially vulnerable. The route they took through Afghanistan became known as the Hindu Kush, the "slayer of Indians." All those slaves would of course have been non-Muslims. Not long afterward, the conqueror Timur boasted of having killed several *lakhs* of Indian infidels—that is, several hundred thousand people—as he wielded the "proselytizing sword."[26]

Other conquerors were scarcely more merciful. Babur, founder of the Mughal dynasty, slaughtered countless thousands of Hindus. In the later seventeenth century, his Mughal successor Aurangzeb (1658–1707), who by that point ruled most of the subcontinent, was savagely intolerant of other faiths, which was all the more striking as his personal beliefs were strongly aligned with the Sufis. Aurangzeb destroyed Hindu temples in their thousands, persecuted Sikhs and other minority faiths, and actively tried to prohibit those other religions' practices and public celebrations. In 1679, he reimposed the *jizya*, the tax demanded of infidels, and imposed many penalties and restrictions of varying degrees of severity. He penalized Muslim schools of thought he found heretical.[27]

Advancing the Faith

But repression was in no sense consistent. Other emperors exercised generous tolerance, freely patronizing Hindu and Muslim shrines and places of worship. As we will see in chapter 9, the great sixteenth-century ruler Akbar sought to unite all religions into one universalist creed. In most cases, Muslim influence spread through peaceful means, including the efforts of powerful lords and their courts. As empires established themselves, so they opened the door to the Sufi orders with their dedication to missionary work among middling and lower ranks, as well as elites. No later than the ninth century, the Sufis were achieving widespread conversions in India's northwestern regions and the lands that in modern times would become Pakistan. Adding to their attraction for ordinary people, their rich devotional life used vernacular languages, rather than the formal tongues of court and administration. Those influences became still more powerful under the Mughal rulers, most of whom strongly favored the Sufis over other Islamic traditions. One venture in particular proved highly successful. In the sixteenth century, the Mughals undertook major agricultural reforms in Bengal, an area for which they had a special love. This involved the cultivation of land and the building of new settlements surrounding Sufi centers. That move marks the decisive advance of Islam as a popular faith in the region, where it subsequently flourished. That success created a foundation for later growth, especially with the stunning demographic expansion of the twentieth century.[28]

The trajectory of Mughal history helps explain the limitations of that success. Compared with the situation elsewhere, the dynasty occupied a much shorter hegemony, over just some two centuries. Although the Mughals remained in power from the 1520s through 1857, they lost most political power after 1707 and suffered a catastrophic defeat at the hands of the Persian conqueror Nadir Shah in the 1730s. Nadir was himself a devout Muslim, but his intervention had the effect of preventing the Mughals from significantly advancing that faith much farther than they already had in the subcontinent. Thereafter, the Mughal emperors remained figureheads with little ability to impose their will over multiple other kingdoms drawn from a variety of religious faiths. It simply was not possible to attempt anything like the Bengal venture on a much larger scale. If the Mughals had sought to Islamicize India at the same rate that their counterparts did in such lands as Persia or Egypt, we would have to imagine a process spanning seven or eight centuries, and Indian conditions offered them no such luxury.[29]

Gunpowder Empires

As we have seen, Islamic powers continued their history of expansion and conquest long after the initial times of the caliphate, so that issues involving the absorption of new and unbelieving populations continued to arise into the early modern period and beyond. These later empires faced dilemmas about religious toleration and compulsion that would have been very familiar to their predecessors. Over and above spreading Islam, these realms ensured which particular forms of the faith would prosper, and the global maps of Sunni and Shia adherence.[30]

From the mid-fifteenth century, technological advances allowed the growth of three diverse and aggressive Islamic empires, each of which fundamentally transformed the religious realities of the lands it conquered. Because of their reliance on cannons and artillery, which made obsolete older concepts of defensive walls and fortifications, these are known as the gunpowder empires: the Ottomans in the West, the Safavid dynasty in Persia, and the Mughals in India. Together, these three spanned the world from Vienna and Algiers to the frontiers of Burma. The three realms were intimately connected, as deadly enemies, but were also bound together through cultural and religious links.[31]

Together, the three drew the religious maps of the Muslim world, particularly on the frontiers of that faith. I have already described the efforts of the Mughals, and how they were cut short by political decline. In the West, the triumphant Ottoman expansion into the Mediterranean and southeastern Europe not only extended Islamic power but also created new centers of Islamic population. From the late fourteenth century into the nineteenth, the Ottomans occupied significant European lands, which reached their greatest extent between the 1520s and the start of the eighteenth century. The Ottomans captured Constantinople in 1453, and in 1517 their defeat of the Egyptian Mamluks allowed them to claim the title of caliphs of Islam. For the next half millennium, mosques throughout the world acknowledged the Ottoman caliph week by week in their Friday prayers.[32]

Much like their Arab predecessors, the Ottomans made few attempts at forcible conversion, and both Christians and Jews remained numerous in the empire. Each minority community, in fact, constituted an acknowledged entity, a millet, with substantial powers of self-government. So large was the Christian community alone that the empire during the seventeenth century constituted one of the world's largest "Christian" states, as measured by population. Even so, the empire provided the context for Muslim growth, through migration and conversions, and substantial communities developed across many areas of the Balkans. Some of them were later eliminated, either through massacres during successive wars of liberation or else forced population exchanges in modern times, but Islam retains a solid European presence in Albania, Bosnia, and Bulgaria. Through much of its history, the Ottoman Empire sponsored Sufi orders, mainly the Bektashis, which achieved significant conversions, especially among former Christians in the Balkans, as well as in Asia Minor, which under the Byzantine Empire had been an ancient center of Christian loyalty.[33]

The Shia World

The gunpowder empires determined the borders between the Sunni and Shia branches of that faith. Ironically, it was in these intra-Muslim conflicts that we see the harshest examples of persecution and naked compulsion of a kind that critics of Islam would often cite as so typical of that faith, although in these cases, the targets of official violence were themselves all Muslim.

Although Islam traditionally generated many different schools of thought, one fundamental division involved the early schism between Sunni and Shia. During the seventh century, Muslims were bitterly divided over the succession to the caliphate and whether it should be based on family succession to the Prophet Muhammad himself. Those who supported such a succession were the Shia, the "partisans" or followers of the Caliph Ali, while the other position became known as Sunni, "lawful" or orthodox. Although the Shia tradition is a minority in modern Islam, it commands the loyalty of at least two hundred million Muslims, over 10 percent of the whole. If it were a free-standing faith, it would by itself constitute one of the world's largest religions. Political tensions between Sunni and Shia states continue to provoke some of the bitterest conflicts, and indeed open wars, in the region.[34]

The relative success of each tradition in different eras was heavily determined by the rise and fall of empires. Although the Abbasid caliphate was Sunni, from the tenth century through the twelfth, it lost most of its western territories to an independent Shia caliphate that we usually name after Fatima, the daughter of Muhammad, who married Ali. They were thus the Fatimid or Alid dynasty. When the Fatimids fell in their turn, so the Shia cause declined, and the prevailing Islamic powers of the following three centuries were Sunni. If later empires had continued to follow those allegiances, then the modern balance of traditions would be very different from what we actually see.[35]

Critical to the modern Shia story was the creation of Persia's Safavid Empire. The empire was founded in 1501 by Ismail, a hereditary sheikh or head of a Sufi tariqa, who traced his origins to that country's far northwest. A brilliant general, he conquered the whole of Persia, proclaiming himself Shahanshah, King of Kings, and beginning a dynasty that lasted until 1736. He established Shia Islam as the official religion and enforced it through savage repression of all rivals. To be precise, this was not just Shia Islam, but that faith in its so-called Twelver form, from the number of imams or successors to Muhammad acknowledged in this tradition. Ismail destroyed Sunni mosques and uprooted their institutions, especially their Sufi orders, while lavishing the resources that he seized on their Shia counterparts. He thus created a whole new religious establishment utterly dependent on his will, without facing the rivalry of the very powerful Sunni scholars and sages. Ismail pursued an effective campaign to annex the country's religious memory: he removed the graves of venerated Sunni leaders and insisted that Persians ritually curse those long-dead foes. As he conquered new territories in Iraq and Azerbaijan, he extended his anti-Sunni violence to those lands.[36]

Partly, Ismail's decision to launch a domestic religious war reflected his bitter rivalry with the Ottoman Empire, against which he fought repeatedly. But there is no reason to doubt his absolute conviction. The policy moreover strengthened the wider interests of his new empire and asserted the credentials of a man of mixed ethnic origins, without links to traditional royal lines. His new Shia-based ideology meshed well with his theocratic ideals. Although deeply invested in Islamic history and tradition, he rooted his authority in Persia's pre-Islamic history, including the Sasanian dynasty. He was entranced by the great historical epic of the *Shahnameh*, which recounted that history in such loving detail, to which we shall return in chapter 9.[37]

As so often occurs during such revolutionary movements, the violence was mainly concentrated in its opening phases, while later phases were marked by gradual assimilation to the new regime and its ideals. Through the mass importation of Shia scholars from Arab lands such as Lebanon, Ismail and his Safavid successors created a faithful new official clergy, with a thriving network of schools and mosques. A century after Ismail's time, his still-mightier successor, Abbas the Great, decisively turned Persia into a Twelver Shia state, with its awe-inspiring center at his imperial capital of Isfahan, with its superb new mosques. All proclaimed the glory of the Safavid dynasty and the Shia faith with which it was indissolubly linked. Although the process of conversion was not completed overnight, and indeed continued for generations, it ultimately triumphed. The formerly Sunni land of Persia became thoroughly Shia, which it remains today. In modern times, the close linkage between Iran and the Shia population of Lebanon has been a critical fact in regional politics, with the Lebanese serving as surrogates or agents of the powerful Iranian state. Five centuries ago, it was the Shia of tiny Lebanon who carved out a spiritual empire in the Persian precursor of today's Iran.[38]

Between them, Ismail and Abbas achieved one of the most sweeping and enduring acts of forced conversion in history. This was a thoroughly top-down transition, dictated for the purpose of reinforcing imperial needs, and at every stage the story strongly recalls the better-known example of Ismail's near-contemporary Christian counterpart, Henry VIII of England. Henry had his Reformation; Ismail presided over his Shia Revolution.

The success of Shia Islam in Persia had vital implications for India, in a way that seems counterintuitive. The Mughals themselves were Sunni, and Aurangzeb hated Shia Muslims even more than Hindus. But cultural connections were strong. Like their predecessors among India's Muslim invaders, the Mughals traced their origins to the country's northwest and to Afghanistan, so that the dynasty always looked to Persian culture and traditions and to the Persian language. For centuries, Persian enjoyed the status of a lingua franca in Islamic India, the tongue of both culture and faith. To give a Western example, we might think of the position of French in Enlightenment Europe, as the medium of cultured discourse, but Persian also occupied a prestige parallel to Latin. To use a modern term, Persia exercised a high degree of "soft power" through an extensive sphere of cultural influence. (In chapter 9, I will return to the continuing cultural power of Persian culture and political ideologies, which had many parallels to the persistence of Roman ideals in the Christian West.) India's secular and religious authorities alike often looked to Persia, from which they imported scholars and teachers, as well as administrators, and that remained true through the nineteenth century. As they drew on Persia, they strengthened the Shia presence in the land.[39]

Those connections have left a potent religious legacy. Today, the largest concentration of Shia Muslims is found in Iran, with some seventy-five million believers, but the second center is the Indian subcontinent, with perhaps fifty million in India and Pakistan combined. Like so many other religious communities around the world, they too are phantoms of empire.

In terms of duration, the story of Islam constitutes a large share of the whole history of civilization. Obviously, then, the practice of Islamic empires and rulers has varied greatly, and some have genuinely compelled subjects in particular religious directions. Most have not. In fact, the most striking examples of such compulsion, and the ones with the largest consequences for the world's religious atlas today, were the work of Christian empires, which at least in theory were pursuing mission, rather than jihad.

PART TWO

Worldwide Empires and Unintended Consequences

Most things are never meant.

Philip Larkin, "Going, Going"

6
Empires and Christian Mission

Still, with the spirit's vision clear,
I saw Hell's empire, vast and grim,
Spread on each Indian river's shore,
Each realm of Asia covering o'er.
There, the weak, trampled by the strong,
Live but to suffer—hopeless die;
There pagan-priests, whose creed is Wrong,
Extortion, Lust, and Cruelty,
Crush our lost race—and brimming fill
The bitter cup of human ill.

Charlotte Brontë, "The Missionary," 1846 [1]

One frequently reproduced image of the British Empire at its zenith is Thomas Jones Barker's painting entitled *The Secret of England's Greatness* (1863), which shows Queen Victoria presenting a Bible to a humbly grateful East African chieftain. The African is happy, we presume, to be released from the bondage of hell's empire, to pass to the benevolent rule of the British Empire. To modern eyes, the painting is intolerably condescending in its portrayal of the relationship between the races, and it seems to use a hypocritical justification for imperial exploitation. More charitable views are possible, not least because of the phenomenal growth of Christianity outside Europe and North America in modern times, to which we shall return in chapter 10.[2]

With that caveat, Barker's painting strongly underlines the connections, both material and ideological, between global empire and Christian missions, but we should emphasize how surprising that linkage might have appeared in earlier times. We are so used to stereotypes of European triumphs worldwide that we easily forget how remarkable they were in an era when Europe seemed so clearly outmatched by the mighty gunpowder empires of Islam. The new global system first became possible in the early modern period, when European states began their far-flung discoveries and encounters, which laid the foundation for empires of unprecedented scale and wealth. For the first time, Christian states could move beyond merely resisting further Islamic expansion to projecting Christianity on a worldwide scale. And so they did, sometimes by means of missions that amounted to ruthless forced conversions.[3]

Christian missions advanced the interests of those emerging empires and indeed justified their existence. Commonly, the linkage worked to the interests of both sides: the cross followed the flag, and the flag followed the cross. Yet the imperial context was by no means simple. If missions and missionaries were indeed the vanguard of worldly empires, this would compromise the spiritual content of the message they were preaching. It posed the danger that external societies would dismiss missions solely as pawns or tools of hostile empires and strike back at them accordingly.[4]

The story of these missions falls neatly into two portions, an earlier Catholic-led phase before 1750 and a later stage in which Protestants took the lead, most obviously in the long nineteenth century. I will divide this chapter accordingly between the two stages and the different imperial interests that each represented. But as we see in both eras, although the relationship between empires and missions could be complex, the role of empires is fundamental to any account of the history of those missions, which in turn lie at the heart of Christian history.[5]

Iberian Empires

At the end of the fifteenth century, Christian numbers were largely concentrated in Europe, with some outlying populations in the Middle East and some more distant concentrations in Ethiopia and southern India. Many of those believers were politically subject to Muslim regimes, particularly the Mamluk sultanate of Egypt and the Ottoman Turks. The prospects for Christianity then changed, quite suddenly, bringing the faith to a far larger global stage and creating something like the religious map we know today.[6] Spain and Portugal extended their power on a worldwide scale, through the Americas and across the Pacific, into India and the Philippines, and with ambitions on Japan. If we seek a symbolic date for the beginning of true globalization, we might point to the year 1578, when the Roman Catholic church established a diocese in Manila, as a suffragan see of Mexico City: both centers, of course, fell under Spanish power. The name "Philippines" was a tribute to the Habsburg prince who would later rule Spain as Philip II. For the first time in history, "world empires" could be truly global, rather than merely Eurasian. (During the Iberian golden age, between 1580 and 1640, Portugal itself was de facto part of the Spanish Empire.)[7]

Each of the great empires formally grounded its power in religious justifications and rhetoric, so that the projection of Christian power of necessity implied spreading the faiths as defined by these states. Spanish and Portuguese ventures in the New World were blessed by the pope, who demanded evangelism and mission as part of the imperial project. That doctrine was formally consecrated in what still remains an egregious historical scandal. In 1513, the Spanish created a document that was to be read to newly contacted nations and tribes, to demand their instant submission, regardless of their literacy or knowledge of European customs and rhetoric. This *Requerimiento* demanded a solid grounding in canon law, as well as the principles of contemporary Spanish feudal practice, and it was to be read in Latin, untranslated. The Spanish explained that God had given all power in the world to one man, the pope, who was based in Rome as the most suitable center from which to rule that dominion. The current pope had given the New World to the kings of Spain and Portugal, who had now come to receive the submission of their subjects. Those subjects were required to permit the preaching of the Catholic faith, although without any actual compulsion to join the church. Any who resisted these demands were subject to military assault, and as rebellious vassals, they were liable to enslavement. Adding to the absurdity, the *Requerimiento* was often read to empty beaches, or the document was merely left as a parchment. Even so, the invaders now felt they had good legal title to the new lands and ample religious justification for their aggression.[8]

This scarcely implied mission in anything like the paternalistic sense that we see portrayed in Thomas Barker's painting. At this stage, the Christian states were far more committed to religious conformity and homogeneity than were their Muslim neighbors. The Iberian nations had long memories of struggles with Muslim powers and were deeply concerned about possible subversion by surviving Muslim or Jewish elements in their own realms. Inevitably, the conquest of new populations meant compulsion, of a harsh and systematic kind. The Iberians did not have to deal with any of the very gradual processes and interactions that we have seen to be so effective in the establishment of Muslim loyalties: rather, they simply rejected any possible rival faiths as enemies, and crushed them wherever possible. Nothing in this grim story could have been accomplished without the wholehearted support of imperial administrators and soldiers.

Conquest and Compulsion

Both in the Americas and the Philippines, the empires established Catholic Christianity as the sole tolerated religion—and, moreover, in its contemporary Iberian form—while church authorities ensured that no rival faiths or systems were tolerated. Among the peoples of Mexico, Central America, and Peru, the conquerors immediately destroyed Native temples and their priestly hierarchies, prohibiting rituals and sacrifices and eradicating books wherever they could be found. In 1562, the fanatical Bishop Diego de Landa collected all the Maya texts he could find and burned them in a grand ceremony. After all, he said, they contained nothing but lies and superstitions of the devil. Today, only four Maya codices survive, out of libraries that would once have contained thousands of books. The spiritual conquest of the Maya was not accomplished overnight, and independent Maya societies continued to operate until the 1690s. But all public religious manifestations were suppressed as swiftly as the conquerors could manage.[9]

Where possible, the conquerors absorbed older Native religious structures into new churches and cathedrals. The great temple of the Aztec metropolis of Tenochtitlan supplied the foundation for the new cathedral of Mexico City. The Catholic cathedral at Cholula stands high atop an Aztec sacred site, which was once the largest pyramid in the Western Hemisphere. An intrusive inquisition sought out practices that could be identified as Jewish, Protestant, or outright diabolical. Even had Native peoples wished to struggle harder to retain their ways, the effects of disease and ruinously steep population declines utterly disrupted the old social and religious orders.[10]

It is only a pallid defense of this imposed religious revolution that in practice, a surprising number of aspects of those older religions actually survived within the new framework, even following what was notionally the total conversion of New World societies. Few indeed were the customs and habits of old Indigenous religions that could not be integrated into new Catholic devotions, with old deities transmogrified into saints, with the appropriate feast days. Such backstories are readily found for the various manifestations of the Virgin Mary that exist across these societies. In practice, converted Native believers might retain practices not unlike what they had always known, in premises or sites that had enjoyed an older sanctity. Even priestly and ritual societies maintained a shadow existence, under the guise of Catholic confraternities. To spread the faith, the missionaries needed common languages, which they found by cultivating and standardizing preexisting Native tongues such as Nahua (Mexico), and Quechua and Guaraní in their South American possessions. Their work actually made these languages even more widespread and familiar than they would have been under the older Aztec and Inka realms.[11]

In part, accepting pre-Christian survivals was a pragmatic response to a situation in which European Christians would be massively outnumbered by Native believers. But it also grew from very long-standing Catholic practice, which drew a sharp line between a religious system aimed at the worship of other gods and the cultural and spiritual behaviors used for these purposes. Once the overarching system was abolished—once hell's empire had been defeated—the practices could readily be adapted to the true faith. Even if they originated in some alien religious environment, the behaviors themselves were neutral and readily lent themselves to appropriation.[12] Much depended on the definition of "religion." For most Christians of that era, and long afterward, newly encountered religions were largely defined by their resemblance to the known monotheistic faiths. As such, they would be expected to have organized clergy and rituals that were performed in special places or buildings, and critically, those alternate religions would be literate, with acknowledged scriptures. Applying this rule, Spanish conquistadors immediately recognized the religious structures of their Aztec or Maya subjects, even if that faith was directed toward the devil, and they moved swiftly to eradicate this pernicious rival to Christianity. Unlike modern anthropologists, they did not recognize an assemblage of customs and practices as constituting "a religion" in any sense worthy of the name, and so those systems could be tolerated, with suitable modifications.[13]

At least to official satisfaction, the peoples of the New World were Christianized, and on the lines demanded by the Catholic empires. Latin America still remains the world's most Catholic region in terms of numbers, with the Philippines a virtual extension of that system.

Spiritual Conquistadors

Although the Spanish and Portuguese notionally held political control over vast areas of the Americas, it was very difficult to exercise that authority outside major population centers. But clergy and missionaries strove both to reinforce the religion among the new Christian populations and to undertake further expansion. Like the Sufi orders of Islam, these Catholic missionaries operated at the frontiers of empire, both literal and figurative.

The empires introduced the full panoply of Catholic institutions and structures, including religious orders such as the Dominicans and Franciscans, who aimed to make Native peoples accept the new religious regime.

In these projects, missionaries made full use of the frameworks supplied by the political empires. Like their predecessors, the Iberian realms created standardized systems of communication across their inconceivably large possessions. They built new cities on the lines familiar to Catholic Europe, where every aspect of the landscape and its public architecture proclaimed the dominance of the new Christian culture. Mexico City and Lima, the vital centers of imperial administration, were the hubs of church life. Opulent churches abounded in the mining boomtown of Potosí, in modern Bolivia, which at the height of the silver boom was probably the fifth-largest city in the whole Christian world and was pivotal to the Spanish economic world system. In the second rank, but still vibrant, were such centers as Havana, Quito, and Cuzco, each with its glorious cathedral and religious houses. Critically too, the empires operated on the two main European languages, Spanish and Portuguese, which were used by officials of both state and church, as well as settlers and immigrants. Those hegemonic tongues gradually spread throughout the whole society—without, of course, eliminating Native languages.[14]

Missionaries of various orders, Jesuits and others, built Catholic structures and devotional life throughout the empire, and their efforts were often heroic. Just to take one ambitious example, in the 1630s the Jesuit Antonio Ruiz de Montoya led what he termed the "spiritual conquest" of vast stretches of the upper Amazon, of "Paraguay, Paraná, Uruguay, and Tape." In North America likewise, other Jesuits advanced the Catholic cause through New France, often facing the risk of bloody martyrdom. In areas like New Mexico, Franciscan clergy organized Native people into communities where they were would learn to be loyal and hardworking as well as faithfully Catholic. The most famous of these mission ventures occurred in California, where the Spanish of the eighteenth century had only small populations to control vast territories, which faced challenges from rival empires, the British and Russians.[15]

Of course, these missions are deeply controversial in modern historical writing. The clergy were ruthlessly authoritarian, forcing Native peoples into economic and social structures that were at variance with their traditions, while dragooning people into controlled settlements encouraged the spread of destructive diseases. Spiritual oppression was explicit. When Natives rebelled, as they did with great success in New Mexico in 1680, they made no distinction between the clergy and the empire's secular officials. Missionaries and clergy were an intrinsic part of imperial administration.[16]

Pastures New

The communication routes on which the empires depended to move officials and soldiers presented perfect opportunities for missionary endeavors. Central to the story was the empire's transpacific route, the Ruta de la Plata, or "Silver Way," which shipped New World silver to China, in exchange for silk and porcelain. This route united Acapulco with Manila, and it was as vital to global commerce as the Silk Routes had been centuries before. The Spanish-milled dollar, the legendary "pieces of eight," became the world's first global currency. Like those Silk Routes of old, the Silver Way was crucial to Christian expansion. That Pacific connection created amazing new possibilities for Catholic expansion, in lands far removed from Iberian political control. That context offered both dangers and advantages for the missions. While they could not rely on imperial protection, neither were they encumbered by the intimate association with those empires and the oppression they implied. They represented something like the classic Western stereotype of missionaries, as heroic adventurers, often alone, pressing deeply into truly alien regions and cultures, and accommodating to them as best they could.[17]

Symbolizing Catholic hopes was the career of St. Francis Xavier (1506–1552), who undertook daring missionary work in India and dreamed of a near-limitless further expansion into China and Japan. All these realms of course lay outside the reach of European imperial powers, but the missionaries used the framework of sea routes and entrepôts created by those empires, such as the cities of Goa and Macau. The century following Francis' death was marked by repeated triumphs, including the establishment of a flourishing mission in Japan. The number of local converts here ran into the hundreds of thousands, including some important aristocrats.[18]

As the world's most populous and powerful nation, China offered still more intoxicating hopes. Jesuits established a strong influence at the Ming court from the start of the seventeenth century, using their expertise in astronomy and some European technologies to prove their usefulness to the emperors. Some conversions followed, including among elite figures. Recalling the history of the Roman Empire, Catholics dreamed that China might produce a convert ruler who would be a "New Constantine." That further raised the prospect of pushing Christianity into the neighboring realms within China's cultural orbit. Initially, the Vatican was happy to support the Chinese mission, approving the bold accommodations that Jesuits made to translate Christianity and its liturgy into terms accessible to educated Chinese.[19]

Agents of Empire

The prospects for future success seemed enormous, but missionaries soon encountered the paradoxes of their imperial connection. While those contexts allowed Jesuits and other religious orders to reach those distant lands and to operate from regional bases, they raised suspicions among the powerful nations that were the setting for their activities.

East Asian governments were understandably puzzled at the intentions of these new visitors. In their own minds, the missionaries were traveling the world for purely religious reasons, but such a project seemed incomprehensible to societies that had long forgotten the heroic ages of Buddhist mission. Beyond being widely traveled, these Europeans possessed obvious skills, especially in languages, and they assiduously studied every aspect of the lands in which they traveled. It was hard not to imagine them as political agents or spies serving some foreign dominion, which in a sense they were. Their travels would have been impossible without the direct support of European empires, and the spiritual sovereign they served, the pope, was throughout this era heavily dependent on those same global powers, especially the Habsburg dynasts. Moreover, the information the missionaries collected was indeed being consumed avidly in European capitals, as political intelligence as well as for new cultural observations.[20]

Missionaries genuinely did engage in activities that were unequivocally political. To secure entrée to new lands, they parlayed the skills they knew, which in Japan meant introducing new kinds of weaponry that substantially changed the balance of power. Their linguistic abilities made missionaries valuable as intermediaries between Asian kingdoms, giving Latin a surprising new role as a diplomatic language in the region. When in 1689 Russian and Chinese envoys met to conclude a peace treaty and draw up new borders, no obvious common language suggested itself as a natural means of communication. By default, Latin was used, with the Chinese side represented by European Jesuits.[21]

Missionaries became essential intermediaries between nations and cultures that hitherto had been utterly unknown to each other. In the seventeenth century, Jesuits established themselves in the powerful nation of Siam, or Thailand. Through their activities, the ambitious French king Louis XIV became aware of this distant royal counterpart, and diplomatic missions were exchanged in the 1680s. Naturally, Jesuits abounded in the embassies sent by both sides, as indispensable interpreters of language and culture. The Siamese embassy to France in 1686 created a sensation in the Europe of its day, with lasting ramifications for fashion and technology, not to mention mutual racial stereotypes. It also gave rich fodder for the intellectual discussions of Enlightenment thinkers. Still more significant, the exchange created an enduring French interest in Southeast Asia, which (as we will see) would later be manifested in that country's imperial adventures.[22]

Against such a background, the question obviously arose, What was the missionaries' own focus of political loyalty?

Pawns and Scapegoats

Missionaries were often less than frank about their own imperial associations. In southern India, Jesuit Robert De Nobili adopted the guise of a Hindu guru to carry out evangelism more effectively. Suspicious Indians asked whether he was a Farangi, which to them clearly meant a European Christian, and presumably a Portuguese agent, which he firmly denied. When other Europeans rebuked him for this falsehood, he implausibly claimed that he thought he was being asked whether he was from France. Christian missionaries in Japan or China said little about their homelands, and only very gradually in the later seventeenth century did the Chinese court realize, with some alarm, that the Jesuits whom they had welcomed might be subject to commands from foreign potentates, whether emperors or popes. That issue came to a head when the Vatican changed its policy and forbade the liturgical compromises, the "Chinese Rites," leading the Chinese to scale down the missions massively and ultimately to persecute Catholics. As the Chinese emperor told the missionaries, quite prophetically, his people had no wish to become the subjects of European sovereigns.[23]

The association with rival empires proved still more calamitous in Japan. Catholic missions in that nation had established themselves during a time of very weak central government, but a new and more powerful regime soon reestablished itself, one that was naturally concerned about possible external threats. At the same time, some missionaries reportedly boasted about how they would soon see the expansion of Spanish power into the region, so that Japan would become subjugated as thoroughly as the Philippines. The Japanese began a fearsome persecution not just of foreign missionaries but of their native converts, and many thousands died in subsequent repressions and rebellions. By the mid-seventeenth century, Christianity in Japan was apparently rooted out, although remarkable communities of crypto-Catholic believers have persisted into the present day.[24]

The Japanese disaster is well known in popular culture through Shusaku Endo's famous novel *Silence*, and the 2016 film based on it. Less celebrated, but quite similar, were the near-contemporary events in the empire of

Ethiopia, which followed Christianity but in a distinctive Orthodox form, with many divergences from European practice. From the 1540s, Ethiopian rulers had repeatedly turned to the Portuguese and Spanish for military help against Muslim rivals, and such aid had largely saved the empire from military jihads. In the 1620s, facing multiple rebellions and military threats, the emperor Susenyos converted to Catholicism and brought in Iberian clergy to establish the new faith. This promised to draw Ethiopia ever closer into the Spanish imperial system, as a de facto subject king, in much the same ways that religion had served this purpose on Roman frontiers in earlier times. This was good imperial policy: following the faith of empire would surely align the smaller state politically and militarily. But as in contemporary Japan, disappointment soon followed. The heavy-handed efforts of the missionaries to enforce European ways in their most rigid form stirred ferocious opposition and outright revolt, as Ethiopians struggled for independence—political, cultural, and religious. The country's Catholic regime lasted barely a decade, and any stubborn Jesuits or converts who remained in the country faced persecution or martyrdom.[25]

Neither for the first time nor the last, missionaries benefited from the global and cosmopolitan connections that empires made possible but then suffered for those very contexts. They became the scapegoats of empire.

Missions against Empire?

Catholic missionaries, and especially Jesuits, plunged wholeheartedly into the cultures of the societies they evangelized, and in the process they often changed those host cultures quite dramatically. As a means of gaining influence and winning souls, the tactic was admirable, but on occasion, it pointed to another of the conflicts endemic to mission: When did immersion in a foreign or subject culture lead to defiance of imperial authority? Jesuits not only became thoroughly familiar with such Asian languages as Vietnamese and Tamil but, as will see, actually redefined the ways that former tongue was written.[26]

In that instance, the missionary contribution did not contradict the goals or policies of Western empires, but conflicts did arise, and sometimes quite spectacularly. On occasion, missionaries attacked imperial practices because they violated the spiritual values on which the Christian empires were supposedly founded. In the early phases of the Spanish conquest of the Caribbean and Mexico, clergy and friars naturally arrived to evangelize the natives. At least a few were horrified by the atrocities they witnessed and spoke out against those crimes, which were causing extraordinary levels of death and suffering. A humanitarian campaign began with the Dominican friar Antonio de Montesinos, who influenced the famous bishop Bartolomé de Las Casas.

Although Las Casas could not entirely prevent the violence, he established the legal and philosophical doctrine that Natives were fully human and that the law should regulate their treatment. Reading the notorious *Requerimiento*, he said that he did not know whether to laugh or cry. The best evidence for the effectiveness of his advocacy for Native peoples was the furious opposition that he aroused among Spanish settlers and imperial officials, and his ideas left a potent heritage in later international law. Las Casas' career has one notorious footnote, in that at one stage, he hoped to safeguard the Natives by bringing in labor from an alternative source, namely African slaves, a policy that both Portuguese and Spanish were soon to pursue enthusiastically. But with that exception, which he came to regret, Las Casas played an exemplary role as a continuing thorn in the side of empire and officialdom.[27]

In some instances, missionary protests became still more daring, most sensationally in the territory that we today call Paraguay, together with neighboring portions of Argentina, Brazil, and Bolivia. In the early seventeenth century, Spanish and Portuguese rule of South America was marked by extreme ill treatment of Native peoples, bringing millions into forced labor, serfdom, or slavery. Large sections of the continent were open to the depredations of private armies and militias, of bandits, mercenaries, and slave traders. Well-intentioned Jesuits attempted to bring Natives into protected reserves or reductions, but gathering Natives into poorly defended settlements merely gave slavers the opportunity to grab larger groups of victims in a single raid.[28]

From the 1630s, the Jesuits developed a more muscular approach, as they expanded the reductions. The Jesuits issued their converts with firearms and trained them in modern tactics. The fathers organized well-armed Native forces several thousand strong, which successfully resisted slave raiders and on occasion even defeated Spanish armies. The expanded reductions were theocratic communities, with urban layouts designed to promote a communist Utopia. The result was a virtually independent Indian Christian state larger in area than most European kingdoms, with populations in the hundreds of thousands. Far from imposing European languages on their converts, the Jesuits actively cultivated the Native language of Guaraní. In effect, the Jesuits used the frameworks of the Iberian empires to carve out their own independent empires, run on principles radically contrary to those official policies.[29]

By the 1750s, the missions faced existential crisis. Both Spain and Portugal coveted the vast and prosperous mission lands, and a series of wars devastated the reductions and forced the abandonment of many. Meanwhile, the Jesuit order itself was under constant attack from both religious and political critics. In 1767, Jesuits were expelled from Spanish possessions, before the order was wholly suppressed in 1773. The reductions were now terminated, although their heritage was not utterly destroyed. In the following century, Guaraní thrived in the new nation of Paraguay, where today it is spoken by many of European descent as well as those of Indigenous heritage.

As we will see, that was by no means the last occasion on which missions would develop goals radically at odds with those of the prevailing empires.

The New Age of Empire

Before 1750, Catholics overwhelmingly dominated the story of Christian mission. Despite the disaster in Japan and the setback in China, Catholic orders continued to wander the world, wherever the Iberian empires spread their influence. Anglophone historians tend to understate the persistence of those once-great powers, forgetting that the Spanish Empire in particular endured for centuries longer than its more celebrated British counterpart. Nor does the French part of the story commonly attract the attention it merits. The French Society of Foreign Missions of Paris (Société des Missions Etrangères de Paris, or MEP) dates from 1658, and it maintained its efforts through the following century. France's Indian colony of Pondicherry served the same function as a base for Asian Catholic ventures as Goa and Macau did for the Portuguese before them.[30]

In the seventeenth century, Catholic polemic vaunted such globalization, pointing out the embarrassing contrast to the paltry endeavors of their rivals. Protestants, they wryly noted, ate herring; Catholics had pineapples, oranges, and coconut. Who could doubt which side had God's favor? Indeed, Protestant missions began on a much smaller scale. The English conquerors of eastern North America undertook some missions to Native peoples, and there were strictly limited Danish ventures in India. In 1701, the Church of England formed the Society for the Propagation of the Gospel in Foreign Parts. Well into the nineteenth century, however, the British rulers of much of India were the East India Company, which had no interest whatever in introducing Christianity and actively discouraged missionaries. Indeed, one religious outcome of this rule was to pull elite British figures into the orbit of Islam or Hinduism: a few actively converted.[31]

The other mighty European empire in Asia was the Dutch, which Anglophone historians so often neglect. In fact, Dutch Calvinist clergy worked closely with the country's East India Company, the VOC, serving as chaplains and moreover establishing networks of schools and missions. If the enterprise was much smaller than the Catholic contemporaries, its geographical span was impressive, stretching from Indonesia and Malaysia to Ceylon and Southern India, and southern Africa, and indeed, to New Netherland, the later New York. Like the Spanish before them, the Dutch developed and standardized local languages for mission use, including Malay and Tamil. The Protestant situation changed fundamentally from the 1790s, as the British Empire expanded its power across much of Africa and Asia. One early effect was the absorption of most Dutch territories outside the East Indies strictly defined. Although the Dutch continued their religious efforts, they (like the British) were nervous about spreading Christian influences that could infuriate local Muslims and thus interfere with making profits.[32]

The British, meanwhile, became far more committed to extending their formal empire and to building missions. In its early phases, British power was exercised through informal means rather than formal annexation, but there was always a sense that British gunboats and soldiers lay conveniently close over the horizon, ready to intervene if needed. Increasingly during the nineteenth century, rivalry from other aspiring powers drove the British to make their territorial claims explicit. By the end of the century, several European powers had officially proclaimed immense imperial possessions that included almost all of Africa, together with large expanses of Asia and Oceania.[33]

The Great Commission

The great age of European imperialism during the long nineteenth century was the golden age of Christian missions. As in older times, the new empires facilitated this task through their networks of trade routes, of centers of commerce and administration, and of the military power that preserved the order on which safe communication depended. From the 1790s, moreover, the various Protestant churches and denominations became far more committed to missionary enterprise across the imperial possessions. The Church of England created a new series of bishops to supervise colonial territories, which ultimately formed the basic structure of the modern-day Anglican Communion. In 1814, a bishop was established for Calcutta, the base for Britain's expanding Indian possessions. He was followed by episcopal colleagues in the West Indies in 1824 and Australia in 1836.[34]

Enthusiasts linked such mission ventures to the fundamental Christian identity of their respective societies. Best known were the Protestant evangelicals, who now placed a heavy emphasis on mission and on the subversion of hell's empire. Hudson Taylor, legendary missionary to China, popularized the term "the Great Commission" to describe Christ's command in the Gospel of Matthew to carry the good news to all nations. In 1819, the Anglican cleric Reginald Heber warned against being seduced by the tropical beauties of the imperial possessions:

> What though the spicy breezes
> Blow soft on Ceylon's isle;
> Though every prospect pleases,
> And only man is vile;
> In vain with lavish kindness
> The gifts of God are strown;
> The heathen, in his blindness,
> Bows down to wood and stone.

In 1823, Heber became bishop of Calcutta.[35]

India now became a flourishing field of Protestant mission, followed shortly afterward by China. Africa likewise attracted fervent interest, due in part to the great age of exploration that was now under way. In 1799 Mungo Park's *Travels in the Interior Districts of Africa* alerted European Protestants to the vast mission field awaiting harvest in the western parts of the continent. When the British established themselves politically at the Cape of Good Hope in 1806, Protestant mission work began in earnest across Southern Africa.[36] Beyond their impact in such overseas territories, the new commitment to mission stirred real enthusiasm among Christians in the metropolitan lands, where fundraising and the support of missions gave ordinary believers an exciting sense of participation in the great global enterprise. Heroic accounts of women missionaries had a special appeal for home congregations.[37]

Catholics too rediscovered their missionary enthusiasm, which they associated with their own imperial ventures. The French, the other great power of the day, launched their own imperial projects, equally supported by new generations of Catholic missions. The MEP enjoyed a vigorous new lease of life. To varying degrees, Belgians, Portuguese, and Italians all followed suit, to create what has become known as the great Mission Century, which lasted until 1914. When the (Protestant) World Missionary Conference was held in Edinburgh in 1910, it seemed wholly plausible to declare the goal of "the evangelization of the world in this generation."[38]

European missions unabashedly associated their Christianity with a powerful cultural and ideological package, which they planned to impose on targeted societies. As suggested by the Brontë poem that I quoted at the beginning of this chapter, missionaries firmly believed that those pagan or heathen faiths were literally of the devil. The famous abolitionist William Wilberforce characterized Hinduism as "one grand abomination, a dark and bloody superstition." But beyond their raw spiritual evil, those other religions were associated with the worst kinds of social and political exploitation that were such a central focus of liberal activism in Europe at this time. Pagan priests were tyrants and brutal exploiters, in this world and the next. England, in contrast, was viewed as a Christian society, destined to rescue and elevate those people. Europeans had a moral and religious obligation to share their cultural and spiritual wealth—to spread education, literacy, and human liberation, to elevate and empower the weak, especially women. Through the work of empire, Christianity would bring salvation, modernity, and liberation.[39]

Enlightenment philosophers such as the Marquis de Condorcet had preached that Europeans had a holy duty to bring the blessings of European civilization to other societies, through what became known as the *mission civisilatrice*. Although that did not necessarily imply Christian conversion, the two concepts of "mission," Christian and civilizing, were hard to separate, and they grew together during the nineteenth century. Scarcely less intermingled were ideas of race and religion. In the rhetoric of the time, light (modernity) was to eliminate the darkness of primitivism and superstition, and the concepts had no necessary racial implication. But in the thought world of the late nineteenth century, it was difficult to avoid the suggestion that light and Christian civilization were aspects of whiteness, while pagan Black Africa was the heart of darkness.[40]

Missionary Imperialism

Establishing and protecting mission activities became a significant point of imperial policy and diplomacy. This was historically new. Earlier empires had been quite frank about the religious motives for their conquests, which advanced Christianity: conversion would follow conquest.

But nineteenth-century empires used a subtler rhetoric, which at least superficially did not directly threaten a non-Christian state, unless and until it endangered Christians, whether they were subject populations or the missionaries who sought to bring enlightenment to dark corners of the globe. This approach was ideologically valuable in a more democratic era, in providing a justification for imperial aggression that was acceptable to a home audience: conquests were being undertaken for the cause of progress and Christian civilization, and indeed of religious freedom.

Several imperial nations deployed the politics of persecution in this way. The Russians used the protection of Christians living under Turkish rule as a central justification for expansion, with a thinly disguised goal of ultimately absorbing the whole Ottoman realm. As we will see in the next chapter, the resulting conflicts repeatedly threatened European peace. In some ways, the missionary issue was still more useful, and more flexible, because it need not be applied only to countries with old, established Christian minorities. It could indeed be applied to any corner of the world touched by missionaries, so that non-Western countries that were scarcely conscious of a Christian presence suddenly found themselves demonized as persecutors and thus liable to military assault. In the US context, those themes pervaded the critical debate that followed the country's defeat of Spain in 1898 and the subsequent proposal to annex the Philippines (which were overwhelmingly Catholic). Supporters of the new imperialism commonly cited the expansion of Protestant missions as a major justification for the expansion, and for the war that the United States now waged against its insurgent subjects. Speaking of the newly conquered Philippines, US president William McKinley declared "that there was nothing for us to do but to take them all, and to educate the Filipinos, and uplift and civilize and Christianize them." Such rhetoric appalled such anti-imperial critics as Mark Twain, who ruthlessly mocked appeals to the supposed needs of "the Person who Sits in Darkness."[41]

France, Missions, and Empire

The protection of Christians—both communities and missionaries—was a central theme in the growth of the French overseas empire in the century after Napoleon Bonaparte, when the nation was struggling to match the seemingly unstoppable global march of its British rival. The British had bested the French for control of North America in the mid-eighteenth century, while the Haitian revolt of the 1790s had removed one of France's richest and most productive possessions. Only after 1830 did a Second French Empire emerge, and repeatedly, missions and missionary rhetoric supplied the crucial excuses for expansion.[42]

In 1830, the French conquered Algiers and progressively expanded their power over the whole of what would become the nation of Algeria. In the process, they had to fight a decades-long series of savage wars against Arab Muslim forces. That territory remained the heart of France's imperial dream until the 1960s, and in theory, it was fully absorbed into the metropolitan homeland. The French aggressively deployed the language of Christian mission to justify their presence. In 1838, Algiers became the seat of a Catholic bishop. From 1867, thc archbishop of Algiers was Cardinal Charles Lavigerie, who had wildly romantic dreams of restoring the ancient Christianity of North Africa that had been shattered a millennium before. He held the honorary title of primate of Africa. Missionary orders now spread their message across the region, fulfilling Lavigerie's vision of something like a revival of the crusader spirit.[43]

Like the British, the French acquired global missionary ambitions, which they supported with the armed forces they judged necessary. In 1838, the alleged mistreatment of French missionaries in Tahiti provoked a French naval intervention, which evolved into a full-scale war in the following decade. Annexations duly followed, and neighboring islands learned the danger of resistance. Thus was the French Pacific empire born. Those events set a powerful precedent for later decades, in far wealthier and more extensive lands.[44]

Religious rhetoric justified the French occupation of Indochina, where the stories of empire and mission are indissolubly intertwined. Vietnam was an ancient and a powerful empire in its own right. Jesuit missionaries such as the heroic Alexandre de Rhodes had established a presence here in the seventeenth century, but Catholics repeatedly suffered persecution, often on a large scale. Those episodes indicated the poor prospects of the church without some degree of political protection. Deep political divisions within Vietnam during the late eighteenth century presented opportunities for French missionary priests, some of whom became heavily involved in Vietnamese politics, supporting the claims of the prince Nguyen Phuc Ánh against the then-emperor. One priest, Pierre Pigneau de Behaine, literally became an emperor maker. In 1787, France formally concluded an alliance with Nguyen, and French forces were sent to his support. From 1802, the prince became the founder of the Nguyen dynasty, which ruled the country until 1945.[45]

Despite the Catholic contributions to establishing the dynasty, later emperors became concerned about the missionary presence, and severe persecutions followed sporadically. In 1858, the Vietnamese emperor tried to expel the missionaries once and for all. These actions gave the pretext for French involvement, which specifically cited the need to protect missionaries, and direct political control developed from the 1860s. By 1867, the French had secured essentially the whole of the later nation of South Vietnam, and further gains soon followed: by the early 1890s, the French united Vietnam, Cambodia, and Laos under their rule. Without the MEP and its lobbying in Paris, the French Empire in this region would have developed in nothing like the way it actually did, and probably would have been unthinkable.[46]

The aggressive intervention in Vietnam in the decade after 1858 reflected the policies of the country's emperor Napoleon III (1852–1871), the nephew of the famous conqueror. The later and lesser Bonaparte used his far-reaching global adventures to shore up political support in a profoundly divided nation. Besides southeast Asia, French forces fought in Mexico, in North Africa, and in the Levant. Napoleon III often used French missions as an excuse for such imperial interventions, presenting himself as a champion of Catholicism as much as of French grandeur.[47]

This policy was evident in China. Western powers had insisted on treaties allowing missionaries to reside. At first, such rights were notional, but as Western influence grew, the Chinese became less able to confine and restrain those foreign arrivals. In 1856, the execution of a MEP priest by Chinese authorities supplied the justification for French involvement in the Second Opium War, in which the Anglo-French alliance won decisively. The war concluded with the Treaty of Tientsin/Tianjin, which forbade Chinese persecutions of Christians and allowed missionary activity and settlement. A major expansion of such missions followed. Other persecutions of Korean Christians in the following decade opened the door to a French military intervention in that nation. Although these actions did not result in major expansions of the formal French Empire—both China and Korea remained independent—they indicated the likely spheres of interest in which the French military would be active in coming years.[48]

Another area of French empire building was in the Levant, in the lands that today are known as Syria and Lebanon. In the mid-nineteenth century, the region was controlled by the Ottoman Empire, and it was home to several competing religions, including ancient Christian communities. In 1860, Christians became the target of extensive massacres by Druze and

Muslim mobs and militias. That precipitated a humanitarian intervention by European powers, aggressively led by France, which began a policy of building up a separate Christian territory under its own dominance. That culminated following the collapse of the Ottoman Empire during the First World War, when that Christian homeland became the basis of a newly defined nation of Lebanon. From 1923 through 1946, Syria and Lebanon were controlled by France under a mandate from the League of Nations, which in effect brought them under imperial control.[49]

Missions and Liberation

For non-Euro-Americans, the concatenation of empire and mission inevitably caused the two forces to become intertwined, if not wholly merged. In many regions, that imperial dimension naturally invited a hostile reaction during eras of violence and resistance. Following the Treaty of Tientsin, outbreaks of anti-missionary violence became a common feature of the Chinese political landscape, with several massacres and "incidents," culminating in the sweeping Boxer Rebellion (1899–1901). In part, that focus on missionaries arose because they were the Europeans most readily available for the expression of popular anger in remote sections of the country, but moreover, they represented the combination of imperial oppression and the assault on traditional ways and beliefs. They were the visible faces of empire and of the Western culture that it sought to promote—and often, of racial arrogance. Anti-missionary violence naturally attracted retaliation by the imperial powers, which further reinforced the perceived linkage between those missions and the prevailing empires of the time.

This lengthy history has tainted the history of missions, especially in Africa. In southern Uganda, Catholics were colloquially known as *baFaransa* (the French), and Protestants were *baIngerezza* (the English). The Gikuyu people of Kenya declared that "There is no difference between missionary and settler." African opponents of empire often told a concise history of missions: "When the missionaries came to Africa they had the Bible and we had the land. They said 'Let us pray.' We closed our eyes. When we opened them, we had the Bible and they had the land." The original remark has been variously attributed to Jomo Kenyatta and Desmond Tutu.[50]

It is easy enough to draw up an indictment of missionaries as de facto agents of empire. Other accounts are much more favorable, and many Africans offer due credit to those missionaries for building what became extraordinarily flourishing churches. But for those empires too, the missions were by no means a simple blessing. They could offer criticisms of imperial rule, and arguably, they contributed powerfully to the demise of those seemingly immortal structures. We have already seen the activism of Bartolomé de Las Casas in protesting the injustice of Spanish imperial rule in the New World. Of course, the central position that he holds in most accounts of this era diverts attention from the countless other clergy who observed similar horrors but for whatever reason failed to speak out, or actively contributed to the atrocities. Nothing about being a missionary or a cleric necessarily gave any given individual any kind of moral superiority. But the nature of missions did contribute to actions that inevitably conflicted with imperial interests. One, obviously, was that their international connections gave them the power to make their criticisms known widely, independent of the empire's own administrative channels and hierarchies. Las Casas, for example, could appeal to the international Dominican order or to the Papacy.

In other ways too, the nature of missions raised subversive questions. One concerned the status of baptized Christians. If vanishingly few Christian thinkers taught anything like the social or political equality of believers, many did hold that those believers, of whatever race, should be imbued with certain rights in the face of oppression or maltreatment. Las Casas certainly applied this principle to Native peoples who had accepted baptism. The question was still more sensitive for enslaved Africans, who from the seventeenth century were so fundamental to the development of imperial economies in the Americas. Although the issue was fiercely controversial, at least some Protestant churches in plantation colonies eventually decided to baptize slaves, which at least in theory granted them equal status within the Christian community and gave them a claim for emancipation. For that very reason, slaveowners bitterly contested any such move, and so did their clerical allies in the churches. In the Anglophone world, that conflict was resolved by making race rather than religion the basis of free status and the rights that accompanied it, with all the consequences that implied for later generations.[51]

The Perils of Christianity

Particularly during the high noon of mission activities in the long nineteenth century, missionaries faced an intractable dilemma. Avowedly, they sought not just to convert Native peoples but to raise them up so that they accepted Western standards of education and general "civilization." At a minimum, that implied education and widespread literacy. For Protestants, such teaching was an essential part of the mission enterprise, as it allowed converts to enter fully into reading and understanding the Bible.

More gradually, Catholic missions also gave priority to literacy. But once someone learned to read, it was impossible to ensure that the material they pursued would be strictly confined to approved religious texts and interpretations. The Bible easily lent itself to radical or revolutionary interpretations, especially for slaves. Antislavery activism of necessity posed a direct threat to the larger political structure, and to empires themselves. All informed people recalled the slave revolt in Saint-Domingue in the 1790s, which resulted in disaster for the French Empire.[52]

It would be pleasant, but misleading, to suggest that missionaries and imperial clerics were so transformed by the Christian message that they inevitably fought against slavery. In fact, many such figures actually supported the institution for those very religious reasons, to rescue Africans from the thrall of hell's empire. When the legendary evangelical George Whitefield visited the American colonies in the 1740s, he not only failed to denounce slavery but actually supported its expansion into the new colony of Georgia. Only from the 1780s did Protestant and evangelical clergy, virtually all with mission connections, lead the great abolitionist campaign that persuaded Britain to end slavery in its empire, a victory eventually secured in the 1830s. As those abolitionists emphasized, their goal was not to harm empire but rather to purify it morally, so that it could advance to still greater ends.[53]

Through much of this period, the vast majority of those resisting slavery were themselves slaves and people of color who had absorbed the biblical teachings in forms very different than their teachers intended. Both in North America and the British Caribbean, the Bible inspired several nineteenth-century slave revolts. In US history, the year 1831 is famous for the revolt in Virginia led by Nat Turner, who was inspired by his own idiosyncratic readings of the Bible. But in that very year, Jamaica was the setting for the largest slave revolt that ever occurred in the British West Indies. The uprising was chiefly led and organized by Baptists, and throughout this "Baptist war," we see the leadership of mission-trained activists. In the aftermath of such events, slaveowners feared the influence of missionaries and mission schools, and missionaries suspected of even slight sympathy for slaves easily found themselves arrested or removed. In fairness to their concerns, the slaveowners' fears were not wholly groundless.[54]

Mission ventures created believing populations and gave them ideological tools they could use to resist empires. We see in this the idea of scripturalization as framed by scholar Vincent Wimbush. According to this view, the process of building empire uses the scriptures of dominant

Western religions as a means of asserting and enforcing truth claims, to control and suppress vernacular and commonly nonliterate cultures. The (written) word conquers all, at least until those vernacular cultures appropriate some or all of those scriptures for themselves and use them as sites of resistance. The empires write (and read) back.[55]

Prophets and Nationalists

Beyond encouraging resistance to slavery, the new autonomous forms of Christianity posed a direct challenge to empires themselves. Of course, the conversion of a new society to Christianity did not of itself portend the creation of new radical or apocalyptic movements, but around the world, such a development has often marked the moment at which the religion passes from being something received from the missionaries to sinking authentic new roots. Often, those movements were associated with self-described prophets or even messiahs.

In Black Africa, the crucial transition came during and after the First World War, with an upsurge of apocalyptic and millenarian churches, most dedicated to spiritual healing. Some of these movements focused on prophetic or messianic leaders, whose appearance terrified imperial authorities that they might inspire overt nationalism. In the Belgian Congo, the most prominent figure was Simon Kimbangu, whom the Belgians imprisoned from 1921 until his death in 1951. Some of these religiously motivated leaders actually did fulfill those imperial fears. In 1915, the Baptist minister John Chilembwe led an anti-colonial uprising in Nyasaland (modern Malawi), a movement that has come to be seen as key in the making of modern independent Africa. Even when such insurgent movements were not overtly revolutionary in any political sense, they assuredly took Christianity in ways deeply uncongenial to the imperial authorities that had placed such high hopes in missionary ventures. Today, those African-Initiated Churches appeal to tens of millions.[56]

The fact of literacy gave individuals a powerful sense of confidence and self-reliance, which could not fail to have political consequences. When independence movements developed in Africa during the mid-twentieth century, the leaders had usually been trained in mission schools, and some themselves came from clerical families. As the churches became increasingly native in composition and leadership, so they offered effective structures for organization and communication. But the role of missions was not confined to such educational work, however crucial it might have been. Particularly in the British context, many white missionaries came to sympathize actively with the aspirations of the people they had converted and trained. We inevitably think back to the Jesuits of the Amazon region in previous centuries, who supported and defended their faithful Native believers against the excesses of the empires of their day.[57]

Because they had seen the injustices of empire at first hand, the children of missionary families produced some ringing condemnations of those evils. To take one powerful example, Olive Schreiner was the daughter of a Wesleyan missionary in southern Africa. In 1897, she published the short novel *Trooper Peter Halket of Mashonaland*, which through the years has become a classic of anti-imperialism. The story depicts a wild young adventurer who has seen countless horrors committed against the native Black population on the empire's fast-expanding frontier in Southern Africa. His life is utterly changed by an encounter with a stranger, who turns out to be Christ himself, who is visiting the region to condemn the savagery and exploitation. Peter Halket learns that he must resist empire, even at the price of martyrdom.[58]

Some missionary clergy advocated passionately on behalf of Native rights and interests, much like Las Casas in an earlier era. During and after the First World War, one conspicuous figure was Frank Weston, the Anglican bishop of Zanzibar, who applied his Christian and socialist principles across racial lines. He fiercely condemned the German empire's treatment of its Black African subjects but was just as willing to denounce British policies that amounted to demanding forced labor by Africans. His 1920 pamphlet *The Serfs of Great Britain* remains a noble monument of anticolonial protest. Ideas like Weston's gained importance from the 1950s as rising nationalist movements came into conflict with imperial authorities, whose responses could be heavy handed, if not brutal. It was particularly through the efforts of missionaries that such encounters reached the attention of the wider world, where they contributed to a swelling hostility against colonialism. If Las Casas could reach a transcontinental stage through the structures of his church, latter-day missionaries fully exploited the news media of their time.[59]

Christian missions build and extend empires; but they also help end them.

7
Worlds in Motion

How shall we sing the Lord's song in a strange land?

Psalm 137:4, KJV

Large portions of the Hebrew Bible concern the deportation of the Hebrew people to the imperial capital of Babylon. We hear of the events leading up to that disaster, of the prophetic responses to it, and the aftermath, but one unusual text records the strictly contemporary experience of one victim of that traumatic uprooting. Written during that exile, the speaker in Psalm 137 expresses his theological bafflement in the words quoted in the epigraph to this chapter. As with most early societies, his religious life was grounded in a particular landscape, with its temple and all its sacred places, its mountains and rivers and wilderness, as recorded in tradition, legend, and scripture, where the ritual calendar was closely attuned to the seasons and harvests of that terrain. How can he adjust to his new world? He denounces his captors with the savage imprecation, "Happy is he who repays you for what you have done to us—he who seizes your infants and dashes them against the rocks."[1]

As we know, that deportation would ultimately end in restoration and vindication, and it would promote a revived faith and consciousness in what became the religion of Judaism. Without that disaster, the faith would have developed very differently, and it would have been slower to develop the universalism that became such a characteristic of all the Abrahamic faiths. However dreadful the effects on individual believers, episodes of exile transform religions, and in unpredictable ways.

When historians recount the spread of religions, they commonly focus on deliberate mission and evangelism, mainly because official agencies that undertake such work have the most accessible records. But diffusion and growth often occur without such conscious intent, for instance, through the migration or deportation of populations. Of their nature, empires are very good at moving peoples, even redistributing whole nations, often far from their original homes and with varying degrees of enticement or compulsion. This involves acts both of settlement and removal, of addition and subtraction. Such movements have the effects of relocating not just individuals and communities but also the religious systems they espouse. The consequences are readily visible around the modern world and are often mapped through the spread of languages. In some cases, movements even extend to the crushing or destruction of whole peoples and their faiths.

In pursuing what they conceive as their interests, those empires have vastly expanded the world's religious diversity, bringing once-localized faiths literally to the other side of the world. In the process, they sometimes force those religious systems to detach themselves from a landscape and cultural setting, making them more open and translatable to wider contexts. Religions actually do learn to sing in strange lands, sometimes in new tongues. In the nineteenth century, Lord Acton famously remarked, "Exile is the nursery of nationality." It can also be the nursery of world religions.[2]

Settling Faith

Many and varied are the motivations that drive empires to settle populations in given areas. At a minimum, empires have moved populations to defend frontiers and to consolidate and extend newly conquered possessions. Greek cities were seeding new settlements at least from the ninth century BC, and they created a world of shared language and cultures, of common gods and cults, stretching across much of the Mediterranean world and the Black Sea region. Colonies supported the development of trade and commerce. Later empires made such plantings an integral part of their organization. Even with all their skills in improving communications, premodern empires found it hard to defend the whole length of an extended frontier and could not hope to rush armies to protect an area from sudden attack. That made it necessary to build up local communities to protect such pressure points. New settlements create residents with a vested interest in fighting for their new homes. Once placed in new territories, those administrators and soldiers provided a nucleus for later growth.[3]

Later empires too planted sizable populations from the metropolis to create a facsimile of that original homeland and to consolidate their possessions. Commonly, such expansion was marked by placenames that reproduce familiar landscapes of home. This is what the Spanish did in their New World possessions, and the British in colonial North America, and later Canada, Australia, and New Zealand. The French likewise made a similar effort in Algeria, which as we have seen, they treated as a wholly integrated component of the metropolitan nation. Such settlements had obvious and far-reaching religious consequences in bringing the faith of the metropolis to new lands. In the long term, this kind of project depended on the relative success of the empires in question, and particularly the existing environments on which they were imposed. In some cases, the newly arrived faith proved to be no more than a light veneer, which was easily removed when imperial structures failed, but where settler colonialism succeeded, the transplanting was thorough. Australia, New Zealand, and Canada became overwhelmingly Christian lands, and that faith shaped these societies, however much religious practice declined over time. Of its nature, the settler revolution is a religious revolution.[4]

Even so, colonies did not and could not reproduce the original homeland with any degree of precision, as interactions with Native populations, and with other settlers, made those new worlds quite diverse both ethnically and religiously. Such territories generated new social and racial hierarchies, over and above imported structures of class and wealth. Relationships to the homeland further created new hierarchies of privilege, according to whether people were born in the metropolis or the new territory. There would be settlers and metropolitans, creoles and "half breeds." As we will see, highly successful colonies attracted new waves of migration, further enhancing diversity and making ever more difficult to reproduce the organic communities of the Old World, with its religious aspects. The fact of empire always left its mark.[5]

New England, New Russia

In some cases, colonial expansion and settlement was explicitly framed in religious terms. Overtly religious motivations were not a major force in the making of several of Europe's colonies in the Americas, the later New France and New Netherland. English colonies varied in their degree of religious inspiration, although some became nuclei for dissident religious traditions. The New England colonies were the most famous examples, with their Puritan and Baptist origins, followed later by the diverse sects and churches that settled Quaker Pennsylvania. Religious visions underlay such cities as Boston, Philadelphia, and Providence, which became vital centers of the eighteenth-century British Empire. Besides strengthening frontier territories in the face of Native and French challenges, such colonies offered a safety valve for the home country, by encouraging the export of its nonconforming groups.[6]

A New Russia likewise reflected spiritual aspirations. From the 1770s, the Russians won many victories over the Muslim Turks in southern Russia, Ukraine, and the Caucasus. Among other acquisitions, they conquered and annexed Crimea, which had hitherto been ruled by a Muslim khanate with historic roots in Mongol times, which subsequently became an Ottoman protectorate. These victories encouraged imperial authorities to build a whole new Christian geography in the conquered lands, a Novorossiya, with faithful new Orthodox believers to replace Muslims and other precursors. (We will return to the implications of these conflicts for the religious maps of the region.) Russian elites at this time were entranced by apocryphal medieval prophecies that imagined a true Orthodox sovereign reestablishing Christian rule across the former Roman Empire, and in Constantinople itself. At the height of the Turkish wars in the 1770s, the empress Catherine the Great christened one of her grandsons Constantine. New Russia would be a base and a bridge to that goal.[7]

The Russians sought deep historical precedents for their venture by littering the maps with Greek-derived place names that at least superficially looked Roman and Byzantine. Most had a *-polis* element, from the Greek word for "city." There was a Royal or Augustan City (Greek, Sevastopol). There was a City of Victory, Nikopol; a City of the Cross, Stavropol; and many counterparts, most of which survive on present maps. Although the regions affected had indeed had a remote Greek and Roman past, there were no lineal connections to this brave new geography. It was, in a sense, a fictional landscape. Reinforcing that impression of theatricality, the chief imperial minister guiding this process was Prince Grigory Potemkin, who became legendary for erecting deceptively Utopian villages for the empress to witness as she passed, the so-called Potemkin villages, which were all show and no substance. So, in its origins, was the newly mapped landscape of New Russia.[8]

Over time, the new lands became extremely important to Russian and indeed global affairs. In 1795, the Russians created a new city named for an ancient Greek colony that supposedly stood nearby, Odessos, and they called it Odessa. It boomed as an outlet for the region's wheat production, becoming the empire's fourth-largest city by the end of the century. Odessa was a center of modernizing improvement that appeared very American and was often compared to San Francisco or Chicago. The brand-new landscape boomed impressively—although as I will show, not exactly on approved religious lines.[9]

Against Their Will

Most such planned settlements were voluntary, and participants responded enthusiastically to offers of new land and opportunity. But empires frequently moved groups or peoples as a form of punishment. This fate might be inflicted on a restive or rebellious people, such as the Jews removed to ancient Babylonia, or else against a community of dubious loyalty who could not safely be permitted to dwell on a sensitive frontier. Nor were such tactics confined to distant antiquity. In the 1950s, British governments forcibly removed whole populations to break up potential centers of rebellion in Malaya and Kenya. In the latter instance, more than a million were displaced, perhaps a seventh of the whole population. Those modern removals were relatively short lived, but their ancient predecessors were long term or even permanent. From an imperial point of view, those movements achieved a double goal, securing the existing frontier and potentially improving the development of some marginal new land. Often, as we have seen, the group affected took its religious system along with it and gave it a fresh planting in new soil. The long Jewish history of Babylonia and later Iraq is testimony to this phenomenon.[10]

Throughout history, imperial wars have resulted in population transfers, through the deportation and enslavement of sizable communities. I have already described the role of such mass movements in spreading Christianity within the Persian Empire, but individual captives could serve as unwitting missionaries. The Bible tells the story of the captive Daniel who, together with his friends, defended the faith at the court of the Babylonian Empire. If that story is not historical, plenty of other instances suggest the role of slaves and captives in spreading religious faith as latter-day Daniels. One famous such case is St. Patrick, abducted by Irish raiders from fifth-century Britain, who later became the missionary of his new homeland. Almost certainly, the Roman-Persian wars of the fourth century caused the enslavement of a young woman called Nino, who found herself in the pagan Caucasian kingdom of Georgia. When the Georgian queen became sick, Nino healed her, and that in turn led to a royal conversion. Georgia then became Christian, which it remains to this day. Nino is remembered as the Enlightener, "equal to the apostles," and she remains Georgia's national heroine.[11]

The Byzantine Empire produced a famous instance in the mid-ninth century. From the seventh century through the ninth, the strong pagan kingdom of the Bulgars posed a deadly threat to the Byzantines, creating a potent rival empire of its own. It was a turning point in the history of European Christianity when the Bulgar khan Boris converted to the Christian faith, and moreover in its Eastern and Orthodox form. Captives again played a pivotal role. Repeated wars produced many captives and slaves who spread Christian beliefs within the pagan realm. The Byzantines, meanwhile, captured the princess Anna, Boris' sister, who became a fervent Christian. When she was returned in a prisoner exchange, "she did not cease inspiring and pleading and sowing the seeds of faith [in Boris]." For centuries to come, the Bulgarian Empire became a rich center of Christian culture, art, and architecture.[12]

Removal

I have described how actions by empires against subject and conquered peoples can on occasion build and expand religions, sometimes contrary to official intentions. Those inspiring events become occasions for celebrating national identity and faith. But throughout history, empires have eliminated communities and even whole populations, together with their religious traditions. In the process, they have built up complete new landscapes unrecognizable to traditional believers, with new peoples and new faiths. Rarely is it possible to build a New England or a New Russia on virgin soil, where there are no troublesome residents already in place. In US history, the removal of Native populations to reservations and to designated "Indian Territory" is an all too familiar story.

Such removal is a common precursor to full-scale settler colonialism. In the British Isles, the model example was the English policy of removing Irish Catholics from large portions of the island in the seventeenth century, with new expropriations and displacements following each new wave of wars. In the notorious words of Oliver Cromwell, displaced Catholics could go "to Hell or Connaught." The lands they forfeited were then given to new Protestant settlers, chiefly from Scotland, who thoroughly recreated the occupied lands. The descendants of those Protestants played a comparable role in aggressively expanding British settlements in North America, where they are commonly remembered as the Scotch-Irish, the vanguard of Manifest Destiny. On the other side of the struggle, among Irish Catholics, the expulsions and resettlements left a heritage of ethnic and religious grievance that continued to spark violence until very recent times.[13]

In many cases, acts of this kind have received little historical attention when the populations thus victimized could be dismissed as primitive or numerically insignificant. When we write the history of religion in Australia, we do not normally present it as the destruction of a continent-wide network of spiritual practices dating back tens of thousands of years—or at least, it is only very recently that scholars have written in those terms.[14]

Genocide

Removal need not necessarily involve physical killing and actual genocide, although in the case of the Australian province of Tasmania, the genocide was literal, rather than merely cultural. The most notorious examples of religious genocide—or genocide with unavoidable religious implications—included the slaughter of Christian Armenians by the Ottoman Turks, in the 1890s and again in 1915, and the Shoah of European Jews by the German Third Reich. Such actions transformed the religious landscape, purging not just peoples but also their institutions and the placenames that had marked the older landscape. Within decades, the older world was so forgotten that it becomes difficult to recall an era when ancient Christian communities still dominated large areas of the Near East; when Muslims were far more numerous in Balkan lands; or when much of eastern and central Europe had a vigorous Jewish character.[15]

Actions of this kind are not confined to empires, as opposed to other kinds of polities, like kingdoms or republics, but the nature of empire makes them much more likely in these settings. The diversity of subject populations, and the existence of religious minorities, poses real issues, especially when they are located in key frontier territories or even straddling borders. Although this in no sense excuses the crime against the Armenians, the act must be understood in this imperial context, and especially the severe pressure that the Ottomans were facing from the Russians. As we have seen, Russia had since the late eighteenth century been advancing steadily into the Black Sea region and the Caucasus, building up its Christian New Russia. More Russian campaigns and victories followed through the nineteenth century, posing an existential threat to the Ottoman state.[16]

Religious subject populations played a steadily increasing role in these imperial conflicts. The Ottomans ruled large Christian populations, especially throughout the Balkans, and many of them followed the Orthodox faith. As such, they could notionally fall under the protection of the Russian czar. From the Russian point of view, ten million Orthodox believers were endangered by Ottoman tyranny and needed protection. A Russian invasion in 1853 provoked war not just with the Ottomans but with England and France. Another crisis ensued in the 1870s. When Bulgarian Christians rebelled against the Ottomans, the Turks replied with brutal and indiscriminate violence, raising the prospect of a Russian intervention that would potentially mean the conquest of the whole Balkan region. That in turn invited British action against Russia and a general European war. Although that was prevented, the issue of religious minorities continued to be explosive. When a new Bulgarian state was established, it adopted a vigorously Christian identity, resulting in severe maltreatment and expulsions of Muslim residents. As Ottoman power disintegrated in the Balkans over the following generation, newly ascendant Christian states increasingly targeted Muslims for massacre or deportation.[17]

When Russia and the Ottomans went to war in 1914, the Turks became deeply concerned about their Christian Armenian minority, who might sympathize actively with Russian invaders. Initially, in 1915, the Turks ostensibly intended to remove Armenians en masse to areas farther removed from any direct military challenge, following the model that other predecessor empires had so often done through history. Only gradually did it become clear that those being deported were not expected to survive the ordeal, and certainly never to return to their former homes. Over and above the Armenians, the policy evolved to slaughter other once-sizable Christian populations in sensitive regions, including the Assyrians and Maronites.[18]

In the German case, the Nazis were not only annihilating those they perceived as racial enemies but preparing the ground for a massive program of colonial resettlement. Had the Nazi regime endured, the extinction of European Jews would have been followed by mass killings of Slavs to clear the way for new German settlement. In justifying such sweeping atrocities, Nazi leaders explicitly cited the bloody achievements of other colonial empires overseas, including the US removal of Native Americans and the British suppression of Australian Aborigines. But if the declared goals of neither Ottomans nor Nazis were religious in character, their acts certainly redrew the religious maps, and with an appalling degree of success.[19]

Refugee Religion

In other less-familiar cases, empires promoted their own official faith by striking at rival adherents, sometimes to the point of wholesale elimination. While nineteenth-century Americans were pursuing what they considered their manifest destroy to rule a continent, so were Russians pushing into Central Asia and the Caucasus, in this case, in the name of a passionate Orthodox Christian faith with overtly mystical and messianic elements. But the opponents were very different. Americans faced a Native foe that was far less advanced than they were technologically, and moreover was gravely weakened by disease; the Russians encountered well-established and populous Muslim communities, with robust military traditions. The Russians tried to counterbalance this presence by promoting the influx of ethnic Russians and other Christian populations, while encouraging Muslim emigration to Persia and the Ottoman realm. In some cases, the Orthodox empire resorted to the outright removal of such stubborn resisters as the Circassians and the Crimean Tatars, who were deported in dreadful conditions that claimed many lives. Perhaps half a million were deported in the 1860s alone.[20]

We might write the history of such events in terms of the purging of a given religion in its former homeland and the literal conversion of that land to the uses of a new faith. But atrocities of this kind cannot fail to have their impact on the survivors of expulsions in their new homes, and the quality of their religious belief. Few indeed were the exile communities who responded to their sufferings with forgiveness or charity: we recall the anonymous psalmist whom I quoted at the beginning of this chapter.

One large but seldom-told part of European history over the past 250 years concerns the once-substantial Muslim populations that existed within the Ottoman imperial possessions in the southeastern parts of that continent, which included many ordinary subjects, besides officials and soldiers. As Ottoman power shrank steadily in the face of Christian nationalist movements, so those Muslim populations suffered repeated blows, through massacre, deportation, or forced population exchange, as well as forced Christianization. Between 1775 and 1915, perhaps five million Ottoman Muslims were forced to relocate. Not surprisingly, the survivors of the failed empire who returned to the Turkish heartland commonly expressed their bitterness through a much harder-edged and more intolerant kind of religious politics than had been customary in earlier generations. Families of those refugee populations were prominently represented in the violent actions against Armenians and other Christians. During the Armenian genocide of 1915, Muslim exile communities like the Circassians provided many of the most lethal police and paramilitary units.[21]

Moving Things and Moving People

Quite apart from such critical issues of the settlement and removal of whole nations, empires opened the way to extensive voluntary migration of smaller but still influential populations, many of whom did not share the officially approved religious system. Such movements tended to create religious diversity. Some of those transplanted groups had long been subjects of the empire in question but came from poorer and marginal geographical areas. The Basques were usually at the forefront of both Spanish and French colonial and naval enterprise, giving them a transcontinental presence. In the British context, both Scots and Irish played a comparable role, and some prospered spectacularly as soldiers, administrators, and merchants.[22]

At least to modern eyes, such groups shared a racial and linguistic identity with the imperial elites, although nineteenth-century British writers often depicted the Irish in particular as members of a separate race. But the opportunities opened by empires attracted many races of very diverse geographical origins. Simplistic stereotypes to the contrary, most empires were complex and quite nuanced societies with many intervening stages between pure imperial overlords and native peasants: empires were seldom painted in black and white. There were merchants, shopkeepers, and traders, entrepreneurs and middlemen. There were mixed-race communities, marginal races and peoples, and many were newly arrived in the land in question. In most cases, such movements were voluntary and responded to imperial systems of free (or relatively free) commerce and trade. Empires varied as to how easily they allowed such new arrivals to assimilate to the imperial order, to seek the privileges of regular subjects or citizens.

Issues of class and ideology meant that the groups most deeply involved in such movements were ethnic and religious minorities in a given society. Historically, the founders of empire commonly espoused martial and aristocratic values, and at least notionally, despised trade and commerce. That presented opportunities to nonelite groups who were not affiliated with those ideals and who were happy to operate in trade and commerce.

Diasporas

Jewish history has repeatedly been shaped by its encounters with empires, both friendly and hostile. Since early modern times, Jews often served the role of traders and intermediaries, and in the process, they expanded the presence of that religion, as well as the people. Frequent persecutions of Jews made it perilous for them to invest in fixed properties that could be easily seized, such as landed estates, which placed a high premium on developing skills in commerce and finance. At the same time, Jews found it all but impossible to advance through the political or administrative structures of the various Christian or Muslim states. Commercial careers were left as the obvious channel for gaining and preserving wealth. Jews were wholly excluded by the Iberian empires, but they took full advantage of the more tolerant British, Dutch, and French.[23]

British territories proved the most fertile for Jewish enterprises. By the early twentieth century, British-ruled South Africa had acquired a substantial Jewish community, so that Johannesburg was colloquially known as "Jewburg." India too attracted Jewish families, especially from Baghdad, as the extraordinarily wealthy house of Sassoon extended its connections from Bombay throughout South Asia and China: the family is often called the "Asian Rothschilds." In India, the opium trade was their great staple, before they made the leap to developing booming Shanghai. Many lesser families followed to India, to develop thriving communities. Britain's great Indian city of Calcutta had a small but influential community of Baghdadi Jews, who built several impressive synagogues. Jews participated intensely in the French settlement of North Africa, building on ancient communities, and they became numerous in Algeria. Even in the chillier environment of imperial Russia, Jews wholeheartedly entered into the world of "New Russia." Odessa itself acquired one of the empire's largest and most successful Jewish communities, constituting some 30 percent of the population by the end of the nineteenth century. Whatever they intended to do on the religious front, empires in practice globalized Judaism.[24]

Other diasporic communities found their own prizes in these new imperial worlds. Under the Ottoman Empire, Greek Christians developed far-reaching enterprises in trade and shipping that extended far beyond the Mediterranean world. Until the twentieth century, Greek was a valuable lingua franca in most of the world's imperial cities. As with the Jews, those international contacts demanded familiarity with the customs and languages of other nations, skills that made the Greeks valuable as imperial diplomats and intermediaries for their Ottoman masters. From the quarter in which these Greek Christian minorities lived, the Phanar, these elite families were known as the Phanariots, and for much of Ottoman history, they were essential to administration. But Greeks of humbler origin could be found throughout the empire's far-flung trading and shipping networks. Also within the Ottoman Empire were the Syrians, a term that until quite modern times included what we would call the Lebanese. Syrians, like Greeks, traveled, traded, and settled throughout the global empires, bringing with them their own religious legacies, both Christian and Muslim.[25]

The other great cosmopolitan minority was the Armenians. Armenia was an ancient Christian kingdom, one of the very first to make Christianity its official religion, and a center of deeply impressive art and scholarship. In the sixteenth century, Armenia stood on a hard-fought borderland between the empires of the Ottomans and Safavid Iran, and from 1604, the Iranian shah Abbas forcibly relocated much of the population—probably several hundred thousand in all—to create a military no-man's-land. From the shah's point of view, the ruthless deportation had the added advantage of building up his spectacular new imperial capital of Isfahan, where Armenians settled in their own quarter of New Julfa. Abbas was sympathetic to Christians, and he actively encouraged them to pursue their existing trading activities, particularly in silk. Under the patronage and protection of Iran's Safavid dynasty, Christian Armenians developed trade networks through the Middle East, South and East Asia, and the Mediterranean world. The New Julfa network collapsed in the eighteenth century, following the fall of the Safavid house, but Armenian traders and merchants built on those precedents in the new imperial worlds of the British and Dutch. Christian communities, and their churches, followed in their footsteps. In modern times, the actions of another and far harsher empire, the Ottomans, drove sizable new waves of Armenian exiles.[26]

The cities that emerged on the frontiers of empire of necessity grew rapidly. In the British context, we think of Melbourne, Cape Town, Bombay, and Singapore, but the Dutch had such flourishing cities as Batavia and Surabaya, the French had Dakar and Hanoi. Melbourne, for instance, founded on a virgin site in the 1830s, had a population of half a million by the 1880s, and the state of Victoria, of which it was the heart, was richer than California. Some of these cities became very diverse as centers of multiple overlapping diasporas. The overlapping imperial interests and trade routes of multiple empires brought wealth, and broad diversity, to such cosmopolitan cities as Shanghai. The rate of globalization accelerated greatly with the completion of the two great canal projects, at Suez (1869), which was initially a French project and which then became critical to British activity, and the US-created Panama Canal, after 1914.[27]

Faiths in Motion

Empires need physical labor, and more particularly labor located in sites of high demand. The resulting migrations have further diversified religion worldwide, spreading faiths that were originally confined to one region. Much like the ancient Hebrew religion that I outlined at the start of this chapter, those religions began as closely bound to a given landscape, but they were transplanted successfully across oceans.

Before quite modern times, empires usually made extensive use of slavery, the most notorious version of which was the transatlantic trade that between the sixteenth century and the nineteenth brought some twelve million Africans to the New World. (That is distinct from the substantial numbers taken by Islamic powers and brought to the Middle East.) As we have seen, the most obvious religious impact of that upheaval was to bring millions of Africans within the orbit of Christians churches, Protestant and Catholic. In modern times, some 180 million people in the Americas are descended from the victims of that traffic, and overwhelmingly, they are at least formally adherents of Christian churches. This African diaspora constitutes a very significant share of the whole Christian world, and it is often described in that religious context.[28]

But the slavery phenomenon also brought African religions to the Americas, so that we can legitimately speak of an African religious diaspora. That may sound strange in a US context, as it is commonly assumed that few older religious systems were able to survive the catastrophe of slavery. But from a wider perspective, which includes both North and South America, the picture is very different. Throughout the slavery era, this trade was a key part of imperial enterprise and economic life, as respective powers fought and negotiated for access to the best sources of human merchandise. In no case did the various powers grant any kind of religious liberty to the slave populations, and in most cases, they demanded conformity to some form of Christianity. The cultural and religious consequences, however, proved very different in different areas. Exactly which imperial power was responsible determined the later cultural, linguistic, and religious fate of those enslaved masses and their descendants. What happened to those affected depended on the specific empire involved, its distinctive attitudes, traditions, and religious outlook. In terms of religious destiny, it mattered crucially whether the official religion of those empires was Protestant or Catholic.

As in the case of Native American populations (discussed in the previous chapter), Catholic societies exercised great latitude to African religious behaviors and customs, precisely because those imperial masters did not acknowledge those nonliterate behaviors as constituting a religion in any valid sense. Hence, overtly African devotions and practices survived widely under French, Spanish, and Portuguese rule, with only fig-leaf concealment. Even specific deities and god names persisted. Primal or traditional religions accommodated easily to those Catholic imperial regimes. There is a straight segue from West African Vodun to the everyday practices of slave societies in the (Catholic) New World. A West African god like Ogun enjoyed a long and distinguished history in the New World, with only a light patina of Catholic sanctity painted over his original face. A vigorous scholarly literature traces the flourishing state of Yoruba religion in the New World, through Brazilian Candomblé or Umbanda or Cuban Santería. Together, those faiths still command the loyalty of tens of millions.[29]

Because of their Protestant assumptions, the British and their American inheritors behaved very differently. While they assuredly did not acknowledge African practices as authentically religious, they were deeply hostile to anything that could be construed as syncretism. Predictably, then, explicitly African-derived religions did not survive in North America in anything like the way they did in Haiti, Cuba, or Brazil. American Hoodoo involves African-derived practices and traditions, but with nothing like the same explicit content of religious worship and deities. Nor does Jamaican Obeah. The only possible US exception to this rule is significant, in that Louisiana Voodoo looks much more African and overtly religious than any of its North American counterparts. But Louisiana's slave society had strongly Catholic and French roots, reinforced powerfully by Catholic refugees from Saint-Domingue and the Caribbean.[30]

To state the crucial distinction: African *practices and customs* survived under Protestant realms; African *religions* survived under Catholic empires. Decisions made by empires centuries ago continue to shape contemporary religious realities.

Traveling to Work

Quite apart from chattel slavery and forced servitude, empires often used indentured labor of a kind that, at its worst, could indeed look much like slavery. In the British context, that involved drawing on Chinese and Indian workers who found themselves in odd and unexpected parts of the world. The Caribbean was a major destination, as empires scrambled to replace labor lost following the abolition of Black slavery, but new enterprises emerged widely. As communities of laborers grew, so they were followed by others from the homelands, merchants, artisans, and shopkeepers. They also brought their religious ways.[31]

Neither the British nor the Dutch Empires intended to bring Asian faiths onto the larger global stage, but in practice, this is what they accomplished. Through such historic population movements, Hindus today represent a quarter of the populations of Trinidad and Suriname, 40 percent of Fiji's population, half of Mauritius. Illustrating the demographic consequences of imperial decisions is the Caribbean nation of Guyana, the former British Guiana, with its capital of Georgetown named for King George III. Today, people of Native American descent account for just 10 percent of the country's eight hundred thousand residents. Thirty percent claim African origin, the descendants of slaves imported by the Dutch or British Empires, but the largest single contingent are people of Indian ancestry, at 40 percent. (A further 20 percent are of mixed ethnicity.) Although Christians predominate, 25 percent of Guyanese are Hindus, and 7 percent Muslims.[32]

Other peoples from the Indian subcontinent, Sikhs and Muslims, likewise found themselves in quite new and distant territories, in Cape Town or Vancouver. At the height of empire, South Asian communities (Hindu, Muslim, and others) appeared in such British-ruled African nations as Kenya and Uganda, although they were expelled after those nations secured their independence in the 1960s. One diaspora segued painfully into another. Those communities then moved to other parts of the world, especially to Britain itself. As I will note in chapter 10, some prospered splendidly.[33]

The Chinese were no less mobile. The territories that we now know as Malaysia and Indonesia were early centers of the swelling Chinese diaspora, which was wholly conditioned by the needs of the two great European empires in the region, the British and Dutch. From the seventeenth century, the Dutch imported sizable numbers of Chinese people as builders and as workers in the tin mines, while others became merchants. At the end of the nineteenth century, the Dutch imperial capital of Batavia (later Jakarta) recorded 116,000 residents, almost a quarter of whom were Chinese, and 8 percent European. The British encouraged mass migration with the development of Malaya and Borneo from the end of the eighteenth century and the growth of new industries in tin and in spice production. In 1819, Singapore was founded on what was essentially a virgin site, and it became the hub of British power throughout the region. By the 1850s, the scientist Alfred Wallace found the harbor there

> crowded with men-of-war and trading vessels of many European nations, and hundreds of Malay praus and Chinese junks. . . .

> [T]he town comprises handsome public buildings and churches, Mahometan mosques, Hindoo temples, Chinese joss-houses, good European houses, massive warehouses, queer old Kling and China bazaars, and long suburbs of Chinese and Malay cottages. By far the most conspicuous of the various kinds of people in Singapore, and those which most attract the stranger's attention, are the Chinese, whose numbers and incessant activity give the place very much the appearance of a town in China.

Today, Malaysia, Indonesia, and Singapore together have some thirteen million people of Chinese descent: they make up a quarter of the population of modern Malaysia and 75 percent of Singapore. Singapore itself is a perfect exemplar of the religious consequences of this kind of imperial-driven migration. Besides churches, imposing Hindu temples and mosques are a notable part of the urban landscape, and so are a diverse range of Chinese places of worship, including Daoist and Buddhist shrines. Singapore represents in miniature the religious globalization facilitated by British imperium.[34]

Other regions followed similar trajectories. In the nineteenth century, more than half a million Chinese migrated to European imperial territories, working on Caribbean plantations or in gold rush settlements. The United States was an early destination, and we have observed the debate as to whether it constituted an empire at this time. But if San Francisco was the original Gold Mountain of Chinese ambitions, British-ruled Melbourne was the successor to that title, the New Gold Mountain. South Africa succeeded to that role at the end of the century. Although grand Chinese temples were not commonplace in these regions of later settlement, at least in any number, less imposing joss houses were found widely.[35]

Canada offers another example. In the late nineteenth century, that area that we today call southern British Columbia was one of the most strategic, and threatened, portions of the British Empire. The whole coast was potentially vulnerable to powerful outside enemies, initially the Russians and later the Americans. In response, the Royal Navy developed a critical naval base at Esquimalt, on Vancouver Island, which became the headquarters for the Pacific Fleet. The building of the Canadian Pacific Railway in the 1880s made the fortunes of the new city of Vancouver, which was as much an imperial upstart as Singapore. Vancouver attracted what soon became Canada's largest Chinese community, and a small Sikh settlement followed. Both groups flourished, and already by the 1920s, white Rightists were lamenting the "Oriental occupation of British Columbia." The Chinese component was further boosted in the 1990s when the British colony of Hong Kong was transferred to Chinese sovereignty—in effect, was restored from one failed empire to the original imperial owner. Today, people of East Asian origin (mainly Chinese) constitute almost a quarter of the population of the Vancouver metropolitan area, with South Asians at 14 percent. At 43 percent, people of European origin are in the minority. Various Asian religions are of course well represented, but so are a great many Christian churches serving East Asian congregations.[36]

Languages of Empire

This enormous mobility is reflected in the linguistic innovations of the imperial age. Of course, empires usually spread the languages of the self-described master races, such as English or Spanish, just as occurred with Greek and Latin in earlier eras, and we have already seen the crucial impact of those languages on Western religious developments. The means by which those languages spread are obvious enough. These are the languages of administration and government, of commerce and trade, and they are commonly associated with new settler populations. Both cities and armies diffuse elite tongues, especially when armies recruit heavily among populations from the imperial frontiers. Today, a map of the world's most-spoken languages is in large measure founded on the relative scale and endurance of empires. If we chart the world's most popular languages in terms of the total number of speakers (both as first and second language) then English, Spanish, French, Russian, and Portuguese all appear in the leading ten tongues. Except in the case of Russia, far more people speak the language outside the traditional metropolitan homeland than within it. Some three billion people speak one of the five European imperial languages, out of a global population of eight billion.[37]

But our knowledge of modern Western imperialism should not make us see these changes as solely a matter of spreading Western or European patterns around the world. Often, the older-established languages that those Western imports were challenging were themselves the product of earlier eras of imperial expansion and inculturation, with the religious consequences that we might expect. In their day, those non-Western languages had similarly displaced or even eliminated older local competitors.

Just to take one example, Vietnamese is obviously an Asian language, which in modern times is associated with anti-colonial resistance. The language originated in one small area in the north of the present country before spreading through conquest and consolidation over the centuries. Prolonged Chinese imperial influence further transformed it into the form we find in the later Middle Ages, which was adopted by other ethnic groups throughout the country. European influences then defined how the language was written and read. In the seventeenth century, the Jesuit Alexandre de Rhodes prepared a scholarly grammar and in 1651, a Vietnamese-Latin-Portuguese dictionary. In his time, Vietnamese was normally written in characters adapted from Chinese, but Portuguese missionaries had developed a Latin alphabet, which de Rhodes appropriated for purposes of popular evangelization. Through his example, that alphabet in turn developed into script that became standard under later French imperial rule. The twentieth-century Vietnamese nationalists who accepted and promoted that Latinized script did so with full knowledge that they were using a system devised by Jesuit fathers. Today, this is the nation's common and officially sanctioned system that is used by the seventy million speakers of that language, which multiple empires have created and recreated over time.[38]

The Language of the Camp

Other languages likewise retain the imprint of older empires. To take one of the world's most widely distributed languages, Arabic spread together with the imperial power of Islam, often to cultures that were already highly literate in still older languages such as Coptic and Syriac; both declined precipitously as spoken tongues. Today, some four hundred million people speak Arabic as a first or second language, not including the many Muslims who must read and know the Qur'an in that language, even if it is not part of their daily life. Moreover, the languages of Islamic empires, Arabic and Persian, interacted with other tongues, with lasting cultural and religious consequences.[39]

Another of the great languages of modern Islam is Urdu, which is spoken by more than two hundred million in the Indian subcontinent, if we include native speakers and those with a good working knowledge. The language is very much an imperial legacy; it is, in fact, the heir of multiple empires, both Islamic and Christian. Urdu is a version of the Hindustani language but with extensive Persian and Persianized borrowings. Those additions and minglings reflect the activities of successive Islamic invaders and imperial conquerors from India's northwest, but the Mughal period created much the most fertile environment for linguistic evolution. By the early eighteenth century, it came to be known as "the language of the imperial camp," *zaban-e Urdu-e shahi*, using a Turkic word that found its way into English as "horde." We might even say that Urdu is "the language of the horde." It became a sophisticated literary language with a major poetic tradition and a strong emphasis on religious themes.[40]

The language enjoyed its greatest success and distribution because of its adoption as the standard tongue of the East India Company, and subsequently of the British Raj. Wherever the British ruled in the subcontinent, they took Urdu with them, and if administrators and soldiers could not speak good Urdu, they had no place in government. Imperial Britain itself borrowed extensively from Urdu, importing many words into the English language. In the great days of the British Empire, in the late nineteenth century, Urdu was its most commonly spoken language—more so even than English. Queen Victoria herself learned enough Urdu to make formal speeches to Indian visitors. As so often through world history, armies are commonly the means by which languages spread across empires, through a process of two-way transmission. The British army wore uniforms that were "soil-colored," or in Urdu, *khaki*. In the First World War, British soldiers overseas famously wanted to get back to their home country, to Blighty. Soldiers prayed quietly for a "Blighty wound," something not serious enough to kill or maim permanently but enough to get them sent back home to peace and safety. Although the word appears to suggest pristine Englishness, it is taken from the Urdu *bilayati*, which in turn comes from the Arabic *wilayat*, meaning a country or kingdom.[41]

Although not all its speakers today are Muslim, Urdu is the official language of Pakistan, and it is very common among Indian Muslims. Respectively, Pakistan and India are the world's second- and third-largest Muslim nations by population. Urdu is one of the primary means by which Muslims discuss and spread their faith and in which they practice their devotion.

The world's most populous Islamic nation is Indonesia, where the standard language is a variant of Malay. If we include that Indonesian variant, some 290 million people speak a version of Malay, about the same total as for the world's French speakers. This tongue also has multiple imperial strata in its history, beginning with Buddhist Srivijaya, which we encountered in chapter 4, and it was in turn actively promoted by the Dutch and British Empires. The translation of the Bible into Malay (1733) was a major accomplishment of the Calvinist missions intimately associated with the Dutch VOC. As Malay became standardized and near universal throughout what would become Indonesia and Malaysia, so it offered the ideal medium for Islamic communication, debate, and religious mission.[42]

The Swahili of East Africa is a comparable imperial offspring. Muslim traders from the Arabian Peninsula mingled with the Bantu-speaking Africans of this region, where they created a hybrid language that in Arabic was called "of the coast," *sawahili*. Today, at least 20 percent of the vocabulary of this Swahili language is made up of Arabic loanwords. A hundred million speak the language. This area of East Africa was never part of a formal caliphate or empire run from Arabia or Baghdad, but the imperial influence was apparent in language and religion. The Islam introduced by traders was taught to native Africans in madrasas, through the medium of Swahili, which at this stage was written in Arabic script: the first written documents date from the early eighteenth century. In the late nineteenth century, the then-dominant European powers appropriated Swahili for Western use. The Germans began writing the language in Latin script, and British authorities standardized spelling practices. In 1928, a conference of all the main East African territories ruled by Britain agreed to adopt the Zanzibar dialect as the norm throughout the region. These changes were immensely useful to Christian missionaries, who translated the Bible into Swahili, which became a vehicle for Christian devotion as much as Muslim. As part of their broadly successful struggle to appropriate the language, Christians formed a vigorous tradition of Swahili hymns and sacred music, which still flourishes.[43]

Lascars and Askaris

Some words of military origin illustrate these linguistic evolutions over time through successive imperial orders, spanning continents. One well-traveled term was the Persian *sipahi*, soldier, which was adopted by both the Ottoman and Mughal Empires. The word retained that approximate meaning in a dozen languages from the Adriatic to the Bay of Bengal, although exactly what kind of fighter it suggested varied considerably. It is best known from the sepoys employed by the British and French in their Indian territories, but the French were still operating armored *spahi* units in the Gulf War of the 1990s. From a Western perspective, Iran's Revolutionary Guard units are a deadly menace to international stability and peace, and as such are regularly condemned in the media. The word translated as "Guards" in their title is actually *sipahi*.[44]

A word with a similarly broad history appears variously in British English as *lascar* and *askari*, recalling the Persian term *lashkar*, "army," while *lashkari* signified "soldier." During the Mughal Empire, that term entered India, where it became firmly part of the emerging

Urdu language. The Portuguese in turn borrowed the word during their Indian encounters, when it became *lascari* and applied to sailors mainly hired in the Indian subcontinent who served as sailors around the world for multiple European empires. Others were enlisted in Somaliland or the Arabian Peninsula.

Lascars acquired a new significance with the growth of steam technology, as they were thought to be fitted for the oppressively hot work of engine rooms, which was unacceptable to Europeans. Lascars accounted for some 18 percent of sailors on British merchant ships: they were essential to the communication networks that spanned the globe. Lascars remained a global phenomenon from the seventeenth century through the mid-twentieth, and they were a standard fixture of the worlds of Rudyard Kipling or Joseph Conrad. The lascars were overwhelmingly Muslim by faith, and those humble believers spread Islam to many corners of the world. In Britain, one of the oldest Muslim communities is in the seaport of Cardiff, one of the world's greatest trading centers in the age of coal and steam power.[45]

But the *lashkari* had other uses for European empires. In Arabic, Swahili, and Somali, the loanword *askari* meant "soldier." As European empires spread in Africa, they enlisted large numbers of local people to fight for them, as askari soldiers and police. They became a standard part of European rule in Africa, for the British above all but also for the Germans, Belgians, and Portuguese. In the First World War, huge numbers of African askaris died in the service of the various empires. Askari forces traveled far from their homelands, and they acquired new ideas, and often new religions. They became a major force for cultural and religious diffusion, bringing both Islam and Christianity with them on their return to their home communities.[46]

Of Species, and of Faiths

However surprising such an analogy might at first appear, there are many points of comparison between a map of the world's religions and that of its plants and other creatures of nature. Around the world, we see many examples of invasive plants and animals, many of which were introduced deliberately, others by accident, but the critical variant in deciding their distributions is empires and colonialism. Imperial representatives, and other settlers, have often tried to reconstruct their new world on the lines of the old. In the introduction, I discussed the role of the Roman Empire in bringing new species and crops into the territories they occupied. In modern times too, we see territories that were occupied by particular empires, such as the British, French, or Dutch, sharing the same range of nonnative and invasive plants, and those "invasions" became more abundant the longer those empires endured. In most cases, empires encouraged such invasions because at some bygone time, the plants were thought to have some economic value and even supplied a whole rationale for the economic exploitation of particular regions.[47]

At every point, religious analogies abound, including how similarities between regions occupied by the same imperial power grow over time. In both cases, biological and religious, the success of any given "planting" depends on its suitability to local conditions and the presence of local rivals. But once successfully installed, they behave as if they had always been native to that setting. They might well grow far beyond the wishes or expectations of the original planters.

Such comparisons can be perilous, not least the idea that any religion is "invasive" in any given area. In modern India, for instance, extreme nationalists claim that both Islam and Christianity are in effect invasive faiths, which deserve to be removed. But the analogy usefully reminds us that religion is not an abstract force that spreads mysteriously across maps. Rather, it is carried by and with people and nations, and those biological entities do not necessarily have control of their own movements. They are conditioned by imperial needs and preferences and a sense of what would serve the goals of empire. Over time, those new arrivals become so thoroughly entrenched in the social landscape that it is impossible to imagine a time when they were not there. To that extent, transplanting religions has often been very successful. But often, those empires have a poor long-term sense of the effects of their actions and the possible harms that might arise.

8
Faith against Empire

> Islam was not a modern power; it was inhibited by the centuries of the past. It did not possess the spirit of new creations. It did not open our eyes to the world outside. . . . European dynamism had a tremendous impact on our static minds.
>
> ***Rabindranath Tagore***[1]

In 1915, Lord Bryce published a still valuable analysis of the relationship between religion and empire, drawing examples from several historical eras. He was convincing in his account of religious passion as an unpredictable wild card in imperial affairs, a point he likely learned from observing the interplay of Hindus and Muslims in the British India of his time:

> [Religious sentiment] acted upon the whole mass of a people, and more powerfully upon the lower than upon the more educated class. It touched those whom ordinary political discontents or aspiration might scarcely affect. When it acted, it was apt to act suddenly and violently like an explosive substance. These characteristics made it formidable and all the more formidable because often unpredictable in its action. Emotional forces usually are unpredictable. Economic grievances and aspirations can be to some extent observed and measured, and their results can therefore be more or less foreseen. Religious passion, working obscurely and silently in masses of men, may easily escape notice, and no one can tell beforehand to what temperature it may rise.[2]

As Bryce knew well, time and again, religious movements had proved very dangerous to successive empires. Those obscure and silent religious passions could manifest in active anti-imperial resistance and in extreme cases, spawned revolts and revolutions.

Imperial rulers and policymakers should have paid very close attention to Bryce's opinions about religious motivations. Repeatedly, as we have seen, empires have moved populations and have made possible far-flung movement and migration, spreading peoples and their religions around the globe. But frequently, such actions have resulted in the growth of ideas or movements that were hostile to those empires and that served to undermine them. By the unintended promotion of religious belief systems, empires themselves have done much to promote anti-imperial resistance. This goes far beyond the familiar idea that persecution can encourage a minority movement in its doctrines, that the blood of martyrs can prepare a fertile soil for later growth. Rather, imperial policies have projected dissident movements onto an international and even a global stage.[3]

Although the faith of Islam is far too significant to be presented as such a marginal movement, the workings of European Christian empires reshaped and transformed Islam, and in ways that made it an effective source of resistance to Western supremacy. Those empires did much to shape that religion as it exists today.

Persecution and Resistance

Imperial regimes had from early times had an enduring concern about potential resistance rooted in religious dissidence. For all the many enemies they faced, Roman writers stressed the singular dangers posed by the fanaticism attributed to the Jews and to the druids of Celtic Europe. The thorough suppression of both became an urgent imperial priority. In later eras, Christian and Muslim regimes alike persecuted nonconforming religions, and in some cases succeeded in eliminating them but only after long and hard-fought struggles.[4]

Through bitter experience, empires knew that persecution could have the effect not of suppressing a surging minority faith but rather of strengthening it, making it more militant and revolutionary. That was the well-known experience of early Christianity, and later examples abounded in the Christian empires of the eighteenth and nineteenth centuries. This was the situation faced by the British in their dealings with Irish Catholics. The greater the repression the Russians exercised against their Muslim populations, the more militant and determined those societies became. Populations that were suppressed in this way developed elaborate forms of clandestine organization commonly linked to religious faith, such as the Sufi orders among Russia's Islamic populations. To adapt Bryce's words, obscurity and silence could be valuable strategies against empire. Such groups developed strongly military traditions.[5]

Another example involves the Sikh religion, which began as a reformist movement in India in the early sixteenth century, under the leadership of a series of teachers or gurus. Sikhism taught broad tolerance and accommodation of other religions, but during the seventeenth century, the Mughal Empire became increasingly determined to enforce strict Muslim orthodoxy. That threat became existential under Aurangzeb, who executed the ninth guru for his resistance to forced conversions. In 1699, the tenth guru responded by creating a special order of devout initiates, the Khalsa, which became a warrior elite. As a survival strategy, this enjoyed great success, which long outlasted the power of the Mughals themselves. By the nineteenth century, the Sikhs ruled a powerful kingdom with a fearsome military tradition, which provided stubborn opposition to all potential foes, Hindu, Muslim, or Christian. Through that militant resistance, Sikhism endured and prospered, and today counts some thirty million followers. Even today, faithful Sikh men wear a ritual sword that recalls the original formation of the Khalsa.[6]

Risky Transplants

Even when they have not persecuted religious minorities, empires have unintentionally contributed to their survival and growth. Imperial military policies have often served such a role, especially in the context of frontier regions.

Empires need armed forces to advance their territorial possessions and to buttress vulnerable borderlands from external rivals. To find such fighters, regimes have often turned to peoples occupying a marginal status within the metropolis itself but who were valued for their military prowess. The British famously used Scottish and Irish soldiers as a mainstay of their armed forces, while in India, British rulers identified particular peoples as "martial races," in sharp contrast to other groups who were labeled as effete or effeminate. Usually, in India and elsewhere, such peoples derived from border regions, which demanded fighting skills in order to survive, and that stereotype of the tough highland warrior long predated British times. The Sikhs were granted the enviable title of a "martial race," although it would be more accurate to characterize them as a dissident religious tradition that needed to produce warriors to withstand persecution. Once absorbed into the empire, such peoples were well rewarded for defending it.[7]

The perennial problem faced by many empires was that such warrior societies did not necessarily share the ideology of the metropolis and retained religious beliefs that were stigmatized or suppressed elsewhere. Dissident and controversial religious ideas flourished on the edges of empire, where enforcement mechanisms were weak, so relying on such outsiders could pose real dangers. Empires ran the grave risk of strengthening and even spreading religious systems that were viewed as alien or seditious.

Ancient and medieval empires alike were firm believers in the concept of "martial races," and the Roman Empire, and its Byzantine successor, drew heavily on marginal or barbarian tribes from remote border territories. Unfortunately for imperial authorities, moving such warriors could, in effect, mean moving those troubling ideas into whole new regions, where they could burgeon. One instance illustrates the quite far-reaching possible consequences. Around 650 AD, in the Christian border kingdom of Armenia, a new sect arose that closely resembled many early Christian heresies and strands of the larger gnostic worldview. The new movement, Paulicianism, had dualist elements, (probably) teaching that Christ represented the God of the New Testament while rejecting the Old Testament. Although the movement's exact ideas are open to some debate, they certainly followed the precedents of such notorious early dissidents as Marcion. From the standpoint of the established Christian churches of the time, such positions were extremely radical and thoroughly toxic. On occasion, Roman emperors persecuted what they called the "Manicheans," killing thousands. From the mid-eighth century, the Byzantine emperors tried a new policy, using the Paulicians as military surrogates in their western territories, particularly in the Balkans, which were gravely endangered by barbarian assaults. The resettlement process was spread over a lengthy period, and the number affected reputedly ran into the hundreds of thousands. Most were relocated to the land we now call Bulgaria.[8]

If the empire achieved its immediate security goals, so that the frontier did indeed hold fast, the long-term effects were alarming. Paulician ideas spread rapidly through the Balkans, where they generated a very influential new sect called the Bogomils. Like the Paulicians before them, their views harked back to the long-stigmatized heresies of the early Christian era, including gnostic and dualist survivals. In retrospect, such a development seems so natural that it is almost incredible that no imperial official sounded the alarm before relocating those heretics to new territories. From the point of view of the Orthodox/Catholic institutional churches, this sudden heretical eruption was disastrous, but worse was to come.

During the eleventh century, views very much like those of the Paulicians and Bogomils increasingly appeared in southern France and Italy, where there arose the movement of the Albigensians, or (as they were often known) the Bulgarians. In the thirteenth century, the crusade against the Albigensians devastated much of southern France, and the struggle to suppress the heresy provoked a fearsome new tactic in the form of the church's inquisition. Albigensians persisted at least into the 1320s. That whole dreadful story began with the imperial need to strengthen its western frontier several centuries before.[9]

Then Shall Religion to America Flee

Relocating a dissident population offered multiple advantages, avoiding the danger of civil conflict at home, while simultaneously bolstering the imperial frontiers. Yet as the Paulician experience suggested, relocated dissenters could build a new and flourishing base for their ideas. As I have suggested, the fact of global empire makes diasporas possible, but these can be dangerous to the empires that create them.

The British Empire suffered from the means it used to build its power. From the 1530s, the established religion of the English state was firmly Anglican and Protestant, with no tolerance for dissidents or dissenters either Catholic or Protestant. After the Stuart dynasty gained power in 1603, the new state also acquired an established Presbyterian regime in Scotland, but again, this heralded no slackening in the enforcement of orthodoxy. Prior to the seventeenth century, dissidents had little option but to accept the official regime, with whatever qualms, or else to risk life and property through rebellion. Matters changed when dissidents could be exported to colonial possessions, where they provided invaluable aid to the imperial project of expanding settlement. Ideally, that provided a double benefit, for the church establishment at home and for the dissidents themselves. Writing in the fevered year of 1776, Thomas Paine argued for a providential link between religious dissidence and imperial exploration: "The Reformation was preceded by the discovery of America: As if the Almighty graciously meant to open a sanctuary to the persecuted in future years, when home should afford neither friendship nor safety."[10]

The obvious example here is the creation of the New England settlements from the 1620s onward, which provided so attractive to the Dissenting Protestants who had become increasingly militant in recent decades. Those highly motivated settlers did an excellent job of defending and expanding imperial territories in the New World, defeating Native rivals, and establishing missions. Even the devout Anglican George Herbert saw the New World as a refuge for true faith at a time of threats to it in the home country:

> Then shall Religion to America flee:
> They have their times of Gospel, ev'n as we.[11]

At the same time, the new territories served as a bastion for radical Puritan ideas and practices, which provided a model for radical reformers and revolutionaries in the British Isles themselves. When royal power collapsed in England in the 1650s, the new regime drew heavily on New England ministers and doctrines to provide the template for the spiritual renewal of the old nation.[12]

Of course, those Puritans represented only a portion of the migrants from the British Isles, most of whom were motivated by economic rather than religious concerns and who traveled to other parts of British America. But religion continued to play its part. Again in the 1680s, civil disorder and religious radicalism drove new migration and imperial expansion. A climate-driven subsistence crisis inflicted severe privation and political turmoil on many parts of western Europe, in a period marked by multiple rebellions, persecutions, and conspiracies. This resulted in mass emigrations to imperial territories—by British and Irish Quakers and Baptists to Pennsylvania, where they were soon joined by German Protestant sects. Large areas of Britain that previously had been strongholds of radical dissent now saw most of their activists relocated to the New World. Other countries suffered similar turbulence, with like results. Persecutions of Protestants in France led the Huguenots of that country to seek their own refuges in overseas empires, whether in British America or Dutch South Africa.[13]

In each case, those colonial settlements became a seedbed for later growth, which was especially concentrated among faith groups who at home would have been at best tolerated dissidents, at worst persecuted victims. This included radical Presbyterian groups from Scotland and Northern Ireland, who were often descendant from the settlers that governments had used to displace Ireland's Catholics in earlier times (as we have seen in chapter 7). Yet those Presbyterians themselves were also deeply dissatisfied with the religious regimes in their homelands. Colonial Pennsylvania boomed as Philadelphia became a vital center of imperial wealth and commerce. But in very few cases were the people leading the expansion across the state and farther west faithful Anglicans. Rather, it was Presbyterians who built their networks of forts and settlements across Pennsylvania and ventured beyond into Ohio and Kentucky. When

America revolted in the 1770s, the revolutionary movement had its spiritual and ideological heart in Puritan New England, but British attention was no less directed against the religious communities concentrated in Pennsylvania and the border country. British observers described the surging national movement as a "Presbyterian Rebellion." Anglicanism barely survived in the new republic, following a profound restructuring that eventually created the Episcopal Church.[14]

Planting in New Soil

As the European empires often found, even victories and territorial gains might shift the balance of religious forces in troubling ways. As empires grew, their ever-expanding subject populations came to outnumber the metropolitan, so that the faith of the homeland was reduced to minority status. Although such a change did not necessarily lead to unrest or subversion, it forced imperial states to come to terms with those alien faiths as something other than targets for evangelism. That was true both of Christian and non-Christian traditions.

After the loss of America, there emerged a Second British Empire, which by 1900 would be the largest imperial realm that has ever existed. But in its religious coloring, that empire was anything but uniform or, in elite terms, orthodox. In 1900, Hindus made up over half the four hundred million subjects of Queen Victoria, Muslims a quarter, and Christians barely 15 percent. As we have seen, British rule in practice certainly expanded the reach of Christianity, but it also promoted the worldwide dissemination of other faiths, including Judaism and Hinduism.[15]

Alarmingly for the British religious establishment, imperial success sparked the growth of rival Christian churches, especially of Roman Catholicism. Many factors drove that process, including the heavy involvement of Irish Catholics in the imperial armed forces that spanned the globe. One ironic part of this story involved convict transportation and the creation of the new colony in Australia. The early modern British state operated a draconian criminal code that potentially inflicted the death penalty on a very large number of offenders, to the horror of growing humanitarian sentiment. Imperial expansion offered the prospect of removing such malefactors permanently from British shores, literally to the other side of the world. Over time, that transportation policy acquired a strong religious dimension, as Catholic and Irish offenders were so well represented, some but not all because of political misdeeds. The new Australia that emerged in the later nineteenth century had a powerful Irish and Catholic presence, which today represents around a quarter of the whole population. If the

British Empire did not intend to create a vital new Catholic presence in the Southern Hemisphere, that was the consequence.[16]

Returning to Zion

The Jewish experience illustrates the role of empires in spreading faiths that would become the focus of anti-imperial struggle. We have already seen how Jewish populations took advantage of the global opportunities opened by the European colonial empires, but on occasion, diasporas could have a clandestine and even forbidden quality. After the Spanish kings united the peninsula in the fifteenth century, they became increasingly intolerant of the large Jewish population and forced them to convert or flee. A great many Jews accepted notional conversion but maintained their faith covertly. From the sixteenth century, many of those crypto-Jews migrated in substantial numbers to many parts of the Americas, including Mexico and New Mexico. Until the end of the South American Inquisition in the 1820s, investigators repeatedly found traces of that global-but-covert Jewish presence in the forms of secret prayers and fragments of liturgy, of distinctive dietary customs and seasonal rituals.[17]

We can debate the significance of that crypto-Jewish experience for the larger story of the Jewish people and their faith. In contrast, an undeniably critical fact in modern Jewish history has been the emergence of Zionism, the movement that in the 1890s declared its aspiration for the Jewish people to build a national homeland in Palestine. Imperial policies and politics dominated this endeavor at every stage, and so did the principle of unintended consequences. When the movement began, Palestine was clearly part of the Ottoman Empire, and Zionist leaders hoped to put pressure on that regime through their connections with other mightier powers, the Germans and British. After the First World War, the British Empire became the crucial player in the region and the essential interlocutor for any progress on the Zionist project.[18]

The British had to balance their actions carefully, facing competing and indeed incompatible demands on behalf of the Jews and of Palestine's Arab population. Having said that, the establishment of a Jewish homeland in some form meshed well with imperial interests as British elites understood them. Beyond generating goodwill in the United States, placing a Western-oriented community in this location promised strategic benefits. It would ideally strengthen British interests in the region of the Suez Canal and so valuably close to the areas of oil production that were assuming such crucial economic and military importance. The idea of placing a friendly population in a sensitive frontier region would have made wonderful sense to many other empires through history. But as in many earlier cases, such imperial plans and dreams went awry. As the Jewish presence grew rapidly in the area, Britain found itself fighting a bloody and unpopular war against Zionist insurgents, leading to a humiliating withdrawal in 1948.[19]

Like other minorities and diaspora communities through history, Jews exploited the opportunities that were opened by the workings of empire and turned them decisively to their own advantage. In this instance, the imperial setback contributed to a thorough restructuring of the world's religious map. In 1900, only a tiny proportion of the world's Jews lived in the territory of Palestine. Today, the comparable figure is almost half the global total, some seven million out of fifteen million.

Islam and the European Empires

Globally, the greatest unintended beneficiary of imperial policies and structures was the faith of Islam, which for more than a millennium dominated much of the globe. Islam existed in intimate alliance with kingdoms, and often with sprawling Muslim empires. During the nineteenth century, however, Islamic political power shrank calamitously in the face of multiple European Christian empires, forcing Muslims to confront the bitter realities of political subjection and inferiority. Seemingly, the very existence of the faith stood in peril. The fact that Islam survived, and that an Islamic political order was restored, must be viewed in the context of interactions with those European empires and the reconstructions that followed. European imperial advances sparked potent and widely successful reactions.[20]

At least in its initial stages, much of the European imperial project involved the subjection of Muslims. When the British arrived in India, most of the subcontinent was subject to Islamic states and empires. Russian expansion to the south and east was usually at the expense of Muslim neighbors, and the French plunged into North Africa. Many of the pivotal episodes in the military history of the European empires involved confrontation with Muslim forces. The decline of Islamic political power accelerated sharply from the 1850s onward, with the British suppression of the Indian Mutiny and the termination of the Mughal dynasty. Meanwhile, Persia came under the shared hegemony of Britain and Russia. In the 1870s, Ottoman rule faced deadly challenges in the Balkans and Caucasus. From that point on, Europeans progressively absorbed Ottoman lands, as Westerners pushed to establish Christian missions and schools throughout Islamic territories.[21]

At the start of the twentieth century, the vast majority of the 240 million Muslims worldwide lived under European rule. With the exception of a few isolated kingdoms operating under the protection of one or another European power, there were just three independent Muslim states in the world, namely the Ottoman Empire, Persia, and Afghanistan. The three countries combined had populations of only around forty million, of whom perhaps thirty-five million were Muslim. In contrast, the British Empire was what Sir John Seeley termed "the greatest Mussulman Power in the world," with some seventy-five million Muslims in the Indian subcontinent, in addition to twenty-five million more in Africa and the rest of Asia. By 1914 the Dutch East Indies was home to perhaps forty million Muslims. The French likewise ruled more Muslims than did any of the three explicitly Islamic states, while Russians, Italians, and Spaniards all dominated sizable Muslim populations. European expansion was still continuing at the beginning of the twentieth century as imperial powers completed their conquest of North Africa. The Christian empires had well-known ambitions on the remaining portions of the Ottoman Empire, not just of conquering it politically but of settling it with European colonists, as was occurring in Algeria.[22]

The continuing series of disasters made informed Muslims painfully aware of European superiority in scientific, technological, and military matters, and naturally created an urgent interest in modernizing reform. But while the European empires were asserting their political control, their actions also had an impact on concepts of the faith of Islam itself. The empires made Muslims aware of a larger Islamic world in ways that had never been possible before, and thereby enabled a remodeling and strengthening of that faith.

Recreating Islam

Across most of the Islamic world, the faith that had prevailed for centuries was strongly attuned to local realities. It was usually dominated by broad-minded Sufi orders that formed easy accommodations with neighboring religions, Hindus, animists, and Buddhists, with a high degree of syncretism. The Sufi orders were the centerpiece of lived faith in North Africa and Central Asia. In India, ordinary believers easily divided their devotion between the shrines of Hindu gods and Sufi sheikhs and saints. In the Dutch East Indies, Islam enjoyed a languid syncretistic relationship with both Hinduism and Chinese religions. Rigid fundamentalists and purists did exist, but such radical voices only slowly gained influence on a wider scale. The extreme vicissitudes of travel made it very difficult for Islamic communities to have any great sense of how far their practices were diverging from those in other parts of the world. Existing as the faith did in such very diverse manifestations, Muslims found it difficult to find common cause and certainly to cooperate politically.[23]

For their own ends, European empires utterly changed those conditions, introducing the telegraph, cheap printing, and newspapers, while railroads and steamships made far-flung travel a familiar reality. As the British and Dutch imperial navies suppressed the pirate fleets that had cursed the region for so long, they made it far easier for Muslims from remote territories to make the once near-impossible pilgrimage to Mecca and even to travel more widely through the Muslim Middle East. Joseph Conrad's novel *Lord Jim* (1900) suggests how normalized such pilgrimage had become by the late nineteenth century. Moreover, the empires used Muslims in their armed forces, to a very large extent in the cases of the British and French. In the twentieth century especially, such service greatly expanded the geographical and cultural horizons of ordinary Muslims, and their local communities, but the imperial impact had been obvious long before this.[24]

As empires sought to secure the loyalty of their Muslim subjects, they unwittingly exposed them to far wider and more modern worlds than they had ever known. In Russia, the empire ruled a diffuse range of communities with very different histories and outlooks. In the 1780s, the government created a new Muslim spiritual assembly with jurisdiction over most of the eastern territories, headquartered in Orenburg. It formalized clerical structure in a new "muftiate," a far more formal and bureaucratic arrangement than known hitherto. What had once been the Tatar Muslim city of Kazan became a thriving Russian city, and in 1804 it acquired a prestigious university charged with promoting the study of the Islamic "Orient" to further imperial advances to the east. In 1801, the Qur'an was printed in Kazan. Although the Russians' ultimate goals were imperial and Christian, such innovations forced Muslims to reconsider their relationship to modernity and gave them new means to do so. Orientalism struck back.[25]

The impact of imperial globalization was obvious at the turn of the nineteenth century, when the militant fundamentalist Wahhabi movement became a major force in the Arabian Peninsula, briefly seizing Mecca and Medina. These events caused both shock and excitement around the Muslim world, where the news traveled far and fast, and they had a special impact in British India. Wahhabi-inspired movements spread under the leadership of the visionary reformer Sayyid Ahmad, who imported his revolutionary jihadi ideas from Arabia itself, where he and his close allies had undertaken the hajj, the pilgrimage. In the 1820s, in India's northwest territories, his mujahidin briefly created a revolutionary Islamic state under Shariah law, until his death in battle in 1831 earned him the status of a martyr. Throughout the mid-century, British authorities in India described their restive Islamist foes by the imported Arabian term, Wahhabis.[26]

In the Dutch East Indies likewise, the imperial protection of trade routes encouraged pilgrimage to Mecca, where the faithful discovered just how far their own customs and practices had strayed from the realities of contemporary Islam in regions with a strong claim to continuity from the earliest days of the faith. This discovery began a fundamental reorientation of Indonesian Islam to a stricter and more exclusive variety and also marked a new emphasis on rediscovering Arabic as the authentic language of faith. Modern Islamic politics in the East Indies date from 1912, when the progressive Muhammadiyah movement was formed to resist syncretism and Western culture, and the Sarekat Islam organization began political activism. Both would enjoy huge influence, to the point that Muhammadiyah today claims some twenty-five million members.[27]

Today, Indonesia is by far the world's largest Muslim nation, with a reported 230 million believers, comparable to the total world population of Muslims as it had existed in 1900. Assuredly, that leap to orthodox Islam is not what the Dutch Empire had in mind when it began addressing the piracy problem. Nor did Dutch officials think that their promotion of the Malay language would offer such a boon to Islamic clerics and thinkers seeking to transcend local cultural divisions.[28]

Islam and the British

If the British suffered mixed consequences from their establishment of safe and speedy travel and communications, they also had cause to regret the well-connected cities that benefited from those changes. Intellectually, the two greatest centers of the Muslim world were in Egypt and India, both heavily exposed to the latest forms of Western modernity, especially in the cities that boomed under imperial influence. Such was British-founded Calcutta, which from 1772 through 1911 was the capital of imperial India. It was also a booming cultural center of publishing, printing, and social mobilization—in fact, a pan-Asian capital for media and communications. Calcutta's printers worked in Arabic, Malay, and Persian, circulating books that served the purposes of Muslims and Hindus, no less than Christians. The city naturally provided the heartbeat of nationalist conspiracy and militancy, mainly among radical Hindus, but Islamic activism thrived.[29]

Although India was a long-standing British possession, British and French empires jostled for influence in Egypt, until the British ultimately secured hegemony here, dreaming of an African empire stretching from "the Cape to Cairo." Cairo in fact became another vital cultural base and a center for publishing and newspapers. With their widespread communications, those imperial cities made it easy to find books and periodicals from all parts of Europe and the Islamic world, making possible a newly globalized approach to Islam and its current dilemmas.[30]

Metropolitan capitals were no less critical to this process. As the heart of the British Empire, London was where dissidents and rebels of all shades and races went to plot the overthrow of that and other empires, and to exchange ideas and beliefs, including communism and anarchism. In religious terms, the city offered the first venue in Islamic history where one could find representatives of each and every Muslim school, strand, and movement, and Paris was at least as accommodating.[31]

Back to the Ages of Faith

Through such means, it became possible to imagine a transnational Muslim public opinion. Writers and theorists imagined a restoration of Islamic political authority, although they differed on how far any such move would take account of modern concepts of democracy or nationalism. Many also linked these political views to Arabizing reforms in religious practice and attacked what they saw as Sufi accretions to the faith.

As in the Dutch East Indies, Indian Muslims who rejected open revolution and armed jihad formed new schools and movements designed to restore Islam to what reformers believed to have been the early and authentic form of the faith, even to the days of the Prophet himself. In the words of the fourteenth-century scholar Ibn Taymiyyah, Muslims should return to the pristine faith of *al-salaf al-salih*, the "pious forefathers," of Salafism. That faith would ideally be enforced by a pure Islamic state, possibly a theocracy. India now produced a series of separatist reform movements that looked back to the Wahhabi pioneer Sayyid Ahmad, including the very strict Indian Ahl i-Hadith, the Way of the Traditions. In 1866, a fundamentalist movement created the madrassa or seminary at Deoband, an enormously influential base that spawned many offshoots, which still exercises its power today (the Taliban grow out of the Deobandi tradition). The Barelvis, another Indian reformist movement that nevertheless incorporated Sufi influences, followed in the 1880s.[32]

Using the structures and facilities so helpfully offered by the European conquerors, reformers spread their views to distant lands. One key figure who urged global Islamic unity and sweeping modernization was Sayyid Jamal al-Din, known from his place of origin as al-Afghani, who left a substantial imprint on later Islamist thought and activism. With the support of the Ottoman sultan, from the 1860s through the 1890s al-Afghani roamed freely across South Asia, the Middle East, North Africa, and even Europe. The influence of al-Afghani's many disciples and pupils survives in the modern-day Salafi movement.[33]

Of course, al-Afghani traveled the routes blazed by the British, but he made even more direct use of their institutions for his own ends. Since the early eighteenth century, British and French merchants, administrators, and seafarers had spread Freemasonry across the lands through which they traveled, and their lodges were very significant in imperial social life. Besides supplying fellowship in remote settings, the lodges offered what a later generation might term easy networking. They played a progressive role in their advocacy of education and technological advance and the blessings of modernity. Masonry features prominently in the writings of Rudyard Kipling, as one of the vital forces binding together the British imperial enterprise. It is ironic, then, that al-Afghani used Egypt's Masonic lodges as key vehicles for his spiritual reform and his political schemes. In the lodges, he found a ready-made system of clandestine societies, which could easily serve as organizational bases against Egypt's own government, and against Europeans and Christians. Also deeply involved in Freemasonry was his Islamist pupil, the Egyptian Muhammad Abduh. From Egypt, reformers used the lodges to extend their activism to Damascus and Beirut.[34]

Islam, Ancient and Modern

The move to construct a new Islamic order was galvanized after the fall of the Ottoman Empire and the abolition of the caliphate in 1924. Although that final act was not the work of any one European empire, it was the logical culmination of generations of pressure on the Ottoman realms by the British, Russians, and others. Muslim reformers responded with a wave of new activist movements, designed to promote pan-Islamism and to organize the Muslim world against imperial rule. In each case, the new currents grew directly from the innovations of the previous century, which I have already discussed.

As before, India and Egypt formed an axis of revivalist militancy. In 1926, Indian Deobandi Muslims formed the Tablighi Jamaat, the Society of Preachers, whose members were intended to wander the world calling believers back to the faith in its sternest and simplest forms. Egypt's Muslim Brotherhood was formed in 1928 and took its ideas of radical political Islamism to a vast public. Similar ideas were developed in India by Maulana Maududi, who is today viewed as a cofounder of the global Islamist movement. Through the mid-twentieth century, Islamist theories spread "obscurely and silently." However anti-modern such views generally were, their circulation and growth would have been inconceivable without the environments created by the various European empires.[35]

Since the 1970s, Islamist radicalism has played a prominent and often sensational role in world affairs, with the growth of terrorist violence, most obviously symbolized by an event like the attacks of September 11, 2001. Scholars naturally trace the origins of those currents in earlier anti-imperial movements and explore how, in a sense, those empires created their own deadliest enemies. But Islamists and Salafists represent only a small fraction of the Islamic world. Less noticed in those histories is the very substantial change that the imperial experience wrought on what we might call the everyday or "normal" experience of Islamic faith for ordinary believers worldwide. Compared to earlier centuries, that practice is far less marked by the work of Sufi orders, with their attendant focus on shrines and local pilgrimage, and the celebration of holy figures that in a Christian context would be called saints. Around the Muslim world, religious practice has drawn ever closer to Arab and Middle Eastern norms, a change reflected in the architectural styles commonly used for mosques. If not totally, religious practice has become far more standardized and uniform, and that change must be understood as the consequence of the imperial encounter. The European empires essentially shaped what is today the world's second-largest religion, which in the not too distant future might (arguably) be the largest.[36]

Empires create the conditions for religions to grow and spread, and those conditions can enjoy a lengthy afterlife. But in no sense can the empire control or even comprehend the directions that those religious movements might take.

9
How Empires Remake Religions

Graecia capta ferum victorem cepit.
(Conquered Greece herself conquered her fierce ruler.)

Horace[1]

In the Middle Ages, the Roman Catholic church used a precious vessel to display objects of special sanctity, such as the eucharistic host or the relic of a saint. From the Latin word *monstrare*, "to show," they were known as monstrances. Already in the fifteenth century, a few were using a sunburst design, but in the following century, that spectacular model became vastly more popular, and indeed standard until quite modern times. The change followed the Spanish conquest of Mexico, when missionaries found it valuable to associate the power of the new faith with the solar-based devotion of Native people. Aztec art often depicted sunburst designs. That Mexican form of the monstrance spread to Europe, where examples were commonly made in gold seized from the New World. Devout Catholics in Ireland or Poland were bowing before objects rooted in a quite alien Meso-American culture, which was imported as a consequence of an imperial religious project.[2]

Empires bring local and national communities onto a much larger stage, and in modern times, that has meant the whole world. Such a development has many consequences for religious traditions. At a most basic level, religions import ideas and practices from that world. That might include a few incidental practices, like the monstrance, but the implications might be much further reaching. As religions globalize, they must determine their relationship to the other faiths they encounter, which might be radically different in all their assumptions. Depending on circumstances, they might seek some accommodation that involves an extensive reconstruction of beliefs and worldviews. Some empires have provided a fertile environment for attempts to combine and integrate religious traditions, to create some new synthesis suitable for a global community. Universal empires can produce universal creeds. But universalism can be counterproductive, and it easily inspires critics who complain of syncretism or pollution. Imperial encounters force religious traditions to define themselves and to draw frontiers between themselves and other systems. As we have seen in the Jewish case, it was the moves to Hellenization that inspired the violent nationalist reaction and a ferocious new emphasis on exclusivism. Some religions seek to return to ancient and primitive forms of faith as they reassert original teachings and sources, a *ressourcement*, and Islam is by no means alone in that.

Such transformations can be sweeping, to a degree that can be counterintuitive. As religions usually claim to be rooted in timeless realities, they are reluctant to admit how fundamentally they have changed through history, and indeed, through quite recent history. We are today used to a canonical list of five or six great world religions, each with its own characteristic beliefs and practices, and its particular geographical focus, but such a conventional picture is anything but inevitable. It is in large measure a modern construct, and it owes much to the consequences of empire, both benevolent and negative. If empires do not exactly make or create world religions, faiths such as Hinduism, Buddhism, Confucianism, and Shinto would be inconceivably different without those imperial structures, and the worlds they created.[3]

Mingling Gods

Such interfaith borrowings have a very long history. We have already seen the rise of the great Hellenistic empires between the fourth and the second centuries BC, which promoted transcontinental cultural and religious exchanges within the *oikoumenē*. An inquiring person in the Mediterranean world could sample from a luxurious buffet of beliefs, including Egyptian, Mesopotamian, Jewish, and Indian ideas. It was tempting to merge and mingle the new faiths. To appeal to both his Egyptian and Greek subjects, the first Ptolemy deliberately created the new Greek-styled cult of Serapis. This new god merged the ancient native cults of Osiris and Apis into a composite figure in the best Greek mode, and he attracted a widespread following throughout the Greek and Roman worlds. Images of Serapis, this immigrant Egyptian deity, were created in the finest classical style. The Egyptian goddess Isis, meanwhile, was combined with multiple female Greek deities to construct an all-powerful queen of heaven. In the new imperial environment, rulers knew that they must try to satisfy the religious needs and preferences of their diverse subject populations. Syncretism was excellent policy.[4]

Those innovations reshaped Greek religion and its Roman successors. Various mystery cults permeated the Greco-Roman world, including the Persian belief in the god Mithras, and both Isis and Serapis acquired followers far beyond Egypt's shores. In a well-connected city such as Thessaloniki on the Via Egnatia, Mithras, Isis, and Serapis coexisted with older Greek deities like Apollo. As newer gods became domesticated in the Greco-Roman world, so they became unmistakably classical in terms of visual depiction, and their worship came to depend on the Greek or Latin languages. Of course, such innovations appalled conservative Romans. In a diatribe against superstitious Egyptians and bloodthirsty Africans, the satirist Juvenal asked, rhetorically, "Who knows not what monsters demented Egypt worships?" Even so, these cults, and the technical language they developed, are often recalled in the New Testament and in other early Christian writings.[5]

At the start of this chapter, I quoted the sentiment that the Roman poet Horace expressed at the end of the first century BC, as he remarked how thoroughly his own society had succumbed to Greek culture: the captives captured the conquerors. In fact, Horace might have said the same not just of Greece but of the wider eastern Mediterranean world: Syria also took its own prisoners. Over the following centuries, the Roman Empire borrowed extensively from Eastern and Persian concepts and ideology, as the emperors became more explicitly godlike in their rhetoric and iconography, with all the attendant court ceremony. Roman emperors were ever more regularly shown wearing the radiate solar crown, which linked them to concepts of divinity that had originated in Hellenistic Egypt. The process of exalting the monarchy and court can be mapped by the spread of the institution of the court eunuch, who could serve as a trusted imperial servant because of his inability to form dynastic ambitions. Eunuchs were mainstays of the Assyrian and Persian courts, but only from the later third century did they became a familiar part of the Roman imperial circle, becoming essential to court life in late Roman and Byzantine times.[6]

When Christianity came to dominate that empire, it naturally borrowed its depictions of Christ and the saints from that same repertoire of divine imperial figures, which shaped the art of countless paintings and mosaics, icons, and church domes. The figure of Isis nursing her son Horus provided the foundation for myriad devotional images of the Virgin Mary.[7]

Empires to the East

In other regions too, the Greeks both borrowed from the religions with which they came into contact and also transformed them. Imperial encounters ensured that Greek ties with Buddhism were surprisingly close. In the third century BC, the Indian emperor Ashoka sent Buddhist envoys to his fellow rulers in Alexandria and Antioch, and they responded with their own ambassadors to Pataliputra. In 20 BC, an Indian envoy to the Roman emperor Augustus created a sensation when he ritually burned himself to death in Athens. We do not know whether he stemmed from the Hindu or Buddhist tradition. Probably, St. Paul was recalling that disturbing incident when he wrote the famous words about gaining nothing from acts performed without *agape*, love, even if he went so far as giving his body to be burned.[8]

Some Greek empire builders in India and Central Asia accepted Buddhism, and one, Menander, became the hero of a long dialogue that attained the status of scripture. Forgotten in the West, he is remembered fondly as the inquiring King Milinda, who learns humbly from a Buddhist sage. Greek elites applied their own aesthetic traditions so enthusiastically to Buddhism that they utterly changed the visual universe of that faith. In the process, the Greek dynasts birthed a major new trend of Greco-Buddhism. For centuries thereafter, depictions of the Buddha closely followed Greek aesthetic tastes, an encounter preserved in countless sculptures.[9]

Such East-West contacts included mutual borrowings of literary themes and religious stories. But the most important result was the emergence of the whole new religion of Manichaeism, which (as we saw in chapter 3) integrated Buddhist as well as Christian and Zoroastrian insights. Without the spiritual crucible supplied by the Persian Empire, such a development would have been inconceivable.

The Caliphs and Their Subjects

The early Arab empires were likewise captured by their subjects, including in religious matters. In the century following 630, the Muslim conquerors built an empire extending from Spain to the borders of China and incorporating most of the great civilizations of the ancient world. In those territories, they found multiple well-established religions, including Christianity,

Judaism, and Zoroastrianism. The religious beliefs and practices of those Muslims evolved very rapidly during the course of building that empire. To take an example far removed from any essential theology, the earliest Muslims did not practice the kind of prostration that we today think of as so characteristic of prayer in that tradition, and indeed they scorned such a practice as unworthy or absurd. Prostration was, however, a standard practice in the Christian Church of the East, the monks and clergy of which were such a fixture of the religious landscape in the newly conquered lands. Arab Muslims themselves soon appropriated the custom.[10]

A similar emulation was apparent in the construction of religious buildings. As the Arabs had little tradition of monumental architecture in their homelands, they were strongly influenced by the structures they now encountered, especially in such great Roman-ruled cities as Damascus and Jerusalem. One common building was the martyrium, a major church intended to house the relics of a major saint, and that supplied the template for most early mosques, although of course with all the crosses, icons, and Christian imagery removed. When the conquerors did build significant new mosques, they relied heavily on Byzantine or Syrian artisans, reinforcing the tendency to reproduce older Christian models.[11]

As we have seen, the new Muslim empire destroyed Persia's Zoroastrian faith, but they still borrowed heavily from its extremely rich and deep-laid culture. Like the Romans before them, Arab rulers appropriated Persia's exalted traditions of sacred kingship, which profoundly affected concepts of government and also the concept of the caliph. The revolution in concepts of religious and political authority was symbolized by the triumph of the long-enduring Abbasid Caliphate in the 750s. The Umayyads had generally made Damascus their capital, contributing to a westward political orientation and a deep interest in Roman precedents and styles. The Abbasid regime moved the capital to the new city of Baghdad, conveniently close both to ancient Babylon and to the old Sasanian capital of Seleucia-Ctesiphon. The court ceremonial acquired unmistakable Persian characteristics, creating a deeply impressive model of monarchy that attracted many later Islamic rulers, whatever their ethnic origins. Through such means, the ancient Sasanian world enjoyed an afterlife scarcely less enduring than that of Rome itself.[12]

Persian influences were transmitted through the epic poem of the *Shahnameh*, the Book of Kings, written in the late tenth century by the Persian poet Ferdawsi, in the time of the conqueror Mahmud of Ghazni. This work recounted and revived the history of the ancient Persian Empire and made those stories integral to the thought of later Islamic dynasties and rulers. Not only did the work recount the deeds of such heroic Sasanian kings as Ardashir, Shapur, and Khosrau, but throughout, the context is resolutely pre- or non-Islamic, often only barely Islam-adjacent. This is the world of Seleucia-Ctesiphon at its glorious height, when Persia threatened to destroy the power of Rome itself. When the Muslim Arab forces finally overwhelm Persia, the tale is told from the viewpoint of the heroic warriors who defend a noble doomed civilization against those scorned outsiders. For centuries, the *Shahnameh* became a manual for empire across Islamic South and Central Asia, and across the Caucasus—for the Mongol successor states, for the Mughals, and for many lesser rivals. Those monarchs aspired to the special divine glory attached to imperial rule since Persian times, the *farr* that shone forth in the face of the true sovereign. Each great dynasty patronized artwork and manuscripts of the whole epic or reflecting its stories. The work wielded special power in Safavid Persia itself, under the conqueror Ismail and his successor Tahmasp. Under their patronage, the artists in the imperial capital of Tabriz created the glorious manuscript known as the *Shahnameh* of Shah Tahmasp, which remains one of the splendors of Islamic and specifically Persian art. In 1568, it was gifted to the Ottoman sultan, as an unabashed proclamation of the glories of the Persian monarchy through the millennia.[13]

Conquered Persia took its own revenge on its conquerors.

Akbar's Faith

Through most of Islamic history, empires and rulers had little doubt of the superiority of their own faith, and at best, they granted toleration as a gracious favor. Realistically, not until quite modern times could Christians plausibly pose any serious political danger to states such as the Ottoman Empire. But in Islam, like other religions, some empires did indeed adopt broader and even universalist ideas, which profoundly changed both the dominant faith and its neighbors.

It was in India that external influences were most pervasive, and seductive. Pre-Islamic India had magnificent traditions of art and architecture, which were profoundly associated with the glorification of royal power, and it was natural that new Islamic rulers would fall prey to the temptations of assimilation. Hindu religious traditions were no less potentially attractive, and they exercised a special appeal to the Mughal emperors. That empire was of course wholly based on military conquest by Islamic nations and tribes, which at various stages had wrought massive destruction on India's older religions. Matters changed fundamentally under Akbar, who ruled from 1556 through 1605 and who acknowledged the power of the extravagantly diverse cultures and faiths over which he ruled. He created a strong imperial system focused on his and his family's power, and closely linked to an Indo-Persian cultural inheritance. He preached a new syncretic religion, which he called Dīn-i-Ilāhī, the Faith of God, which drew its beliefs from Hindu, Buddhist, and Zoroastrian sources, as well as Islam, and even made gestures toward Christianity. His court patronized art with Christian themes.[14]

The Faith of God did not long endure, although at least some of Akbar's successors followed his tolerance. As we have seen in other instances, universalism also generated a serious reaction, as Muslims questioned such excessive generosity. Half a century after Akbar's death, his successor Aurangzeb began a career of fearsome repression. But such actions could not reverse the significant blurring of religious loyalties and practices across much of Mughal society. Increasingly, believers divided their attention between holy places and individuals of both Hindu and Muslim background, and through the eighteenth century, Muslim sultans happily patronized Hindu temples and priests. Viewed globally, these close interactions were so significant because the subcontinent was home to so large a proportion of the world's Muslims.

Remaking South Asian Religions

I have described how dominant religions could be transformed by the faiths they conquered, but a reverse process also occurred, in which empires reshape those subordinate faiths. Historically, that pattern has been profoundly influential. We know a religious world in which Hindus, Buddhists, and Muslims constitute a massive presence on the spectrum of believers. Together, the three faiths account for perhaps 3.5 billion adherents, over 40 percent of global population. Given the importance of those groups, we might assume that they are all sharply differentiated from each other, but those lines have in the past been far less starkly obvious than they later became. As we have seen, the frontiers between Buddhism and Hinduism were only gradually drawn in early India. In modern times, the experience of subjection to European empires transformed the practice of Islam, making it much more difficult to allow accommodations with other religions that purists viewed as syncretistic.

Imperial interventions caused a thoroughgoing transformation of Hinduism, making it stand in much sharper contrast to its neighboring creeds. British imperial rule forced a radical rethinking of the nature of India's enormously diverse religious currents. As we have seen, British rulers did not initially promote Christian missions, but that changed from the early nineteenth century. In response, Hindu elites had to justify and defend their practices and beliefs in a way that had not been necessary in the past, while seeking to explain the obvious success of Western rule and its technologies. Hindus faced exactly the same questions that Muslims were likewise addressing in these years. The necessity for change was obvious, but did adaptation mean accepting Western ways or returning to older customs and practices?[15]

This dilemma forced Indian thinkers to rethink their most basic assumptions, during what is called the Bengal Renaissance, and for Muslims and Hindus alike, the booming imperial city of Calcutta proved very fertile ground for discussing and circulating new ideas. From 1816, it was a leader of this progressive movement, Ram Mohan Roy, who popularized the then fairly novel term "Hinduism." Roy himself founded a reformist movement of universalist principles, the Brahmo Samaj, which soon evolved away from any kind of orthodox Hinduism and indeed became recognized as a separate religion in its own right. But this was only one of multiple reform movements and sects that now emerged. From the 1860s, the Aryo Samaj preached modernization on the basis of total reliance on the scriptural authority of the Vedas. Initially at elite levels, Hindus became more markedly and recognizably what we would think of as Hindu.[16]

Rediscovering India's Past

The British themselves contributed greatly to the revival and to the rediscovery of Indian culture. Historians rightly mock Western claims to have "discovered" other cultures that were very well known to the native peoples of those lands: Columbus' so-called discovery of the Americas is a prime example. But in the Indian case, British and European scholars genuinely did raise awareness among Hindus about their long-forgotten cultural treasures and just how highly they stood in a global context. A lengthy and substantial dialogue profoundly affected the views of Hindus themselves, particularly the reformers, as well as Western observers of India. Famously, it was the British imperial official Sir William Jones who began the academic study of the Sanskrit language and scriptures, which he compared very favorably to Greek and Latin parallels, and he noted the ancient unity of the Indo-European languages. Jones sponsored a new Asiatic Society (1784), based in Calcutta, which promoted scholarship of all kinds and collected ancient manuscripts in vast profusion. Jones himself translated some of the Indian classics. He published some extracts from the Vedas and Upanishads, creating real excitement among contemporary British and European intellectuals. His translation of Kalidasa's ancient play *Shakuntala* fascinated European authors, and Goethe borrowed from it in *Faust*.[17]

Ethnographic and archaeological studies proliferated, as scholars proved the existence of Indian empires long forgotten by Indians themselves. The extensive work of the Asiatic Society provided the essential foundation for the Archaeological Survey of India, in 1861, which revolutionized understanding of India's past and its complex religious legacies. Such scholarly work had a natural appeal in its own right, but some of the leading figures had very conscious British and imperial goals in mind. The first director of the Archaeological Society was Sir Alexander Cunningham, who had long advocated a very ambitious archaeological survey of the whole country. He explicitly declared that such an enterprise would show that past Indian states had usually been petty chiefdoms, and that only under a strong united regime would the country be strong and secure against invasion. He also hoped to show

> that Brahmanism [i.e., modern Hinduism], instead of being an unchanged and unchangeable religion which had subsisted for ages, was of comparatively modern origin, and had been constantly receiving additions and alterations; facts which prove that the establishment of the Christian religion in India must ultimately succeed.[18]

His point about the historical development of Hindu religion was well taken, given what was only then being recognized as the country's extensive Buddhist heritage.

As events developed, the historical discoveries were rather taken to support Hindu claims and causes. British-directed excavations and archival research now identified the sites of some of the key cities of ancient India and uncovered sequences of lost empires. As British scholars interpreted these finds, they showed a special predilection for those eras in which India had been wholly or largely united under a single dynasty, such as the Mauryas or Guptas, while underplaying times of division and decentralization. Empires like to study empires. Nationalists and Hindu advocates alike relished these new insights, and the evidence of bygone cultures that they saw as far superior to anything that the Christian West might produce.[19]

That process continued until the latter days of the British Raj, in the mid-twentieth century. In the 1920s, British and Indian scholars together uncovered the ancient cities of the Indus Valley culture, India's first great urban civilization. Because they showed the extreme antiquity of something so recognizably Indian, Hindu enthusiasts used these remains to denounce scholarly suggestions that Hindu civilization was in any sense a later importation. From this perspective, Indian, and Hindu, civilization was built wholly on local roots, an argument enthusiastically proclaimed by extreme religious nationalists.[20]

Hinduism as World Religion

The creation of well-established shipping routes between Europe and India made possible the Western academic study of Indian thought and religion, and of this now-fascinating topic of "Hinduism." Although he never ventured near India, the great German-born scholar Max Müller (1823–1900) used such materials to formulate a sweeping theory of Hindu thought and the prospects for that faith (from 1850, Müller held a prestigious professorship at Oxford University). Like other Westerners of his day, Müller viewed other religions through a Judeo-Christian lens and sought to impose structures, hierarchies, orthodoxies, and worldviews where, commonly, nothing of the kind existed. In the words of scholar Ann Della Subin, Müller could make a religion out of "anything that sufficiently resembled Christianity."[21]

Accustomed as he was to a Western world where familiar boundary fences marked the respective territories of Jews, Christians, and Muslims, he assumed that such clarity must be found just as easily in Asian faiths. Among other things, that meant elevating scriptural and mystical aspects of religions over vernacular practices, which were readily dismissed as folk religion, or even as superstitious accretions to authentic faith. It was especially through his work, which laid the foundation for the discipline of religious studies, that Europeans extended their listing of the "world religions" to include not just Hinduism but also Buddhism, Confucianism, and Daoism. Müller was the first directing editor of the *Sacred Books of the East*, a fifty-volume collection of translations that appeared between 1879 and 1910.

Hindu reformers were deeply influenced by these scholarly ideas and were delighted to integrate Western discoveries about the glories of bygone Hindu civilizations and their scriptures. Those thinkers claimed a degree of distinctiveness and consistency in Hindu practice that was at some variance with historical experience. In the process, reformers accommodated Western prejudices about the superiority of an absolute monotheism that supposedly stood above the teeming diversity of the various deities. Particularly valuable in this regard were the Upanishads, which so often preached an ultimate reality over and above the various deities as they appeared in popular devotion. Latin translations of the Upanishads were available in Europe from the start of the nineteenth century, and they greatly impressed influential intellectuals. Hindus themselves placed a special focus on accessible key scriptures that could be used as a retort to the pocket New Testaments distributed by Christian proselytizers. The *Bhagavad Gita* proved ideal for this task, and it has ever since been used in this way.[22]

Hindu reformers developed the idea of that package of beliefs as a great religion, with powerful universalist and mystical aspirations. In that guise, Hinduism achieved worldwide recognition as (at least) a worthy counterpart to Christianity or Islam. Leading the spiritual revival was the Bengali mystic Ramakrishna (1836–1886), who explored most of the currents of mysticism and devotion available in the India of his day, including Tantra, Vedanta, and even Sufi Islam. He not only praised other faiths like Islam and Christianity but saw them all as valid paths to a common goal. Over the next century, many religious and political thinkers saw Ramakrishna as one of the greatest holy figures of his age, in any faith, and he was, of course, a splendid recommendation for the virtues of Hinduism. The new vision of that faith found a charismatic global face in his disciple, Swami Vivekananda, at the end of the nineteenth century, and subsequently in Mahatma Gandhi. Vivekananda traveled and lectured around the world, and was a star of the World's Parliament of Religions held in Chicago in 1893 (to which we shall return shortly). Responding to an ovation at this event, Vivekananda thanked the cosmopolitan crowd "in the name of the mother of religions." But as has been aptly observed, "Vivekananda might have styled himself as an avatar of timeless Eastern wisdom, but he was a creature of steam trains and ocean liners. . . . [His] was a steam-powered pilgrimage." Although devoted to Indian culture, he spoke warmly of what the British had contributed to modernization: he hoped that "an admixture of the two civilizations would give birth to an ideal society in India and a new age would be ushered into the world."[23]

To that extent, Hinduism in its modern guise originated as a direct response to the Western and Christian challenge, but other British actions had a very direct effect on the ordinary followers of that faith. In the early twentieth century, rising nationalist agitation raised the prospect of an independent India, which would be strongly dominated by Hindus, and in the recently resurgent form of that faith. This naturally alarmed Muslims, who began their own campaigns for political representation and protection. But any talk of representation in elected assemblies depended on a clear and explicit sense of whether families or individuals should properly be counted as Hindu, or Muslim, or one of India's other religious constituencies. From 1919, under the auspices of British bureaucracy, Indians began a sweeping process of self-identification, which in practice forced people to accept unequivocal religious identities of a kind that had never been needed in the past. Hindus and Muslims became more sharply marked as communities, a process that would culminate in the bitter civil violence that accompanied the end of British rule in 1947. That partition, and the disasters that accompanied it, resulted in a far starker drawing of religious lines than ever in Indian history.[24]

If imperial regimes did not "invent" Hinduism, they did much to mold it into the shape in which is conventionally understood today. That is certainly true of the vision of Hinduism as one of the world faiths.[25]

Rediscovering Buddhism

An even better case can be made for the imperial "invention" of another great faith, namely Buddhism. Prior to the early nineteenth century, Buddhist societies flourished across much of Asia, although no longer in India itself. Generally, those societies had few religious interactions with each other and operated strictly according to local and national traditions. Unlike in earlier eras, they were little attracted by the once-legendary pilgrim shrines of northern India, where the thriving Buddhist universities were forgotten. There were few, if any, latter-day successors to the Chinese or Indian monks who had wandered so freely over the Buddhist realms in the fifth and sixth centuries. Through the reports of diplomats and Jesuit missionaries, meanwhile, Europeans recognized the existence of some widespread common faith that had manifestations as far afield as China, Japan, Siam, Mongolia, the East Indies, and "Tartary." Even so, they were almost wholly ignorant of the Buddha and his teachings. It was chiefly British scholars of the nineteenth century who observed all these diverse religious phenomena and hypothesized that they were all remnants of one common framework of "Buddhism."[26]

Most significant, the British rediscovered the ancient Indian sources from which that Buddhist world had sprung, and in the process they uncovered what was in effect a civilization as dead as that of the ancient Assyrians or Babylonians. Initially through chance finds, British officials and soldiers found the copious remains of various Buddhist cultures across India, in areas from which the faith had vanished a millennium previously. The treasures of the Ajanta Caves were rediscovered around 1820, and their existence was publicized worldwide. At about the same time, a British administrator in Java ordered an expedition that found the forgotten site of Borobodur. The academic study of the Pali language, the common tongue of the earliest scriptures, dates from English and French scholars of the 1820s. In 1837, James Prinsep achieved a stunning breakthrough when he deciphered the Brahmi writing system that many early empires had used for their monumental inscriptions. Together, these discoveries allowed the reading of ancient texts, including the rock inscriptions in which the emperor Ashoka proclaimed to the world his Buddhist faith and the new social organization that he intended to build upon it. Although scholars of many nations participated in these explorations, their activities were wholly made possible by British political rule, and the scholarship found an effective organizing base in the Asiatic Society. Prinsep himself was the director of the East India Company's Bengal mint.[27]

The development of archaeology from the mid-century encouraged a new respect for the major centers of the region, such as Sarnath and Bodh Gaya, but more important, it showed just how startlingly common Buddhist shrines and temples had once been in all parts of the subcontinent. In 1819, a British officer announced a pioneering discovery of what had once been the country's very widespread stupas. Contemplating images of Sarnath's ruins, a "*Boodh* monument," in 1832, English poet Letitia Landon saw vestiges of a lost religion:

> Forgotten utterly; and of their faith,
> No memory, but fallen monuments,
> Haunted by dim tradition.

She asserted that Indian Buddhists had been fiercely persecuted by Hindu brahmins, which was not too far from the truth. Landon then speculated about the sheer scale of the surviving faith. Although ruined in India, the Buddhist sect's "doctrines extend over Ceylon, Thibet, Tonquin, Cochin

China, throughout China, exists largely in Japan, and is without doubt the religion which has the most numerous followers in the world." It was eminently worth studying.[28]

Reforming Buddhism

As with Hindus, Western "discoveries" found a ready audience among Buddhists themselves, who from the 1860s entered a period of rapid modernization in response to imperial and Christian pressures. All the main Buddhist-dominated states were affected by movements for reconstruction and reformation. One common theme in such efforts was a return to more primitive kinds of religious authority, although just how such a movement might be interpreted differed enormously in each society. In some areas, the changes amounted to a cultural revolution. Korean Buddhists, for instance, revived an ancient tradition of propagation of teaching, coupled with a greater role for the laity, in an obvious response to Protestant missionary pressures.[29]

Reformist activism was vigorous in Burma, which was under direct threat of British conquest, with hard-fought wars in the 1820s and again in the 1850s. Following the loss of much of the country to the British in 1853, the new king Mindon Min launched a program of systematic modernization, with a potent spiritual dimension. As was happening with other faiths at the time, reform involved a return to the most primitive manifestations of the faith. Buddhist history recorded four ancient councils as pivotal moments in the definition of the faith, the last of which was held at the turn of the Common Era. Daringly, King Mindon convened what he billed as a fifth council, which met at Mandalay in 1871. The chief goal was to examine and purify the scriptures, to determine a new and authoritative version of the Pali Canon. In reality, this so called fifth council attracted little attention outside Burma, but the sheer audacity was notable. It was akin to a modern-day Christian leader summoning a new General Council at Nicaea or Chalcedon.[30]

Buddhism also experienced new growth in Vietnam, after long centuries of suppression by Confucian regimes. As the country fell under ever more direct French control, Buddhists benefited from the discrediting of older elites and a new freedom of religious practice. They used these opportunities to rebuild, and a national revival began in the 1920s. The well-organized and militant Buddhist movements that the Americans notoriously encountered in that land in the 1960s were of quite recent growth, and ironically, they were products of European rule.[31]

Japan: Restoration and Revolution

In Japan, one of the ancient Buddhist centers, *ressourcement* produced utterly different effects, with an attempt to return to pre-Buddhist times. From the 1850s, the country faced frightening pressures from expanding empires, notably the United States, and the country's elites decided that salvation could come only from urgent modernization, to beat those empires at their own game. This is what occurred after 1868, under the Meiji Restoration, as a renewed Japanese empire began a period of aggressive expansionism. That revival had a powerful spiritual dimension, in a land where Buddhist and Shinto practice had long coexisted. Prior to 1868, Buddhists had enjoyed many advantages, to the point of framing the gods and spirits of Shinto as lesser beings within its own cosmic hierarchies. In this condescending vision, Shinto was portrayed at best as a folk religion, a poor relation of the great Buddhist faith. Buddhist priests practiced in Shinto shrines.

Under the Meiji Restoration, the government began a ferocious persecution of Buddhists, as part of a campaign to draw sharp and rigid lines between the two faiths. The movement is remembered through the slogan, *Haibutsu kishaku*, "Abolish Buddhism!" and it swiftly developed a character much like that of the European Reformation centuries before. Tens of thousands of temples were destroyed or seized. Buddhist scriptures were burned, temple bells melted down, and there was mass iconoclasm. Although Buddhism survived, much of its activism was concentrated in a series of new Buddhist movements, most of which were strongly associated with Japanese patriotism. So was the older school of Zen Buddhism, which enthusiastically adapted to the new environment. Under government pressure, many Buddhists moved away from such fundamental practices as clerical celibacy. When Japan annexed Korea, the conquerors imposed that new and more secularized system on their new possession, in a land where Buddhism dated back some 1,600 years.[32]

The Japanese Buddhism that Westerners discovered in the twentieth century was the product of this imperial crisis. The other aspect of the religious revolution involved Shinto itself, which the reformers understood as the authentic religion of the land, in need of restoration to its primitive glories, freed of the foreign pollutions of Buddhism. Shinto became much more sharply defined, with a fervent devotion to the emperor and to nationalist causes. In its aspect of State Shinto, it became an ideal imperial ideology. Shinto duly joined Western academic lists of acknowledged world religions.

The Missionary

Elsewhere, the encounter with empire had more beneficial, and lasting, effects for Buddhism. In British-ruled Ceylon (Sri Lanka), confrontations with Christian missionaries forced Buddhist monks to develop new structures and apologetic techniques. Among other manifestations, Ceylon became the birthplace of a powerful modernizing movement that is known as Buddhist modernism or, significantly, Protestant Buddhism. Its most famous representative was Anagarika Dharmapāla, the son of a wealthy family who was educated in a series of Christian schools and colleges that had been established under British auspices. He guided the religious revival in his own country and carried his mission into India and China, and to Europe and the United States. It was the imperial framework of steamships and trains that made such ventures possible. Dharmapāla visited China to revive Buddhism in what should by any numerical standard have been a teeming center of the faith. In practice, he managed to reach only Shanghai, the entrepôt where the diverse empires active in the region met.[33]

His Indian visit was especially important as a conscious return to the roots of the faith. In ancient times, the most venerated Buddhist shrine had been at Bodh Gaya, which had fallen badly into disrepair and had effectively been converted into a Shaivite Hindu shrine. That situation drew the attention of Sir Edwin Arnold, a British scholar who faithfully served the Raj in India and fought against the rebels during the Indian Mutiny. Arnold, however, had strong sympathies for Indian culture, and in 1879 he published a hugely influential bestseller *The Light of Asia*, an epic poem on the Buddha's life. Through Arnold's work, Dharmapāla made his own discovery of Bodh Gaya, and the two worked to revive the country's Buddhist shrines. As so often with India's other monuments in this era, restoration work was commonly approved and undertaken by imperial administrators. The two men together—the British imperial servant and the Ceylonese scholar—marked the beginnings of a Buddhist revival in India itself. They also spread awareness of Buddhism as a global faith, a concept that would have been incomprehensible at the start of the nineteenth century.[34]

A New Buddhist State

In modern times, Westerners interested in Buddhism often turn to Tibetan versions of the faith. The fourteenth Dalai Lama has become a universally recognized symbol of spirituality, arguably even more so than the incumbent pope. Such prominence is remarkable given the remoteness of the region, which was very poorly known to the West before the end of the nineteenth century, and one moreover with a tiny population. It was multiple imperial interventions that transformed the situation and made Tibetan Buddhism appear as something like the norm of that faith.[35]

From the 1720s, the Chinese Qing dynasty conquered Tibet, which remained an integral part of its empire until the start of the twentieth century. As China declined, so British and Russian pressures grew, and the British invaded Tibet in 1903–1904. This forced the thirteenth Dalai Lama into exile in Mongolia, where he restored long-dormant ties with the Buddhist communities of that region, sparking new Buddhist growth. Already, Tibet's spiritual leader was becoming a visible figure in the transnational Buddhist world. In 1912, Tibet gained independence as a Buddhist theocracy under the Dalai Lama. That independence was made possible by the reluctance of both Britain and Russia to see its rival taking control of the region, while a gravely weakened China was unable to assert its claims. Buddhist Tibet remained independent for almost forty years.[36]

In 1950, China was under a Communist regime, but one that still behaved exactly like its imperial predecessors in terms of its distant possessions. In the previous chapter, we saw how imperial pressures have often driven marginal groups to flee to new lands and how faiths grew even stronger in exile, and that is exactly what happened in Chinese-ruled Tibet. Official repression has focused on the Buddhist institutions and persecutions that authorities see as the heart of Tibetan cultural and national identity. Rebellions and bloodshed have driven many into exile. The overall numbers are not large in global terms, running as they do into the hundreds of thousands, but that is a sizable share of the population.[37]

The effects have been quite disproportionate in bringing Tibetan Buddhism to global consciousness. Although Western enthusiasm for Buddhism dates back to the mid-nineteenth century, only in very modern times has it become relatively simple for interested followers to seek out Tibetan practice, in the exile communities in India, particularly the city of Dharamsala, and also in Western nations. The situation is quite different from that of earlier times, when only the most intrepid could dream of venturing to the ferociously inaccessible Tibetan homeland. These developments have helped advance Buddhist causes very widely in Western nations—much to the horror of the Chinese who sought to extirpate the pretensions of that faith within their "imperial" dominions.[38]

The idea of Buddhism as a world religion is an imperial invention, or rather a rediscovery.

How Asian Religions Became Religions

Other religions besides Buddhism were likewise transformed as they responded to the imperial challenge, and one fundamental change involved absorbing Western definitions of the concept of "religion" and "a religion." However natural such language might appear to Christians, it poses grave difficulties in Asian cultures where people might follow multiple traditions at once, some (but not all) of which involved concepts of worship or devotion. In China, it was quite possible and even expected that individuals would follow practices and customs that we might variously classify as Buddhist, Confucian, or Daoist. Those systems might not have anything recognizable as "God" in the Judeo-Christian sense, nor did they necessarily have a canonized scripture. As Western powers forced Japan to open to external contact and commerce, they insisted on "freedom of religion," which raised the intriguing question of just what that latter word might imply. In response, Japanese scholars invented the new category of *shūkyō*, to delineate religion as opposed to morality or civic ethics. This new terminology fed into the ongoing debates that we have encountered about defining the increasingly distinct worlds of Buddhism and Shinto. Each was now "a religion," an -ism, and was duly differentiated from vernacular practices that were now downgraded to superstitions. Such a taxonomy could not have emerged without the imperial intrusion.[39]

In China similarly, the philosophical, ethical, and political tradition associated with the ancient teacher Kong Qiu—Kong Fuzi, or Master Kong—became a religion, and indeed a world religion, under the title of Confucianism. The process began with the European Jesuits who were the West's main conduits of information on Chinese matters from the sixteenth century onward. Those Europeans focused on the singular figure of Confucius in a way that had not hitherto been common, to make him as central a figure in his tradition as Jesus, Muhammad, or Zoroaster were in theirs. Like those other founders, Confucius too had his distinctive body of scriptures, in the *Analects*. Even if we do not see this process as a simple tale of "manufacturing" Confucianism, to use the title of one controversial modern history, those Catholic missionaries did indeed profit from this new formulation. The more Christianized Confucius appeared, the easier it was to depict actual Christianity as filling a natural place in Chinese thought. The process of assimilation entered a new phase from the end of the eighteenth century as British diplomats sought the establishment of relations with China as a natural extension of their imperial interests in India. Meanwhile, Christian missionaries began the process of translating Confucian texts: by 1814, English speakers had access to (flawed) translations of most of the key writings. But if Confucianism was now constructed as a religion, it was a deeply problematic one, and Western empires exploited this negative image for their own purposes. When the British confronted China in the Opium Wars, the common Western stereotype depicted Confucian China as inflexible and resistant to modernity, and special blame attached to effete Confucian sages.[40]

New imperial perspectives affected the perceptions of Asian thinkers themselves, to the point of actually creating "Confucians." By the end of the nineteenth century, Chinese reformers had to confront their country's growing subjection to imperial powers—to Western states of course, and increasingly to a predatory Japan. As they agonized over this existential crisis, some influential thinkers turned to Confucianism as a means of reconstructing Chinese pride and consciousness. At every stage, these thinkers were shaped by their observations of Western Christianity, as they understood it, with the established Christian churches that were so prominent a feature of the leading Western powers. In response, Chinese intellectuals defined Confucianism as "a religion," a concept that really had no direct Chinese translation. One leading reformer, Kang Youwei, used the older word *jiao* for this purpose, so that Confucianism became *kongjiao*. Kang dreamed of a true national faith (*guojiao*) which would be taught in Confucian churches across the Chinese Empire, as a means of fostering national unity and identity. Kang's followers built on his insights to develop the terminology of *zongjiao*, which has become the modern Chinese word for "religion": the word is actually borrowed from the Japanese *shūkyō*. Beyond reshaping religions, empires actually carried the ideas of religion to vast areas of the globe.[41]

Empire as the Mother of Theology

Empires, and the Christian missions they made possible, transformed the religions of subject peoples. The encounters also inspired new visions of Christianity itself: while missions carry with them the assumptions of the imperial metropolis, they can also import beliefs and customs from the peripheries back to that core. Historians of Christian mission often quote Martin Kahler's maxim that mission is "the mother of theology."[42]

Many examples through Christian history illustrate this pattern, but during the great era of imperial mission, it had a special impact on concepts of the boundaries dividing individual traditions and on visions of church unity. Missionaries in remote societies had to deal with alien spiritual traditions, but scarcely less demanding, they also had to live alongside fellow Christians from other churches, in a setting where Christians of any kind were a tiny minority. Logically, such a situation called for close cooperation in a common cause, but that was difficult when members of the respective churches regarded their rivals as having strayed so far from orthodox truth. In some cases, followers of one church regarded other missionaries as scarcely Christian in any worthwhile sense.[43]

Such qualms faded in the conditions of frontier mission, and specifically in the closing days of the British rule in India. As national independence approached in the 1940s, Christians faced challenging questions about their place in the emerging order. In 1947, in the southern half of India, a broad range of churches agreed to an act of unification that would have appeared breathtaking or even unthinkable in Europe or North America. The new Church of South India (CSI) incorporated four main traditions, the Anglican, Methodist, Presbyterian, and Congregational. The CSI is thus a full member of the Anglican Communion but also the World Methodist Council. For its motto, the church adopts Jesus' words "that they all may be one." Over the following decades, the CSI experiment was followed in other parts of the subcontinent, most significantly by the Church of North India (CNI), created in 1970. Over and above the founding denominations of the CSI, its northern counterpart also included Baptists and Disciples of Christ. Those innovations, and especially the original CSI, excited and inspired advocates of ecumenism, who dreamed of reproducing them in the Protestant nations of the Global North.[44]

Contacts with other religions forced Christian Churches to try to place those faiths in a theological context that went beyond older assumptions that they were all diabolical deceits or (as in the case of Islam) Christian heresy. Such interactions were particularly troubling in South Asia, where Christians found a range of highly literate faiths teaching doctrines and practices that they themselves found seductive and intoxicating. But any such interfaith theorizing was perilous. If indeed other faiths were all valid in their own right—if each was a legitimate road to salvation—then any such acknowledgment had a devastating effect on essential Christian doctrines of the unique role of Christ and his church.

Although Christians had engaged in dialogues of a sort with Judaism and Islam from early times, it was only during the great age of European empires that these conversations incorporated other great faiths and attempted to move beyond confrontation and diatribe. The first great monument of this new phenomenon was the World's Parliament of Religions, which was part of the Columbian Exposition held in Chicago in 1893. This assembly featured delegates of most of the great religions, with Dharmapāla and Vivekananda speaking respectively for Theravada Buddhism and Hinduism: several other branches of both traditions were also represented, as well as Jainism, Islam, and various Christian traditions. At least at the level of church elites and academics, interfaith dialogues continued through the following century. They achieved a historic degree of recognition when in 1965 the Roman Catholic Church issued the historic statement *Nostra Aetate*, which enumerated the positive aspects of other faiths, including Hinduism and Buddhism, concluding that "the Catholic Church rejects nothing of what is true and holy in these religions." However obvious and even anodyne such a statement may seem today, in the long history of the Christian Church, it constituted a theological revolution.[45]

Flowing West

The discovery of Asian religious glories had an immense impact on Western nations, and on Western religious thought, far beyond the professional theologians or the ecclesiastical bureaucrats. The situation strongly recalls the passion that "Oriental" mysteries and devotions stirred in the ancient Roman world. Conquered India acquired a Western reputation as a global heart of spirituality.

During the nineteenth century, many educated Europeans and Americans were profoundly disenchanted with Judeo-Christian religion, which had been subjected to so many scholarly and philosophical attacks during the Enlightenment. They were still thirsty for mystical or spiritual inspiration, which they found abundantly provided in Eastern religions, as these were selectively imported. Unitarians, rationalists, and transcendentalists alike easily identified with the awe-inspiring visions of an ultimate Reality lying beyond reality that they found in Hinduism and Buddhism alike. If few Westerners wholeheartedly accepted those religions in their entirety (some did), Indian-derived ideas became a massive presence on the Euro-American cultural stage. Sanskrit texts generated real excitement when they were translated into Western languages. The Asiatic Society made the *Bhagavad Gita* available in English in 1785, and shortly after that it appeared in French and German. The philosopher Arthur Schopenhauer declared, "In the whole world there is no study so beneficial and so elevating as that of the Upanishads." Friedrich von Schlegel believed that "India is superior in everything—intellectually, religiously, even Greek heritage seems pale in comparison."[46]

Such new insights sharply contradicted the common Christian tendency to judge and condemn non-Christian faiths. By the 1840s, Henry David Thoreau reported:

> In the morning I bathe my intellect in the stupendous and cosmogonal philosophy of the Bhagvat Geeta [*sic*], since whose composition years of the gods have elapsed, and in comparison with which our modern world and its literature seem puny and trivial. . . . The pure Walden water is mingled with the sacred water of the Ganges.[47]

By way of context, Thoreau was writing at very much the same time as Charlotte Brontë published her poem "The Missionary," which as we saw imagined Hinduism in terms of hell's empire. To take another synchronicity, the Indian Mutiny of 1857 led British observers to denounce what they saw as the ruthless savagery of "Oriental" cultures. But in that same year, the American transcendentalist Ralph Waldo Emerson published his once very popular poem "Brahma," which offered a short and accessible summary of the teachings of Vedanta, of the *Bhagavad Gita* and the Katha Upanishad:

> Far or forgot to me is near;
> Shadow and sunlight are the same;
> The vanished gods to me appear;
> And one to me are shame and fame.

The poem served as a gateway drug for generations of mystically inclined Westerners seeking Eastern wisdom.[48]

Theosophy and the Quest for Wisdom

The subsequent Western appropriation of "Oriental" spirituality is a vast theme, which has been the subject of much academic study. In the Theosophical Society (1875), Anglo-American thinkers devised a new religious synthesis rooted thoroughly in Hindu and Buddhist ideas (the group's main prophet was the Russian Helena Blavatsky). Theosophical teachings incorporated reincarnation, karma, and gurus, as well as the sacred bodhisattvas of Mahayana Buddhism. Some leaders, like the American colonel Henry Olcott, proclaimed themselves Buddhists and worked closely with Buddhist reformers like Dharmapāla. (Dharmapāla eventually abandoned his Western allies because their universalist message failed to give adequate recognition to the distinctive teachings of the Buddhist religion.)[49]

Despite its indisputably imperial context, Theosophical leaders strongly supported Indian national aspirations, and with surprising effects. In 1889, two (white) English Theosophists in London asked a young Indian visitor for help understanding Sanskrit words in the *Bhagavad Gita*. The young man, who later earned fame as Mahatma Gandhi, was ashamed to admit that he had never read the work in any language and was enormously impressed when he eventually read it in the English translation of Sir Edwin Arnold. The *Gita* went on to be a foundation of his whole religious life. Gandhi, of course, would play a key role in the overthrow of British rule in India. Another of the leading British radicals of the day, Annie Besant (1847–1933), was at once a prominent Theosophist and a vigorous activist for Indian independence. Her other great cause was Freemasonry, which we have already seen as both a consequence of imperial-driven globalization and a vehicle for its subversion. In the 1920s, she supported the messianic claims of the young Indian Jiddu Krishnamurti, who attracted a passionate following across Europe and North America.[50]

Not until much later in the century would Hindu and Buddhist populations swell in the metropolitan nations themselves, and even then, that was mainly the consequence of mass immigration, rather than the conversion of Euro-Americans themselves. Even so, the World's Parliament of Religions allowed some Asian faiths, including Hinduism and Zen Buddhism, to achieve a foothold in the West and among white Western believers. That further aroused interest in Theosophy, which had a very large impact on Western cultural and religious thought. Right up to the Second World War, Theosophy had an inordinate influence on Western thinkers and thoroughly permeated literature, music, and the visual arts.

More broadly, from the end of the nineteenth century, this fascination with Asian spirituality left its mark on Western concepts of Christianity. Liberal and progressive thinkers found much to admire in Buddhism especially and speculated freely about possible Asian influences on the earliest church. Influential new pseudo-gospels recounted Jesus' acquisition of such Eastern teachings, especially reincarnation. Such theories acquired mainstream status through best-selling novels and works of popularization. Although many of these ideas were the work of US or German authors, they soon found a home in Britain, the seat of the empire that had made this kind of contact possible.[51]

During the twentieth century, occult and esoteric sects transmitted these themes to a mass audience, culminating in the very popular New Age movement of the 1970s. These teachings had a startling influence on the mainstream population: by some estimates, up to 30 percent of US Christians believe in reincarnation.[52]

Christian empires did succeed, very largely, in spreading their own faith, but they also caused the growth and development of other belief systems that they would have defined as alien or hostile. I have noted Horace's remark about the ultimate victory of the conquered, the captives, but we might put this in more colloquial form: empires really do strike back.

10
The Ends of Empire

Far-called, our navies melt away;
    On dune and headland sinks the fire:
Lo, all our pomp of yesterday
    Is one with Nineveh and Tyre!

Rudyard Kipling[1]

Even when empires end, religions flourish in their aftermath. Historians of mission often cite St. Patrick, who lived in the post-Roman Britain of the fifth century and whose endeavors expanded that older cultural ambience to whole new territories barely touched by Rome itself. Throughout, he communicated in the Latin language of the older regime. The Irish church that he helped to found would in later centuries become a vital missionary presence across western Europe, vastly strengthening the power of that other imperial phantom, the Roman Papacy. In so many ways, that instance foreshadows the experience of many later empires as they fade and perish but are resurrected in religious form.

This theme of religious continuity might be illustrated by a verse beloved by generations of patriotic British imperialists. In 1782, William Cowper's poem "Boadicea" imagined the rebellious British Celtic queen of that name facing a hopeless struggle against the Roman conquerors. A Druid comforts her with the prophetic assurance that

Regions Caesar never knew,
    Thy posterity shall sway,
Where his eagles never flew,
    None invincible as they.[2]

Religions, like nations, can push far beyond the frontiers known by secular Caesars and their legions. And in faith as in political matters, the conquered and subordinate peoples of one generation might come to dominate future eras.

Europe's colonial empires were largely extinct by the 1970s, but they left a potent religious legacy, both through the survival of language and through mass migration. That impact has been particularly evident in the case of Christianity, but also of Islam and the religions of South Asia. Each in its separate way reached regions and populations barely imagined a century ago. In each case too, that postimperial movement transformed religious life in the metropolitan homelands. Without those imperial memories, our present religious world would be unimaginably different.[3]

The Captains and the Kings Depart

Empires rarely end neatly, although narrative convenience often portrays events in such a way. It is all too tempting to find a single spectacular incident or battle to mark the end of a given empire. Nonspecialist historians commonly imagine the "Fall of Rome" in terms of an apocalyptic sack of the city, with the date 476 much cited. In reality, there were two sacks by barbarians, in 410 and 455, and 476 was chiefly a matter of administrative convenience, as the very powerful continuing empire in Constantinople decided to end the formality of a separate Western ruler. In reality, Roman power in the West maintained a shadowy existence for centuries to come, and the Eastern Empire survived for another millennium. As late as the tenth and eleventh centuries AD, the Roman Empire was still a formidable military power, capable of expansion into Muslim territories. As I have mentioned, the decisive end came only in 1453, with the Turkish capture of Constantinople, but by that point, the empire itself had long since ceased to function far beyond the immediate confines of that once-glorious capital.[4]

Beyond the formality of political control, the structures and opportunities created by empires long outlive any sense of political identity. That includes modes of transport and communication, common languages, and the role of great cities. In such Western Roman territories as Britain or Gaul, Roman buildings and roads remained in use for centuries after the withdrawal of Roman administration and armed forces. More broadly, many cultural aspects of former empires also continue to exercise a kind of soft power throughout former possessions. Memories and myths prove very stubborn.[5]

Nor in most cases do the religions associated with empires simply evaporate when the last imperial flag is taken down. Conquerors might expel the adherents of defeated faiths, as so often occurred when the Ottoman Empire was driven from Europe. There were also precedents for religions being so closely associated with settler groups, and so little connected with native populations, that they evaporated when those settlers withdrew. This is what happened to the once-thriving Christianity of North Africa, which disappeared utterly when Roman settlers and Latin speakers fled before the approaching forces of Islam. But commonly, religions survive the departure of the empires that had introduced them. Even if they begin as invasive species, they sink deep roots.[6]

The Fall of a World System

When the European empires eventually ended, those events were just as untidy as their ancient predecessors, and themes of persistence and continuity were equally in evidence. In terms of territorial extent, the European empires reached their apogee in the years between the two world wars. The second of those wars irreversibly weakened all of those entities, leading to the creation of many new nations around the world. Crucial moments included the establishment of India and Pakistan in 1947 and Indonesia in 1949 and the collapse of French rule in Indochina in 1954. Despite hopes that European power might survive longer in Black sub-Saharan Africa, the British, French, and Belgian Empires were all substantially liquidated in the decade after 1957. The Portuguese persisted only into the mid-1970s. In some cases, the process of achieving African independence involved prolonged violence and armed resistance, most bitterly in the Algerian war against French rulers. The sequence of liberation wars culminated in the campaigns against the two white-ruled states of Rhodesia and South Africa.[7]

Although most scholars were content to date the end of that great historical phase of empire to African events of the 1970s, observers reluctantly conceded that the Soviet Union was in fact an empire in very much the classical mold, and only with its fragmentation in 1991 could we plausibly speak of the end of empires. Activists in particular regions might be even more conservative about that older language: nationalist opponents of British rule in Northern Ireland, for instance, portrayed their struggle as yet another phase in the age-old war against empire, and that rhetoric survives today.[8]

As in earlier eras, the withdrawal of imperial systems was a very mixed phenomenon. In some regions, such as the Dutch East Indies, imperial power was removed quite suddenly, and thoroughly. Here especially, nationalist militants targeted civilian groups for mass killing and torture, including Dutch citizens, mixed-race Eurasians, Chinese, and native Christians. In contrast, although the French colonial empire suffered a bloody catastrophe with the loss of Algeria in 1962, in all essential aspects, that country's dominance of its African territories lasted for several decades thereafter: we might even question whether that control ever ended. Not only did France exercise substantial control within its African sphere of influence, of Françafrique; it actually expanded its power over former Belgian territories. That influence was repeatedly manifested in military interventions. To take a symbolic illustration of this continuing power, air travel between France's former African colonies often assumes routing through Paris, rather than any more logical local travel.[9]

What Empires Left Behind

Elsewhere, the long endurance of ancient Roman roads finds a modern parallel in the survival of the vitally important rail networks that the British created over the Indian subcontinent. As in earlier eras, military forces have often served as the vessels of imperial memory, as is illustrated by the remarkable and continuing diffusion of Scottish bagpipes across the armed forces of many African and Asian nations. Far more significant, the European empires long retained their strong economic stakes in their various former territories, provoking lively debates about the nature of "neo-colonialism."[10]

Some of the most striking survivals of empire proved to be among the most pernicious, especially in matters of the borders acquired by newly independent states. When empires withdrew from particular regions, rarely was it easy to identify the proper and natural boundaries of the successor nation-states, which were usually new creations heavily influenced by imperial needs and interests. The withdrawing empires played a critical role in shaping those new entities, which sometimes meant lumping together populations that had previously been separate, or else separating older communities that historically had shared a common identity. The most notorious example involved the religious-based partition of the Indian Empire into the nations of India and Pakistan, a traumatic event that claimed millions of lives. In the process, it thoroughly transformed the religious geography of South Asia.[11]

That example is well known, but similar histories can be traced in many other regions, and often with religious consequences. Commonly, the newly drawn borders made little sense in terms of local geography or of demographic realities. The new nation of Nigeria, for instance, closely followed the outline of the older colonial possession, which combined tribal and religious groups with very different histories and interests. The country's subsequent history of religious violence was a natural outcome. In the enormous country of Sudan, likewise, it was a British decision that originally left an Islamic government in charge of many Christian areas. Across Africa, the postindependence decades were often marked by outbreaks of massacre and civil war that were variously portrayed as ethnic or religious, which led Western observers to despair about the supposedly primitive tribal loyalties that still seemed so commonplace. In reality, the imperial legacy explains why such diverse communities found themselves within a single state.[12]

Religious Continuities

The ends of empire aroused grave concern about the fate of religious structures and above all, of Christianity, which seemed particularly vulnerable in an era of postimperial turmoil. In some areas, anti-colonial and anti-Western violence targeted the religious symbols of empire. Missionaries and nuns suffered dreadfully in the violence that overwhelmed the former Belgian Congo. Virtually nowhere in Islamic territories did European Christian powers achieve any significant conversion of Muslim populations, and Christian endeavors scarcely survived the end of empire. Algeria offered perhaps the most telling example of a decisive breach, as virtually all European settlers were forced to flee, facing the stark choice of "the suitcase or the coffin," at a stroke, removing almost all the Christian and Jewish population. Much as had occurred in Roman Africa many centuries before, the removal of the Christian veneer opened the door to revived Islam. Algerian cities are littered with buildings that were intended to be the churches and cathedrals of a new Catholic order, which today are either disused or have been repurposed as mosques. Christian institutions and buildings were uprooted just as thoroughly by the Communist revolution in China.[13]

In some regions, the Christianity introduced by imperial missions survived as the faith of postcolonial elites. When the French withdrew from Indochina, the anti-Communist elite in the new South Vietnam was aggressively Catholic and sought to govern in the interests of that minority faith. The resentment that stirred among the Buddhist majority provoked serious conflict, which opened the door for Communist insurgency, and thus for later US intervention. After the Communist victory in 1975, Catholicism survived in the new united Vietnam, but in much reduced form, as a great many of its adherents joined the flood of refugees heading to Australia and the United States.[14]

Elsewhere, where transitions of power were more respectful of continuity, as in India or Pakistan, splendid cathedrals and churches survived as places of Christian worship, but often serving aging expatriate congregations. In such contexts, Christianity seemed like a ghost religion, as far removed from the actual religious mainstream of the society in question as the ancient Mithraic temples being excavated in London and elsewhere on the old Roman frontier. In both cases, it seemed, the attentive listener could hear the melancholy, long, withdrawing roar of a failing faith. It should be said that the faith as a whole was actually much stronger in India than these superficial impressions might suggest, as new forms of evangelical and Pentecostal faith were making serious inroads in the post-imperial years. But the rather staid older churches, and their buildings, presented a sad picture of irrelevance and decline.[15]

African Christianity

Pessimistic observers feared a similar fate for Christianity in many other regions, in Asia and especially in Black Africa, where the recently introduced faith was seemingly so dependent on European empire, and on the missionaries those authorities supported. Could it even survive in an independent environment? In pessimistic scenarios, the new African nations would be secular and (likely) socialist, or else they would increasingly turn to the Islam that had deeper roots in the continent. Making prospects even worse, the British had tended to favor Islamic elites in successor states, to the disadvantage of Christian populations. In reality, such expectations proved wildly inaccurate. The explosive growth of Christianity in Africa and Asia has been one of the most significant stories in modern religious history. In Africa alone, the number of Christian believers in 1900 was just 10 million, but it rose to 360 million by the end of the twentieth century, and by 2050 it is projected to grow to over 1 billion. That would make Africa the most Christian continent in terms of population, and even that figure does not include many more millions in the global African diaspora.[16]

That revolutionary transformation is reshaping all Christian denominations. In 1900, the whole of Africa had just a couple of million Catholics, but that number grew to 130 million by the end of the century, and today it approaches 200 million. By the 2040s, there will be some 460 million

African Catholics. Around 2030, we will cross a historic milestone when the number of Catholics in Africa will exceed the number in Europe.[17]

Much of that Christian growth in Africa resulted from demographic factors and the steep rise in the continent's overall population, but evangelism and conversion were also vital. As a proportion of African population, Christians grew from 10 percent in 1900 to a little under half by 2000, and that figure seems likely to be sustained. To take the example of Africa's most populous nation, in 1900, the territories that would become Nigeria had a population of some 16 million, of which barely 100,000 were Christian. Today, the country's total population exceeds 200 million, and the likely number of Christians is more than 90 million: both numbers could double by 2050. The Democratic Republic of the Congo—the former Belgian Congo—has 100 million people, of whom 90 percent identify as Christian. Both Nigeria and the DRC will soon be counted among the nations with the largest Catholic populations, besides all their other churches.[18]

The reasons for this triumphant growth are many, and only some are directly connected with the imperial legacy. That linkage is most obvious in the case of the churches and denominations that have grown most dramatically in particular regions. Of course, denominations such as the Anglicans and Presbyterians flourished in such British-ruled territories as Nigeria, Ghana, and Uganda, but Catholicism also enjoyed a boom in those very countries, and so did many independent denominations and sects. These alignments did not indicate any kind of bow to secular authority. New African believers accepted Christianity because it provided spiritual answers that were much in demand, especially in a world beset by constant dangers of otherworldly evil and of real-world disease. In different regions, many accepted membership in one of the mission churches, while others adhered to newer churches based on local traditions, such as the diverse African-Initiated Churches.[19]

Whatever qualifications we might offer, the crucial fact remains that the European empires had planted the seeds of that growth, establishing networks of churches and schools across the continent and protecting missions. They thus made Christian institutions so widely familiar across the continent, and so readily accessible. But as with St. Patrick, the greatest growth occurred after the withdrawal of formal political power, to a degree that startled many Western observers at the time. Suddenly, Thomas Barker's painting of the African chieftain receiving the Bible seemed far less absurd than it might once have.

Languages of Faith

The imperial heritage did much to shape the diverse forms of Christianity that were exploding across the Global South in these years, and that was nowhere truer than in matters of language. As Christianity was rising in Africa and Asia in the 1960s, Western observers imagined that it would be expressed chiefly in local languages. In response to this expected development, the Roman Catholics and other liturgically oriented communities devoted much effort to translating services into those languages, and with appropriate adaptations of local custom and belief, as part of inculturation. Much of that work was relevant and useful, but what those observers missed was just how critical the colonial languages would remain after independence, especially in societies with multiple local tongues.[20]

That usage is obvious in the vast culture of revivals and miracle crusades that have done so much to make Christianity a fundamental part of Africa's cultural landscape, usually through promises of healing, well-being, and prosperity. Such events virtually always use those old colonial languages as a means of crossing local ethnic and tribal boundaries, rather than (as might have been expected) depending on multiple simultaneous translators. That also has the effect of making English (or the other European-derived tongues) seem like the normal means of communication in faith. This story is evident in Nigeria, where Christian revivals can easily draw crowds in excess of a million, and the medium is English, albeit in forms and dialects that British native speakers can find puzzling.[21]

Those imperial languages have "gone native," just as Latin did after the collapse of the Roman Empire in the West, in Patrick's time. To take Nigeria again, the country became an independent state in 1960, and the median age of its population today is around eighteen. Only 8 percent of Nigerians are aged over fifty-five. Only the very old have the slightest recollection of the British Empire or think of English as the language of imperial administration. For most Nigerians (or Ugandans, or Kenyans), English is an African language, and it always has been. It is also, naturally, a language of faith. The same is true of attitudes toward French and Portuguese in other areas of the continent.[22]

Such common languages also provide the basis for missionary endeavors across Africa, and indeed farther afield. The use of Portuguese permits Brazilian churches to undertake mission in such African nations as Angola and Mozambique. Shared languages make it easy to distribute evangelistic materials in the forms of pamphlets or videos.[23]

Migration and Faith

Empires have also driven mass migration, which has so transformed religious maps around the world. When empires were at their height, they often moved populations around the world as cheap labor, and as we have seen, that created new religious minorities of Hindus and others far from their homelands. After the Second World War, many people in Africa and the Caribbean decided to migrate to Europe, a process that the imperial connection initially made simple. Afro-Caribbean people who lived in British-ruled territories like Jamaica were aware of Britain through the educational system, and many had served in British imperial forces during the war. For such imperial subjects, entry visas or documents were no issue. Critically too, those migrants spoke English. The arrival of a new cohort of people of color, and a new phase in British history, is symbolized by the arrival of the migrant ship *Windrush*, in 1948. Britain developed a sizable Afro-Caribbean population, as did that other former British imperial territory of Canada. It was just as natural for citizens of the former Indian Empire to make the same movement to Britain from the 1950s onward.[24]

Britain remained just as attractive a destination even after the passport and citizenship requirements were tightened dramatically in the 1960s. Once immigrant communities established themselves in a particular city or center, others followed through the well-known phenomenon of chain migration. By 2021, 18 percent of the residents of England and Wales traced their ancestry to Africa, South Asia, or the Caribbean. Asians alone accounted for 9 percent.[25]

Similar imperial connections directed the residents of former possessions and colonies to their particular "homelands," and again, the question of language was vital. French-speaking Moroccans and Algerians found their way to France just as naturally as Jamaicans and Trinidadians—and later Nigerians and Ghanaians—went to Britain. Many of those migrants had served in the French armed forces, or else their forebears had, often through multiple generations. Other Francophone Africans went to Belgium. Still other former imperial subjects went to the Netherlands or Portugal. In each case, the country that became their destination was not a matter of random choice: it was largely determined by questions of language and ease of entry, which were consequences of empire. The picture is somewhat more complicated than I am suggesting, and it was not merely a case of migrants from French colonies (say) inevitably coming to France. Immigrant peoples often moved on beyond those first countries of settlement, a transition that was relatively easy with the relaxation of border controls in a uniting Europe. Hence Moroccans, for instance, found their way to the Netherlands or Sweden. Lacking imperial ties, at least in recent times, Germany and Scandinavia found workers in Turkey and thereby acquired the bases of what would later become major immigrant settlements. But generally, the imperial connections were very influential.[26]

Those multiple migrations have had a long-term religious impact. One very visible fact in modern Europe is the acquisition of significant communities from non-Judeo-Christian traditions, and these religious innovations were built on imperial foundations. It was Britain, rather than any other nation, that acquired major Hindu and Sikh settlements, a direct legacy of the long Indian connection. Britain itself is now home to around a million Hindus, some of whom are strikingly successful and wealthy: the country's wealthiest family is the multibillionaire Hindujas. Hindu temples are commonplace in Britain. Initially, communities adapted existing secular structures, but more recently some have constructed whole new buildings that faithfully replicate the finest Indian models. Neasden, in London, is the home of the impressive Shri Swaminarayan Mandir, the stone construction of which declares both confidence and permanence. In 2022, the practicing Hindu Rishi Sunak became prime minister of Great Britain: when he took his oath as a member of the House of Commons, he did so on the *Bhagavad Gita*. Indian newspapers greeted the new prime minister at the commencement of what they termed the "Sunak Raj." Sunak's own parents were part of the Indian diaspora to East Africa, which I described in chapter 7, and they subsequently found their way to Britain. Similar backgrounds produced other leading contemporaries of Sunak's in the British Conservative Party, including highly placed members of the cabinet.[27]

Other Indians migrated elsewhere within the British dominions, especially to Canada, where Indo-Canadians make up over 5 percent of the national population. The country has some eight hundred thousand Hindus and a slightly larger number of Sikhs. Numerically, British Columbia has the most Sikhs of any province or administrative division in the world, with the exception of the Indian regions of Punjab and Chandigarh. Sikhs are very well represented in particular cities and regions, and many are active in public life. Jagmeet Singh, for example, currently leads the country's New Democratic Party, one of the major political groupings. Counting Canadians of Pakistani origin would add another percentage point to the numbers derived from the subcontinent. Although they have until recently been far less visible than in Canada, Indians have also migrated to Australia in sizable numbers, and Hindus and Sikhs comprise about 3 percent of the population.[28]

Imperial connections alone do not wholly explain this globalization of faiths, as so many diverse believers found their way to the United States, which had never had a formal political hold in Africa or South Asia. But in many cases, migrants followed the old imperial maps and trade routes.

Migrant Islam

One familiar aspect of the religious impact of migration has been the spread of Islam, especially in Europe. At the start of the twentieth century, Muslim communities in Europe were chiefly found in the southeast of the continent, in former Ottoman territories. Since the 1950s, new communities have planted roots across western Europe, largely in consequence of the imperial heritage. Exact numbers are controversial, because estimates are based on culture rather than active religious commitment, and they count as Muslims many people who might be thoroughly secular in orientation.[29]

But even given those caveats, Islam has expanded impressively: there are now some 27 million European Muslims, some 5.5 percent of the continental population. Among the key former imperial powers, Great Britain now has 2.7 million Muslims, around 5 percent of the population. The French probably stands between 4 and 6 million, some 7 or 8 percent of the total population. (Some estimates range much higher.) Since 2016, London's mayor has been the Muslim Sadiq Khan, whose family origins lie in the Indian city of Lucknow, which among other things was pivotal to the struggles of the Indian Mutiny in 1857. Across the whole of Europe, the Muslim share of the population currently varies between 5 and 8 percent in countries like Germany, Austria, Belgium, the Netherlands, Denmark, and Sweden, with a heavy concentration in urban areas. Muslims probably comprise 12 percent of Greater London and a somewhat larger proportion of the Paris metropolitan area.[30]

The fact that the proportions are far higher among children and young adults means that European Islam will become an even larger part of the social landscape. By 2050, the Muslim proportion of European population will exceed 10 percent. Islam has also expanded in Canada, which for present purposes should equally be considered as another postimperial territory. Presently, about 5 percent of Canadians are Muslim, which is equivalent to the numbers of that country's Hindus and Sikhs combined.[31]

In recent decades, the threat of "Islamization" has been much heard in European political life, but it is in Russia that the most substantial religious effects of imperial overreach are being felt. As we have seen, most of that country's imperial expansion was directed into Muslim territories, in Central Asia and the Caucasus, and many of those territories broke free of central control in 1991. But Muslims remain numerous in the regions that are still part of the Russian Federation, the new nation that emerged from that collapse. Muslim numbers are strong in the Caucasus, but they also have a strong and visible presence in the great cities, especially Moscow itself. Muslims make up at least 15 percent of the Russian population, some twenty-two million people, a far larger share than in Britain or France. Russia's grand mufti places the number at twenty-five million, or 18 percent of the whole, and further projects that the proportion could exceed 30 percent by the mid-2030s. By some projections, Russia could acquire a Muslim majority by the end of the present century.[32]

While most European nations found themselves with Islamic populations, the particular kind of Islam that now appeared differed enormously according to the national origins of those immigrant communities. French Islam is still mainly rooted in North Africa, in the countries of the Maghreb. In contrast, Muslims in Britain looks mainly to the Indian subcontinent, to Pakistan and Bangladesh. Actually, it is even more localized than that. An impressive 70 percent of Britain's Pakistanis (who are overwhelmingly Muslim) come from just one tiny and remote area, namely the highly conservative Mirpur, so that we speak of the Mirpuri diaspora. That fact goes far toward explaining the religious, political, and social outlook of that very large component of British Islam. Contrary to Western stereotypes, the customs and outlook of British Muslims differ greatly from those of, say, French Algerian communities, and still more from the Sufi-dominated faith of French West Africa; and it is no less at variance with the Sufi traditions of Russian Islam.[33]

Migrant Christians

Such diversity caused by migration patterns is especially obvious within Christianity. Although Islamic immigration has received so much emphasis in media coverage in Europe, a large share of the post–World War II arrivals were in fact Christian, and that was true in France and the Netherlands as well as Britain. Besides African and Afro-Caribbean people, they also included migrants from the ancient Christian communities of southern India, communities such as the St. Thomas Christians.[34]

The relative importance of such immigrant Christians grew enormously from the 1960s onward as levels of belief and practice plummeted among Europe's old-stock populations. As overall numbers of immigrant believers rose, so they constituted an ever larger share of active and practicing Christians. Some of those immigrants were conspicuous in their evangelistic activities in their new homeland. In Britain, the most successful and visible new churches belong to African or Afro-Caribbean traditions, usually of a Pentecostal or charismatic kind. Francophone variants of these traditions are strong in France or Belgium, where immigrant-based megachurches flourish. British megachurches tend to look to Nigerian or Ghanaian pastors and spiritual entrepreneurs; Francophone counterparts turn to Congolese or Madagascarian. In each case, immigrant-derived communities maintain close ties with their countries of origin, so that London, for instance, plays a pivotal role in the organization of many transnational churches, not to mention the global gospel music industry. Paris and Brussels retain their role as capitals of spiritual empires.[35]

Such immigrant churches are numerous, and conspicuous, in the old imperial metropolises. So predictable are the connections between ethnicity and faith that it is possible to use an ethnography of foods to map religious practice in a particular area. Observing the foods on offer at local markets and grocery stores in a European city gives an excellent idea of the religious denominations and services active in the area and (commonly) from which parts of the historic empires the congregations derive. Yams, plantains, and cassava indicate African origins, and African churches, and some linkages are still more direct. An area in which jollof rice is popular is certain to have West African Pentecostal congregations and African-Initiated Churches, all marked by long and energetic services with a strong focus on healing. Other foods indicate the particular kind of Islam that flourishes locally and whether its roots are Middle Eastern or Turkish or South Asian. Food and faith alike map religious concentrations and imperial legacies.

That immigrant role is not just true of the Protestant or Pentecostal worlds. For Catholics and other liturgical churches, the influx of Global South Christians to the imperial metropolis has contributed to revival of faith, and of a quite traditional kind. In Britain, such believers have revived many of the country's medieval pilgrim shrines, as regular pilgrimages draw heavily from southern Indians and Sri Lankans, as well as Christians from Africa and the West Indies. Such communities have also increasingly supplied clergy, including some at the churches' highest ranks. In 2005, Ugandan John Sentamu became archbishop of the Anglican archdiocese of York, which traces its line of episcopal succession to the 620s AD. Imported clergy have been evident in the Catholic context. As vocations to the Catholic priesthood dried up so sharply in the late twentieth century, the church had to turn to foreign-born priests. In Britain, that commonly meant Nigerians or Southern Indians. In France, it meant Francophone Africans, especially Congolese, as well as Vietnamese. Again, this demonstrates just how much language matters in guiding religious developments.[36]

Anglican Empires

Regardless of the intentions of policy makers, imperial maps often survive the loss of actual rule. When the British Empire wound up, successive London governments hoped to retain some kind of authority through the loose structure of the British Commonwealth, which has enjoyed mixed success. Although the organization continues, and has actually grown over time, its political role is negligible. But other networks also continue, notably the global religious structure of the Anglican Communion, which as its name suggests was English in origin. Recent controversies within that organization well illustrate the persistent religious impacts of empire, and their paradoxes.[37]

As we have seen, the Anglican Church pursued its missionary ventures within the imperial framework, and at least in theory, it extended its ecclesiastical networks far beyond British shores. In the mid-nineteenth century, English, US, and Canadian leaders formed the idea of regular episcopal meetings within the larger communion, under the overall guidance of the archbishop of Canterbury, and the Lambeth Conferences began in 1867. During the twentieth century, Anglican growth continued vigorously, but the communion acquired a very different ethnic and geographical foundation from anything its founders had contemplated.

Today, the Anglican communion claims some ninety million adherents, making it the third-largest Christian tradition, after the Catholic and Orthodox Churches. At least notionally, the largest component is still the Church of England, with twenty-six million members, although the actual number who practice the faith in that land is closer to one or two million. The other giant in the Anglican world is the church of Nigeria (eighteen million), followed by the provinces of Uganda, Kenya, South Sudan, South India, Southern Africa, and Tanzania, all of which were once part of the old British Empire. Together, those latter six claim twenty-seven million adherents. Besides the church in Great Britain itself, we do find some old, established bodies with predominantly white memberships in the United

States (the Episcopal Church), as well as Canada and Australia, but they are dwarfed by the explosive growth in Africa and Asia. Yet if the Anglican Communion reproduces the contours of the defunct British Empire, the balance of regional power is almost precisely inverted. The communion itself is ever more clearly the preserve of those regions Caesar never knew.[38]

In recent decades, the shift of Anglican numbers has attracted intense public attention from observers not normally interested in that denomination. Debates over sexuality, and especially gay issues, have shown the great strength of the Global South churches, which in virtually all cases hold very conservative views on such matters. Although the conservative cause is mainly rooted in African churches, it also finds a powerful voice in the Asian primates of provinces such as Singapore. Global North churches have found themselves in a minority within the communion as a whole. In some cases, dissident conservative factions in Northern churches—mainly white by race—have seceded to form new congregations accepting leadership from African or Asian bishops. Such developments constitute a near-revolutionary reversal of familiar stereotypes about race and the global distribution of power within churches.[39]

These lessons are reinforced by similar developments in other denominations that aspire to global reach, such as Methodists and Lutherans, which have also faced North-South schisms over issues of sexuality and morality. As in the Anglican case, old-stock Christian believers in the metropolitan nations find their assumptions increasingly challenged by a surging faith in the old colonial possessions. To return to Thomas Barker's painting, the symbolic chieftain was not only receiving the new faith but would use it to transform societies in ways that the old empires might not have approved.

Particularly in the Anglican context, the rhetoric of empire and imperialism surfaced often, and acrimoniously, in these church debates. Conservative African and Asian critics of gay rights and gay ordination asserted that their own views represented the authentic traditions of their own societies, which they upheld in the face of overbearing pressure from the liberal Global North, in a kind of moral neo-imperialism. Liberals, in contrast, deny that anti-gay views are in any sense natural to Africa or Asia, and suggest that it was British attitudes and legislation that suppressed older and more tolerant attitudes. The anti-gay legislation that characterizes many societies of the former British Empire is usually based on the strict British models and precedents of bygone years. For both sides, the suggestion that a doctrine or opinion was the consequence of empire is believed to discredit it.

Such recent controversies obviously owe much to globalization, and the global media resources and easy travel that make such intercontinental interactions so easy. But at every stage, these debates bear the unmistakable hallmark of empire not only in the language of debate but also in the territorial and cultural maps on which those contests take place. Empires seldom end neatly.

Conclusion

The empires of the future are the empires of the mind.

Winston Churchill[1]

Following the British annexation of the Punjab in 1849, the conquerors built new military and administrative settlements from which to govern. One of these was founded by Major James Abbott, a figure that no novelist would have dared invent. He was a key player in the Great Game, the prolonged British effort to prevent the Russians extending their power into South Asia. Abbott enjoyed a sensational career as a soldier, diplomat, and spy, wandering through the Islamic borderlands between British and Russian Empires in Central Asia: one painting portrays him in the garb of an Afghan noble. His new settlement was duly named Abbottabad, which he commemorated lovingly in a poem that is, by common consent, one of the most embarrassing literary productions of the era. In Abbott's defense, he probably composed it in Urdu, so that the flaws lie in the translation rather than the original composition. After a long history as a British military base, Abbottabad transferred to the control of the new nation of Pakistan in 1947. In the 1980s, the northwest regions of Pakistan acquired a vital strategic significance as a base for Islamist resistance against the Soviet occupation of Afghanistan, in that later phase of the Great Game and through the following years Abbottabad itself attracted radicals and terrorists. In 2011, it earned worldwide notoriety when a US special forces unit undertook a raid to kill the terrorist commander Osama bin Laden, who had been living in a compound there.[2]

Although the killing of bin Laden was not commonly reported as an imperial adventure, the context made it hard to resist such connotations, from the world of James Abbott himself to that of bin Laden, who in his earlier days struggled against Russian imperial control of the Islamic land of Afghanistan. That conflict in turn had broad global implications for the fate of Islam, and for its relations with other faiths. Reports of the death of empires may, in fact, been greatly exaggerated.

In most past societies, empires have had an immense influence on the development of religion, and religions. This naturally invites the question of whether that now represents a closed phase in history. Have empires actually ended, as a standard form of social organization, and if so, what might replace their role in religious change?

Have Empires Really Ended?

At first glance, the question of whether empires still continue seems straightforward: surely, they are long gone, one with Nineveh and Tyre. Yet by the definitions I offered in chapter 1, several nations today earn this tainted label. Russia and China still exercise their unpopular rule over minority peoples in vast lands acquired by conquests in earlier centuries. In 2022, Russia's invasion of Ukraine was intended as the opening salvo in an expansive campaign to restore the older Soviet Union and its imperial rule over neighboring states, including those of eastern Europe. A renewed Chinese imperial system is likewise emerging in the South China Sea and across much of Asia and Africa. Presently, this expansion takes the form of financial and commercial power, through the country's wildly ambitious Belt and Road initiative, but already, the scheme is being reinforced by military bases and warships. Chinese bases operate in such old imperial centers as Sri Lanka, Pakistan, and Djibouti. It is difficult to avoid the famous American maxim: westward the course of empire takes its way.[3]

Meanwhile, enthusiasts for a united Europe increasingly use imperial rhetoric. Some speak overtly of "a new empire," although they imagine any new entity as wholly committed to liberal and humanitarian goals, and they hark back longingly to the romanticized multiethnic harmony of the Habsburg realm. In the title of a recent book, this was "yesterday's world; tomorrow's world."[4]

Even apart from formal expansion, much recent history powerfully recalls earlier epochs of empire. Over the past three centuries, it is difficult to find a decade in which at least a couple of leading Western powers were not at war with Islamic nations or movements, often on the frontiers of empires, and the supposed "end of empire" has made little difference to that rule. A Rip Van Winkle who fell asleep as recently as 2000 would be startled to find that just a few years later, he would awake to a world in which US and British soldiers were fighting a very familiar kind of guerrilla war in Afghanistan, with Australian and Canadian allies, and that names such as Kandahar were very much in the news. The story of Abbottabad puts such memories into even sharper focus. Even that multifaceted imperial word *lashkar* returned as a term used by Islamist militants seeking to create a holy army of Islamic "warriors." The best-known example is the Lashkar-e-Taiba, Army of the Righteous, which was originally designed to combat the "imperial" occupation of Afghanistan by the Soviets and was funded by bin Laden. It was subsequently responsible for some of the deadliest mass terror attacks in the Indian sub-continent. If the French colonial empire in Africa is theoretically extinct, that country's armed forces are still highly active across much of West Africa, fighting Islamist guerrillas who might well be the lineal descendants of earlier generations of anti-imperial resisters. The landscapes of imperial struggle have changed remarkably little.[5]

Nor would it be difficult for earlier generations of metropolitan news consumers to understand the rhetoric arising from such struggles. At the start of the twentieth century, the British and other nations were locked in a vicious and prolonged war against the Somali Muslim leader they knew contemptuously as the Mad Mullah: in part, that alleged madness consisted of his not wishing to succumb to imperial rule. If official rhetoric has become more serious and more respectful since that point, popular understandings have been slower to change, as we see from depictions of such figures as Osama bin Laden.

In 2021, Richard Overy published his important book on the imperial dimensions of the Second World War, which I have already noted. The British edition was entitled *Blood and Ruins: The Great Imperial War 1931–1945*, but the US edition subtly altered the subtitle to *The Last Imperial War 1931–1945*. Given the fact that the US edition appeared just at the time of Russia's Ukrainian adventure, that adjustment seems highly optimistic. If only . . .[6]

Using Religion

So many recent examples further suggest that the ideological justifications for empire have not changed as much as we might suspect. At least in appearance, the continuities are startling.

Russia might be an outlier in this regard, but the official justifications for its Ukrainian adventure were strikingly retrograde. President Vladimir Putin explicitly compares himself to the country's great empire builders of earlier eras, especially the czar Peter the Great. The regime drew on nineteenth-century doctrines of mystical nationalism, reinforced by a close alliance with a grovelingly loyal Orthodox Church. The Russian branch of that church, under the leadership of the patriarch of Moscow, harked back to long traditions when it asserted its rights against Ukraine's rival patriarchate, centered in Kyiv, raising the specter of a new religious war. Russian bishops and priests blessed banners and military equipment for the struggle, and distributed cherished relics. Russian clergy issued theological pronouncements asserting that soldiers who sacrificed their lives for their country would in effect become martyrs: that benefit applied only to those fighting for the true holy and Orthodox cause, which was that of Russia. But like so many previous empires, that Christian realm fought its battles through the martial races of other faiths, including Chechen Muslims, and Central Asians of both Muslim and Buddhist backgrounds. Tolstoy would immediately have understood these military arrangements, as would Kipling.[7]

Scarcely less archaic have been the ambitions of the modern Turkish government, which since 2003 has been dominated by Recep Tayyip Erdoğan, who successively served as both prime minister and president, as head of the Islamist AKP party. Under Erdoğan, Turkey has retreated massively from its old doctrines of official secularism and has actively promoted Islam to the point of giving it a favored role in the state. In 2020, Erdoğan declared Hagia Sophia a mosque once more, for the first time since the building's secularization in 1934. In domestic and foreign politics alike, the country's policies have been described as a reversion to Ottoman principles and ambitions, with a series of military interventions in such old Ottoman spheres of influence as Syria and the Caucasus. Erdoğan has made disturbing allusions to the previous extent of Ottoman power throughout the Balkan lands and Greece. Meanwhile, Ottoman themes surface regularly and sympathetically in the nation's popular culture. If Putin looks nostalgically to an older imperial Russia, modern Turkish Islamists can legitimately be described as neo-Ottoman. Imperial habits die hard.[8]

In other cultural contexts, imperial memories and fantasies continue to drive militant religious movements of real significance. We think of the Islamic State with its attempted revival of the caliphate, which dreamed of asserting authority wherever Islamic banners have ever flown, including in Spain. More realistically, the movement received archaic-sounding oaths of fealty from militant groups across the Middle East, North Africa, and beyond. Conversely, Hindu ultranationalists in India are no less determined to extirpate the memories of those once-mighty Islamic empires. In 2023,

India's educational authorities introduced new school textbooks that omitted or severely underplayed the existence of past Muslim rulers on the subcontinent, including, most egregiously, the Mughal Empire.

Empire and Religion: A True Ending?

Empires, in various forms, will continue to rise and fall, and as we know, their influence can last long after their formal dissolution. Conceivably, that influence could take religious forms. As in previous eras, aspiring empires persecute and expel rival believers, forcing them to relocate to new and unsuspected parts of the world. Even operating on a small geographical scale, the would-be caliphate of the Islamic State drove many thousands of Middle Eastern Christians to seek more congenial homes. Also profoundly affected were adherents of the ancient minority faith of the Yazidis, who hitherto has lived within a narrowly defined geographical area. Refugees from the Ukraine war, who are likewise victims of imperial aspirations, will assuredly strengthen Orthodox Churches across Europe and beyond.

Even so, we should not expect that any latter-day empires will have anything like the structural effects on religious affairs of the kind that I have outlined in this book. In earlier eras, the greatest achievement of empires was in overcoming obstacles to communication between territories and cultures, allowing the dissemination of ideas and beliefs. Empires thus laid the essential foundation for globalization, but that process acquired a momentum of its own quite apart from any imperial contexts. What we might call non-imperial globalization is a very familiar reality in its own right, marked by the easy movement of people and ideas, and faiths. If empires once brought remote and peripheral populations into a world system, any such role is now superfluous.

For better or worse, cellphones and the internet have vastly reduced the once-insurmountable barriers between distant regions, between core and periphery. So has the spread of global languages, above all English. Religion, as much as commerce, has been profoundly affected by the hugely enhanced and accelerated means of conveying ideas. Within Christianity, we see, for instance, the rapid spread of Pentecostal styles of worship and practice. The same media have permitted the growth of simpler and more rigorous forms of Islam, often with a political emphasis.

We speak metaphorically of media empires, and we use the same term for the inconceivably gigantic technology companies, but the language is more appropriate than we might suspect. In most ways, those technological enterprises are fulfilling in the modern world the same functions that historically were the work of true political empires. In Churchill's words, the improvements in communication and understanding offered by those new empires of the mind promised "far better prizes than taking away other people's provinces or lands or grinding them down in exploitation."[9]

The Essential Imperial Dimension

But if empires will not again fulfil those ancient roles, this does not mean that they are no longer relevant to understanding the world's religions, often in unexpected ways. Scholars of religion are well used to going far beyond the texts and teachings of great faiths in order to understand them, to explore the social and cultural reasons that determine why particular movements succeed or fail. Of course, politics plays its part, and faiths that are resolutely backed by states and kings have an enormous advantage over their competitors. But that cannot be the only answer, or else Christianity would not have survived the persecutions in either Rome or Persia. Accordingly, scholars acknowledge a diversity of pressures and concerns, psychological, social, and economic. Recognizing the role of religion in assisting people during disease-related crises, they pay attention to the history of medicine and epidemiology or to climate-related factors. Demographics also play a critical role.

Any or all of those factors have some validity, but when we consider the history of religions on a transcontinental or global scale, we must explore not just the role of political power in general but specifically of the imperial dimension. Such a perspective seems critically relevant in a world where churches in Africa debate moral issues with counterparts in the United States or England; where Muslim television personalities use their bases in England to speak to faithful audiences in Egypt; where the likely candidates for a papal succession are African or Asian; or where a practicing Hindu heads the government of Great Britain, while a Muslim is mayor of London—in short, in a time of intense religious globalization.

Among other lessons, such an imperial perspective teaches us how and why given religions reached their current geographical limits and reminds us that no religion has a natural or, as we might say, a God-given right to any territorial distribution. Those limits were shaped by imperial actions and policies. In some cases, those imperial decisions determined the particular forms of faith that would survive and grow.

Today more than ever, scholars of religion need to understand the workings of empire.

Notes

Introduction

1 Thomas Hobbes, *Leviathan: With Selected Variants from the Latin Edition of 1668*, ed. Edwin Curley (Indianapolis: Hackett, 1994), 483.

2 Gina A. Zurlo, *Global Christianity: A Guide to the World's Largest Religion from Afghanistan to Zimbabwe* (Grand Rapids: Zondervan, 2022).

3 Michael Angold, ed., *Eastern Christianity*, vol. 5 of *The Cambridge History of Christianity* (New York: Cambridge University Press, 2006).

4 Philip Jenkins, *The Great and Holy War: How World War I Became a Religious Crusade* (San Francisco: HarperOne, 2014).

5 Swami Vivekananda is quoted from his letter to Francis Leggett, July 6, 1896, https://www.swamivivekananda.guru/2017/06/20/6th-july-1896/. From the substantial contemporary literatures on empires through history, see, for instance, Herfried Münkler, *Empires: The Logic of World Domination from Ancient Rome to the United States* (London: Polity, 2007); John Darwin, *After Tamerlane: The Rise and Fall of Global Empires, 1400–2000* (London: Bloomsbury, 2009); Jane Burbank and Frederick Cooper, *Empires in World History: Power and the Politics of Difference* (Princeton, N.J.: Princeton University Press, 2010); Jim Masselos, ed., *The Great Empires of Asia* (Berkeley: University of California Press, 2010); Robert Aldrich and Kirsten McKenzie, eds., *The Routledge History of Western Empires* (Abingdon, UK: Routledge, 2014); Heather Streets-Salter and Trevor R. Getz, *Empires and Colonies in the Modern World: A Global Perspective* (New York: Oxford University Press, 2015); Myles Lavan, Richard E. Payne, and John Weisweiler, eds., *Cosmopolitanism and Empire: Universal Rulers, Local Elites, and Cultural Integration in the Ancient Near East and Mediterranean* (New York: Oxford University Press, 2016); Krishan Kumar, *Visions of Empire: How Five Imperial Regimes Shaped the World* (Princeton, N.J.: Princeton University Press, 2017); Yuri Pines, Michal Biran, and Jörg Rüpke, eds., *The Limits of Universal Rule: Eurasian Empires Compared* (New York: Cambridge University Press, 2021); Andrew Phillips, *How the East Was Won:*

Barbarian Conquerors, Universal Conquest and the Making of Modern Asia (New York: Cambridge University Press, 2021).

For Somewheres and Anywheres, see David Goodhart, *The Road to Somewhere: The New Tribes Shaping British Politics* (London: Penguin, 2017).

6 Metaphors of ghosts and phantoms are common in the current literature on empires. From many possible examples, see Kwasi Kwarteng, *Ghosts of Empire: Britain's Legacies in the Modern World* (London: Public Affairs, 2012); or Dina Gusejnova, *European Elites and Ideas of Empire, 1917–1957* (New York: Cambridge University Press, 2016).

7 See the numerous essays in Peter Fibiger Bang, C. A. Bayly, and Walter Scheidel, eds., *The Oxford World History of Empire*, 2 vols. (New York: Oxford University Press, 2021).

8 From the very extensive literature on the British Empire, see, for example, William Roger Louis, ed., *The Oxford History of the British Empire*, 5 vols. (New York: Oxford University Press, 1998–99); Ronald Hyam, *Britain's Imperial Century, 1815–1914: A Study of Empire and Expansion*, 3rd ed. (New York: Palgrave Macmillan, 2002); Ronald Hyam, *Understanding the British Empire* (Cambridge: Cambridge University Press, 2010); John Darwin, *The Empire Project: The Rise and Fall of the British World-System, 1830–1970* (New York: Cambridge University Press, 2011); John Darwin, *Unfinished Empire: The Global Expansion of Britain* (London: Bloomsbury, 2012); P. J. Cain and A. G. Hopkins, *British Imperialism: 1688–2015* (Abingdon, UK: Routledge, 2016); Bernard Porter, *British Imperial: What the Empire Wasn't* (London: I. B. Tauris, 2015); and Bernard Porter, *Empire Ways: Aspects of British Imperialism* (London: I. B. Tauris, 2020); Joseph E. Inikori, ed., *British Imperialism and Globalization, c. 1650–1960: Essays in Honour of Patrick O'Brien* (Woodbridge, UK: Boydell and Brewer, 2022); John MacKenzie, *A Cultural History of the British Empire* (New Haven, Conn.: Yale University Press, 2023); Matthew Parker, *One Fine Day: Britain's Empire on the Brink: September 29, 1923* (London: Public Affairs, 2023). For the transition to the early independent United States, see Sean X. Goudie, *Creole America: The West Indies and the Formation of Literature and Culture in the New Republic* (Philadelphia: University of Pennsylvania Press, 2006).

9 Robert Aldrich, *Greater France: A History of French Overseas Expansion* (London: Palgrave Macmillan, 1996); Alice L. Conklin, Sarah Fishman, and Robert Zaretsky, *France and Its Empire since 1870*, 2nd ed. (New York: Oxford University Press, 2011); Roger Crowley, *Conquerors: How Portugal Forged the First Global Empire* (New York: Random House, 2015); Pieter C. Emmer and Jos J. L. Gommans, *The Dutch Overseas Empire, 1600–1800* (New York: Cambridge University Press, 2021).

10 Edward W. Said, *Orientalism* (New York: Vintage Books, 2003). Since that book's first appearance in 1978, literally hundreds of titles have been published on the general theme of Orientalism and empires. Jennifer Yee, *Exotic Subversions in Nineteenth-Century French Fiction* (Leeds, England: Legenda; London: in association with Modern Humanities Research Association and Maney, 2008); Richard Scully and Andrekos Varnava, eds., *Comic Empires: Imperialism in Cartoons, Caricatures, and Satirical Art* (Manchester: Manchester University Press, 2020); MacKenzie, *A Cultural History of the British Empire*.

11 For the distinctions between sea and land empires, see Andrew Lambert, *Seapower States: Maritime Culture, Continental Empires and the Conflict That Made the Modern World* (New Haven, Conn.: Yale University Press, 2018); Larry Wolff, *The Idea of Galicia: History and Fantasy in Habsburg Political Culture* (Stanford, Calif.: Stanford University Press, 2010); Pieter Judson, *The Habsburg Empire: A New History* (Cambridge, Mass.: Belknap Press of Harvard University Press, 2016).

For Germany, see Michael Perraudin and Jürgen Zimmerer, with Katy Heady, eds., *German Colonialism and National Identity* (Abingdon, UK: Routledge, 2011); Bradley Naranch and Geoff Eley, eds., *German Colonialism in a Global Age* (Durham, N.C.: Duke University Press, 2014); Matthew Fitzpatrick, *The Kaiser and the Colonies: Monarchy in the Age of Empire* (New York: Oxford University Press, 2022); Adam A. Blackle, *An Imperial Homeland: Forging German Identity in Southwest Africa* (University Park: Pennsylvania State Press, 2022).

12 Robert D. Crews, *For Prophet and Tsar* (Cambridge, Mass.: Harvard University Press, 2006); Michael David-Fox, Peter Holquist, and Alexander Martin, eds., *Orientalism and Empire in Russia* (Bloomington, Ind.: Slavica, 2006); David Schimmelpenninck van der Oye, *Russian Orientalism: Asia in the Russian Mind from Peter the Great to the Emigration* (New Haven, Conn.: Yale University Press, 2010); Simon Sebag Montefiore, *The Romanovs: 1613–1918* (London: Weidenfeld & Nicolson, 2016); Jeff Eden, *Slavery and Empire in Central Asia* (Cambridge: Cambridge University Press, 2018); Shoshana Keller, *Russia and Central Asia: Coexistence, Conquest, Convergence* (Toronto: University of Toronto Press, 2019); Alexander Morrison, *The Russian Conquest of Central Asia: A Study in Imperial Expansion, 1814–1914* (New York: Cambridge University Press, 2020). For Russia's cities, see Daniel R. Brower, *The Russian City between Tradition and Modernity, 1850–1900* (Berkeley: University of California Press, 1990).

13 Bang, Bayly, and Scheidel, *The Oxford World History of Empire*. For the great Eurasian empires, see Christopher I. Beckwith, *Empires of the Silk Road: A History of Central Eurasia from the Bronze Age to the Present* (Princeton, N.J.: Princeton University Press, 2009); John Man, *Empire*

of Horses: The First Nomadic Civilization and the Making of China (London: Pegasus Books, 2020); Peter Fibiger Bang and C. A. Bayly, eds., *Tributary Empires in Global History* (New York: Palgrave Macmillan, 2011); Anthony Sattin, *Nomads: The Wanderers Who Shaped Our World* (London: John Murray, 2022); Christopher I. Beckwith, *The Scythian Empire: Central Eurasia and the Birth of the Classical Age from Persia to China* (Princeton, N.J.: Princeton University Press, 2023).

14 Abdelmajid Hannoum, *The Invention of the Maghreb: Between Africa and the Middle East*, (Princeton, N.J.: Princeton University Press, 2021); Ashley L. Cohen, *The Global Indies: British Imperial Culture and the Reshaping of the World, 1756–1815* (New Haven, Conn.: Yale University Press, 2021); Nile Green, *How Asia Found Herself: A Story of Intercultural Understanding* (New Haven, Conn.: Yale University Press, 2023).

15 Jeffrey Mankoff, *Empires of Eurasia: How Imperial Legacies Shape International Security* (New Haven, Conn.: Yale University Press, 2022); Alasdair Roberts, *Superstates: Empires of the 21st Century* (Cambridge: Polity, 2023). For postcolonialism, see John McLeod, ed., *The Routledge Companion to Postcolonial Studies* (Abingdon, UK: Routledge, 2007); Graham Huggan, ed., *The Oxford Handbook of Postcolonial Studies* (New York: Oxford University Press, 2013). For the BRICs and other recent acronyms, Valeria Lauria and Corrado Fumagalli, "BRICS, The Southern Model, and the Evolving Landscape of Development Assistance: Toward a New Taxonomy," *Public Administration and Development* 39, nos. 4–5 (2019): 165–244.

16 Bang, Bayly, and Scheidel, *The Oxford World History of Empire*. I will discuss changing concepts of the imperial nature of US history in chapter 1. In 2023, the National Portrait Gallery in Washington, DC, organized a groundbreaking exhibition, *1898: U.S. Imperial Visions and Revisions*, which placed a sharp new focus on US imperial history and its legacies: https://1898exhibition.si.edu/.

17 Richard Overy, *Blood and Ruins: The Great Imperial War 1931–1945* (London: Allen Lane, 2021).

18 Richard Drayton, *Nature's Government: Science, Imperial Britain, and the "Improvement" of the World* (New Haven, Conn.: Yale University Press, 2000); Londa Schiebinger, *Plants and Empire: Colonial Bioprospecting in the Atlantic World* (Cambridge, Mass.: Harvard University Press. 2004); Sujit Sivasundaram, *Nature and the Godly Empire: Science and Evangelical Mission in the Pacific, 1795–1850* (New York: Cambridge University Press, 2005); Tanja Hammel, *Shaping Natural History and Settler Society: Mary Elizabeth Barber and the Nineteenth-Century Cape* (Cham, Switzerland: Springer International, 2019); and Andrew Goss, ed., *The Routledge Handbook of Science and Empire* (Abingdon, UK: Routledge, 2021).

For medicine, see Londa Schiebinger, *Secret Cures of Slaves: People, Plants, and Medicine in the Eighteenth-Century Atlantic World* (Stanford,

Calif.: Stanford University Press, 2017); Zachary Dorner, *Merchants of Medicines: The Commerce and Coercion of Health in Britain's Long Eighteenth Century* (Chicago: University of Chicago Press, 2020); and Jim Downs, *Maladies of Empire: How Colonialism, Slavery, and War Transformed Medicine* (Cambridge, Mass.: Belknap Press of Harvard University Press, 2021).

19 William Beinart and Lotte Hughes, *Environment and Empire*, Oxford History of the British Empire Companion Series (Oxford: Oxford University Press, 2007); Ulrike Kirchberger and Brett M. Bennett, eds., *Environments of Empire: Networks and Agents of Ecological Change* (Chapel Hill: University of North Carolina Press, 2020).

20 Carlos A. Driscoll, Juliet Clutton-Brock, Andrew C. Kitchener, and Stephen J. O'Brien, "The Taming of the Cat," *Scientific American* 300, no. 6 (2009): 68–75, https://www.ncbi.nlm.nih.gov/pmc/articles/PMC5790555/; Dan Eatherley, "What Have the Romans Done for Us?" *History Today*, July 7, 2019, at https://www.historytoday.com/history-matters/what-have-romans-done-us.

21 John Charles Griffiths, *Tea: The Drink That Changed the World* (London: Andre Deutsch, 2007); Dan Koeppel, *Banana: The Fate of the Fruit that Changed the World* (New York: Penguin, 2008); Rebecca Earle, *The Body of the Conquistador: Food, Race and the Colonial Experience in Spanish America, 1492–1700* (New York: Cambridge University Press, 2012); Amitav Ghosh, *The Nutmeg's Curse: Parables for a Planet in Crisis* (Chicago: University of Chicago Press, 2021); Jonathan Saha, *Colonizing Animals: Interspecies Empire in Myanmar* (Cambridge: Cambridge University Press, 2021); Ali Humayun Akhtar, *1368: China and the Making of the Modern World* (Stanford, Calif.: Stanford University Press, 2022); Jennifer Regan-Lefebvre, *Imperial Wine: How the British Empire Made Wine's New World* (Berkeley: University of California Press, 2022); Ulbe Bosma, *The World of Sugar: How the Sweet Stuff Transformed Our Politics, Health, and Environment over 2,000 Years* (Cambridge, Mass.: Harvard University Press, 2023).

22 Clare Anderson, *Subaltern Lives: Biographies of Colonialism in the Indian Ocean World, 1790–1920* (New York: Cambridge University Press, 2012); Tessa Murphy, *The Creole Archipelago: Race and Borders in the Colonial Caribbean* (Philadelphia: University of Pennsylvania Press, 2021).

23 Grace Moore, *Dickens and Empire: Discourses of Class, Race and Colonialism in the Works of Charles Dickens* (Abingdon, UK: Routledge, 2004); Griffiths, *Tea*; Andrew F. Smith, *Sugar: A Global History* (London: Reaktion Books, 2015); Jennifer Yee, *The Colonial Comedy: Imperialism in the French Realist Novel* (New York: Oxford University Press, 2016); Alexander Bubb, *Asian Classics on The Victorian Bookshelf: Flights of Translation* (Oxford: Oxford University Press, 2023).

24 James Walvin, *A World Transformed: Slavery in the Americas and the Origins of Global Power* (Oakland: University of California Press, 2022); Padraic X. Scanlan, *Slave Empire: How Slavery Built Modern Britain* (London: Robinson, 2022); Jori Lewis, *Slaves for Peanuts: A Story of Conquest, Liberation, and a Crop That Changed History* (New York: New Press, 2022); Maxine Berg and Pat Hudson, *Slavery, Capitalism and the Industrial Revolution* (London: Polity 2023).

25 Stephanie Barczewski, *Country Houses and the British Empire, 1700–1930* (Manchester University Press, 2014); Shashi Tharoor, *Inglorious Empire: What the British Did to India* (London: Hurst, 2017). For urban history, see Tristram Hunt, *Cities of Empire: The British Colonies and the Creation of the Urban World* (New York: Metropolitan Books, 2014); Annemarie Jordan Gschwend and K. J. P. Lowe, eds., *The Global City: On the Streets of Renaissance Lisbon* (Chicago: University of Chicago Press, 2016); Philip J. Stern, *Empire, Incorporated: The Corporations That Built British Colonialism* (Cambridge, Mass.: Harvard University Press, 2023).

26 Philip M. Conti, *The Pennsylvania State Police: A History of Service to the Commonwealth, 1905 to the Present* (Harrisburg, Pa.: Stackpole Books, 1977); C. A. Bayly, *Empire and Information: Intelligence Gathering and Social Communication in India, 1780–1870* (New York: Cambridge University Press, 1996); James Hevia, *The Imperial Security State: British Colonial Knowledge and Empire-Building in Asia* (New York: Cambridge University Press, 2012); Kathleen Keller, *Colonial Suspects: Suspicion, Imperial Rule, and Colonial Society in Interwar French West Africa* (Lincoln: University of Nebraska Press, 2018); Amit Prakash, *Empire on the Seine: the Policing of North Africans in Paris, 1925–1975* (New York: Oxford University Press, 2022).

27 Colin Kidd, *The Forging of Races: Race and Scripture in the Protestant Atlantic World, 1600–2000* (New York: Cambridge University Press, 2006); Marilyn Lake, *Drawing the Global Colour Line: White Men's Countries and the International Challenge of Racial Equality* (New York: Cambridge University Press, 2008); Harald Fischer-Tiné and Susanne Gehrmann, eds., *Empires and Boundaries: Rethinking Race, Class, and Gender in Colonial Settings* (Abingdon, UK: Routledge, 2009); Sathnam Sanghera, *Empireland: How Imperialism Has Shaped Modern Britain* (London: Viking, 2021).

Sexuality is the theme of very active scholarship within the larger history of empires: Ronald Hyam, *Empire and Sexuality: The British Experience* (Manchester: Manchester University Press, 1991); Chelsea Schields and Dagmar Herzog, eds., *The Routledge Companion to Sexuality and Colonialism* (London: Routledge, Taylor & Francis Group, 2021).

For the imperial history of gender, see Philippa Levine, ed., *Gender and Empire* (New York: Oxford University Press, 2004); Tracey Rizzo and Steven Gerontakis, *Intimate Empires: Body, Race, and Gender in the Modern World* (New York: Oxford University Press, 2016); Ulrike Lindner and Dörte Lerp, eds., *New Perspectives on the History of Gender and Empire: Comparative and Global Approaches* (London: Bloomsbury Academic, 2018).

28 Caroline Elkins, *Imperial Reckoning: The Untold Story of Britain's Gulag in Kenya* (London: Jonathan Cape, 2005); Robert J. Blyth and Keith Jeffery, eds., *The British Empire and Its Contested Pasts* (Dublin: Irish Academic Press, 2009); Richard Gott, *Britain's Empire: Resistance, Repression and Revolt* (London: Verso, 2011); Jon Wilson, *India Conquered: Britain's Raj and the Chaos of Empire* (New York: Simon and Schuster, 2016); Philip Dwyer and Amanda Nettelbeck, eds., *Violence, Colonialism and Empire in the Modern World* (Cham, Switzerland: Palgrave Macmillan, 2018); Priyamvada Gopal, *Insurgent Empire: Anticolonial Resistance and British Dissent* (London: Verso, 2019); Priya Satia, *Time's Monster: History, Conscience and Britain's Empire* (London: Allen Lane, 2020); Sujit Sivasundaram, *Waves across the South: A New History of Revolution and Empire* (Chicago: University of Chicago Press, 2020); Caroline Elkins, *Legacy of Violence: A History of the British Empire* (London: Penguin Random House, 2022); David Veevers, *The Great Defiance* (London: Ebury Press, 2023).

29 Walter Reid, *Empire of Sand: How Britain Made the Middle East* (Edinburgh: Birlinn, 2011); Guy Vanthemsche, *Belgium and the Congo, 1885–1980* (New York: Cambridge University Press, 2012); David van Reybrouck, *Congo: The Epic History of a People* (New York: Ecco, 2014); J. P. Daughton, *In the Forest of No Joy: The Congo-Océan Railroad and the Tragedy of French Colonialism* (New York: Norton, 2021).

30 Robert Aldrich, *Vestiges of the Colonial Empire in France: Monuments, Museums and Colonial Memories* (New York: Palgrave Macmillan, 2005); Annie Coombes, ed., *Rethinking Settler Colonialism: History and Memory in Australia, Canada, Aotearoa New Zealand and South Africa* (Manchester: Manchester University Press, 2006); Dietmar Rothermund, ed., *Memories of Post-imperial Nations: The Aftermath of Decolonization, 1945–2013* (Cambridge: Cambridge University Press, 2015); Thomas Houlton, *Monuments as Cultural and Critical Objects: From Mesolithic to Eco-queer* (New York: Routledge, 2022); Britta Timm Knudsen, John Oldfield, Elizabeth Buettner, and Elvan Zabunyan, eds., *Decolonizing Colonial Heritage: New Agendas, Actors and Practices in and beyond Europe* (Abingdon, UK: Routledge, 2022).

31 Robert Gildea, *Empires of the Mind: The Colonial Past and the Politics of the Present* (New York: Cambridge University Press, 2019); Berny Sèbe and Matthew G. Stanard, eds., *Decolonising Europe? Popular Responses to the End of Empire* (Abingdon, UK: Routledge, 2020); Charlotte Lydia

Riley, *Imperial Island: A History of Empire in Modern Britain* (London: Bodley Head, 2023). For more favorable views of empire, see, for instance, Kwarteng, *Ghosts of Empire*; Kartar Lalvani, *The Making of India: The Untold Story of British Enterprise* (London: Bloomsbury, 2016); Nigel Biggar, *Colonialism: A Moral Reckoning* (London: William Collins, 2023).

32 Louis B. Wright, *Religion and Empire: The Alliance between Piety and Commerce in English Expansion, 1558–1625* (1943; New York: Octagon Books, 1965); Brian Stanley, *The Bible and the Flag: Protestant Missions and British Imperialism in the Nineteenth and Twentieth Centuries* (Leicester: Apollos, 1990); Gerald Studdert-Kennedy, *Providence and the Raj: Imperial Mission and Missionary Imperialism* (Walnut Creek, Calif.: Altamira, 1998); David Hempton, *Methodism: Empire of the Spirit* (New Haven, Conn.: Yale University Press, 2005); Susan Thorne, "Religion and Empire at Home," in *At Home with the Empire: Metropolitan Culture and the Imperial World*, ed. Catherine Hall and Sonya O. Rose (New York: Cambridge University Press, 2006), 143–65; Hilary M. Carey, *God's Empire: Religion and Colonialism in the British World, c. 1801–1908* (New York: Cambridge University Press, 2010); Hilary M. Carey and John Gascoigne, ed., *Church and State in Old and New Worlds* (Leiden: Brill, 2011); Haig Z. Smith, *Religion and Governance in England's Emerging Colonial Empire, 1601–1698* (London: Palgrave Macmillan, 2022).

33 Katherine Carté, *Religion and the American Revolution: An Imperial History* (Williamsburg: Omohundro Institute of Early American History and Culture / University of North Carolina Press, 2021); Tisa Wenger and Sylvester A. Johnson, eds., *Religion and US Empire: Critical New Histories* (New York: New York University Press, 2022).

34 James Bryce, "Religion as a Factor in the History of Empires," *Journal of Roman Studies* 5 (1915): 1–22; John Gascoigne, "Introduction: Religion and Empire, an Historiographical Perspective," *Journal of Religious History* 32, no. 2 (2008): 159–79; Amira K. Bennison, "Empire and Religion," in Bang, Bayly, and Scheidel, *Oxford World History of Empire*, 1:318–41.

1 What Is an Empire?

1 Vergil, *Bucolics, Aeneid, and Georgics of Vergil*, ed. J. B. Greenough (Boston: Ginn, 1900), https://www.perseus.tufts.edu/hopper/text?doc=Perseus%3Atext%3A1999.02.0055%3Abook%3D6%3Acard%3D801; Dryden's translation is quoted from https://www.perseus.tufts.edu/hopper/text?doc=Perseus%3Atext%3A1999.02.0052%3Abook%3D6%3Acard%3D801.

2 Cornelius Tacitus, *De vita Iulii Agricolae*, ed. Henry Furneaux (Oxford: Clarendon Press, 1900), http://www.perseus.tufts.edu/hopper/text?doc=Perseus%3Atext%3A1999.02.0084%3Achapter%3D30%3Asection%3D6; Loveday Alexander, ed., *Images of Empire* (Sheffield, UK: Sheffield Academic Press, 1991).

3 Adrian Goldsworthy, *Pax Romana: War, Peace, and Conquest in the Roman World* (New Haven, Conn.: Yale University Press, 2016); Jan Morris, *Pax Britannica: The Climax of an Empire* (New York: Harcourt, Brace & World, 1968).

4 Bryce, "Religion as a Factor in the History of Empires," 3; Amira K. Bennison, "Empire and Religion," in Bang, Bayly, and Scheidel, *The Oxford World History of Empire*, 1:318–341; Stephen Howe, *Empire: A Very Short Introduction* (New York: Oxford University Press, 2002), 15.

5 Dominic Lieven, *In the Shadow of the Gods: The Emperor in World History* (London: Allen Lane, 2022); Olivier Hekster, *Caesar Rules: The Emperor in the Changing Roman World (c.50 BC–AD 565)* (Cambridge: Cambridge University Press, 2023).

6 Winfried Baumgart, *Imperialism: The Idea and Reality of British and French Colonial Expansion, 1880–1914* (New York: Oxford University Press, 1982); Alice L. Conklin, *A Mission to Civilize: The Republican Idea of Empire in France and West Africa, 1895–1930* (Stanford, Calif.: Stanford University Press, 1997); J. P. Daughton, *An Empire Divided: Religion, Republicanism, and the Making of French Colonialism 1880–1914* (New York: Oxford University Press, 2006). Seeley is quoted from John R. Seeley, *The Expansion of England: Two Courses of Lectures* (London: Macmillan, 1914), 89. For the Soviets, see for instance Graham Smith, ed., *The Nationalities Question in the Soviet Union*, 2nd ed. (London: Longman, 1995); Andreas Kappeler, *The Russian Empire: A Multiethnic History* (New York: Routledge, 2001).

7 Andrew C. Johnston, *The Sons of Remus: Identity in Roman Gaul and Spain* (Cambridge, Mass.: Harvard University Press, 2017).

8 Mary Beard, *SPQR: A History of Ancient Rome* (New York: Liveright, 2015).

9 Benedict Anderson, *Imagined Communities: Reflections on the Origin and Spread of Nationalism*, 2nd ed. (London: Verso, 2006).

10 Kris Manjapra, *Colonialism in Global Perspective* (New York: Cambridge University Press, 2020); Lorenzo Veracini, *Colonialism: A Global History* (New York: Routledge, 2023).

11 Turgot is quoted from J. R. Seeley, *The Expansion of England* (1883; Cambridge University Press, 2010). Caroline Elkins and Susan Pedersen, eds., *Settler Colonialism in the Twentieth Century: Projects, Practices, Legacies* (New York: Routledge, 2005); James Belich, *Replenishing the Earth: The Settler Revolution and the Rise of the Angloworld, 1780–1939* (New York: Oxford University Press, 2009); Robert Bickers, ed., *Settlers and Expatriates: Britons over the Seas*, Oxford History of the British Empire Companion Series (Oxford: Oxford University Press, 2010); Edward Cavanagh and Lorenzo Veracini, eds., *The Routledge Handbook of the History of Settler Colonialism* (Abingdon, UK: Routledge, 2017).

12 Paul Frymer, *Building an American Empire: The Era of Territorial and Political Expansion* (Princeton, N.J.: Princeton University Press, 2017); A. G. Hopkins, *American Empire: A Global History* (Princeton, N.J.: Princeton University Press, 2018); Allan Greer, *Property and Dispossession: Natives, Empires and Land in Early Modern North America* (New York: Cambridge University Press, 2018); Katharine Bjork, *Prairie Imperialists: The Indian Country Origins of American Empire* (Philadelphia: University of Pennsylvania Press, 2019); Todd Miller, *Empire of Borders: The Expansion of the US Border around the World* (London: Verso, 2019); Daniel Immerwahr, *How to Hide an Empire: A History of the Greater United States* (New York: Macmillan, 2019).

13 Kappeler, *Russian Empire*; Anthony Cross, ed., *St. Petersburg, 1703–1825* (Basingstoke: Palgrave Macmillan, 2003).

14 F. Harrison Rankin, *The White Man's Grave: A Visit to Sierra Leone, in 1834* (London: Richard Bentley, 1836).

15 John Julius Norwich, *Venice: The Rise to Empire* (London: Allen Lane, 1977).

16 Seeley, *The Expansion of England*; Gregory A. Barton, *Informal Empire and the Rise of One World Culture* (London: Palgrave Macmillan, 2014); William Dalrymple, *The Anarchy: The Relentless Rise of the East India Company* (London: Bloomsbury, 2019); Andrew Phillips and J. C. Sharman, *Outsourcing Empire: How Company-States Made the Modern World* (Princeton, N.J.: Princeton University Press, 2020); Callie Wilkinson, *Empire of Influence: The East India Company and the Making of Indirect Rule* (Cambridge: Cambridge University Press, 2023).

17 Matthew Brown, ed., *Informal Empire in Latin America: Culture, Commerce and Capital* (Oxford: Blackwell, 2008); John Fisher, *Outskirts of Empire Studies in British Power Projection* (Abingdon, UK: Routledge, 2019).

18 Rolf Strootman, Floris van den Eijnde, and Roy van Wijk, eds., *Empires of the Sea: Maritime Power Networks in World History* (Leiden: Brill, 2020).

19 Hunt, *Cities of Empire*.

20 Bang and Bayly, *Tributary Empires in Global History*.

21 Heather Streets-Salter, *Martial Races: The Military, Race, and Masculinity in British Imperial Culture, 1857–1914* (Manchester: Manchester University Press, 2004); Georg Christ, Patrick Sänger, and Mike Carr, eds., *Military Diasporas: Building of Empire in the Middle East and Europe (550 BCE–1500 CE)* (New York: Routledge, 2023).

22 Nicholas Ostler, *Empires of the Word: A Language History of the World* (New York: Harper Collins, 2010).

23 Ann McGrath and Lynette Russell, eds., *The Routledge Companion to Global Indigenous History* (Abingdon, UK: Routledge, 2022).

24 See, for instance, José Moya, ed., *Atlantic Crossroads: Webs of Migration, Culture and Politics between Europe, Africa, and the Americas, 1800–2020* (Abingdon, UK: Routledge, 2021).

25 Thomas M. Wilson and Hastings Donnan, eds., *A Companion to Border Studies* (Malden, Mass: Wiley Blackwell, 2012); Omer Bartov and Eric D. Weitz, eds., *Shatterzone of Empires: Coexistence and Violence in the German, Habsburg, Russian, and Ottoman Borderlands* (Indianapolis: Indiana University Press, 2013); Marcus Rediker, Titas Chakraborty, and Matthias van Rossum, eds., *A Global History of Runaways: Workers, Mobility, and Capitalism 1600–1850* (Oakland: University of California Press, 2019); Benjamin D. Hopkins, *Ruling the Savage Periphery: Frontier Governance and the Making of the Modern State* (Cambridge, Mass.: Harvard University Press, 2020); Farhana Ibrahim and Tanuja Kothiyal, eds., *South Asian Borderlands: Mobility, History, Affect* (New York: Cambridge University Press, 2021); James Crawford, *The Edge of the Plain: How Borders Make and Break Our World* (New York: Norton, 2022).

For maritime "borderlands," see, for instance, Christian J. Koot, *Empire at the Periphery: British Colonists, Anglo-Dutch Trade, and the Development of the British Atlantic, 1621–1713* (New York: New York University Press, 2011); Kit Candlin, *The Last Caribbean Frontier, 1795–1815* (London: Palgrave Macmillan, 2012); Karwan Fatah-Black, *White Lies and Black Markets: Evading Metropolitan Authority in Colonial Suriname, 1650–1800* (Leiden: Brill, 2015); Bram Boonhout, *Borderless Empire: Dutch Guiana in the Atlantic World, 1750–1800* (Athens: University of Georgia Press, 2020).

26 For shatter zones, see, for instance, Robbie Franklyn Ethridge and Sheri Marie Shuck-Hall, eds., *Mapping the Mississippian Shatter Zone: The Colonial Indian Slave Trade and Regional Instability in the American South* (Lincoln: University of Nebraska Press, 2009); Timothy Snyder, *Bloodlands: Europe between Hitler and Stalin* (New York: Basic Books, 2012); Alfred J. Rieber, *The Struggle for the Eurasian Borderlands from the Rise of Early Modern Empires to the End of the First World War* (New York: Cambridge University Press, 2014); Ben Raffield, "Broken Worlds: Towards an Archaeology of the Shatter Zone," *Journal of Archaeological Method and Theory* 28 (2021): 871–910.

27 The scene is quoted at "Scene 10: Before the Romans Things Were Smelly," in *Life of Brian Script, Another Bleedin' Monty Python Site*, http://montypython.50webs.com/scripts/Life_of_Brian/10.htm.

28 Peter Jackson, *The Mongols and the Islamic World; from Conquest to Conversion* (New Haven, Conn.: Yale University Press, 2017).

29 The Testament of Ardashir is quoted from Bennison, "Empire and Religion," 324; compare Abolqasem Ferdowsi, *Shahnameh: The Persian Book of Kings*, trans. Dick Davis (New York: Viking, 2006), 569. Geoffrey W. Conrad and Arthur Demarest, *Religion and Empire: The Dynamics of Aztec and Inca Expansionism* (New York: Cambridge University Press, 1984); Jiang Yonglin, *The Mandate of Heaven and the Great Ming Code*

(Seattle: University of Washington Press, 2011); Mu-chou Poo, H. A. Drake, and Lisa Raphals, eds., *Old Society, New Belief: Religious Transformation of China and Rome, ca. 1st–6th Centuries* (New York: Oxford University Press, 2017).

30 Bennison, "Empire and Religion."

31 Hugh Kennedy, *Caliphate: The History of an Idea* (New York: Basic Books, 2016).

32 Jenkins, *Great and Holy War*; Ian Campbell, *Holy War: The Untold Story of Catholic Italy's Crusade against the Ethiopian Orthodox Church* (London: Hurst, 2021).

33 Elizabeth A. Foster, *Faith in Empire: Religion, Politics, and Colonial Rule in French Senegal, 1880–1940* (Stanford, Calif.: Stanford University Press, 2013).

34 Maxim Waldstein and Sanna Turoma, eds., *Empire De/Centered: New Spatial Histories of Russia and the Soviet Union* (Abingdon, UK: Routledge, 2013); Jenkins, *Great and Holy War*; Brian Glyn Williams, *The Crimean Tatars: From Soviet Genocide to Putin's Conquest* (New York: Oxford University Press, 2016); Caryl Emerson, George Pattison, and Randall A. Poole, eds., *The Oxford Handbook of Russian Religious Thought* (New York: Oxford University Press, 2020).

35 Fritz-Heiner Mutschler and Achim Mittag, eds., *Conceiving the Empire: China and Rome Compared* (New York: Oxford University Press, 2008); Elena Muñiz Grijalvo, Juan Manuel Cortés Copete, and Fernando Lozano Gómez, eds., *Empire and Religion: Religious Change in Greek Cities under Roman Rule* (Leiden: Brill, 2017); Filippo Marsili, *Heaven Is Empty: A Cross-Cultural Approach to "Religion" and Empire in Ancient China* (Albany: State University of New York Press, 2018); Harriet I. Flower, ed., *Empire and Religion in the Roman World* (New York: Cambridge University Press, 2021).

36 Kyle Smith, *Constantine and the Captive Christians of Persia: Martyrdom and Religious Identity in Late Antiquity* (Oakland: University of California Press, 2016).

37 Bryce, "Religion as a Factor in the History of Empires"; Bennison, "Empire and Religion."

38 Roger Crowley, *Empires of the Sea: The Final Battle for the Mediterranean 1521–1580* (London: Faber, 2008).

39 Malcolm Ebright and Rick Hendricks, *The Witches of Abiquiu: The Governor, the Priest, the Genízaro Indians, and the Devil* (Albuquerque: University of New Mexico Press, 2006).

40 John M. D. Pohl and Claire L. Lyons, eds., *Altera Roma: Art and Empire from Mérida to México* (Los Angeles: Cotsen Institute of Archaeology Press, 2016); David Charles Wright-Carr and Francisco Marco Simón, eds., *From Ancient Rome to Colonial Mexico: Religious Globalization in the Context of Empire* (Denver: University Press of Colorado, 2023).

41 Andrew Fear, *Mithras* (New York: Routledge, 2022). For Greco-Buddhism, see Warwick Ball, *The Monuments of Afghanistan: History, Archaeology and Architecture* (London: I. B. Tauris, 2008).

42 "John Dee's Spirit Mirror," Collection Items, British Library, https://www.bl.uk/collection-items/john-dees-spirit-mirror; Peter J. French, *John Dee: The World of an Elizabethan Magus* (London: Routledge and Kegan Paul, 2002).

43 Philip Meadows Taylor, *Confessions of a Thug* (1839; London: Richard Bentley, 1858); Kim A. Wagner, *Thuggee: Banditry and the British in Early Nineteenth-Century India* (London: Palgrave Macmillan, 2007).

44 Gananath Obeyesekere, *Cannibal Talk: The Man-Eating Myth and Human Sacrifice in the South Seas* (Berkeley: University of California Press, 2005).

45 Percy Bysshe Shelley, "Ozymandias," https://www.poetryfoundation.org/poems/46565/ozymandias.

46 David Damrosch, *The Buried Book: The Loss and Rediscovery of the Great Epic of Gilgamesh* (New York: Henry Holt, 2007); Shawn Malley, *From Archaeology to Spectacle in Victorian Britain: The Case of Assyria, 1845–1854* (Burlington, Vt.: Ashgate, 2012).

47 Beate Pongratz-Leisten, *Religion and Ideology in Assyria* (Berlin: De Gruyter, 2015); Benjamin R. Foster, *The Age of Agade: Inventing Empire in Ancient Mesopotamia* (London: Routledge / Taylor and Francis, 2016); Lavan, Payne, and Weisweiler, *Cosmopolitanism and Empire*; Lieven, *In the Shadow of the Gods*.

48 Betty De Shong Meador, ed., *Inanna, Lady of Largest Heart: Poems of the Sumerian High Priestess Enheduanna* (Austin: University of Texas Press, 2000); Steven W. Holloway, ed., *Orientalism, Assyriology and the Bible* (Sheffield, UK: Sheffield Phoenix Press, 2007). Sargon is recalled in the Bible, in Genesis 10:8–10, which recalls his city of Agade/Akkad.

49 Karen Radner and Eleanor Robson, eds., *The Oxford Handbook of Cuneiform Culture* (New York: Oxford University Press, 2011); Eleanor Robson, *Ancient Knowledge Networks: A Social Geography of Cuneiform Scholarship in First-Millennium Assyria and Babylonia* (London: University College London Press, 2019); Eckart Frahm, *Assyria: The Rise and Fall of the World's First Empire* (New York: Basic Books, 2023).

50 Peter Heather, *The Restoration of Rome: Barbarian Popes and Imperial Pretenders* (New York: Oxford University Press, 2014); Johannes Fried, *Charlemagne* (Cambridge, Mass.: Harvard University Press, 2016); Wouter Bracke, Jan Nelis, and Jan De Maeyer, eds., *Renovatio, Inventio, Absentia Imperii: From the Roman Empire to Contemporary Imperialism* (Brussels: Academia Belgica, 2018); Joanna Story, *Charlemagne and Rome: Alcuin and the Epitaph of Pope Hadrian I* (Oxford: Oxford University Press, 2023).

51 Angold, *Eastern Christianity*; Diana Mishkova, *Rival Byzantiums: Empire and Identity in Southeastern Europe* (Cambridge: Cambridge University Press, 2023).

52 Edward Shawcross, *The Last Emperor of Mexico: A Disaster in the New World* (London: Faber, 2022).

53 Robert Aldrich and Cindy McCreery, eds., *Crowns and Colonies: European Monarchies and Overseas Empires* (Manchester: Manchester University Press, 2016); Jean Lartéguy, *The Centurions* (New York: Dutton, 1962); Lartéguy, *The Praetorians* (New York: Dutton, 1963).

54 Deborah L. Nichols and Enrique Rodríguez-Alegría, eds., *The Oxford Handbook of the Aztecs* (New York: Oxford University Press, 2017).

55 Anderson, *Imagined Communities*.

56 Ian Anderson, "Sitting Bull and the Mounties," *Wild West* 10, no. 5 (February 1998), https://www.historynet.com/sitting-bull.

2 The Kingdoms of God

1 Zvi Ben-Dor Benite, *The Ten Lost Tribes: A World History* (New York: Oxford University Press, 2009); Giovanni B. Lanfranchi and Simo Parpola, eds., *Correspondence of Sargon II* (Winona Lake, Ind.: Eisenbrauns, 2014); Josette Elayi, *Sargon II, King of Assyria* (Atlanta: SBL Press, 2017); Frahm, *Assyria*.

2 Leo G. Perdue and Warren Carter, *Israel and Empire: A Postcolonial History of Israel and Early Judaism*, ed. Coleman A. Baker (London: Bloomsbury T&T Clark, 2015); Martin Goodman, *A History of Judaism* (Princeton, N.J.: Princeton University Press, 2018).

3 Richard Elliott Friedman, *The Exodus* (San Francisco: HarperOne, 2017).

4 These figures about word occurrence are derived from the New International Version, https://www.biblegateway.com/. Craig W. Tyson and Virginia R. Herrmann, eds., *Imperial Peripheries in the Neo-Assyrian Period* (Louisville: University Press of Colorado, 2018).

5 Holloway, *Orientalism, Assyriology and the Bible*; Malley, *From Archaeology to Spectacle in Victorian Britain*; Agnès Garcia-Ventura and Lorenzo Verderame, eds., *Perspectives on the History of Ancient Near Eastern Studies* (University Park, Pa.: Eisenbrauns, 2020). Jan Christian Gertz, Angelika Berlejung, Konrad Schmid, and Markus Witte. eds., *T&T Clark Handbook of the Old Testament: An Introduction to the Literature, Religion and History of the Old Testament* (London: T&T Clark, 2012).

6 W. D. Davies and Louis Finkelstein, eds., *Introduction: The Persian Period*, vol. 1 of *The Cambridge History of Judaism* (New York: Cambridge University Press, 1984); Philip Jenkins, *Crucible of Faith: The Ancient Revolution That Made Our Modern Religious World* (New York: Basic Books, 2017); Yonatan Adler, *The Origins of Judaism: An Archaeological-Historical Reappraisal* (New Haven, Conn.: Yale University Press, 2022).

7 "Let us make Man" is from Genesis 1:26. Mark S. Smith, *The Early History of God: Yahweh and the Other Deities in Ancient Israel* (Grand Rapids: Eerdmans, 2002); Mark S. Smith, *The Origins of Biblical Monotheism: Israel's Polytheistic Background and the Ugaritic Texts*, new ed. (New York: Oxford University Press, 2003); Francesca Stavrakopoulou and John Barton, eds., *Religious Diversity in Ancient Israel and Judah* (New York: Continuum, 2010); Thomas Römer, *The Invention of God* (Cambridge, Mass.: Harvard University Press, 2015); Jenkins, *Crucible of Faith.*

8 C. L. Crouch, *Israel and the Assyrians: Deuteronomy, the Succession Treaty of Esarhaddon, and the Nature of Subversion* (Atlanta: SBL Press, 2014).

9 Jenkins, *Crucible of Faith.*

10 Baruch Halpern, *From Gods to God*, ed. M. J. Adams (Tübingen: Mohr Siebeck, 2009).

11 Matt Waters, *Ancient Persia: A Concise History of the Achaemenid Empire, 550–330 BCE* (New York: Cambridge University Press, 2014); Jonathan Stökl and Caroline Waerzeggers, eds., *Exile and Return* (Boston: De Gruyter, 2015); Matt Waters, *King of the World: The Life of Cyrus the Great* (Oxford: Oxford University Press, 2022).

12 Isaiah 14:12–17; Jenkins, *Crucible of Faith*; Frahm, *Assyria.*

13 Timothy H. Lim, *The Formation of the Jewish Canon* (New Haven, Conn.: Yale University Press, 2013).

14 David J. Shepherd and Christopher J. H. Wright, *Ezra and Nehemiah* (Grand Rapids: Eerdmans, 2018); Lloyd Llewellyn-Jones, *Persians: The Age of the Great Kings* (New York: Basic Books, 2022).

15 Jenkins, *Crucible of Faith.*

16 Shaul Shaked, "Iranian Influence on Judaism," in Davies and Finkelstein, *Introduction: The Persian Period*, 308–25.

17 F. W. Walbank et al., eds., *The Cambridge Ancient History*, vol. 7, pt. 1, *The Hellenistic World*, 2nd ed. (New York: Cambridge University Press, 1984); Edward M. Anson, *Alexander's Heirs: The Age of the Successors* (Malden, Mass: Wiley-Blackwell, 2014); Hans Hauben and Alexander Meeus, eds., *The Age of the Successors and the Creation of the Hellenistic Kingdoms (323–276 B.C.)* (Leuven: Peeters, 2014); Paul J. Kosmin, *The Land of the Elephant Kings* (Cambridge, Mass.: Harvard University Press, 2014); Ian Worthington, *Ptolemy I: King and Pharaoh of Egypt* (New York: Oxford University Press, 2016).

18 W. D. Davies and Louis Finkelstein, eds., *The Hellenistic Age*, vol. 2 of *The Cambridge History of Judaism* (New York: Cambridge University Press, 1990); Günther Hölbl, *A History of the Ptolemaic Empire* (New York: Routledge, 2001); Justin Pollard and Howard Reid, *The Rise and Fall of Alexandria* (New York: Penguin Books, 2007).

19 M. Dandamayev, "The Diaspora," in Davies and Finkelstein, *Introduction: The Persian Period*, 326–400; Harald Hegermann, "The Diaspora in the

Hellenistic Age," in Davies and Finkelstein, *The Hellenistic Age*, 115–66; Erich S. Gruen, *Diaspora: Jews amidst Greeks and Romans* (Cambridge, Mass.: Harvard University Press, 2002); John R. Bartlett, ed., *Jews in the Hellenistic and Roman Cities* (New York: Routledge, 2002); Shai Secunda, *The Iranian Talmud: Reading the Bavli in Its Sasanian Context* (Philadelphia: University of Pennsylvania Press, 2014).

20 Glenn R. Bugh, ed., *The Cambridge Companion to the Hellenistic World* (New York: Cambridge University Press, 2006); Graham Shipley, *The Greek World after Alexander* (New York: Routledge, 2000); Peter Thonemann, *The Hellenistic Age* (New York: Oxford University Press, 2016); Lavan, Payne, and Weisweiler, *Cosmopolitanism and Empire*.

21 Jenkins, *Crucible of Faith*.

22 John J. Collins and J. G. Manning, eds., *Revolt and Resistance in the Ancient Classical World and the Near East: In the Crucible of Empire* (Leiden: Brill, 2016); Jenkins, *Crucible of Faith*.

23 William Horbury, W. D. Davies, and John Sturdy, eds., *The Early Roman Period*, vol. 3 of *The Cambridge History of Judaism* (New York: Cambridge University Press, 1999); Alexander, *Images of Empire*; Jerry L. Walls, ed., *The Oxford Handbook of Eschatology* (New York: Oxford University Press, 2008).

24 Steven T. Katz, ed., *The Late Roman-Rabbinic Period*, vol. 4 of *The Cambridge History of Judaism* (New York: Cambridge University Press, 2006); Adrian Goldsworthy, *Rome and Persia: The Seven Hundred Year Rivalry* (New York: Basic Books, 2023).

25 Charlotte Elisheva Fonrobert and Martin S. Jaffee, eds., *The Cambridge Companion to the Talmud and Rabbinic Literature* (New York: Cambridge University Press, 2007); Seth Schwartz, *The Ancient Jews from Alexander to Muhammad* (New York: Cambridge University Press, 2014); Moulie Vidas, *Tradition and the Formation of the Talmud* (Princeton, N.J.: Princeton University Press, 2014); Goodman, *History of Judaism*.

26 "A decree went out" is from Luke 2:1.

27 E. Badian, *Publicans and Sinners: Private Enterprise in the Service of the Roman Republic* (Ithaca, N.Y.: Cornell University Press, 1972).

28 Another possible word for "emperor" (as opposed to "king") is *sebastos*, which occurs in Acts, with specific reference to Augustus: "σεβαστός," *Blue Letter Bible*, https://www.blueletterbible.org/lexicon/g4575/kjv/tr/0-1/. For *basileia*, see "Basileia," *Bible Hub*, https://biblehub.com/greek/932.htm.

29 For the coin story, see Matthew 22:15–22; Mark 12:13–17; Luke 20:20–26.

30 Revelation 13; 17:9, for the interpretation of the seven heads. But see also Drew W. Billings, *Acts of the Apostles and the Rhetoric of Roman Imperialism* (Cambridge: Cambridge University Press, 2017).

3 Making Christianity

1 Rudyard Kipling, "The Church That Was at Antioch," in *Limits and Renewals* (London: Penguin Classics, 1987).

2 Margaret M. Mitchell and Frances M. Young, eds., *Origins to Constantine*, vol. 1 of *The Cambridge History of Christianity* (New York: Cambridge University Press, 2006); Jaś Elsner, ed., *Empires of Faith in Late Antiquity: Histories of Art and Religion from India to Ireland* (New York: Cambridge University Press, 2020).

3 Andrea U. De Giorgi and Asa Eger, *Antioch: A History* (New York: Routledge, 2021).

4 Philip Jenkins, *The Many Faces of Christ: The Thousand-Year Story of the Survival and Influence of the Lost Gospels* (New York: Basic Books, 2015).

5 Steven J. Friesen, Daniel N. Schowalter, and James C. Walters, eds., *Corinth in Context: Comparative Studies on Religion and Society* (Leiden: Brill, 2010); Robin Waterfield, *Taken at the Flood: The Roman Conquest of Greece* (New York: Oxford University Press, 2014).

6 Acts 18:15; Rudyard Kipling, "Gallio's Song," *Poetry Lovers Page*, https://www.poetryloverspage.com/poets/kipling/gallios_song.html.

7 Jenkins, *Many Faces of Christ*.

8 Robin Lane Fox, *Pagans and Christians* (San Francisco: HarperSanFrancisco, 1986), 274–75; Marietta Horster and Nikolas Hächler, *The Impact of the Roman Empire on Landscapes: Proceedings of the Fourteenth Workshop of the International Network Impact of Empire (Mainz, June 12–15, 2019)* (Leiden: Brill, 2022).

9 Leonard A. Curchin, *Roman Spain: Conquest and Assimilation* (New York: Routledge, 1991); Pieter Houten, *Urbanisation in Roman Spain and Portugal: Civitates Hispaniae in the Early Empire* (Abingdon, UK: Routledge, 2021).

10 Philip Jenkins, *Jesus Wars: How Four Patriarchs, Three Queens, and Two Emperors Decided What Christians Would Believe for the Next 1,500 Years* (San Francisco: HarperOne, 2010).

11 Sarah Bassett, ed., *The Cambridge Companion to Constantinople* (Cambridge: Cambridge University Press, 2022); Philip Jenkins, *A Storm of Images: Iconoclasm and Religious Reformation in the Byzantine World* (Waco, Tex.: Baylor University Press, 2023).

12 Augustine Casiday and Frederick W. Norris, eds., *Constantine to c.600*, vol. 2 of *The Cambridge History of Christianity* (New York: Cambridge University Press, 2007); Flower, *Empire and Religion in the Roman World*.

13 Virginia Burrus, *The Making of a Heretic: Gender, Authority, and the Priscillianist Controversy* (Berkeley: University of California, 1995); Peter Heather, *Christendom: The Triumph of a Religion, AD 300–1300* (New York: Alfred A. Knopf, 2023).

14 Jenkins, *Jesus Wars*; Fried, *Charlemagne*.
15 W. H. C. Frend, *The Rise of Christianity* (Philadelphia: Fortress, 1984); Peter Brown, *The Rise of Western Christendom: Triumph and Diversity, A.D. 200–1000* (Malden, Mass.: Blackwell, 2003); Lamin Sanneh, *Disciples of All Nations: Pillars of World Christianity* (New York: Oxford University Press, 2007); Casiday and Norris, *Constantine to c.600*; Diarmaid MacCulloch, *Christianity: The First Three Thousand Years* (New York: Viking, 2010); Sarris, *Empires of Faith*.
16 Thomas F. X. Noble and Julia M. H. Smith, eds., *Early Medieval Christianities, c.600–c.1100*, vol. 3 of *The Cambridge History of Christianity* (New York: Cambridge University Press, 2008).
17 Peter Brown, *The Rise of Western Christendom*; Sanneh, *Disciples of All Nations*; MacCulloch, *Christianity*.
18 Chris Wickham, *Framing the Early Middle Ages: Europe and the Mediterranean 400–800* (Oxford: Oxford University Press, 2005).
19 Heather, *Restoration of Rome*; Rosamond McKitterick, *Rome and the Invention of the Papacy: The "Liber Pontificalis"* (Cambridge: Cambridge University Press, 2020); Maya Maskarinec, *City of Saints: Rebuilding Rome in the Early Middle Ages* (Philadelphia: University of Pennsylvania Press, 2022). For Augustine, see J. E. Merdinger, *Rome and the African Church in the Time of Augustine* (New Haven, Conn.: Yale University Press, 1997).
20 "Diocese," *Catholic Encyclopedia*, https://www.newadvent.org/cathen/05001a.htm.
21 Jenkins, *Storm of Images*.
22 John Milton, "On the Morning of Christ's Nativity," Poetry Foundation, https://www.poetryfoundation.org/poems/44735/on-the-morning-of-christs-nativity. For Persia, see Ehsan Yarshater, ed., *The Cambridge History of Iran*, vol. 3, *The Seleucid, Parthian and Sasanid Periods* (New York: Cambridge University Press, 1983); D. T. Potts, ed., *The Oxford Handbook of Ancient Iran* (New York: Oxford University Press, 2013); Lavan, Payne, and Weisweiler, *Cosmopolitanism and Empire*.
23 Martin Sprengling, *Third Century Iran, Sapor and Kartir* (Chicago: Oriental Institute, 1953); Michael Stausberg and Yuhan Sohrab-Dinshaw Vevaina, eds., *The Wiley Blackwell Companion to Zoroastrianism* (Hoboken, N.J.: John Wiley & Sons, 2015). Kartir's inscription can be found at "Kartir KZ," Avesta—Zoroastrian Archives, http://www.avesta.org/mp/kz.html.
24 D. T. Potts, *Mesopotamia, Iran and Arabia from the Seleucids to the Sasanians* (Farnham: Ashgate Variorum, 2010).
25 Peter Brown, *Rise of Western Christendom*; Philip Jenkins, *The Lost History of Christianity: The Thousand-Year Golden Age of the Church in the*

Middle East, Africa, and Asia—and How It Died (San Francisco: HarperOne, 2008); *Sources for the History of the School of Nisibis*, trans. Adam H. Becker (Liverpool: Liverpool University Press, 2008).

26 Craig Benjamin, ed., *The Cambridge World History*, vol. 4, *A World with States, Empires and Networks 1200 BCE–900 CE* (New York: Cambridge University Press, 2015); Eberhard W. Sauer, ed., *Sasanian Persia: Between Rome and the Steppes of Eurasia* (Edinburgh: Edinburgh University Press, 2017); Michael Bonner, *The Last Empire of Iran* (New York: Gorgias Press, 2020).

27 Michael H. Dodgeon and Samuel N. C. Lieu, eds., *The Roman Eastern Frontier and the Persian Wars AD 226–363: A Documentary History* (Abingdon, UK: Routledge, 2002); Geoffrey Greatrex and Samuel N. C. Lieu, *The Roman Eastern Frontier and the Persian Wars AD 363–628* (Abingdon, UK: Routledge, 2005); and Beate Dignas and Engelbert Winter, *Rome and Persia in Late Antiquity: Neighbours and Rivals* (New York: Cambridge University Press, 2007).

28 Jenkins, *The Many Faces of Christ*; James Howard-Johnston, *The Last Great War of Antiquity* (New York: Oxford University Press, 2021).

29 Christoph Baumer, *The Church of the East* (New York: I. B. Tauris, 2006); Jenkins, *Lost History*; Kyle Smith, *Constantine and the Captive Christians of Persia.*

30 Jes Peter Asmussen, "Christians in Iran," in Yarshater, *The Cambridge History of Iran*, 924–48; Richard E. Payne, *A State of Mixture Christians, Zoroastrians, and Iranian Political Culture in Late Antiquity* (Oakland: University of California Press, 2015).

31 S. Frederick Starr, *Lost Enlightenment: Central Asia's Golden Age from the Arab Conquest to Tamerlane* (Princeton, N.J.: Princeton University Press, 2013); Peter Frankopan, *The Silk Roads: A New History of the World* (London: Bloomsbury, 2015); Susan Whitfield, *Life along the Silk Road*, 2nd ed. (University of California Press, 2015); Valerie Hansen, *The Silk Road: A New History* (New York: Oxford University Press, 2016); Raoul McLaughlin, *The Roman Empire and the Silk Routes: The Ancient World Economy and the Empires of Parthia, Central Asia and Han China* (Barnsley, South Yorkshire: Pen & Sword History, 2016); Khodadad Rezakhani, *ReOrienting the Sasanians: East Iran in Late Antiquity* (Edinburgh: Edinburgh University Press, 2017); Poo, Drake, and Raphals, *Old Society, New Belief*; Hyun Jin Kim, Frederik Juliaan Vervaet, and Selim Ferruh Adalı, eds., *Eurasian Empires in Antiquity and the Early Middle Ages: Contact and Exchange between the Graeco-Roman World, Inner Asia and China* (New York: Cambridge University Press, 2017); Susan Whitfield, *Silk, Slaves, and Stupas: Material Culture of the Silk Road* (Oakland: University of California Press, 2018); Nicola Di Cosmo and Michael Maas, eds., *Empires and Exchanges in*

Eurasian Late Antiquity: Rome, China, Iran, and the Steppe (Cambridge: Cambridge University Press, 2018); Craig Benjamin, *Empires of Ancient Eurasia: The First Silk Roads Era, 100 BCE–250 CE* (New York: Cambridge University Press, 2018).

32 Daniel King, ed., *The Syriac World* (New York: Routledge, 2019).

33 Wolfram Gajetzki, *Greeks and Parthians in Mesopotamia and Beyond* (London: Bristol Classical Press, 2011); Jenkins, *The Many Faces of Christ*; Jenkins, *Crucible of Faith*; Iain Gardner, *The Founder of Manichaeism* (Cambridge: Cambridge University Press, 2020).

34 Ferdowsi, *Shahnameh.*

35 Jenkins, *Lost History*; Nathanael J. Andrade, *The Journey of Christianity to India in Late Antiquity: Networks and the Movement of Culture* (Cambridge: Cambridge University Press, 2018).

36 Jenkins, *Crucible of Faith.*

4 The Light of Asia

1 Ven. S. Dhammika, "The Edicts of King Ashoka," *The Wheel*, publication no. 386/387 (1993), https://www.cs.colostate.edu/~malaiya/ashoka.html.

2 Marijke J. Klokke and Veronique Degroot, eds., *Materializing Southeast Asia's Past: Selected Papers from the 12th International Conference of the European Association of Southeast Asian Archaeologists*, vol. 2 (Singapore: NUS Press, 2013); Marion Dolan, *Decoding Astronomy in Art and Architecture* (Cham, Switzerland: Springer International, 2021).

3 John N. Miksic and Geok Yian Goh, *Ancient Southeast Asia* (London: Routledge, 2017).

4 Donald W. Mitchell and Sarah H. Jacoby, *Buddhism: Introducing the Buddhist Experience*, 3rd ed. (New York: Oxford University Press, 2013); John S. Strong, *Buddhisms: An Introduction* (London: Oneworld, 2015).

5 For the origins of Pali, see Valerie J. Roebuck, ed., *The Dhammapada* (London: Penguin Classics, 2010); Kenneth Roy Norman, *Pali Literature* (Wiesbaden: Otto Harrassowitz, 1983); Johannes Bronkhorst, *Greater Magadha: Studies in the Culture of Early India* (Leiden: Brill, 2007).

6 Burjor Avari, *India, the Ancient Past: A History of the Indian Subcontinent from c. 7000 BC to AD 1200* (New York: Routledge, 2007); Irfan Habib and Vivekanand Jha, *Mauryan India* (New Delhi: Tulika Books, 2015); Benjamin, *The Cambridge World History*; Richard Stoneman, *Megasthenes' Indica: A New Translation of the Fragments with Commentary* (London: Routledge / Taylor & Francis Group, 2021); Hermann Kulke and Bhairabi Prasad Sahu, eds., *The Routledge Handbook of the State in Premodern India* (New York: Routledge / Taylor & Francis Group, 2022); Xinru Liu, *Early Buddhist Society: The World of Gautama Buddha* (Albany: State University of New York Press, 2022).

7 Habib and Jha, *Mauryan India.*

8 G. Srinivasa Murti and A. N. Krishna Aiyangar, eds., *Edicts of Aśoka (Priyadarśin) with English Translation*, 2nd ed. ([Adyar]: Adyar Library, 1951); Patrick Olivelle, Janice Leoshko, and Himanshu Prabha Ray, eds., *Reimagining Aśoka: Memory and History* (New Delhi: Oxford University Press, 2012); Nayanjot Lahiri, *Ashoka in Ancient India* (Cambridge, Mass.: Harvard University Press, 2015); Colleen Taylor Sen, *Ashoka and the Maura Dynasty: The History and Legacy of Ancient India's Greatest Empire* (London: Reaktion Books, 2022).

9 Romila Thapar, *Asoka and the Decline of the Mauryas*, 3rd ed. (New York: Oxford University Press, 2012).

10 Frederick M. Asher, *Sarnath: A Critical History of the Place Where Buddhism Began* (Los Angeles: Getty Research Institute, 2020); Birendra Nath Prasad, *Rethinking Bihar and Bengal: History, Culture and Religion* (Abingdon, UK: Routledge, 2021).

11 Madeleine Hallade, *Gandharan Art of North India* (New York: H. N. Abrams, 1968); Pia Brancaccio and Kurt Behrendt, eds., *Gandharan Buddhism: Archaeology, Art and Texts* (Vancouver: University of British Columbia Press, 2006); Xinru Liu, *The Silk Road in World History* (New York: Oxford University Press, 2010); Benjamin, *Empires of Ancient Eurasia*.

12 Hirakawa Akira, *A History of Indian Buddhism: From Śākyamuni to Early Mahāyāna* (Honolulu: University of Hawai'i Press, 1990); Johan Elverskog, *Buddhism and Islam on the Silk Road* (Philadelphia: University of Pennsylvania Press, 2010); Ladislav Stančo, *Greek Gods in the East: Hellenistic Iconographic Schemes in Central Asia* (Prague: Charles University in Prague / Karolinum Press, 2012); Dorothy C. Wong and Gustav Heldt, eds., *China and beyond in the Mediaeval Period: Cultural Crossings and Inter-regional Connections* (New Delhi: Manohar; Amherst, N.Y.: Cambria Press, 2014); Frankopan, *The Silk Roads*; Whitfield, *Life along the Silk Road*; Hansen, *The Silk Road*; McLaughlin, *The Roman Empire and the Silk Routes*; Poo, Drake, and Raphals, *Old Society, New Belief*; Kim, Vervaet, and Adalı, *Eurasian Empires in Antiquity and the Early Middle Ages*; Whitfield, *Silk, Slaves, and Stupas*; Benjamin, *Empires of Ancient Eurasia*.

13 Richard Foltz, *Religions of the Silk Road: Premodern Patterns of Globalization*, 2nd ed. (London: Palgrave MacMillan, 2010); Jason Neelis, *Early Buddhist Transmission and Trade Networks: Mobility and Exchange within and beyond the Northwestern Borderlands of South Asia* (Leiden: Brill, 2011); T. H. Barrett, "Translation and Transmission of Buddhist Texts" (2019), Discovering Sacred Texts, British Library, https://www.bl.uk/sacred-texts/articles/translation-and-transmission-of-buddhism.

14 Kulke and Sahu, *The Routledge Handbook of the State in Premodern India*; Anne R. Bromberg, Frederick M. Asher, Catherine B. Asher, Nancy Tingley, and Robert Warren Clark, *The Arts of India, Southeast*

Asia, and the Himalayas: At the Dallas Museum of Art (Dallas: Dallas Museum of Art; distributed by Yale University Press, 2013).

15 James Legge, ed., *A Record of Buddhistic Kingdoms: Being an Account by the Chinese Monk Fâ-Hien of His Travels in India and Ceylon (A.D. 399–414) in Search of the Buddhist Books of Discipline Translated and Annotated with a Corean Recension of the Chinese Text* (New York: Dover, 1991); Walter Spink, *Ajanta: History and Development; Defining Features* (Leiden: Koninklijke Brill, 2014); Nishant Tiwary, *Celebrating Bihar: The Heritage of Nalanda* (New Delhi: Oxford University Press, 2014); Pintu Kumar, *Buddhist Learning in South Asia: Education, Religion, and Culture at the Ancient Śrī Nālandā Mahāvihāra* (Lanham, Md.: Lexington Books, 2018).

16 John Keay, *The Spice Route: A History* (London: John Murray, 2005); Elverskog, *Buddhism and Islam on the Silk Road*; Frankopan, *The Silk Roads*; Hansen, *The Silk Road*; Serena Autiero and Matthew Adam Cobb, eds., *Globalization and Transculturality from Antiquity to the Premodern World* (Abingdon, UK: Routledge, 2023).

17 Barbara Kaim and Maja Kornacka, "Religious Landscape of the Ancient Merv Oasis," *Iran: Journal of the British Institute of Persian Studies* 54 (2016): 47–72; Di Cosmo and Maas, *Empires and Exchanges in Eurasian Late Antiquity*.

18 Jeffrey L. Broughton, *The Bodhidharma Anthology: The Earliest Records of Zen* (Berkeley: University of California Press, 1999); Andy Ferguson, *Tracking Bodhidharma: A Journey to the Heart of Chinese Culture* (Berkeley, Calif.: Counterpoint, 2012); Wong and Heldt, *China and beyond in the Mediaeval Period*; Tansen Sen, *Buddhism, Diplomacy, and Trade: The Realignment of India-China Relations, 600–1400* (Lanham, Md.: Rowman & Littlefield, 2015).

19 Red Pine, *The Heart Sutra: The Womb of Buddhas* (Washington, DC: Shoemaker & Hoard, 2004).

20 Andrea Acri, *Esoteric Buddhism in Mediaeval Maritime Asia: Networks of Masters, Texts, Icons* (Honolulu: University of Hawai'i Press, 2016); Jan Westerhoff, *The Golden Age of Indian Buddhist Philosophy* (New York: Oxford University Press, 2018); Andrea Acri and Paolo E. Rosati, eds., *Tantra, Magic, and Vernacular Religions in Monsoon Asia: Texts, Practices, and Practitioners from the Margins* (New York: Routledge, 2023).

21 János Harmatta, B. N. Puri, and G. F. Etemadi, eds., *History of Civilizations of Central Asia: The Development of Sedentary and Nomadic Civilizations; 700 B.C. to A.D. 250* (UNESCO, 1994).

22 Amy McNair, *Donors of Longmen: Faith, Politics, and Patronage in Medieval Chinese Buddhist Sculpture* (Honolulu: University of Hawai'i Press, 2007).

23 D. Christian Lammerts, ed., *Buddhist Dynamics in Premodern and Early Modern Southeast Asia* (Singapore: Institute of Southeast Asian Studies ISEAS, 2015); Acri, *Esoteric Buddhism in Mediaeval Maritime Asia*; Himanshu Prabha Ray, *Coastal Shrines and Transnational Maritime Networks across India and Southeast Asia* (New York: Routledge, 2021); Andrea Acri and Peter Sharrock, eds., *The Creative South: Buddhist and Hindu Art in Mediaeval Maritime Asia*, vol. 1 (Singapore: Institute of Southeast Asian Studies ISEAS—Yusof Ishak Institute, 2022); Acri and Rosati, *Tantra, Magic, and Vernacular Religions in Monsoon Asia*.

24 Takeshi Kobayashi, *Nara Buddhist Art, Todai-ji* (New York: Weatherhill, 1975); Roger Des Forges and John S. Major, *The Asian World, 600–1500* (New York: Oxford University Press, 2005).

25 Andrea Acri, Helen Creese, and Arlo Griffiths, eds., *From Lanka Eastwards: The Ramayana in the Literature and Visual Arts of Indonesia* (Leiden: KITLV Press, 2011); Eric Tagliacozzo, *In Asian Waters: Oceanic Worlds from Yemen to Yokohama* (Princeton, N.J.: Princeton University Press, 2022).

26 Regina Krahl, John Guy, Julian Raby, J. Keith Wilson, eds., *Shipwrecked: Tang Treasures and Monsoon Winds* (Washington, DC: Arthur M. Sackler Gallery, Smithsonian Institution 2010).

27 O. W. Wolters, *The Fall of Śrīvijaya in Malay History* (Ithaca, N.Y.: Cornell University Press, 1970); Kenneth R. Hall, *A History of Early Southeast Asia: Maritime Trade and Societal Development, 100–1500* (Lanham, Md.: Rowman & Littlefield, 2011).

28 Christopher I. Beckwith, *The Tibetan Empire in Central Asia: A History of the Struggle for Great Power among Tibetans, Turks, Arabs, and Chinese during the Early Middle Ages* (Princeton, N.J.: Princeton University Press, 1987); Michael Walter, *Buddhism and Empire: The Political and Religious Culture of Early Tibet* (Leiden: Brill, 2009); Brenton Sullivan, *Building a Religious Empire: Tibetan Buddhism, Bureaucracy, and the Rise of the Gelukpa* (Philadelphia: University of Pennsylvania Press, 2020).

29 Sally Hovey Wriggins, *Xuanzang: A Buddhist Pilgrim on the Silk Road* (Boulder, Colo.: Westview Press, 1996).

30 Philip Jenkins, *Climate, Catastrophe, and Faith: How Changes in Climate Drive Religious Upheaval* (New York: Oxford University Press, 2021); Peter Frankopan, *The Earth Transformed: An Untold History* (London: Bloomsbury, 2023), 229–56.

31 Mandakranta Bose, ed., *The Oxford History of Hinduism: The Goddess* (New York: Oxford University Press, 2018).

32 Natalia Isayeva, *Shankara and Indian Philosophy* (Albany: State University of New York Press, 1993); R. Ramachandran, *A History of Hinduism: The Past, Present, and Future* (New Delhi: Sage India, 2018).

33 James Heitzman, *Gifts of Power: Lordship in an Early Indian State* (Delhi: Oxford University Press, 1997); Charles Allen, *Coromandel: A Personal History of South India* (New York: Little, Brown, 2018); Anirudh Kanisetti, *Lords of the Deccan: Southern India from the Chalukyas to the Cholas* (New Delhi: Juggernaut, 2022).
34 Allen, *Coromandel.*
35 Paul Dundas, *The Jains*, 2nd ed. (New York: Routledge 2002).
36 G. Coedes, *The Indianized States of Southeast Asia*, ed. Walter F. Vella (Canberra, A.C.T.: Australian National University Press, 1975); Masselos, *The Great Empires of Asia*; Hall, *A History of Early Southeast Asia*; Miksic and Goh, *Ancient Southeast Asia*; C. F. W. Higham and Nam C. Kim, eds., *The Oxford Handbook of Early Southeast Asia* (New York: Oxford University Press, 2022).
37 Romila Thapar, *Somanatha: The Many Voices of a History* (London: Verso, 2005); Starr, *Lost Enlightenment*; Richard M. Eaton, *India in the Persianate Age, 1000–1765* (Oakland: University of California Press, 2019); A. C. S. Peacock and Richard Piran McClary, eds., *Turkish History and Culture in India: Identity, Art and Transregional Connections* (Leiden: Brill, 2020).
38 Marc S. Abramson, *Ethnic Identity in Tang China* (Philadelphia: University of Pennsylvania Press, 2008).
39 Michael Aung-Thwin, *Pagan: The Origins of Modern Burma* (Honolulu: University of Hawai'i Press, 1985); Goh Geok Yian, John N. Miksic, and Michael Aung-Thwin, eds., *Bagan and the World: Early Myanmar and Its Global Connections* (Singapore: ISEAS Yusof Ishak Institute, 2018).

5 Persuading to Faith

1 Joyce E. Salisbury, *The Blood of Martyrs: The Impact and Memory of Ancient Violence* (London: Taylor & Francis, 2004).
2 Elizabeth Nash, *Seville, Córdoba, and Granada: A Cultural History* (New York: Oxford University Press, 2005).
3 Throughout this chapter I have used Michael Cook, ed., *The New Cambridge History of Islam*, 6 vols. (New York: Cambridge University Press, 2010).
4 For charges of Islamic intolerance, see Philip Jenkins, *God's Continent: Christianity, Islam and Europe's Religious Crisis* (New York: Oxford University Press, 2007).
5 Malise Ruthven, *Islam in the World*, 3rd ed. (New York: Oxford University Press, 2006).
6 Amira K. Bennison, *The Great Caliphs: The Golden Age of the 'Abbasid Empire* (New Haven, Conn.: Yale University Press, 2009); Tayeb El-Hibri, *The Abbasid Caliphate: A History* (New York: Cambridge University Press, 2021); Hugh Kennedy, *The Prophet and the Age of the*

Caliphates: The Islamic Near East from the Sixth to the Eleventh Century, 4th ed. (New York: Routledge, 2022).

7 Carl F. Petry, ed., *The Cambridge History of Egypt*, vol. 1, *640–1517* (New York: Cambridge University Press, 1998); Michael Brett, *The Fatimid Empire* (Edinburgh: Edinburgh University Press, 2017); Glaire D. Anderson, Corisande Fenwick, and Mariam Rosser-Owen, with Sihem Lamine, eds., *The Aghlabids and Their Neighbours: Art and Material Culture in Ninth-Century North Africa* (Boston: Brill, 2018); K. D'Hulster, G. Schallenbergh, and J. Van Steenbergen, eds., *Egypt and Syria in the Fatimid, Ayyubid and Mamluk Eras: IX, Proceedings of the 23rd and 24th International Colloquium Organized at the University of Leuven in May 2015 and 2016* (Leuven: Peeters, 2019); Jo Van Steenbergen, *A History of the Islamic World, 600–1800: Empire, Dynastic Formations, and Heterogeneities in Pre-modern Islamic West-Asia* (New York: Routledge / Taylor & Francis Group, 2021); Carl F. Petry, *The Mamluk Sultanate: A History* (New York: Cambridge University Press, 2022).

8 Qur'an 2:256.

9 Anver M. Emon, *Religious Pluralism in Islamic Law: Dhimmis and Others in the Empire of Law* (New York: Oxford University Press, 2012); John Andrew Morrow, *The Covenants of the Prophet Muhammad with the Christians of the World* (Tacoma, Wash.: Angelico Press / Sophia Perennis, 2013); Arietta Papaconstantinou, with Neil McLynn and Daniel L. Schwartz, eds., *Conversion in Late Antiquity: Christianity, Islam, and Beyond; Papers from the Andrew W. Mellon Foundation Sawyer Seminar, University of Oxford, 2009–2010* (Burlington, Vt.: Ashgate, 2015).

10 Shaul Shaked, *From Zoroastrian Iran to Islam: Studies in Religious History and Intercultural Contacts* (Brookfield, Vt.: Variorum, 1995); Jenny Rose, *Zoroastrianism: An Introduction* (London: I. B. Tauris, 2011); Stausberg and Sohrab-Dinshaw Vevaina, *The Wiley Blackwell Companion to Zoroastrianism*.

11 Jenkins, *Lost History*; Christophe Picard, *Sea of the Caliphs: The Mediterranean in the Medieval Islamic World* (Cambridge, Mass.: Belknap Press of Harvard University Press, 2018).

12 Starr, *Lost Enlightenment*.

13 Miri Rubin and Walter Simons, eds., *Christianity in Western Europe, c.1100–c.1500*, vol. 4 of *The Cambridge History of Christianity* (New York: Cambridge University Press, 2009); A. S. Tritton, *The Caliphs and Their Non-Muslim Subjects: A Critical Study of the Covenant of 'Umar* (London: Routledge, 2008); Mercedes García-Arenal and Yonatan Glazer-Eytan, eds., *Forced Conversion in Christianity, Judaism and Islam: Coercion and Faith in Premodern Iberia and Beyond* (Leiden: Brill, 2020); Jenkins, *Storm of Images*.

14 A. C. S. Peacock, ed., *Islamisation: Comparative Perspectives from History* (Edinburgh: Edinburgh University Press, 2017); Claire Norton, *Conversion and Islam in the Early Modern Mediterranean: The Lure of the Other* (New York: Routledge, 2017).

15 Chase F. Robinson, *The Formation of the Islamic World, Sixth to Eleventh Centuries*, in Cook, *The New Cambridge History of Islam*; Michael Greenhalgh, *Constantinople to Córdoba: Dismantling Ancient Architecture in the East, North Africa and Islamic Spain* (Leiden: Brill, 2012); Alain George, *The Umayyad Mosque of Damascus: Art, Faith and Empire in Early Islam* (London: Gingko, 2021).

16 Perry, *The Cambridge History of Egypt*; Starr, *Lost Enlightenment*.

17 Jason R. Zaborowski, *The Coptic Martyrdom of John of Phanijōit: Assimilation and Conversion to Islam in Thirteenth-Century Egypt* (Leiden: Brill, 2005); Richard Hitchcock, *Mozarabs in Medieval and Early Modern Spain: Identities and Influences* (Burlington, Vt.: Ashgate, 2008); Cyrille Aillet, *Les Mozarabes: Christianisme et Arabisation en al-Andalus (IXᵉ–XIIᵉ siècle)* (Madrid: Casa de Velázquez, 2010).

18 Jenkins, *Lost History*.

19 Jenkins, *Lost History*.

20 Ruthven, *Islam in the World*; Ayman S. Ibrahim, *Conversion to Islam: Competing Themes in Early Islamic Historiography* (New York: Oxford University Press, 2021).

21 R. Michael Feener and Anne M. Blackburn, eds., *Buddhist and Islamic Orders in Southern Asia: Comparative Perspectives* (Honolulu: University of Hawai'i Press, 2019).

22 Richard W. Bulliet, *Conversion to Islam in the Medieval Period: An Essay in Quantitative History* (Cambridge, Mass.: Harvard University Press, 1979); Milka Levy-Rubin, *Non-Muslims in the Early Islamic Empire: From Surrender to Coexistence* (New York: Cambridge University Press, 2011); Jenkins, *Climate, Catastrophe, and Faith*.

23 Masselos, *The Great Empires of Asia*; Bang and Bayly, *Tributary Empires in Global History*; Eaton, *India in the Persianate Age, 1000–1765*; Pines, Biran, and Rüpke, *Limits of Universal Rule*.

24 William R. Polk, *Crusade and Jihad: The Thousand-Year War between the Muslim World and the Global North* (New Haven, Conn.: Yale University Press, 2018).

25 Eaton, *India in the Persianate Age, 1000–1765*.

26 John F. Richards, *The Mughal Empire* (New York: Cambridge University Press, 1993); Tanvir Anjum, *Chishtī Sufis in the Sultanate of Delhi, 1190–1400: From Restrained Indifference to Calculated Defiance* (Karachi: Oxford University Press, 2011); Nile Green, *Afghanistan's Islam: From Conversion to the Taliban* (Oakland: University of California Press, 2017); Allen, *Coromandel*.

27 Simon Digby, ed., *Sufis and Soldiers in Awrangzeb's Deccan: Malfūzāt-i-Naqshbandiyya* (New Delhi: Oxford University Press, 2001); Audrey Truschke, *Aurangzeb: The Life and Legacy of India's Most Controversial King* (Stanford, Calif.: Stanford University Press, 2017). For continuities from the Timurids through the Mughal period, see Lisa Balabanlilar, *Imperial Identity in the Mughal Empire: Memory and Dynastic Politics in Early Modern South and Central Asia* (London: I. B. Tauris, 2012).

28 Richard M. Eaton, *The Rise of Islam and the Bengal Frontier, 1204–1760* (Berkeley: University of California Press, 1993); Raziuddin Aquil, ed., *Sufism and Society in Medieval India* (New Delhi: Oxford University Press, 2010); Omar H. Ali, *Islam in the Indian Ocean World* (Boston: Bedford / St. Martin's, 2016); Muzaffar Alam, *The Mughals and the Sufis: Islam and Political Imagination in India, 1500–1750* (Albany: State University of New York Press, 2021); Phillips, *How the East Was Won*; Surinder Singh, *Medieval Panjab in Transition: Authority, Resistance and Spirituality c.1500–c.1700* (New York: Routledge, 2022).

29 Michael Axworthy, *The Sword of Persia: Nader Shah, From Tribal Warrior to Conquering Tyrant* (London: I. B. Tauris, 2009).

30 Kumar, *Visions of Empire*; Pines, Biran, and Rüpke, *The Limits of Universal Rule*; Phillips, *How the East Was Won*.

31 David O. Morgan and Anthony Reid, *The Eastern Islamic World, Eleventh to Eighteenth Centuries*, in Cook, *The New Cambridge History of Islam*; Douglas E. Streusand, *Islamic Gunpowder Empires: Ottomans, Safavids, and Mughals* (Boulder, Colo.: Westview Press, 2011); Andrew de la Garza, *The Mughal Empire at War: Babur, Akbar and the Indian Military Revolution, 1500–1605* (New York: Routledge, 2016); Hani Khafipour, ed., *The Empires of the Near East and India: Source Studies of the Safavid, Ottoman, and Mughal Literate Communities* (New York: Columbia University Press, 2019); Sanjay Subrahmanyam, *Empires between Islam and Christianity, 1500–1800* (Albany: State University of New York Press, 2019); Pratyay Nath, *Climate of Conquest: War, Environment, and Empire in Mughal North India* (New York: Oxford University Press, 2019); Ayşe Zarakol, *Before the West: The Rise and Fall of Eastern World Orders* (New York: Cambridge University Press, 2022).

32 Alan Mikhail, *God's Shadow: Sultan Selim, His Ottoman Empire, and the Making of the Modern World* (New York: Liveright 2020).

33 Marc David Baer, *Honored by the Glory of Islam: Conversion and Conquest in Ottoman Europe* (New York: Oxford University Press, 2008); Zeynep Yürekli, *Architecture and Hagiography in the Ottoman Empire: The Politics of Bektashi Shrines in the Classical Age* (Burlington, Vt.: Ashgate, 2012); A. C. S. Peacock, Bruno De Nicola, and Sara Nur Yıldız, *Islam and Christianity in Medieval Anatolia* (Burlington, Vt.: Ashgate, 2015); Tobias P. Graf, *The Sultan's Renegades: Christian-European*

Converts to Islam and the Making of the Ottoman Elite, 1575–1610 (New York: Oxford University Press, 2017); Robert Elsie, *The Albanian Bektashi: History and Culture of a Dervish Order in the Balkans* (London: I. B. Tauris, 2019); Marc David Baer, *The Ottomans: Khans, Caesars, and Caliphs* (New York: Basic, 2021).

34 Ruthven, *Islam in the World*; Lesley Hazleton, *After the Prophet: The Epic Story of the Shia-Sunni Split in Islam* (New York: Doubleday, 2009); Toby Matthiesen, *The Caliph and the Imam: The Making of Sunnism and Shiism* (Oxford: Oxford University Press, 2023).

35 Brett, *The Fatimid Empire*; Laurence Louër, *Sunnis and Shi'a: A Political History of Discord* (Princeton, N.J.: Princeton University Press, 2020).

36 Andrew J. Newman, *Safavid Iran: Rebirth of a Persian Empire* (London: I. B. Tauris, 2006); Rudi Matthee, ed., *The Safavid World* (New York: Routledge / Taylor & Francis Group, 2022).

37 Ferdowsi, *Shahnameh.*

38 David Blow, *Shah Abbas: The Ruthless King Who Became an Iranian Legend* (London: I. B. Tauris, 2009); Willem Floor and Edmund Herzig, eds., *Iran and the World in the Safavid Age* (London: I. B. Tauris, 2012).

39 Justin Jones, *Shi'a Islam in Colonial India: Religion, Community and Sectarianism* (New York: Cambridge University Press, 2012); Eaton, *India in the Persianate Age, 1000–1765*; Sholeh A. Quinn, *Persian Historiography across Empires: The Ottomans, Safavids, and Mughals* (New York: Cambridge University Press, 2021); Matthiesen, *Caliph and the Imam.*

6 Empires and Christian Mission

1 Charlotte Bronte, "The Missionary," *The Complete Poems of Charlotte Brontë*, ed. Clement Shorter, with bibliography and notes by C. W. Hatfield (London: Hodder and Stoughton, 1923), full text available online at HathiTrust, https://www.hathitrust.org.

2 Lynda Nead, "The Secret of England's Greatness," *Journal of Victorian Culture* 19 (2014): 161–82.

3 Norman Etherington, ed., *Missions and Empire* (New York: Oxford University Press, 2005); Sanneh, *Disciples of All Nations.*

4 Studdert-Kennedy, *Providence and the Raj*; Andrew Porter, ed., *The Imperial Horizons of British Protestant Missions, 1880–1914: The Interplay of Representation and Experience* (Grand Rapids: Eerdmans, 2003); Dana L. Robert, ed., *Converting Colonialism: Visions and Realities in Mission History, 1706–1914* (Grand Rapids: Eerdmans, 2008); John H. Darch, *Missionary Imperialists? Missionaries, Government and the Growth of the British Empire in the Tropics 1860–1885* (London: Paternoster, 2009).

5 Lamin Sanneh and Michael J. McClymond, eds., *The Wiley Blackwell Companion to World Christianity* (Hoboken, N.J.: Wiley/Blackwell, 2016).

6 Philip Jenkins, *The Next Christendom: The Rise of Global Christianity*, 3rd ed. (New York: Oxford University Press, 2011).

7 Hugh Thomas, *World without End: Spain, Philip II, and the First Global Empire* (New York: Random House, 2014); Roger Crowley, *Conquerors: How Portugal Forged the First Global Empire* (New York: Random House, 2015); Ernesto Bassi Arevalo, *An Aqueous Territory: Sailor Geographies and New Granada's Transimperial Greater Caribbean World* (Durham, N.C.: Duke University Press, 2016); Fernando Cervantes, *Conquistadores: A New History* (New York: Viking, 2021). For the globalization of religious practices in the new Catholic world, see Karin Vélez, *The Miraculous Flying House of Loreto: Spreading Catholicism in the Early Modern World* (Princeton, N.J.: Princeton University Press, 2018).

8 *Requerimiento*, National Humanities Center, https://nationalhumanitiescenter.org/pds/amerbegin/contact/text7/requirement.pdf; Erin Woodruff Stone, *Captives of Conquest: Slavery in the Early Modern Spanish Caribbean* (Philadelphia: University of Pennsylvania Press, 2021).

9 John Lynch, *New Worlds: A Religious History of Latin America* (New Haven, Conn.: Yale University Press, 2012); David M. Carballo, *Collision of Worlds: A Deep History of the Fall of Aztec Mexico and the Forging of New Spain* (New York: Oxford University Press, 2020); Yolanda Martínez-San Miguel and Santa Arias, eds., *The Routledge Hispanic Studies Companion to Colonial Latin America and the Caribbean (1492–1898)* (New York: Routledge / Taylor & Francis Group, 2021); Matthew Restall, Amara Solari, John F. Chuchiak IV, and Traci Ardren, *The Friar and the Maya: Diego de Landa and the Account of the Things of Yucatan* (Denver: University Press of Colorado, 2023).

10 Cheryl Claassen, *Religion in Sixteenth-Century Mexico: A Guide to Aztec and Catholic Beliefs and Practices* (New York: Cambridge University Press, 2022).

11 Cornelius Conover, *Pious Imperialism: Spanish Rule and the Cult of Saints in Mexico City* (Albuquerque: University of New Mexico Press, 2019); Laura Dierksmeier, *Charity for and by the Poor: Franciscan-Indigenous Confraternities in Mexico, 1527–1700* (Norman: University of Oklahoma Press, 2020); R. Alan Covey, *Inca Apocalypse: The Spanish Conquest and the Transformation of the Andean World* (New York: Oxford University Press, 2020). For the use of languages, see Jaime Lara, *Christian Texts for Aztecs: Art and Liturgy in Colonial Mexico* (Notre Dame, Ind.: University of Notre Dame Press, 2008); David Tavarez, ed., *Words and Worlds Turned Around: Indigenous Christianities in*

Colonial Latin America (Denver: University Press of Colorado, 2017); Nancy Farriss, *Tongues of Fire: Language and Evangelization in Colonial Mexico* (New York: Oxford University Press, 2018); Sonia Alconini and Alan Covey, eds., *The Oxford Handbook of the Incas* (New York: Oxford University Press, 2018).

12 David Lindenfeld, *World Christianity and Indigenous Experience: A Global History, 1500–2000* (New York: Cambridge University Press, 2021).

13 Brent Nongbri, *Before Religion: A History of a Modern Concept* (New Haven, Conn.: Yale University Press, 2013); Santa Arias and Raul Marrero-Fente, eds., *Coloniality, Religion, and the Law in the Early Iberian World* (Nashville, Tenn.: Vanderbilt University Press, 2014). Although it concerns a different time and place, see the comments about defining religion in David Chidester, *Savage Systems: Religion and Colonialism in Southern Africa* (Charlottesville: University of Virginia Press, 1996).

14 Kris Lane, *Potosí: The Silver City That Changed the World* (Berkeley: University of California Press, 2021); María Soledad Barbón, *Colonial Loyalities: Celebrating the Spanish Monarchy in Eighteenth-Century Lima* (Notre Dame, Ind.: University of Notre Dame Press, 2019). Compare Liam Matthew Brockey, ed., *Portuguese Colonial Cities in the Early Modern World* (New York: Routledge, 2008).

15 Barbara Ganson, "Antonio Ruiz de Montoya, Apostle of the Guarani," *Journal of Jesuit Studies* 3 (2016): 197–210; Brandon Bayne, *Missions Begin with Blood: Suffering and Salvation in the Borderlands of New Spain* (New York: Fordham University Press, 2021); Markus Friedrich, *The Jesuits: A History* (Princeton, N.J.: Princeton University Press, 2022).

16 Joseph P. Sánchez, *Pueblos, Plains and Province: New Mexico in the Seventeenth Century* (Denver: University Press of Colorado, 2021).

17 R. Po-chia Hsia, ed., *Reform and Expansion 1500–1660*, vol. 6 of *The Cambridge History of Christianity* (New York: Cambridge University Press, 2007); Liam Matthew Brockey, *The Visitor: André Palmeiro and the Jesuits in Asia* (Cambridge, Mass.: Belknap Press, 2014); Arturo Giraldez, *The Age of Trade: The Manila Galleons and the Dawn of the Global Economy* (Lanham, Md.: Rowman & Littlefield, 2015); Sarah E. Owens, *Nuns Navigating the Spanish Empire* (Albuquerque: University of New Mexico Press, 2017); Peter Gordon and Juan José Morales, *The Silver Way: China, Spanish America and the Birth of Globalisation, 1565–1815* (Sydney: Penguin Australia, 2017); Ronnie Po-chia Hsia, ed., *A Companion to Early Modern Catholic Global Missions* (Leiden: Brill, 2018).

18 Brockey, *Portuguese Colonial Cities in the Early Modern World*; Ananya Chakravarti, *The Empire of Apostles: Religion, Accommodation, and the Imagination of Empire in Early Modern Brazil and India* (New Delhi: Oxford University Press, 2018).

19 George Minamiki, *The Chinese Rites Controversy: From Its Beginning to Modern Times* (Chicago: Loyola University Press, 1985); Liam Matthew Brockey, *Journey to the East: The Jesuit Mission to China, 1579–1724* (Cambridge, Mass.: Harvard University Press, 2017).

20 Sanneh, *Disciples of All Nations.*

21 Colin Thubron, *The Amur River: Between Russia and China* (New York: Harper, 2021); Philip Snow, *China and Russia: Four Centuries of Conflict and Concord* (New Haven, Conn.: Yale University Press, 2023).

22 Abbé de Choisy, *Journal of a Voyage to Siam, 1685–1686*, trans. Michael Smithies (New York: Oxford University Press, 1993); Gabriel Paquette, *The European Seaborne Empires: From the Thirty Years' War to the Age of Revolutions* (New Haven, Conn.: Yale University Press, 2019).

23 Jenkins, *Next Christendom.*

24 Peter C. Phan, ed., *Christianities in Asia* (Malden, Mass.: Wiley-Blackwell, 2011).

25 Philip Caraman, *The Lost Empire: The Story of the Jesuits in Ethiopia, 1555–1634* (London: Sidgwick & Jackson, 1985).

26 For the Vietnamese example, see chapter 7 below. Phan, *Christianities in Asia*; Tara Alberts, *Conflict and Conversion: Catholicism in Southeast Asia, 1500–1700* (New York: Oxford University Press, 2013).

27 David M. Lantigua, *Infidels and Empires in a New World Order: Early Modern Spanish Contributions to International Legal Thought* (New York: Cambridge University Press, 2020).

28 Philip Caraman, *The Lost Paradise: An Account of the Jesuits in Paraguay, 1607–1768* (London: Sidgwick and Jackson, 1975); Hsia, *A Companion to Early Modern Catholic Global Missions.*

29 Julia J. S. Sarreal, *The Guaraní and Their Missions: A Socioeconomic History* (Stanford, Calif.: Stanford University Press, 2014).

30 Carole Blackburn, *Harvest of Souls: The Jesuit Missions and Colonialism in North America, 1632–1650* (Montreal: McGill-Queen's University Press, 2000); Dominique Deslandres, *Croire et faire croire: Les missions françaises au XVIIe siècle* (Paris: Fayard, 2003); Stewart J. Brown and Timothy Tackett, eds., *Enlightenment, Reawakening and Revolution 1660–1815*, vol. 7 of *The Cambridge History of Christianity* (New York: Cambridge University Press, 2006); Bronwen McShea, *Apostles of Empire: The Jesuits and New France* (University of Nebraska, 2019); Benjamin Steiner, *Building the French Empire, 1600–1800: Colonialism and Material Culture* (Manchester: Manchester University Press, 2020).

31 B. Schlenther, "Religious Faith and Commercial Empire," in *The Eighteenth Century*, ed. P. J. Marshall, vol. 2 of Louis, *The Oxford History of the British Empire*; Ian Copland, "Christianity as an Arm of Empire: The Ambiguous Case of India under the Company, c. 1813–1858," *Historical Journal* 49, no. 4 (2006): 1025–54; Carla Pestana, *Protestant Empire:*

Religion and the Making of the British Atlantic World (Philadelphia: University of Pennsylvania Press, 2009); Linda Gregerson and Susan Juster, eds., *Empires of God: Religious Encounters in the Early Modern Atlantic* (Philadelphia: University of Pennsylvania Press, 2011); Penelope Carson, *The East India Company and Religion, 1698–1858* (Woodbridge: Boydell Press, 2012); Rowan Strong, gen. ed., *The Oxford History of Anglicanism*, vol. 2, *Establishment and Empire, 1662–1829*, ed. Jeremy Gregory (New York: Oxford University Press, 2017); Dalrymple, *The Anarchy*; Haig Z. Smith, *Religion and Governance in England's Emerging Colonial Empire, 1601–1698*.

32 Charles H. Parker, *Global Calvinism: Conversion and Commerce in the Dutch Empire, 1600–1800* (New York: Oxford University Press, 2022). For the extraordinary breadth of the Dutch imperial experience, see Petra Groen, Anita van Dissel, Mark Loderichs, Rémy Limpach, and Thijs Brocades Zaalberg, *Krijgsgeweld en kolonie: Opkomst en ondergang van Nederland als koloniale mogendheid 1816–2010* (Amsterdam: Boom, 2021).

33 Andrew Porter, ed., with Alaine Low, *The Nineteenth Century*, vol. 3 of Louis, *Oxford History of the British Empire*; Cain and Hopkins, *British Imperialism*; Hyam, *Britain's Imperial Century, 1815–1914*; Christina Welsch, *The Company's Sword: The East India Company and the Politics of Militarism, 1644–1858* (New York: Cambridge University Press, 2022).

34 C. A. Bayly, *Imperial Meridian: The British Empire and the World, 1780–1830* (London: Routledge, 1989); Stanley, *The Bible and the Flag*; Christopher Hodgkins, *Reforming Empire: Protestant Colonialism and Conscience in British Literature* (Columbia: University of Missouri Press, 2002); Sheridan Gilley and Brian Stanley, eds., *World Christianities c.1815–c.1914*, vol. 8 of *The Cambridge History of Christianity* (New York: Cambridge University Press, 2005); Rowan Strong, *Anglicanism and the British Empire c. 1700–1850* (New York: Oxford University Press, 2007); Rowan Strong, ed., *Partisan Anglicanism and Its Global Expansion, 1829–c.1914*, vol. 3 of Strong, *The Oxford History of Anglicanism*.

35 Bishop Reginald Heber, "From Greenland's Icy Mountains," Victorian Web, https://victorianweb.org/religion/hymns/heber1.html.

36 Studdert-Kennedy, *Providence and the Raj*; Chima J. Korieh and Raphael Chijioke Njoku, eds., *Missions, States, and European Expansion in Africa* (New York: Routledge, 2007); Steven S. Maughan, *Mighty England Do Good: Culture, Faith, Empire, and World in the Foreign Missions of the Church of England, 1850–1915* (Grand Rapids: Eerdmans, 2014).

37 Anna Johnston, *Missionary Writing and Empire, 1800–1860* (Cambridge: Cambridge University Press, 2003); Thorpe, "Religion and Empire at Home"; Janet Wootton, ed., *Women in Christianity in the*

Age of Empire: (1800–1920) (London: Routledge / Taylor & Francis Group, 2022).

38 In 1901, the American Arthur T. Pierson coined a famous description of this era when he published *The Modern Mission Century; Viewed as a Cycle of Divine Working*. A. C. Hill, *Christian Imperialism* (London: Hodder and Stoughton, 1917); For the German role, see Jeremy Best, *Heavenly Fatherland: German Missionary Culture and Globalization in the Age of Empire* (Toronto: University of Toronto Press, 2021).

39 Wilberforce is quoted from Allen, *Coromandel*. Jessica Patterson, *Religion, Enlightenment and Empire: British Interpretations of Hinduism in the Eighteenth Century* (New York: Cambridge University Press, 2022).

40 Baumgart, *Imperialism*; Conklin, *A Mission to Civilize*; Miguel Bandeira Jerónimo, *The "Civilising Mission" of Portuguese Colonialism, 1870–1930* (London: Palgrave Macmillan, 2015); Emily Conroy-Krutz, *Christian Imperialism: Converting the World in the Early American Republic* (Ithaca, N.Y.: Cornell University Press, 2015); Richard Price, *Empire and Indigeneity: Histories and Legacies* (London: Routledge, 2021).

41 John R. Lampe and Ulf Brunnbauer, eds., *The Routledge Handbook of Balkan and Southeast European History* (Milton: Taylor & Francis Group, 2020). Harold H. Kolb Jr., *Mark Twain: The Gift of Humor* (Lanham, Md.: University Press of America, 2014), 310.

42 Pascale Pellerin, ed., *Les Lumières, l'esclavage et l'idéologie coloniale: XVIIIe–XXe siècles* (Paris: Classiques Garnier, 2020).

43 Julia Clancy-Smith, "Islam and the French Empire in North Africa," in *Islam and the European Empires*, ed. David Motadel (New York: Oxford University Press, 2014), 90–111; Herbert Ingram Priestley, *France Overseas: A Study of Modern Imperialism* (London: Taylor and Francis, 2018); Joseph W. Peterson, *Sacred Rivals: Catholic Missions and the Making of Islam in Nineteenth-Century France and Algeria* (New York: Oxford University Press, 2022).

44 Robert Aldrich, *The French Presence in the South Pacific, 1842–1940* (Honolulu: University of Hawai'i Press, 1989); Owen White and J. P. Daughton, eds., *In God's Empire* (New York: Oxford University Press, 2012).

45 Aldrich, *Greater France*; Conklin, Fishman, and Zaretsky, *France and Its Empire since 1870*; Charles Keith, *Catholic Vietnam: A Church from Empire to Nation* (Berkeley: University of California Press, 2012); George E. Dutton, *A Vietnamese Moses: Philiphê Bỉnh and the Geographies of Early Modern Catholicism* (Oakland: University of California Press, 2017); Edward J. Gillin, *Entente Imperial: British and French Power in the Age of Empire* (Amberley, 2022).

46 Kathryn Robson and Jennifer Yee, eds., *France and "Indochina": Cultural Representations* (Lanham, Md.: Lexington Books, 2005).

47 Kristine Ibsen, *Maximilian, Mexico, and the Invention of Empire* (Nashville, Tenn.: Vanderbilt University Press, 2010).

48 Dong Wang, *China's Unequal Treaties: Narrating National History* (Lanham, Md.: Lexington Books, 2005); Sheila Miyoshi Jager, *The Other Great Game: The Opening of Korea and the Birth of Modern East Asia* (Cambridge, Mass.: Harvard University Press, 2023).

49 William Harris, *Lebanon: A History, 600–2011* (New York: Oxford University Press, 2012).

50 Jenkins, *Next Christendom*.

51 Katharine Gerbner, *Christian Slavery: Conversion and Race in the Protestant Atlantic World* (Philadelphia: University of Pennsylvania Press, 2018); Howard W. French, *Born in Blackness: Africa, Africans, and the Making of the Modern World, 1471 to the Second World War* (New York: Liveright, 2021).

52 James Epstein, *Scandal of Colonial Rule: Power and Subversion in the British Atlantic during the Age of Revolution* (New York: Cambridge University Press, 2012).

53 Jon F. Sensbach, *Rebecca's Revival* (Cambridge, Mass.: Harvard University Press, 2005); Brian Stanley, "Christian Missions, Antislavery and the Claims of Humanity, c.1813–1873," in Gilley and Stanley, *World Christianities c.1815–c.1914*; J. R. Oldfield, *Transatlantic Abolitionism in the Age of Revolution: An International History of Anti-slavery, c.1787–1820* (New York: Cambridge University Press, 2013); Thomas Kidd, *George Whitefield: America's Spiritual Founding Father* (New Haven, Conn.: Yale University Press, 2014); Zoë Laidlaw, *Protecting the Empire's Humanity: Thomas Hodgkin and British Colonial Activism 1830–1870* (New York: Cambridge University Press, 2021).

54 Tom Zoellner, *Island on Fire: The Revolt That Ended Slavery in the British Empire* (Cambridge, Mass.: Harvard University Press, 2020).

55 Jonathan A. Draper, ed., *Orality, Literacy, and Colonialism in Southern Africa* (Atlanta: SBL Press, 2003); Phan, *Christianities in Asia*; Vincent L. Wimbush, *White Men's Magic: Scripturalization as Slavery* (New York: Oxford University Press, 2012); R. S. Sugirtharajah, *Jesus in Asia* (Cambridge, Mass.: Harvard University Press, 2018); Gareth Atkins, Shinjini Das, and Brian Murray, eds, *Chosen Peoples: The Bible, Race and Empire in the Long Nineteenth Century* (Manchester: Manchester University Press, 2020); Jione Havea, ed., *Mission and Context* (Minneapolis: Fortress Academic 2021). For subjects appropriating the culture of the elites, see MacKenzie, *Cultural History of the British Empire*.

56 Jenkins, *Next Christendom*; French, *Born in Blackness*.

57 Andrew Porter, *Religion versus Empire? British Protestant Missionaries and Overseas Expansion, 1700–1914* (Manchester: Manchester University Press, 2004).

58 Stephen Neill, *Colonialism and Christian Missions* (New York: McGraw-Hill, 1966); Olive Schreiner, *Trooper Peter Halket of Mashonaland* (London: T. Fisher Unwin, 1897).

59 Frank Weston, *The Serfs of Great Britain* (London: W Knott, 1920).

7 Worlds in Motion

1 Psalm 137:9 NIV.

2 "Exile is the nursery of nationality" is quoted by Benedict Anderson, "Exodus," *Critical Inquiry* 20 (1994): 314–27.

3 See, for example, Gocha R. Tsetskhladze, ed., *Greek Colonisation: An Account of Greek Colonies and Other Settlements Overseas* (Leiden: Brill, 2006).

4 Elkins and Pedersen, *Settler Colonialism in the Twentieth Century*; Belich, *Replenishing the Earth*; Bickers, *Settlers and Expatriates*; Marjory Harper and Stephen Constantine, *Migration and Empire*, Oxford History of the British Empire Companion Series (Oxford: Oxford University Press, 2014); Cavanagh and Veracini, *The Routledge Handbook of the History of Settler Colonialism*.

5 Linda M. Rupert, *Creolization and Contraband: Curaçao in the Early Modern Atlantic World* (Athens: University of Georgia Press, 2012); Murphy, *Creole Archipelago*.

6 Jorge Cañizares-Esguerra, *Puritan Conquistadors: Iberianizing the Atlantic, 1550–1700* (Stanford, Calif.: Stanford University Press, 2006).

7 Brian Davies, *Empire and Military Revolution in Eastern Europe: Russia's Turkish Wars in the Eighteenth Century* (London: Bloomsbury, 2013); Kelly O'Neill, *Claiming Crimea: A History of Catherine the Great's Southern Empire* (New Haven, Conn.: Yale University Press, 2017).

8 Douglas Smith, ed., *Love and Conquest: Personal Correspondence of Catherine the Great and Prince Grigory Potemkin* (DeKalb: Northern Illinois University Press, 2004).

9 Charles King, *Odessa: Genius and Death in a City of Dreams* (New York: Norton, 2011).

10 Elkins, *Legacy of Violence*.

11 Jehu Hanciles, *Migration and the Making of Global Christianity* (Grand Rapids: Eerdmans, 2021).

12 Kiril Petkov, *The Voices of Medieval Bulgaria, Seventh–Fifteenth Century: The Records of a Bygone Culture* (Leiden: Brill, 2008).

13 Roy Foster, ed., *The Oxford History of Ireland* (New York: Oxford University Press, 1992); Colin Barr and Hilary M. Carey, eds., *Religion and Greater Ireland: Christianity and Irish Global Networks, 1750–1950* (Montreal: McGill-Queen's University Press, 2015).

14 Elizabeth Elbourne, *Empire, Kinship and Violence: Family Histories, Indigenous Rights and the Making of Settler Colonialism, 1770–1842* (New York: Cambridge University Press, 2023).

15 Sara E. Brown and Stephen D. Smith, eds., *The Routledge Handbook of Religion, Mass Atrocity, and Genocide* (New York: Routledge, 2022).
16 Jenkins, *Great and Holy War.*
17 Miloš Ković, *Disraeli and the Eastern Question* (New York: Oxford University Press, 2011); Lampe and Brunnbauer, *The Routledge Handbook of Balkan and Southeast European History*; Jonathan Parry, *Promised Lands: The British and the Ottoman Middle East* (Princeton, N.J.: Princeton University Press, 2022).
18 For the mass population (and religious) movements of just a few years afterward, see Bruce Clark, *Twice a Stranger: How Mass Expulsion Forged Modern Greece and Turkey* (London: Granta, 2006).
19 Mechtild Rössler und Sabine Schleiermacher, eds., *Der "Generalplan Ost": Hauptlinien der nationalsozialistischen Planungs- und Vernichtungspolitik* (Berlin: Akademie Verlag, 1993).
20 Amjad Jaimoukha, *The Circassians: A Handbook* (New York: Palgrave, 2001); Williams, *Crimean Tatars.*
21 William H. Holt, *The Balkan Reconquista and Turkey's Forgotten Refugee Crisis* (Salt Lake City: University of Utah Press, 2019); Jeremy Salt, *The Last Ottoman Wars: The Human Cost, 1877–1923* (Salt Lake City: University of Utah Press, 2019).
22 James Livesey, *Civil Society and Empire: Ireland and Scotland in the Eighteenth-Century Atlantic World* (New Haven, Conn.: Yale University Press, 2009); Barr and Carey, *Religion and Greater Ireland*; Jessica Hanser, *Mr Smith Goes to China* (New Haven, Conn.: Yale University Press, 2019); Murray Pittock, *Scotland: The Global History; 1603 to the Present* (New Haven, Conn.: Yale University Press, 2022).
23 Jonathan Karp and Adam Sutcliffe, eds., *The Early Modern World, 1500–1815*, vol. 7 of *The Cambridge History of Judaism* (New York: Cambridge University Press, 2017).
24 King, *Odessa*; Sophie B. Roberts, *Citizenship and Antisemitism in French Colonial Algeria, 1870–1962* (New York: Cambridge University Press, 2017); Mitchell B. Hart and Tony Michels, eds., *The Modern World, 1815–2000*, vol. 8 of *The Cambridge History of Judaism* (New York: Cambridge University Press, 2017); Joseph Sassoon, *The Sassoons: The Great Global Merchants and the Making of an Empire* (New York: Panetheon, 2022).
25 Minna Rozen, ed., *Homeland and Diasporas: Greeks, Jews and Their Migrations* (London: I. B. Tauris, 2008); Lampe and Brunnbauer, *Routledge Handbook of Balkan and Southeast European History.*
26 Sebouh David Aslanian, *From the Indian Ocean to the Mediterranean: The Global Trade Networks of Armenian Merchants from New Julfa* (Berkeley: University of California Press, 2010); Floor and Herzig, *Iran and the World in the Safavid Age.*

27 Belich, *Replenishing the Earth*. Compare Brockey, *Portuguese Colonial Cities in the Early Modern World*. For the British global networks at their height, see Matthew Parker, *One Fine Day: Britain's Empire on the Brink: September 29, 1923* (London: Public Affairs, 2023).

28 Emma Christopher, Cassandra Pybus, and Marcus Rediker, eds., *Many Middle Passages: Forced Migration and the Making of the Modern World* (Berkeley: University of California Press, 2007); Jenkins, *Next Christendom*.

29 Toyin Falola and Matt D. Childs, eds., *The Yoruba Diaspora in the Atlantic World* (Bloomington: Indiana University Press, 2004); Ruth Marie Griffith and Barbara Dianne Savage, eds., *Women and Religion in the African Diaspora: Knowledge, Power, and Performance* (Baltimore: Johns Hopkins University Press, 2006); Cécile Fromont, ed., *Afro-Catholic Festivals in the Americas: Performance, Representation, and the Making of Black Atlantic Tradition* (University Park: Pennsylvania State University Press, 2019); Margarite Fernández Olmos and Lizabeth Paravisini-Gebert, *Creole Religions of the Caribbean: An Introduction*, 3rd ed. (New York: New York University Press, 2022).

30 Diana Paton, *The Cultural Politics of Obeah: Religion, Colonialism and Modernity in the Caribbean World* (New York: Cambridge University Press, 2015); Cécile Vidal, *Caribbean New Orleans: Empire, Race, and the Making of a Slave Society* (Chapel Hill: University of North Carolina Press, 2019).

31 Walton Look Lai and Tan Chee-Beng, eds., *The Chinese in Latin America and the Caribbean* (Leiden: Brill, 2010); Rachel K. Bright, *Chinese Labour in South Africa, 1902–10: Race, Violence, and Global Spectacle* (Houndmills: Palgrave Macmillan, 2013); Anna Suranyi, *Indentured Servitude: Unfree Labour and Citizenship in the British Colonies* (Montreal: McGill-Queen's University Press, 2021); Fae Dussart, *In the Service of Empire: Domestic Service and Mastery in Metropole and Colony* (London: Bloomsbury, 2022).

32 Thomas R. Metcalf, *Imperial Connections: India in the Indian Ocean Arena, 1860–1920* (Berkeley: University of California Press, 2007); Sugata Bose, *A Hundred Horizons: The Indian Ocean in the Age of Global Empire* (Cambridge, Mass.: Harvard University Press, 2009); Office of International Religious Freedom, *2021 Report on International Religious Freedom: Guyana*, June 2, 2022, https://www.state.gov/reports/2021-report-on-international-religious-freedom/guyana/; Suzanne Chazan-Gillig and Pavitranand Ramhota, *Hinduism and Popular Cults in Mauritius: Sacred Religion and Plantation Economy* (New York: Routledge, 2023).

33 Brinsley Samaroo, Primnath Gooptar, Kumar Mahabir, eds., *Global Indian Diaspora: Charting New Frontiers*, vol. 1 (Abingdon: Routledge, 2022).

34 Barbara Watson Andaya and Leonard Y. Andaya, *A History of Malaysia*, 3rd ed. (London: Palgrave, 2017); Alfred Wallace is quoted from his

book *The Malay Archipelago: The Land of the Orang-Utan and the Bird of Paradise* (London: Macmillan, 1869), vol. 1, ch. 2.

35 Manu Karuka, *Empire's Tracks: Indigenous Nations, Chinese Workers, and the Transcontinental Railroad* (Berkeley: University of California Press, 2019); Mae Ngai, *The Chinese Question: The Gold Rushes and Global Politics* (New York: Norton, 2021).

36 Larry DeVries, Don Baker, and Dan Overmyer, eds., *Asian Religions in British Columbia* (Vancouver: University of British Columbia Press, 2010); Andrea Geiger, *Converging Empires: Citizens and Subjects in the North Pacific Borderlands, 1867–1945* (Chapel Hill: University of North Carolina Press, 2022); Tom MacInnes, *Oriental Occupation of British Columbia* (Vancouver: Sun, 1927).

37 David M. Eberhard, Gary F. Simons, and Charles D. Fennig eds., *Ethnologue*, 3 vols., 25th ed. (Dallas: SIL International, 2022).

38 Alexandre de Rhodes, *Histoire du Royaume du Tonkin*, ed. Jean-Pierre Duteil (Paris: Kimé, 1999); Phan, *Christianities in Asia*.

39 David Crystal, *The Cambridge Encyclopedia of Language* (New York: Cambridge University Press, 1987).

40 "A Historical Perspective of Urdu," https://www.urducouncil.nic.in/council/historical-perspective-urdu.

41 Philip Durkin, *Borrowed Words: A History of Loanwords in English* (New York: Oxford University Press, 2014).

42 Rachel Leow, *Taming Babel: Language in the Making of Malaysia* (New York: Cambridge University Press, 2016); Parker, *Global Calvinism*.

43 John M Mugane, "The Story of How Swahili Became Africa's Most Spoken Language," *Conversation*, February 20, 2022, https://theconversation.com/the-story-of-how-swahili-became-africas-most-spoken-language-177259.

44 David Omissi, *The Sepoy and the Raj: The Indian Army, 1860–1940* (Houndmills: Macmillan in association with King's College London, 1994).

45 Rila Mukherjee and Radhika Seshan, eds., *Indian Ocean Histories: The Many Worlds of Michael Naylor Pearson* (New York: Routledge, 2020).

46 Santanu Das, ed., *Race, Empire and First World War Writing* (New York: Cambridge University Press, 2011); Michelle R. Moyd, *Violent Intermediaries: African Soldiers, Conquest, and Everyday Colonialism in German East Africa* (Athens: Ohio University Press, 2014).

47 Dan Eatherley, "What Have the Romans Done for Us?" *History Today*, 2019, https://www.historytoday.com/history-matters/what-have-romans-done-us.

8 Faith against Empire

1 Romit Bagchi, "Rammohan Roy, Vivekananda and Tagore on British Rule," *Pioneer*, February 8, 2015, https://www.dailypioneer.com/2015/state-editions/rammohan-roy-vivekananda-and-tagore-on-british-rule.html.
2 Bryce, "Religion as a Factor in the History of Empires," 2.
3 For resistance against empires, see Antoinette Burton, *The Trouble with Empire: Challenges to Modern British Imperialism* (New York: Oxford University Press, 2015); Sivasundaram, *Waves across the South.*
4 Jonathan J. Price, Margalit Finkelberg, and Yuval Shahar, eds., *Rome: An Empire of Many Nations; New Perspectives on Ethnic Diversity and Cultural Identity* (New York: Cambridge University Press, 2022).
5 Michael A. Reynolds, "Muslim Mobilization in Imperial Russia's Caucasus," in Motadel, *Islam and the European Empires*, 187–212.
6 Amandeep Singh Madra and Parmjit Singh, *Warrior Saints: Three Centuries of the Sikh Military Tradition* (London: I. B. Tauris in association with the Sikh Foundation, 1999); J. S. Grewal, *Guru Gobind Singh, 1666–1708: Master of the White Hawk* (New Delhi: Oxford University Press, 2020); Priya Atwal, *Royals and Rebels: The Rise and Fall of the Sikh Empire* (London: Hurst, 2021).
7 George MacMunn, *The Martial Races of India* (Quetta: Nisa Traders, 1977); Streets-Salter, *Martial Races.*
8 Jenkins, *Storm of Images*. For an argument that the Paulicians were less egregiously heretical than is usually claimed, see Carl Dixon, *The Paulicians: Heresy, Persecution and Warfare on the Byzantine Frontier, c.750–880* (Leiden: Brill, 2022).
9 Yuri Stoyanov, *The Other God: Dualist Religions from Antiquity to the Cathar Heresy* (New Haven, Conn.: Yale Nota Bene, 2000).
10 Thomas Paine, *Common Sense* (New York: P. Eckler, 1918), 25.
11 George Herbert, "Religion Westward Bent," Bartleby, https://www.bartleby.com/400/poem/20.html; Evan Haefeli, *Accidental Pluralism: America and the Religious Politics of English Expansion* (Chicago: University of Chicago Press, 2021).
12 Philip Jenkins, "Infidels, Demons, Witches, and Quakers: The Affair of Colonel Bowen," *Fides et Historia* 49, no. 2 (2017): 1–15.
13 Jenkins, *Climate, Catastrophe, and Faith.*
14 Jenkins, *Climate, Catastrophe, and Faith.*
15 Flora Louise Lugard, "British Empire: Population," in *Encyclopædia Britannica*, ed. Hugh Chisholm, vol. 4, 11th ed. (New York: Cambridge University Press, 1911).
16 Barr and Carey, *Religion and Greater Ireland*; Hilary M. Carey, *Empire of Hell: Religion and the Campaign to End Convict Transportation in the British Empire, 1788–1875* (New York: Cambridge University Press,

2019); Clare Anderson, *Convicts: A Global History* (New York: Cambridge University Press, 2021).

17 Janet Liebman Jacobs, *Hidden Heritage: The Legacy of the Crypto-Jews* (Berkeley: University of California Press, 2002).

18 Abigail Jacobson, *From Empire to Empire: Jerusalem between Ottoman and British Rule* (Syracuse, N.Y.: Syracuse University Press, 2011); Jenkins, *Great and Holy War.*

19 Reid, *Empire of Sand.*

20 Francis Robinson, ed., *The Islamic World in the Age of Western Dominance*, in Cook, *New Cambridge History of Islam.*

21 Robert W. Hefner, *Muslims and Modernity: Culture and Society since 1800*, in Cook, *The New Cambridge History of Islam.*

22 Seeley is quoted from John R. Seeley, *The Expansion of England: Two Courses of Lectures* (London: Macmillan, 1914), 205. A wide-ranging collection of relevant case studies can be found in Motadel, *Islam and the European Empires*; Jenkins, *Great and Holy War.*

23 Knut S. Vikør, "Religious Revolts in Colonial North Africa," in Motadel, *Islam and the European Empires*, 170–86.

24 Benedict Anderson, *The Spectre of Comparisons: Nationalism, Southeast Asia, and the World* (London: Verso, 1998); Eric Tagliacozzo, *The Longest Journey: Southeast Asians and the Pilgrimage to Mecca* (Oxford: Oxford University Press, 2013).

25 Robert P. Geraci and Michael Khodarkovsky, eds., *Of Religion and Empire: Missions, Conversion, and Tolerance in Tsarist Russia* (Ithaca, N.Y.: Cornell University Press, 2001); Crews, *For Prophet and Tsar*; Agnès Nilüfer Kefeli, *Becoming Muslim in Imperial Russia: Conversion, Apostasy, and Literacy* (Ithaca, N.Y.: Cornell University Press, 2014); Mustafa Tuna, *Imperial Russia's Muslims: Islam, Empire and European Modernity, 1788–1914* (New York: Cambridge University Press, 2015); Eileen M. Kane, *Russian Hajj: Empire and the Pilgrimage to Mecca* (Ithaca, N.Y.: Cornell University Press, 2015).

26 W. W. Hunter, *The Indian Musalmans*, 3rd ed. (London: Trübner, 1876); John Slight, *The British Empire and the Hajj, 1865–1956* (Cambridge, Mass.: Harvard University Press, 2015); Chandra Mallampalli, *A Muslim Conspiracy in British India? Politics and Paranoia in the Early Nineteenth-Century Deccan* (Cambridge: Cambridge University Press, 2017).

27 Anderson, *Spectre of Comparisons*; Eric Tagliacozzo, "The Dutch Empire and the Hajj," and also Gerrit Knaap, "Islamic Resistance in the Dutch Colonial Empire," both in Motadel, *Islam and the European Empires*, 73–89 and 213–30; Muhamad Ali, *Islam and Colonialism: Becoming Modern in Indonesia and Malaya* (Edinburgh: Edinburgh University Press, 2016); Farish A. Noor and Peter Carey, eds., *Racial Difference and*

the Colonial Wars of 19th Century Southeast Asia (Amsterdam: Amsterdam University Press, 2021).

28 Carool Kersten, *A History of Islam in Indonesia: Unity in Diversity* (Edinburgh: Edinburgh University Press, 2017).

29 Daniel E. White, *From Little London to Little Bengal: Religion, Print, and Modernity in Early British India, 1793–1835* (Baltimore: Johns Hopkins University Press, 2013); Tim Harper, *Underground Asia: Global Revolutionaries and the Assault on Empire* (Cambridge, Mass.: Belknap Press of Harvard University Press, 2021).

30 Lois A. C. Raphael, *The Cape-to-Cairo Dream: A Study in British Imperialism* (New York: Columbia University Press, 1936); Andrew Beattie, *Cairo: A Cultural History* (New York: Oxford University Press, 2005).

31 Harper, *Underground Asia.*

32 Barbara Daly Metcalf, *Islamic Revival in British India: Deoband, 1860–1900* (Princeton, N.J.: Princeton University Press, 1982); Elizabeth Sirriyeh, *Sufis and Anti-Sufis: The Defense, Rethinking and Rejection of Sufism in the Modern World* (London: Curzon, 1999); Brannon D. Ingram, *Revival from Below: The Deoband Movement and Global Islam* (Oakland: University of California Press, 2018).

33 Umar Ryad, "Anti-Imperialism and the Pan-Islamic Movement," in Motadel, *Islam and the European Empires*, 131–49; Pankaj Mishra, *From the Ruins of Empire: The Intellectuals Who Remade Asia* (New York: Farrar, Straus and Giroux, 2012); Dominic Green, *The Religious Revolution: The Birth of Modern Spirituality, 1848–1898* (New York: Farrar, Straus and Giroux, 2022).

34 Andrew Hammond, *Late Ottoman Origins of Modern Islamic Thought: Turkish and Egyptian Thinkers on the Disruption of Islamic Knowledge* (New York: Cambridge University Press, 2023).

35 Reza Pankhurst, *The Inevitable Caliphate? A History of the Struggle for Global Islamic Union, 1924 to the Present* (London: Hurst, 2013).

36 Ruthven, *Islam in the World*; Roel Meijer, ed., *Global Salafism: Islam's New Religious Movement* (New York: Oxford University Press, 2013).

9 How Empires Remake Religions

1 Horace is quoted from Q. Horatius Flaccus (Horace), *Epistles*, ed. H. Rushton Fairclough, 409, http://www.perseus.tufts.edu/hopper/text?doc=Hor.%20Ep.%202.1&lang=original.

2 Lara, *Christian Texts for Aztecs.*

3 Björn Bentlage, Marion Eggert, Hans Martin Krämer, and Stefan Reichmuth, eds., *Religious Dynamics under the Impact of Imperialism and Colonialism: A Sourcebook* (Leiden: Brill, 2017).

4 Jenkins, *Crucible of Faith*; Lindsey Mazurek, *Isis in a Global Empire: Greek Identity through Egyptian Religion in Roman Greece* (Cambridge: Cambridge University Press, 2022).
5 "Quis nescit, Volusi Bithynice, qualia demens / Aegyptos portenta colat?" Juvenal, Satire 15, Latin Library, https://www.thelatinlibrary.com/juvenal/15.shtml.
6 Jenkins, *Storm of Images*.
7 Jenkins, *Storm of Images*.
8 1 Corinthians 13:3.
9 Rachel Mairs, *The Hellenistic Far East* (Berkeley: University of California Press, 2014); Jenkins, *Crucible of Faith*; Richard Stoneman, *The Greek Experience of India: From Alexander to the Indo-Greeks* (Princeton, N.J.: Princeton University Press, 2019).
10 Jenkins, *Lost History*; Michael Philip Penn, *Envisioning Islam: Syriac Christianity and the Early Muslim World* (Philadelphia: University of Pennsylvania Press, 2015).
11 Jenkins, *Lost History*; Dionigi Albera and Maria Couroucli, eds., *Sharing Sacred Spaces in the Mediterranean: Christians, Muslims, and Jews at Shrines and Sanctuaries* (Bloomington: Indiana University Press, 2012).
12 Bennison, *The Great Caliphs*; Robert G. Hoyland, ed., *The "History of the Kings of the Persians" in Three Arabic Chronicles: The Transmission of the Iranian Past from Late Antiquity to Early Islam* (Liverpool: Liverpool University Press, 2018); El-Hibri, *Abbasid Caliphate*; Kennedy, *The Prophet and the Age of the Caliphates*.
13 Stuart Cary Welch, *A King's Book of Kings: The Shah-Nameh of Shah Tahmasp* (New York: Metropolitan Museum of Art, 1972); Jon Thompson and Sheila R. Canby, eds., *Hunt for Paradise: Court Arts of Safavid Iran, 1501–1576* (Milan: Skira; London: Thames & Hudson, 2003); Ferdowsi, *Shahnameh*; Barbara Brend and Charles Melville, *Epic of the Persian Kings: The Art of Ferdowsi's Shahnameh* (London: I. B. Tauris, 2010).
14 Albrecht Fuess and Jan-Peter Hartung, eds., *Court Cultures in the Muslim World: Seventh to Nineteenth Centuries* (New York: Routledge, 2011); Mika Natif, *Mughal Occidentalism: Artistic Encounters between Europe and Asia at the Courts of India, 1580–1630* (Leiden: Brill, 2018).
15 Ramachandran, *History of Hinduism*.
16 David Kopf, *British Orientalism and the Bengal Renaissance: The Dynamics of Indian Modernization, 1773–1835* (Berkeley: University of California Press, 1969); Arvind Sharma, *Modern Hindu Thought: The Essential Texts* (New York: Oxford University Press, 2002); Subrata Dasgupta, *The Bengal Renaissance: Identity and Creativity from Rammohun Roy to Rabindranath Tagore* (New Delhi: distributed by Orient Longman, 2007); Brian A. Hatcher, *Hinduism before Reform* (Cambridge, Mass.: Harvard University Press, 2020).

17 Stuart Simmonds and Simon Digby, eds., *The Royal Asiatic Society: Its History and Treasures* (Leiden: published for the Royal Asiatic Society by E. J. Brill, 1979); Michael S. Dodson, *Orientalism, Empire, and National Culture: India, 1770–1880* (New York: Palgrave Macmillan, 2007); Michael J. Franklin, *Orientalist Jones: Sir William Jones, Poet, Lawyer, and Linguist, 1746–1794* (New York: Oxford University Press, 2011); Rajesh Kochhar, *Sanskrit and the British Empire* (New York: Routledge, 2021).

18 Alexander Cunningham, "An Account of the Discovery of the Ruins of the Buddhist City of Samkassa," *Journal of the Royal Asiatic Society* 7 (1843): 241–49.

19 Tapati Guha-Thakurta, *Monuments, Objects, Histories: Institutions of Art in Colonial and Postcolonial India* (New York: Columbia University Press, 2004); Michael Falser, ed., *Cultural Heritage as Civilizing Mission: From Decay to Recovery* (Cham, Switzerland: Springer, 2015).

20 Mortimer Wheeler, *Civilizations of the Indus Valley and Beyond* (New York: McGraw-Hill, 1966).

21 Jon R. Stone, ed., *The Essential Max Müller: On Language, Mythology, and Religion* (New York: Palgrave Macmillan, 2002); Lourens P. van den Bosch, *Friedrich Max Müller: A Life Devoted to the Humanities* (Leiden: Brill, 2002); David Chidester, *Empire of Religion: Imperialism and Comparative Religion* (Chicago: University of Chicago Press 2014); Ann Della Subin, *Accidental Gods* (New York: Macmillan, 2021).

22 Mick Brown, *The Nirvana Express: How the Search for Enlightenment Went West* (London: Hurst, 2023).

23 Ruth Harris, *Guru to the World: The Life and Legacy of Vivekananda* (Cambridge, Mass.: Belknap Press of Harvard University Press, 2022); M. Christhu Doss, *India after the 1857 Revolt: Decolonising the Mind* (New York: Routledge, 2023). "Vivekananda might have styled himself" is quoted from Michael Ledger-Lomas, "Against Boiled Cabbage," *London Review of Books*, February 2, 2023. "The admixture" is quoted from Romit Bagchi, "Rammohan Roy, Vivekananda and Tagore on British Rule," *Pioneer* (India), February 8, 2015, https://www.dailypioneer.com/2015/state-editions/rammohan-roy-vivekananda-and-tagore-on-british-rule.html.

24 Peter Gottschalk, *Religion, Science, and Empire: Classifying Hinduism and Islam in British India* (New York: Oxford University Press, 2013); Jenkins, *Great and Holy War*.

25 P. J. Marshall, *The British Discovery of Hinduism in the Eighteenth Century* (New York: Cambridge University Press, 1970); John Keay, *India Discovered* (New York: Harper Collins, 1988); David N. Lorenzen, *Who Invented Hinduism?* (New Delhi: Yoda Press, 2006).

26 Louis Daniel LeComte, *A Compleat History of the Empire of China: Being the Observations of Above Ten Years Travels Through That Country*, 2nd ed. (London: James Hodges, 1739); Charles Allen, *The Buddha and the Sahibs* (London: John Murray, 2002); Allen, *Coromandel*. For Indian scholars and the rediscovery of Buddhism, see Douglas Ober, *Dust on the Throne: The Search for Buddhism in Modern India* (Stanford, Calif.: Stanford University Press, 2023).

27 James Prinsep, *Essays on Indian Antiquities, Historic, Numismatic, and Palaeographic* (New Delhi: Asian Educational Services, 1995); J. Jeffrey Franklin, *The Lotus and the Lion: Buddhism and the British Empire* (Ithaca, N.Y.: Cornell University Press, 2008); Lars Fogelin, *An Archaeological History of Indian Buddhism* (New York: Oxford University Press, 2015); John S. Strong, *The Buddha's Tooth: Western Tales of a Sri Lankan Relic* (Chicago: University of Chicago Press, 2021); Zareer Masani, "How the British Saved India's Classical History," *Spectator*, January 29, 2023.

28 Letitia Landon, "Sarnat," in *The Cento: A Collection of Poetry, Original and Select* (London: Mitchell, 1840), 30.

29 Mark A. Nathan, *From the Mountains to the Cities: A History of Buddhist Propagation in Modern Korea* (Honolulu: University of Hawai'i Press, 2018).

30 E. Michael Mendelson, *Sangha and State in Burma* (Ithaca, N.Y.: Cornell University Press, 1975); Khammai Dhammasami, *Buddhism, Education and Politics in Burma and Thailand: From the Seventeenth Century to the Present* (London: Bloomsbury Academic, 2018). For later Burma, see Alicia Turner, *Saving Buddhism: The Impermanence of Religion in Colonial Burma* (Honolulu: University of Hawai'i Press, 2014); Alexandra Kaloyanides, *Baptizing Burma: Religious Change in the Last Buddhist Kingdom* (New York: Columbia University Press, 2023).

31 Shawn Frederick McHale, *Print and Power: Confucianism, Communism, and Buddhism in the Making of Modern Vietnam* (Honolulu: University of Hawai'i Press, 2004); George E. Dutton, Jayne S. Werner, and John K. Whitmore, eds., *Sources of Vietnamese Tradition* (New York: Columbia University Press, 2012).

32 James Edward Ketelaar, *Of Heretics and Martyrs in Meiji Japan: Buddhism and Its Persecution* (Princeton, N.J.: Princeton University Press, 1990); Thomas David DuBois, *Religion and the Making of Modern East Asia* (New York: Cambridge University Press, 2011).

33 Steven Kemper, *Rescued from the Nation: Anagarika Dharmapala and the Buddhist World* (Chicago: University of Chicago Press, 2015).

34 Sarath Amunugama, *The Lion's Roar: Anagarika Dharmapala and the Making of Modern Buddhism* (New Delhi: Oxford University Press, 2020); Ober, *Dust on the Throne*.

35 Donald S. Lopez Jr., *Prisoners of Shangri-La: Tibetan Buddhism and the West* (Chicago: University of Chicago Press, 1998).

36 Peter Perdue, *China Marches West: The Qing Conquest of Central Eurasia* (Cambridge, Mass.: Belknap Press of Harvard University Press, 2005); Ishihama Yumiko and Alex McKay, eds., *The Early 20th Century Resurgence of the Tibetan Buddhist World: Studies in Central Asian Buddhism* (Amsterdam: Amsterdam University Press, 2021); Lan Wu, *Common Ground: Tibetan Buddhist Expansion and Qing China's Inner Asia* (New York: Columbia University Press, 2022).

37 John Powers, *The Buddha Party: How the People's Republic of China Works to Define and Control Tibetan Buddhism* (New York: Oxford University Press, 2016).

38 Mara Lisa Arizaga, *When Tibetan Meditation Goes Global: A Study of the Adaptation of Bon Religious Practices in the West* (Berlin: De Gruyter, 2022).

39 Jason Ananda Josephson Storm, *The Invention of Religion in Japan* (Chicago: University of Chicago Press, 2012); Nongbri, *Before Religion.*

40 Lionel M. Jensen, *Manufacturing Confucianism: Chinese Traditions and Universal Civilization* (Durham, N.C.: Duke University Press, 1998); Lydia Liu, *The Clash of Empires: The Invention of China in Modern World Making* (Cambridge, Mass.: Harvard University Press, 2004); Chris Murray, *China from the Ruins of Athens and Rome: Classics, Sinology, and Romanticism, 1793–1938* (New York: Oxford University Press, 2020).

41 Rebecca Nedostup, *Superstitious Regimes: Religion and the Politics of Chinese Modernity* (Cambridge, Mass.: Harvard University Press, 2009); Kai-wing Chow, "Imperialism, Reform, and the End of Institutional Confucianism in the Late Qing," in *The Oxford Handbook of Confucianism*, ed. Jennifer Oldstone-Moore (Oxford University Press, 2023), 191–203.

42 Martin Kahler, *Schriften zur Christologie und Mission* (Munich: Christian Kaiser, 1971).

43 David A. Hollinger, *Protestants Abroad: How Missionaries Tried to Change the World but Changed America* (Princeton, N.J.: Princeton University Press, 2017).

44 Geoffrey Wainwright, *Lesslie Newbigin: A Theological Life* (New York: Oxford University Press, 2000); Robert Eric Frykenberg, *Christianity in India: From Beginnings to the Present* (New York: Oxford University Press, 2008).

45 Richard Hughes Seager, *The World's Parliament of Religions: The East/West Encounter, Chicago, 1893* (Bloomington: Indiana University Press, 1995); Edward W. Bristow, ed., *No Religion Is an Island: The Nostra Aetate Dialogues* (New York: Fordham University Press, 1998); Second Vatican Council, "Nostra Aetate: Declaration on the Relationship of the Church to Non-Christian Religions," October 28, 1965, https://www.bc.edu/content/dam/files/research_sites/cjl/texts/cjrelations/resources/documents/catholic/Nostra_Aetate.htm.

46 Philip Jenkins, *Mystics and Messiahs: Cults and New Religions in American History* (New York: Oxford University Press, 2000); Tomoko Masuzawa, *The Invention of World Religions; or, How European Universalism Was Preserved in the Language of Pluralism* (Chicago: University of Chicago Press, 2005); Dominic Green, *The Religious Revolution*; Alexander Bubb, *Asian Classics on The Victorian Bookshelf: Flights of Translation* (Oxford University Press, 2023). Schopenhauer is quoted from Arati Barua, "Schopenhauer's Philosophy of Will and Sankara's Advaita Vedanta: A Comparative Study," *Proceedings of the XXII World Congress of Philosophy* 8 (2008): 23–29. Schlegel is quoted from Nitin Mehta, "A Nation Born Out of Sanskrit, and Still in Love with It," *Daily Guardian* (India), October 17, 2020.

47 Henry David Thoreau, *Walden* (New York: Oxford University Press, 1999).

48 Ralph Waldo Emerson, "Brahma," Poetry Foundation, https://www.poetryfoundation.org/poems/45868/brahma-56d225936127b.

49 Dominic Green, *The Religious Revolution*; Tim Rudbøg and Erik Reenberg, eds., *Imagining the East: The Early Theosophical Society* (New York: Oxford University Press, 2020).

50 M. K. Gandhi, *Gandhi's Autobiography: The Story of My Experiments with Truth* (Washington, DC: Public Affairs Press, 1948), 90–93; Pupul Jayakar, *Krishnamurti: A Biography* (San Francisco: Harper & Row, 1986); Gananath Obeyesekere, *The Buddha in Sri Lanka: Histories and Stories* (London: Routledge / Taylor & Francis Group, 2018).

51 Jenkins, *The Many Faces of Christ*.

52 Jenkins, *Mystics and Messiahs*; Claire Gecewicz, "'New Age' Beliefs Common among Both Religious and Nonreligious Americans," Pew Research Center (2018), https://www.pewresearch.org/fact-tank/2018/10/01/new-age-beliefs-common-among-both-religious-and-nonreligious-americans/.

10 The Ends of Empire

1 Rudyard Kipling, "Recessional," Poetry Foundation, https://www.poetryfoundation.org/poems/46780/recessional.

2 William Cowper, "Boadicea: An Ode," Eighteenth-Century Poetry Archive, https://www.eighteenthcenturypoetry.org/works/o3794-w0400.shtml.

3 Rothermund, *Memories of Post-imperial Nations*.

4 Sarris, *Empires of Faith*.

5 Hendrik W. Dey, *The Afterlife of the Roman City: Architecture and Ceremony in Late Antiquity and the Early Middle Ages* (New York: Cambridge University Press, 2014).

6 Martin Thomas and Andrew Thompson, eds., *The Oxford Handbook of the Ends of Empire* (New York: Oxford University Press, 2018).

7 Raymond F. Betts, *Decolonization*, 2nd ed. (Abingdon, UK: Routledge, 2004); Ronald Hyam, *Britain's Declining Empire: The Road to Decolonisation, 1918–1968* (Cambridge: Cambridge University Press, 2006); W. David McIntyre, *Winding Up the British Empire in the Pacific Islands*, Oxford History of the British Empire Companion Series (Oxford: Oxford University Press, 2014); Tracey Banivanua Mar, *Decolonisation and the Pacific: Indigenous Globalisation and the Ends of Empire* (New York: Cambridge University Press, 2016); Jan C. Jansen and Jürgen Osterhammel, *Decolonization: A Short History* (Princeton, N.J.: Princeton University Press, 2017); Thijs Brocades Zaalberg and Bart Luttikhuis, eds., *Empire's Violent End: Comparing Dutch, British, and French Wars of Decolonization, 1945–1962* (Ithaca, N.Y.: Cornell University Press, 2022).

8 For the impact of the end of empire on European nations, see Elizabeth Buettner, *Europe after Empire: Decolonization, Society, and Culture* (New York: Cambridge University Press, 2016).

9 John Jansen van Galen, *Afscheid van de koloniën: Het Nederlandse dekolonisatiebeleid 1942–2012* (Amsterdam: Atlas Contact, 2013); Sung-Eun Choi, *Decolonization and the French of Algeria: Bringing the Settler Colony Home* (London: Palgrave Macmillan, 2016); Andrew W. M. Smith and Chris Jeppesen, eds., *Britain, France and the Decolonization of Africa: Future Imperfect?* (London: University College London Press, 2017).

10 Judith M. Brown and William Roger Louis, eds., *The Twentieth Century*, in Louis, *The Oxford History of the British Empire*; MacKenzie, *Cultural History of the British Empire*.

11 Amit Ranjan, ed., *Partition of India: Postcolonial Legacies* (Abingdon, UK: Routledge, 2019).

12 Martin S. Shanguhyia and Toyin Falola, eds., *The Palgrave Handbook of African Colonial and Postcolonial History*, 2 vols. (London: Palgrave Macmillan, 2018).

13 Darcie Fontaine, *Decolonizing Christianity: Religion and the End of Empire in France and Algeria* (New York: Cambridge University Press, 2016).

14 Piero Gheddo, *The Cross and the Bo-Tree: Catholics and Buddhists in Vietnam* (New York: Sheed and Ward, 1970).

15 Frykenberg, *Christianity in India*.

16 Hugh McLeod, ed., *World Christianities c.1914–c.2000*, vol. 9 of *The Cambridge History of Christianity* (New York: Cambridge University Press, 2006); Sanneh, *Disciples of All Nations*; Brian Stanley, *Christianity in the Twentieth Century: A World History* (Princeton, N.J.: Princeton University Press, 2018); Zurlo, *Global Christianity*; Elizabeth A. Foster and Udi Greenberg, eds., *Decolonization and the Remaking of Christianity* (Philadelphia: University of Pennsylvania Press, 2023).

17 Giuliana Chamedes and Elizabeth A. Foster, "Decolonization and Religion in the French Empire," *French Politics, Culture and Society* 33, no. 2 (2015): 1–10.

18 Elizabeth A. Foster, *African Catholic: Decolonization and the Transformation of the Church*, roundtable for H-DIPLO, June 22, 2020, https://networks.h-net.org/node/28443/discussions/6202254/h-diplo-roundtable-xxi-47-foster-african-catholic-decolonization.

19 Jenkins, *Next Christendom.*

20 Philip Jenkins, *The New Faces of Christianity: Believing the Bible in the Global South* (New York: Oxford University Press, 2006).

21 Jenkins, *Next Christendom*; Ruth Marshall, *Political Spiritualities: The Pentecostal Revolution in Nigeria* (Chicago: University of Chicago Press, 2009).

22 Philip Jenkins, *Fertility and Faith: The Demographic Revolution That Is Transforming All the World's Religions* (Waco, Tex.: Baylor University Press, 2020).

23 Fernando Arenas, *Lusophone Africa: Beyond Independence* (Minneapolis: University of Minnesota Press, 2011).

24 Jenkins, *Fertility and Faith*; Mike Phillips and Trevor Phillips, *Windrush: The Irresistible Rise of Multi-racial Britain* (London: HarperCollins, 1998).

25 Office for National Statistics, "Ethnic Group, England and Wales: Census 2021," https://www.ons.gov.uk/peoplepopulationandcommunity/culturalidentity/ethnicity/bulletins/ethnicgroupenglandandwales/census2021.

26 Jenkins, *God's Continent.*

27 Gijsbert Oonk, ed., *Global Indian Diasporas: Exploring Trajectories of Migration and Theory* (Amsterdam: Amsterdam University Press, 2007); Claire Alexander, Joya Chatterji, and Annu Jalais, *The Bengal Diaspora: Rethinking Muslim Migration* (London: Routledge / Taylor & Francis Group, 2016).

28 Gurcharn S. Basran and B. Singh Bolaria, *The Sikhs in Canada: Migration, Race, Class, and Gender* (New Delhi: Oxford University Press, 2003); Pashaura Singh, ed., *Sikhism in Global Context* (New Delhi: Oxford University Press, 2011); Kamala Elizabeth Nayar, *The Punjabis in British Columbia: Location, Labour, First Nations, and Multiculturalism* (Montreal: McGill-Queen's University Press, 2012); Peter Beyer and Rubina Ramji, eds., *Growing Up Canadian: Muslims, Hindus, Buddhists* (Montreal: McGill-Queen's University Press, 2013).

29 Helena Vilaça, Enzo Pace, Inger Furseth, and Per Pettersson, eds., *The Changing Soul of Europe: Religions and Migrations in Northern and Southern Europe* (Burlington, Vt.: Ashgate, 2014); Jocelyne Cesari, ed., *The Oxford Handbook of European Islam* (New York: Oxford University Press, 2015).

30 "Europe's Growing Muslim Population," Pew Research Center (2017), https://www.pewresearch.org/religion/2017/11/29/europes-growing-muslim-population/; Ron Geaves, *Islam and Britain: Muslim Mission in an Age of Empire* (London: Bloomsbury Academic, 2018); Jenkins, *Fertility and Faith.*

31 Jenkins, *God's Continent*; Haideh Moghissi, Saeed Rahnema, and Mark J. Goodman, *Diaspora by Design: Muslims in Canada and Beyond* (Toronto: University of Toronto Press, 2009).

32 Simona E. Merati, *Muslims in Putin's Russia: Discourse on Identity, Politics, and Security* (Cham, Switzerland: Palgrave Macmillan, 2017); Jenkins, *Fertility and Faith.*

33 Olivier Roy, *Holy Ignorance: When Religion and Culture Part Ways* (New York: Columbia University Press, 2010); P. Akhtar, *British Muslim Politics: Examining Pakistani Biraderi Networks* (London: Palgrave Macmillan, 2013).

34 Jenkins, *God's Continent.*

35 Frieder Ludwig and J. Kwabena Asamoah-Gyadu, *African Christian Presence in the West: New Immigrant Congregations and Transnational Networks in North America and Europe* (Trenton, N.J.: Africa World Press, 2011).

36 Jenkins, *God's Continent.*

37 William L. Sachs, *Global Anglicanism, c.1910–2000*, vol. 5 of Strong, *The Oxford History of Anglicanism.*

38 Kevin Ward, *A History of Global Anglicanism* (New York: Cambridge University Press, 2006).

39 Miranda K. Hassett, *Anglican Communion in Crisis: How Episcopal Dissidents and Their African Allies Are Reshaping Anglicanism* (Princeton, N.J.: Princeton University Press, 2007); Christopher Craig Brittain and Andrew McKinnon, *The Anglican Communion at a Crossroads: The Crises of a Global Church* (University Park: Pennsylvania State University Press, 2018).

Conclusion

1 Winston Churchill, "The Gift of a Common Tongue," speech delivered at Harvard University, September 6, 1943, International Churchill Society, https://winstonchurchill.org/resources/speeches/1941-1945-war-leader/the-gift-of-a-common-tongue/. Compare Gildea, *Empires of the Mind.*

2 For Abbott, see Riaz Dean, *Mapping the Great Game: Explorers, Spies and Maps in 19th-Century Asia* (Havertown, Pa.: Casemate, 2020). His poem can be found at https://en.wikipedia.org/wiki/Abbottabad_(poem). Peter L. Bergen, *Manhunt: The Ten-Year Search for bin Laden, from 9/11 to Abbottabad* (New York: Crown, 2012).

3 For the new age of global empires, see Alasdair Roberts, *Superstates*; Serhii Plokhy, *The Russo-Ukrainian War: The Return of History* (New York: Norton, 2023).

4 For emerging visions of "imperial Europe," see Bruno Le Maire, *Le nouvel empire: L'Europe du vingt et unième siècle* (Paris: Éditions Gallimard, 2019); Luuk van Middelaar, *The Passage to Europe: How a Continent Became a Union* (New Haven, Conn.: Yale University Press, 2020); Caroline De Gruyter, *Monde d'hier, monde de demain? Un voyage à travers l'Empire des Habsbourg et l'Union Européenne* (Arles, France: Actes Sud, 2023). For the persistence of older racial agendas, see Hans Kundnani, *Eurowhiteness: Culture, Empire and Race in the European Project* (London: Hurst, 2023).

5 C. Christine Fair, *In Their Own Words: Understanding Lashkar-e-Tayyaba* (London: Hurst, 2019).

6 Richard Overy, *Blood and Ruins: The Great Imperial War 1931–1945* (London: Allen Lane, 2021); Richard Overy, *Blood and Ruins: The Last Imperial War 1931–1945* (New York: Viking, 2022).

7 Sarah Rainsford, "Putin and Peter the Great: Russian Leader Likens Himself to 18th Century Tsar," BBC News, June 10, 2022, https://www.bbc.com/news/world-europe-61767191; Hanna Stähle, *Russian Church in the Digital Era: Mediatization of Orthodoxy* (New York: Routledge, 2021).

8 M. Hakan Yavuz, *Erdoğan: The Making of an Autocrat* (Edinburgh: Edinburgh University Press, 2021); "Erdoğan Says 'We Will Bury the Neo-Byzantines'—Provocative Light Show Set Up on Hagia Sophia," *Greek City Times*, May 30, 2022, https://greekcitytimes.com/2022/05/30/erdogan-neo-byzantine-hagia-sophia/.

9 Churchill, "The Gift of a Common Tongue." Henry Farrell and Abraham Newman, *Underground Empire: How America Weaponized the World Economy* (New York: Henry Holt, 2023).

Bibliography

Abramson, Marc S. *Ethnic Identity in Tang China*. Philadelphia: University of Pennsylvania Press, 2008.

Acri, Andrea. *Esoteric Buddhism in Mediaeval Maritime Asia: Networks of Masters, Texts, Icons*. Honolulu: University of Hawai'i Press, 2016.

Acri, Andrea, Helen Creese, and Arlo Griffiths, eds. *From Lanka Eastwards: The Ramayana in the Literature and Visual Arts of Indonesia*. Leiden: KITLV Press, 2011.

Acri, Andrea, and Paolo E. Rosati, eds. *Tantra, Magic, and Vernacular Religions in Monsoon Asia: Texts, Practices, and Practitioners from the Margins*. New York: Routledge, 2023.

Acri, Andrea, and Peter Sharrock, eds. *The Creative South: Buddhist and Hindu Art in Mediaeval Maritime Asia*. Vol. 1. Singapore: ISEAS—Yusof Ishak Institute, 2022.

Adler, Yonatan. *The Origins of Judaism: An Archaeological-Historical Reappraisal*. New Haven, Conn.: Yale University Press, 2022.

"A Historical Perspective of Urdu." National Council for Promotion of Urdu Language. https://www.urducouncil.nic.in/council/historical-perspective-urdu.

Aillet, Cyrille. *Les Mozarabes: Christianisme et Arabisation en al-Andalus (IXe–XIIe siècle)*. Madrid: Casa de Velázquez, 2010.

Akhtar, Ali Humayun. *1368: China and the Making of the Modern World*. Stanford, Calif.: Stanford University Press, 2022.

Akhtar, P. *British Muslim Politics: Examining Pakistani Biraderi Networks*. London: Palgrave Macmillan, 2013.

Akira, Hirakawa. *A History of Indian Buddhism: From Śākyamuni to Early Mahāyāna*. Honolulu: University of Hawai'i Press, 1990.

Alam, Muzaffar. *The Mughals and the Sufis: Islam and Political Imagination in India, 1500–1750*. Albany: SUNY Press, 2021.

Albera, Dionigi, and Maria Couroucli, eds. *Sharing Sacred Spaces in the Mediterranean: Christians, Muslims, and Jews at Shrines and Sanctuaries*. Bloomington: Indiana University Press, 2012.

Alberts, Tara. *Conflict and Conversion: Catholicism in Southeast Asia, 1500–1700*. New York: Oxford University Press, 2013.

Alconini, Sonia, and Alan Covey, eds. *The Oxford Handbook of the Incas*. New York: Oxford University Press, 2018.

Aldrich, Robert. *Greater France: A History of French Overseas Expansion*. London: Palgrave Macmillan, 1996.

———. *The French Presence in the South Pacific, 1842–1940*. Honolulu: University of Hawai'i Press, 1989.

———. *Vestiges of the Colonial Empire in France: Monuments, Museums and Colonial Memories*. New York: Palgrave Macmillan, 2005.

Aldrich, Robert, and Cindy McCreery, eds. *Crowns and Colonies: European Monarchies and Overseas Empires*. Manchester: Manchester University Press, 2016.

Aldrich, Robert, and Kirsten McKenzie, eds. *The Routledge History of Western Empires*. Abingdon, UK: Routledge, 2014.

Alexander, Claire, Joya Chatterji, and Annu Jalais. *The Bengal Diaspora: Rethinking Muslim Migration*. London: Routledge, 2016.

Alexander, Loveday, ed., *Images of Empire*. Sheffield, UK: Sheffield Academic Press, 1991.

Ali, Muhamad. *Islam and Colonialism: Becoming Modern in Indonesia and Malaya*. Edinburgh: Edinburgh University Press, 2016.

Ali, Omar H. *Islam in the Indian Ocean World*. Boston: Bedford/St. Martin's, 2016.

Allen, Charles. *The Buddha and the Sahibs*. London: John Murray, 2002.

———. *Coromandel: A Personal History of South India*. New York: Little, Brown, 2018.

Amunugama, Sarath. *The Lion's Roar: Anagarika Dharmapala and the Making of Modern Buddhism*. New Delhi: Oxford University Press, 2020.

Andaya, Barbara Watson, and Leonard Y. Andaya. *A History of Malaysia*. 3rd ed. London: Palgrave, 2017.

Anderson, Benedict. "Exodus." *Critical Inquiry* 20 (1994): 314–27.

———. *Imagined Communities: Reflections on the Origin and Spread of Nationalism*. 2nd ed. London: Verso, 2006.

———. *The Spectre of Comparisons: Nationalism, Southeast Asia, and the World*. London: Verso, 1998.

Anderson, Clare. *Convicts: A Global History*. New York: Cambridge University Press, 2021.

———. *Subaltern Lives: Biographies of Colonialism in the Indian Ocean World, 1790–1920*. New York: Cambridge University Press, 2012.

Anderson, Glaire D., Corisande Fenwick, and Mariam Rosser-Owen, with Sihem Lamine, eds. *The Aghlabids and Their Neighbours: Art and Material Culture in Ninth-Century North Africa*. Boston: Brill, 2018.

Anderson, Ian. "Sitting Bull and the Mounties." *Wild West* 10, no. 5 (1998). https://www.historynet.com/sitting-bull.

Andrade, Nathanael J. *The Journey of Christianity to India in Late Antiquity: Networks and the Movement of Culture*. Cambridge: Cambridge University Press, 2018.

Angold, Michael, ed. *Eastern Christianity*. Vol. 5 of *The Cambridge History of Christianity*. New York: Cambridge University Press, 2006.

Anjum, Tanvir. *Chishtī Sufis in the Sultanate of Delhi, 1190–1400: From Restrained Indifference to Calculated Defiance*. Karachi: Oxford University Press, 2011.

Anson, Edward M. *Alexander's Heirs: The Age of the Successors*. Malden, Mass.: Wiley-Blackwell, 2014.

Aquil, Raziuddin, ed. *Sufism and Society in Medieval India*. New Delhi: Oxford University Press, 2010.

Arenas, Fernando. *Lusophone Africa: Beyond Independence.* Minneapolis: University of Minnesota Press, 2011.

Arevalo, Ernesto Bassi. *An Aqueous Territory: Sailor Geographies and New Granada's Transimperial Greater Caribbean World.* Durham, N.C.: Duke University Press, 2016.

Arias, Santa, and Raul Marrero-Fente, eds. *Coloniality, Religion, and the Law in the Early Iberian World.* Nashville, Tenn.: Vanderbilt University Press, 2014.

Arizaga, Mara Lisa. *When Tibetan Meditation Goes Global: A Study of the Adaptation of Bon Religious Practices in the West.* Berlin: De Gruyter, 2022.

Asher, Frederick M. *Sarnath: A Critical History of the Place Where Buddhism Began.* Los Angeles: Getty Research Institute, 2020.

Aslanian, Sebouh David. *From the Indian Ocean to the Mediterranean: The Global Trade Networks of Armenian Merchants from New Julfa.* Berkeley: University of California Press, 2010.

Asmussen, Jes Peter. "Christians in Iran." In Yarshater, *The Seleucid, Parthian and Sasanid Periods*, 924–48.

Atkins, Gareth, Shinjini Das, and Brian Murray, eds. *Chosen Peoples: The Bible, Race and Empire in the Long Nineteenth Century.* Manchester: Manchester University Press, 2020.

Atwal, Priya. *Royals and Rebels: The Rise and Fall of the Sikh Empire.* London: Hurst, 2021.

Aung-Thwin, Michael. *Pagan: The Origins of Modern Burma.* Honolulu: University of Hawai'i Press, 1985.

Autiero, Serena, and Matthew Adam Cobb, eds. *Globalization and Transculturality from Antiquity to the Pre-modern World.* Abingdon, UK: Routledge, 2023.

Avari, Burjor. *India, the Ancient Past: A History of the Indian Sub-continent from c. 7000 BC to AD 1200.* New York: Routledge, 2007.

Axworthy, Michael. *The Sword of Persia: Nader Shah, From Tribal Warrior to Conquering Tyrant.* London: I. B. Tauris, 2009.

Badian, E. *Publicans and Sinners: Private Enterprise in the Service of the Roman Republic.* Ithaca, N.Y.: Cornell University Press, 1972.

Baer, Marc David. *Honored by the Glory of Islam: Conversion and Conquest in Ottoman Europe.* New York: Oxford University Press, 2008.

———. *The Ottomans: Khans, Caesars, and Caliphs.* New York: Basic Books, 2021.

Bagchi, Romit. "Rammohan Roy, Vivekananda and Tagore on British Rule." *Pioneer*, February 8, 2015. https://www.dailypioneer.com/2015/state-editions/rammohan-roy-vivekananda-and-tagore-on-british-rule.html.

Balabanlilar, Lisa. *Imperial Identity in the Mughal Empire: Memory and Dynastic Politics in Early Modern South and Central Asia.* London: I. B. Tauris, 2012.

Ball, Warwick. *The Monuments of Afghanistan: History, Archaeology and Architecture.* London: I. B. Tauris, 2008.

Bang, Peter Fibiger, and C. A. Bayly, eds. *Tributary Empires in Global History.* New York: Palgrave Macmillan, 2011.

Bang, Peter Fibiger, C. A. Bayly, and Walter Scheidel, eds. *The Oxford World History of Empire.* 2 vols. New York: Oxford University Press, 2021.

Barbón, María Soledad. *Colonial Loyalties: Celebrating the Spanish Monarchy in Eighteenth-Century Lima*. Notre Dame, Ind.: University of Notre Dame Press, 2019.

Barczewski, Stephanie. *Country Houses and the British Empire, 1700–1930*. Manchester: Manchester University Press, 2014.

Barr, Colin, and Hilary M. Carey, eds. *Religion and Greater Ireland: Christianity and Irish Global Networks, 1750–1950*. Montreal: McGill-Queen's University Press, 2015.

Barrett, T. H. "Translation and Transmission of Buddhist Texts." Discovering Sacred Texts. British Library. https://www.bl.uk/sacred-texts/articles/translation-and-transmission-of-buddhism.

Bartlett, John R., ed. *Jews in the Hellenistic and Roman Cities*. New York: Routledge, 2002.

Barton, Gregory A. *Informal Empire and the Rise of One World Culture*. London: Palgrave Macmillan, 2014.

Bartov, Omer, and Eric D. Weitz, eds. *Shatterzone of Empires: Coexistence and Violence in the German, Habsburg, Russian, and Ottoman Borderlands*. Indianapolis: Indiana University Press, 2013.

Barua, Arati. "Schopenhauer's Philosophy of Will and Sankara's Advaita Vedanta: A Comparative Study." *Proceedings of the XXII World Congress of Philosophy* 8 (2008): 23–29.

Basran, Gurcharn S., and B. Singh Bolaria. *The Sikhs in Canada: Migration, Race, Class, and Gender*. New Delhi: Oxford University Press, 2003.

Bassett, Sarah, ed., *The Cambridge Companion to Constantinople*. Cambridge: Cambridge University Press, 2022.

Baumer, Christoph. *The Church of the East*. New York: I. B. Tauris, 2006.

Baumgart, Winfried. *Imperialism: The Idea and Reality of British and French Colonial Expansion, 1880–1914*. New York: Oxford University Press, 1982.

Bayly, C. A. *Empire and Information: Intelligence Gathering and Social Communication in India, 1780–1870*. New York: Cambridge University Press, 1996.

———. *Imperial Meridian: The British Empire and the World, 1780–1830*. London: Routledge, 1989.

Bayne, Brandon. *Missions Begin with Blood: Suffering and Salvation in the Borderlands of New Spain*. New York: Fordham University Press, 2021.

Beard, Mary. *SPQR: A History of Ancient Rome*. New York: Liveright, 2015.

Beattie, Andrew. *Cairo: A Cultural History*. New York: Oxford University Press, 2005.

Beckwith, Christopher I. *Empires of the Silk Road: A History of Central Eurasia from the Bronze Age to the Present*. Princeton, N.J.: Princeton University Press, 2009.

———. *The Scythian Empire: Central Eurasia and the Birth of the Classical Age from Persia to China*. Princeton, N.J.: Princeton University Press, 2023.

———. *The Tibetan Empire in Central Asia: A History of the Struggle for Great Power among Tibetans, Turks, Arabs, and Chinese during the Early Middle Ages*. Princeton, N.J.: Princeton University Press, 1987.

Beinart, William, and Lotte Hughes. *Environment and Empire*. Oxford History of the British Empire Companion Series. Oxford: Oxford University Press, 2007.

Belich, James. *Replenishing the Earth: The Settler Revolution and the Rise of the Angloworld, 1780–1939*. New York: Oxford University Press, 2009.
Benite, Zvi Ben-Dor. *The Ten Lost Tribes: A World History*. New York: Oxford University Press, 2009.
Benjamin, Craig, ed. *A World with States, Empires and Networks 1200 BCE–900 CE*. Vol. 4 of *The Cambridge World History*. New York: Cambridge University Press, 2015.
Benjamin, Craig. *Empires of Ancient Eurasia: The First Silk Roads Era, 100 BCE–250 CE*. New York: Cambridge University Press, 2018.
Bennison, Amira K. "Empire and Religion." In Bang, Bayly, and Scheidel, *Oxford World History of Empire*, 1:318–41.
———. *The Great Caliphs: The Golden Age of the ʿAbbasid Empire*. New Haven, Conn.: Yale University Press, 2009.
Bentlage, Björn, Marion Eggert, Hans Martin Krämer, and Stefan Reichmuth, eds. *Religious Dynamics under the Impact of Imperialism and Colonialism: A Sourcebook*. Leiden: Brill, 2017.
Berg, Maxine, and Pat Hudson. *Slavery, Capitalism and the Industrial Revolution*. London: Polity, 2023.
Bergen, Peter L. *Manhunt: The Ten-Year Search for bin Laden, from 9/11 to Abbottabad*. New York: Crown, 2012.
Best, Jeremy. *Heavenly Fatherland: German Missionary Culture and Globalization in the Age of Empire*. Toronto: University of Toronto Press, 2021.
Betts, Raymond F. *Decolonization*. 2nd ed. Abingdon, UK: Routledge, 2004.
Beyer, Peter, and Rubina Ramji, eds. *Growing Up Canadian: Muslims, Hindus, Buddhists*. Montreal: McGill-Queen's University Press, 2013.
Bickers, Robert, ed. *Settlers and Expatriates: Britons over the Seas*. Oxford History of the British Empire Companion Series. Oxford: Oxford University Press, 2010.
Biggar, Nigel. *Colonialism: A Moral Reckoning*. London: William Collins, 2023.
Billings, Drew W. *Acts of the Apostles and the Rhetoric of Roman Imperialism*. Cambridge: Cambridge University Press, 2017.
Bjork, Katharine. *Prairie Imperialists: The Indian Country Origins of American Empire*. Philadelphia: University of Pennsylvania Press, 2019.
Blackburn, Carole. *Harvest of Souls: The Jesuit Missions and Colonialism in North America, 1632–1650*. Montreal: McGill-Queen's University Press, 2000.
Blackle, Adam A. *An Imperial Homeland: Forging German Identity in Southwest Africa*. University Park: Pennsylvania State Press, 2022.
Blow, David. *Shah Abbas: The Ruthless King Who Became an Iranian Legend*. London: I. B. Tauris, 2009.
Blyth, Robert J., and Keith Jeffery, eds. *The British Empire and Its Contested Pasts*. Dublin: Irish Academic Press, 2009.
Bonner, Michael. *The Last Empire of Iran*. New York: Gorgias, 2020.
Boonhout, Bram. *Borderless Empire: Dutch Guiana in the Atlantic World, 1750–1800*. Athens: University of Georgia Press, 2020.
Bosch, Lourens P. van den. *Friedrich Max Müller: A Life Devoted to the Humanities*. Leiden: Brill, 2002.
Bose, Mandakranta, ed. *The Oxford History of Hinduism: The Goddess*. New York: Oxford University Press, 2018.

Bose, Sugata. *A Hundred Horizons: The Indian Ocean in the Age of Global Empire*. Cambridge, Mass.: Harvard University Press, 2009.

Bosma, Ulbe. *The World of Sugar: How the Sweet Stuff Transformed Our Politics, Health, and Environment over 2,000 Years*. Cambridge, Mass.: Harvard University Press, 2023.

Bracke, Wouter, Jan Nelis, and Jan De Maeyer, eds. *Renovatio, Inventio, Absentia Imperii: From the Roman Empire to Contemporary Imperialism*. Brussels: Academia Belgica, 2018.

Brancaccio, Pia, and Kurt Behrendt, eds. *Gandharan Buddhism: Archaeology, Art and Texts*. Vancouver: University of British Columbia Press, 2006.

Brend, Barbara, and Charles Melville. *Epic of the Persian Kings: The Art of Ferdowsi's Shahnameh*. London: I. B. Tauris, 2010.

Brett, Michael. *The Fatimid Empire*. Edinburgh: Edinburgh University Press, 2017.

Bright, Rachel K. *Chinese Labour in South Africa, 1902–10: Race, Violence, and Global Spectacle*. Houndmills, UK: Palgrave Macmillan, 2013.

Bristow, Edward W., ed. *No Religion Is an Island: The Nostra Aetate Dialogues*. New York: Fordham University Press, 1998.

Brittain, Christopher Craig, and Andrew McKinnon. *The Anglican Communion at a Crossroads: The Crises of a Global Church*. University Park: Pennsylvania State University Press, 2018.

Brockey, Liam Matthew. *Journey to the East: The Jesuit Mission to China, 1579–1724*. Cambridge, Mass.: Harvard University Press, 2017.

———. *The Visitor: André Palmeiro and the Jesuits in Asia*. Cambridge, Mass.: Belknap Press, 2014.

Brockey, Liam Matthew, ed. *Portuguese Colonial Cities in the Early Modern World*. New York: Routledge, 2008.

Bromberg, Anne R., Frederick M. Asher, Catherine B. Asher, Nancy Tingley, and Robert Warren Clark. *The Arts of India, Southeast Asia, and the Himalayas: At the Dallas Museum of Art*. Dallas: Dallas Museum of Art, 2013.

Bronkhorst, Johannes. *Greater Magadha: Studies in the Culture of Early India*. Leiden: Brill, 2007.

Brontë, Charlotte. "The Missionary." In *The Complete Poems of Charlotte Brontë*, edited by Clement Shorter, with bibliography and notes by C. W. Hatfield. London: Hodder and Stoughton, 1923. Full text available online at HathiTrust, https://www.hathitrust.org.

Broughton, Jeffrey L. *The Bodhidharma Anthology: The Earliest Records of Zen*. Berkeley: University of California Press, 1999.

Brower, Daniel R. *The Russian City between Tradition and Modernity, 1850–1900*. Berkeley: University of California Press, 1990.

Brown Judith M., ed. *The Twentieth Century*. Vol. 4 of Louis, *The Oxford History of the British Empire*.

Brown, Matthew, ed. *Informal Empire in Latin America: Culture, Commerce and Capital*. Oxford: Blackwell, 2008.

Brown, Mick. *The Nirvana Express: How the Search for Enlightenment Went West*. London: Hurst, 2023.

Brown, Peter. *The Rise of Western Christendom: Triumph and Diversity, A.D. 200–1000*. Malden, Mass.: Blackwell, 2003.

Brown, Sara E., and Stephen D. Smith, eds. *The Routledge Handbook of Religion, Mass Atrocity, and Genocide*. New York: Routledge, 2022.

Brown, Stewart J., and Timothy Tackett, eds. *Enlightenment, Reawakening and Revolution 1660–1815*. Vol. 7 of *The Cambridge History of Christianity*. New York: Cambridge University Press, 2006.

Bryce, James. "Religion as a Factor in the History of Empires." *Journal of Roman Studies* 5 (1915): 1–22.

Bubb, Alexander. *Asian Classics on The Victorian Bookshelf: Flights of Translation*. Oxford: Oxford University Press, 2023.

Buettner, Elizabeth. *Europe after Empire: Decolonization, Society, and Culture*. New York: Cambridge University Press, 2016.

Bugh, Glenn R., ed. *The Cambridge Companion to the Hellenistic World*. New York: Cambridge University Press, 2006.

Bulliet, Richard W. *Conversion to Islam in the Medieval Period: An Essay in Quantitative History*. Cambridge, Mass.: Harvard University Press, 1979.

Burbank, Jane, and Frederick Cooper. *Empires in World History: Power and the Politics of Difference*. Princeton, N.J.: Princeton University Press, 2010.

Burrus, Virginia. *The Making of a Heretic: Gender, Authority, and the Priscillianist Controversy*. Berkeley: University of California, 1995.

Burton, Antoinette. *The Trouble with Empire: Challenges to Modern British Imperialism*. New York: Oxford University Press, 2015.

Cain, P. J., and A. G. Hopkins. *British Imperialism: 1688–2015*. Abingdon, UK: Routledge, 2016.

Campbell, Ian. *Holy War: The Untold Story of Catholic Italy's Crusade against the Ethiopian Orthodox Church*. London: Hurst, 2021.

Candlin, Kit. *The Last Caribbean Frontier, 1795–1815*. London: Palgrave Macmillan, 2012.

Cañizares-Esguerra, Jorge. *Puritan Conquistadors: Iberianizing the Atlantic, 1550–1700*. Stanford, Calif.: Stanford University Press, 2006.

Caraman, Philip. *The Lost Empire: The Story of the Jesuits in Ethiopia, 1555–1634*. London: Sidgwick & Jackson, 1985.

———. *The Lost Paradise: An Account of the Jesuits in Paraguay, 1607–1768*. London: Sidgwick and Jackson, 1975.

Carballo, David M. *Collision of Worlds: A Deep History of the Fall of Aztec Mexico and the Forging of New Spain*. New York: Oxford University Press, 2020.

Carey, Hilary M. *Empire of Hell: Religion and the Campaign to End Convict Transportation in the British Empire, 1788–1875*. New York: Cambridge University Press, 2019.

———. *God's Empire: Religion and Colonialism in the British World, c. 1801–1908*. New York: Cambridge University Press, 2010.

Carey, Hilary M., and John Gascoigne, eds. *Church and State in Old and New Worlds*. Leiden: Brill, 2011.

Carson, Penelope. *The East India Company and Religion, 1698–1858*. Woodbridge: Boydell Press, 2012.

Carté, Katherine. *Religion and the American Revolution: An Imperial History*. Williamsburg: Omohundro Institute of Early American History and Culture/University of North Carolina Press, 2021.

Casiday, Augustine, and Frederick W. Norris, eds. *Constantine to c.600*. Vol. 2 of *The Cambridge History of Christianity*. New York: Cambridge University Press, 2007.

Cavanagh, Edward, and Lorenzo Veracini, eds. *The Routledge Handbook of the History of Settler Colonialism*. Abingdon, UK: Routledge, 2017.

Cervantes, Fernando. *Conquistadores: A New History*. New York: Viking, 2021.

Cesari, Jocelyne, ed. *The Oxford Handbook of European Islam*. New York: Oxford University Press, 2015.

Chakravarti, Ananya. *The Empire of Apostles: Religion, Accommodation, and the Imagination of Empire in Early Modern Brazil and India*. New Delhi: Oxford University Press, 2018.

Chamedes, Giuliana, and Elizabeth A. Foster. "Decolonization and Religion in the French Empire." *French Politics, Culture and Society* 33, no. 2 (2015): 1–10.

Chazan-Gillig, Suzanne, and Pavitranand Ramhota. *Hinduism and Popular Cults in Mauritius: Sacred Religion and Plantation Economy*. New York: Routledge, 2023.

Chidester, David. *Empire of Religion: Imperialism and Comparative Religion*. Chicago: University of Chicago Press, 2014.

———. *Savage Systems: Religion and Colonialism in Southern Africa*. Charlottesville: University of Virginia Press, 1996.

Choi, Sung-Eun. *Decolonization and the French of Algeria: Bringing the Settler Colony Home*. London: Palgrave Macmillan, 2016.

Choisy, Abbé de. *Journal of a Voyage to Siam, 1685–1686*. Translated by Michael Smithies. New York: Oxford University Press, 1993.

Chow, Kai-wing. "Imperialism, Reform, and the End of Institutional Confucianism in the Late Qing." In *The Oxford Handbook of Confucianism*, edited by Jennifer Oldstone-Moore, 191–203. New York: Oxford University Press, 2023.

Christ, Georg, Patrick Sänger, and Mike Carr, eds. *Military Diasporas: Building of Empire in the Middle East and Europe (550 BCE–1500 CE)*. New York: Routledge, 2023.

Christopher, Emma, Cassandra Pybus, and Marcus Rediker, eds. *Many Middle Passages: Forced Migration and the Making of the Modern World*. Berkeley: University of California Press, 2007.

Churchill, Winston. "The Gift of a Common Tongue." The International Churchill Society. Speech delivered at Harvard University, September 6, 1943. https://winstonchurchill.org/resources/speeches/1941-1945-war-leader/the-gift-of-a-common-tongue/.

Claassen, Cheryl. *Religion in Sixteenth-Century Mexico: A Guide to Aztec and Catholic Beliefs and Practices*. New York: Cambridge University Press, 2022.

Clancy-Smith, Julia. "Islam and the French Empire in North Africa." In Motadel, *Islam and the European Empires*, 90–111.

Clark, Bruce. *Twice a Stranger: How Mass Expulsion Forged Modern Greece and Turkey*. London: Granta, 2006.

Coedes, G. *The Indianized States of Southeast Asia*. Edited by Walter F. Vella. Canberra, A.C.T.: Australian National University Press, 1975.

Cohen, Ashley L. *The Global Indies: British Imperial Culture and the Reshaping of the World, 1756–1815*. New Haven, Conn.: Yale University Press, 2021.

Collins, John J., and J. G. Manning, eds. *Revolt and Resistance in the Ancient Classical World and the Near East: In the Crucible of Empire*. Leiden: Brill, 2016.

Conklin, Alice L. *A Mission to Civilize: The Republican Idea of Empire in France and West Africa, 1895–1930*. Stanford, Calif.: Stanford University Press, 1997.

Conklin, Alice L., Sarah Fishman, and Robert Zaretsky. *France and Its Empire since 1870*. 2nd ed. New York: Oxford University Press, 2011.

Conover, Cornelius. *Pious Imperialism: Spanish Rule and the Cult of Saints in Mexico City*. Albuquerque: University of New Mexico Press, 2019.

Conrad, Geoffrey W., and Arthur Demarest. *Religion and Empire: The Dynamics of Aztec and Inca Expansionism*. New York: Cambridge University Press, 1984.

Conroy-Krutz, Emily. *Christian Imperialism: Converting the World in the Early American Republic*. Ithaca, N.Y.: Cornell University Press, 2015.

Conti, Philip M. *The Pennsylvania State Police: A History of Service to the Commonwealth, 1905 to the Present*. Harrisburg, Pa.: Stackpole Books, 1977.

Cook, Michael, ed. *The New Cambridge History of Islam*. 6 vols. New York: Cambridge University Press, 2010.

Coombes, Annie, ed. *Rethinking Settler Colonialism: History and Memory in Australia, Canada, Aotearoa New Zealand and South Africa*. Manchester: Manchester University Press, 2006.

Copland, Ian. "Christianity as an Arm of Empire: The Ambiguous Case of India under the Company, c. 1813–1858." *Historical Journal* 49, no. 4 (2006): 1025–54.

Council of Castile (Spain). Requerimiento 1510. National Humanities Center. https://nationalhumanitiescenter.org/pds/amerbegin/contact/text7/requirement.pdf.

Covey, R. Alan. *Inca Apocalypse: The Spanish Conquest and the Transformation of the Andean World*. New York: Oxford University Press, 2020.

Cowper, William. "Boadicea: An Ode." Eighteenth-Century Poetry Archive. https://www.eighteenthcenturypoetry.org/works/o3794-w0400.shtml.

Crawford, James. *The Edge of the Plain: How Borders Make and Break Our World*. New York: Norton, 2022.

Crews, Robert D. *For Prophet and Tsar*. Cambridge, Mass.: Harvard University Press, 2006.

Cross, Anthony, ed. *St. Petersburg, 1703–1825*. Basingstoke: Palgrave Macmillan, 2003.

Crouch, C. L. *Israel and the Assyrians: Deuteronomy, the Succession Treaty of Esarhaddon, and the Nature of Subversion*. Atlanta: SBL Press, 2014.

Crowley, Roger. *Conquerors: How Portugal Forged the First Global Empire*. New York: Random House, 2015.

———. *Empires of the Sea: The Final Battle for the Mediterranean 1521–1580*. London: Faber, 2008.

Crystal, David. *The Cambridge Encyclopedia of Language*. New York: Cambridge University Press, 1987.

Cunningham, Alexander. "An Account of the Discovery of the Ruins of the Buddhist City of Samkassa." *Journal of the Royal Asiatic Society* 7 (1843): 241–49.

Curchin, Leonard A. *Roman Spain: Conquest and Assimilation*. New York: Routledge, 1991.

Dalrymple, William. *The Anarchy: The Relentless Rise of the East India Company*. London: Bloomsbury, 2019.

Damrosch, David. *The Buried Book: The Loss and Rediscovery of the Great Epic of Gilgamesh*. New York: Henry Holt, 2007.

Dandamayev, M. "The Diaspora." In Davies and Finkelstein, *Introduction: The Persian Period*, 326–400.

Darch, John H. *Missionary Imperialists? Missionaries, Government and the Growth of the British Empire in the Tropics 1860–1885*. London: Paternoster, 2009.

Darwin, John. *After Tamerlane: The Rise and Fall of Global Empires, 1400–2000*. London: Bloomsbury, 2009.

———. *The Empire Project: The Rise and Fall of the British World-System, 1830–1970*. New York: Cambridge University Press, 2011.

———. *Unfinished Empire: The Global Expansion of Britain*. London: Bloomsbury, 2012.

Das, Santanu, ed. *Race, Empire and First World War Writing*. New York: Cambridge University Press, 2011.

Dasgupta, Subrata. *The Bengal Renaissance: Identity and Creativity from Rammohun Roy to Rabindranath Tagore*. New Delhi: Permanent Black, 2007.

Daughton, J. P. *An Empire Divided: Religion, Republicanism, and the Making of French Colonialism 1880–1914*. New York: Oxford University Press, 2006.

———. *In the Forest of No Joy: The Congo-Océan Railroad and the Tragedy of French Colonialism*. New York: Norton, 2021.

David-Fox, Michael, Peter Holquist, and Alexander Martin, eds. *Orientalism and Empire in Russia*. Bloomington, Ind.: Slavica, 2006.

Davies, Brian. *Empire and Military Revolution in Eastern Europe: Russia's Turkish Wars in the Eighteenth Century*. London: Bloomsbury, 2013.

Davies, W. D., and Louis Finkelstein, eds. *Introduction: The Persian Period*. Vol. 1 of *The Cambridge History of Judaism*. New York: Cambridge University Press, 1984.

———. eds. *The Hellenistic Age*. Vol. 2 of *The Cambridge History of Judaism*. New York: Cambridge University Press, 1990.

Dean, Riaz. *Mapping the Great Game: Explorers, Spies and Maps in 19th-Century Asia*. Havertown, Pa.: Casemate, 2020.

De Giorgi, Andrea U., and Asa Eger. *Antioch: A History*. New York: Routledge, 2021.

De Gruyter, Caroline. *Monde d'hier, monde de demain? Un voyage à travers l'Empire des Habsbourg et l'Union Européenne*. Arles, France: Actes Sud, 2023.

Des Forges, Roger, and John S. Major. *The Asian World, 600–1500*. New York: Oxford University Press, 2005.

Deslandres, Dominique. *Croire et faire croire: Les missions françaises au XVII*[e] *siècle*. Paris: Fayard, 2003.

DeVries, Larry, Don Baker, and Dan Overmyer, eds. *Asian Religions in British Columbia*. Vancouver: University of British Columbia Press, 2010.

Dey, Hendrik W. *The Afterlife of the Roman City: Architecture and Ceremony in Late Antiquity and the Early Middle Ages*. New York: Cambridge University Press, 2014.

Dhammasami, Khammai. *Buddhism, Education and Politics in Burma and Thailand: From the Seventeenth Century to the Present*. London: Bloomsbury Academic, 2018.

Dhammika, Ven. S. "The Edicts of King Ashoka." *The Wheel*, No. 386/387 (1993). https://www.cs.colostate.edu/~malaiya/ashoka.html.

D'Hulster, K., G. Schallenbergh, and J. Van Steenbergen, eds. *Egypt and Syria in the Fatimid, Ayyubid and Mamluk Eras: IX, Proceedings of the 23rd and 24th International Colloquium Organized at the University of Leuven in May 2015 and 2016.* Leuven: Peeters, 2019.

Di Cosmo, Nicola, and Michael Maas, eds. *Empires and Exchanges in Eurasian Late Antiquity: Rome, China, Iran, and the Steppe.* Cambridge: Cambridge University Press, 2018.

Dierksmeier, Laura. *Charity for and by the Poor: Franciscan-Indigenous Confraternities in Mexico, 1527–1700.* Norman: University of Oklahoma Press, 2020.

Digby, Simon, ed. *Sufis and Soldiers in Awrangzeb's Deccan: Malfūẓāt-i-Naqshbandiyya.* New Delhi: Oxford University Press, 2001.

Dignas, Beate, and Engelbert Winter. *Rome and Persia in Late Antiquity: Neighbours and Rivals.* New York: Cambridge University Prcss, 2007.

Dixon, Carl. *The Paulicians: Heresy, Persecution and Warfare on the Byzantine Frontier, c.750–880.* Leiden: Brill, 2022.

Dodgeon, Michael H., and Samuel N. C. Lieu, eds. *The Roman Eastern Frontier and the Persian Wars AD 226–363: A Documentary History.* Abingdon, UK: Routledge, 2002.

Dodson, Michael S. *Orientalism, Empire, and National Culture: India, 1770–1880.* New York: Palgrave Macmillan, 2007.

Dolan, Marion. *Decoding Astronomy in Art and Architecture.* Cham, Switzerland: Springer International, 2021.

Dorner, Zachary. *Merchants of Medicines: The Commerce and Coercion of Health in Britain's Long Eighteenth Century.* Chicago: University of Chicago Press, 2020.

Doss, M. Christhu. *India after the 1857 Revolt: Decolonising the Mind.* New York: Routledge, 2023.

Downs, Jim. *Maladies of Empire: How Colonialism, Slavery, and War Transformed Medicine.* Cambridge, Mass.: Belknap Press of Harvard University Press, 2021.

Draper, Jonathan A., ed. *Orality, Literacy, and Colonialism in Southern Africa.* Atlanta: SBL Press, 2003.

Drayton, Richard. *Nature's Government: Science, Imperial Britain, and the "Improvement" of the World.* New Haven, Conn.: Yale University Press, 2000.

Driscoll, Carlos A., Juliet Clutton-Brock, Andrew C. Kitchener, and Stephen J. O'Brien. "The Taming of the Cat." *Scientific American* 300, no. 6 (2009): 68–75. https://www.ncbi.nlm.nih.gov/pmc/articles/PMC5790555/.

DuBois, Thomas David. *Religion and the Making of Modern East Asia.* New York: Cambridge University Press, 2011.

Dundas, Paul. *The Jains.* 2nd ed. New York: Routledge, 2002.

Durkin, Philip. *Borrowed Words: A History of Loanwords in English.* New York: Oxford University Press, 2014.

Dussart, Fae. *In the Service of Empire: Domestic Service and Mastery in Metropole and Colony.* London: Bloomsbury, 2022.

Dutton, George E. *A Vietnamese Moses: Philiphê Bỉnh and the Geographies of Early Modern Catholicism.* Oakland: University of California Press, 2017.

Dutton, George E., Jayne S. Werner, and John K. Whitmore, eds. *Sources of Vietnamese Tradition.* New York: Columbia University Press, 2012.

Dwyer, Philip, and Amanda Nettelbeck, eds. *Violence, Colonialism and Empire in the Modern World*. Cham, Switzerland: Palgrave Macmillan, 2018.

Earle, Rebecca. *The Body of the Conquistador: Food, Race and the Colonial Experience in Spanish America, 1492–1700*. New York: Cambridge University Press, 2012.

Eatherley, Dan. "What Have the Romans Done for Us?" *History Today*, July 7, 2019. https://www.historytoday.com/history-matters/what-have-romans-done-us.

Eaton, Richard M. *India in the Persianate Age, 1000–1765*. Oakland: University of California Press, 2019.

———. *The Rise of Islam and the Bengal Frontier, 1204–1760*. Berkeley: University of California Press, 1993.

Eberhard, David M., Gary F. Simons, and Charles D. Fennig, eds. *Ethnologue*. 3 vols. 25th ed. Dallas: SIL International, 2022.

Ebright, Malcolm, and Rick Hendricks. *The Witches of Abiquiu: The Governor, the Priest, the Genízaro Indians, and the Devil*. Albuquerque: University of New Mexico Press, 2006.

Eden, Jeff. *Slavery and Empire in Central Asia*. Cambridge: Cambridge University Press, 2018.

Elayi, Josette. *Sargon II, King of Assyria*. Atlanta: SBL Press, 2017.

Elbourne, Elizabeth. *Empire, Kinship and Violence: Family Histories, Indigenous Rights and the Making of Settler Colonialism, 1770–1842*. New York: Cambridge University Press, 2023.

El-Hibri, Tayeb. *The Abbasid Caliphate: A History*. New York: Cambridge University Press, 2021.

Elkins, Caroline. *Imperial Reckoning: The Untold Story of Britain's Gulag in Kenya*. London: Jonathan Cape, 2005.

———. *Legacy of Violence: A History of the British Empire*. London: Penguin Random House, 2022.

Elkins, Caroline, and Susan Pedersen, eds. *Settler Colonialism in the Twentieth Century: Projects, Practices, Legacies*. New York: Routledge, 2005.

Elsie, Robert. *The Albanian Bektashi: History and Culture of a Dervish Order in the Balkans*. London: I. B. Tauris, 2019.

Elsner, Jaś, ed. *Empires of Faith in Late Antiquity: Histories of Art and Religion from India to Ireland*. New York: Cambridge University Press, 2020.

Elverskog, Johan. *Buddhism and Islam on the Silk Road*. Philadelphia: University of Pennsylvania Press, 2010.

Emerson, Caryl, George Pattison, and Randall A. Poole, eds. *The Oxford Handbook of Russian Religious Thought*. New York: Oxford University Press, 2020.

Emerson, Ralph Waldo. "Brahma." Poetry Foundation. https://www.poetryfoundation.org/poems/45868/brahma-56d225936127b.

Emmer, Pieter C., and Jos J. L. Gommans. *The Dutch Overseas Empire, 1600–1800*. New York: Cambridge University Press, 2021.

Emon, Anver M. *Religious Pluralism in Islamic Law: Dhimmis and Others in the Empire of Law*. New York: Oxford University Press, 2012.

Epstein, James. *Scandal of Colonial Rule: Power and Subversion in the British Atlantic during the Age of Revolution*. New York: Cambridge University Press, 2012.

"Erdoğan Says 'We Will Bury the Neo-Byzantines'—Provocative Light Show Set Up on Hagia Sophia." *Greek City Times*, May 30, 2022. https://greekcitytimes.com/2022/05/30/erdogan-neo-byzantine-hagia-sophia/.

Etherington, Norman, ed. *Missions and Empire*. New York: Oxford University Press, 2005.

Ethridge, Robbie Franklyn, and Sheri Marie Shuck-Hall, eds. *Mapping the Mississippian Shatter Zone: The Colonial Indian Slave Trade and Regional Instability in the American South*. Lincoln: University of Nebraska Press, 2009.

"Europe's Growing Muslim Population." Pew Research Center. November 29, 2017. https://www.pewresearch.org/religion/2017/11/29/europes-growing-muslim-population/.

Fair, C. Christine. *In Their Own Words: Understanding Lashkar-e-Tayyaba*. London: Hurst, 2019.

Falola, Toyin, and Matt D. Childs, eds. *The Yoruba Diaspora in the Atlantic World*. Bloomington: Indiana University Press, 2004.

Falser, Michael, ed. *Cultural Heritage as Civilizing Mission: From Decay to Recovery*. Cham, Switzerland: Springer, 2015.

Farrell, Henry, and Abraham Newman. *Underground Empire: How America Weaponized the World Economy*. New York: Henry Holt, 2023.

Farriss, Nancy. *Tongues of Fire: Language and Evangelization in Colonial Mexico*. New York: Oxford University Press, 2018.

Fatah-Black, Karwan. *White Lies and Black Markets: Evading Metropolitan Authority in Colonial Suriname, 1650–1800*. Leiden: Brill, 2015.

Fear, Andrew. *Mithras*. New York: Routledge, 2022.

Feener, R. Michael, and Anne M. Blackburn, eds. *Buddhist and Islamic Orders in Southern Asia: Comparative Perspectives*. Honolulu: University of Hawai'i Press, 2019.

Ferdowsi, Abolqasem. *Shahnameh: The Persian Book of Kings*. Translated by Dick Davis. New York: Viking, 2006.

Ferguson, Andy. *Tracking Bodhidharma: A Journey to the Heart of Chinese Culture*. Berkeley, Calif.: Counterpoint, 2012.

Fischer-Tiné, Harald, and Susanne Gehrmann, eds. *Empires and Boundaries: Rethinking Race, Class, and Gender in Colonial Settings*. Abingdon, UK: Routledge, 2009.

Fisher, John. *Outskirts of Empire Studies in British Power Projection*. Abingdon, UK: Routledge, 2019.

Fitzpatrick, Matthew. *The Kaiser and the Colonies: Monarchy in the Age of Empire*. New York: Oxford University Press, 2022.

Floor, Willem, and Edmund Herzig, eds. *Iran and the World in the Safavid Age*. London: I. B. Tauris, 2012.

Flower, Harriet I., ed. *Empire and Religion in the Roman World*. New York: Cambridge University Press, 2021.

Fogelin, Lars. *An Archaeological History of Indian Buddhism*. New York: Oxford University Press, 2015.

Foltz, Richard. *Religions of the Silk Road: Premodern Patterns of Globalization*. 2nd ed. London: Palgrave MacMillan, 2010.

Fonrobert, Charlotte Elisheva, and Martin S. Jaffee, eds. *The Cambridge Companion to the Talmud and Rabbinic Literature*. New York: Cambridge University Press, 2007.

Fontaine, Darcie. *Decolonizing Christianity: Religion and the End of Empire in France and Algeria*. New York: Cambridge University Press, 2016.

Foster, Benjamin R. *The Age of Agade: Inventing Empire in Ancient Mesopotamia*. London: Routledge, 2016.

Foster, Elizabeth A. *African Catholic: Decolonization and the Transformation of the Church*. Roundtable for H-DIPLO. June 22, 2020. https://networks.h-net.org/node/28443/discussions/6202254/h-diplo-roundtable-xxi-47-foster-african-catholic-decolonization.

———. *Faith in Empire: Religion, Politics, and Colonial Rule in French Senegal, 1880–1940*. Stanford, Calif.: Stanford University Press, 2013.

Foster, Elizabeth A., and Udi Greenberg, eds. *Decolonization and the Remaking of Christianity*. Philadelphia: University of Pennsylvania Press, 2023.

Foster, Roy, ed. *The Oxford History of Ireland*. New York: Oxford University Press, 1992.

Fox, Robin Lane. *Pagans and Christians*. San Francisco: HarperSanFrancisco, 1986.

Frahm, Eckart. *Assyria: The Rise and Fall of the World's First Empire*. New York: Basic Books, 2023.

Franklin, J. Jeffrey. *The Lotus and the Lion: Buddhism and the British Empire*. Ithaca, N.Y.: Cornell University Press, 2008.

Franklin, Michael J. *Orientalist Jones: Sir William Jones, Poet, Lawyer, and Linguist, 1746–1794*. New York: Oxford University Press, 2011.

Frankopan, Peter. *The Earth Transformed: An Untold History*. London: Bloomsbury, 2023.

———. *The Silk Roads: A New History of the World*. London: Bloomsbury, 2015.

French, Howard W. *Born in Blackness: Africa, Africans, and the Making of the Modern World, 1471 to the Second World War*. New York: Liveright, 2021.

French, Peter J. *John Dee: The World of an Elizabethan Magus*. London: Routledge, 2002.

Frend, W. H. C. *The Rise of Christianity*. Philadelphia: Fortress, 1984.

Fried, Johannes. *Charlemagne*. Cambridge, Mass.: Harvard University Press, 2016.

Friedman, Richard Elliott. *The Exodus*. San Francisco: HarperOne, 2017.

Friedrich, Markus. *The Jesuits: A History*. Princeton, N.J.: Princeton University Press, 2022.

Friesen, Steven J., Daniel N. Schowalter, and James C. Walters, eds. *Corinth in Context: Comparative Studies on Religion and Society*. Leiden: Brill, 2010.

Fromont, Cécile, ed. *Afro-Catholic Festivals in the Americas: Performance, Representation, and the Making of Black Atlantic Tradition*. University Park: Pennsylvania State University Press, 2019.

Frykenberg, Robert Eric. *Christianity in India: From Beginnings to the Present*. New York: Oxford University Press, 2008.

Frymer, Paul. *Building an American Empire: The Era of Territorial and Political Expansion*. Princeton, N.J.: Princeton University Press, 2017.

Fuess, Albrecht, and Jan-Peter Hartung, eds. *Court Cultures in the Muslim World: Seventh to Nineteenth Centuries*. New York: Routledge, 2011.

Gajetzki, Wolfram. *Greeks and Parthians in Mesopotamia and Beyond*. London: Bristol Classical Press, 2011.

Galen, John Jansen van. *Afscheid van de koloniën: Het Nederlandse dekolonisatiebeleid 1942–2012*. Amsterdam: Atlas Contact, 2013.

Gandhi, M. K. *Gandhi's Autobiography: The Story of My Experiments with Truth*. Washington, D.C.: Public Affairs Press, 1948.

Ganson, Barbara. "Antonio Ruiz de Montoya, Apostle of the Guarani." *Journal of Jesuit Studies* 3 (2016): 197–210.

García-Arenal, Mercedes, and Yonatan Glazer-Eytan, eds. *Forced Conversion in Christianity, Judaism and Islam: Coercion and Faith in Premodern Iberia and Beyond*. Leiden: Brill, 2020.

Garcia-Ventura, Agnès, and Lorenzo Verderame, eds. *Perspectives on the History of Ancient Near Eastern Studies*. University Park, Pa.: Eisenbrauns, 2020.

Gardner, Iain. *The Founder of Manichaeism*. Cambridge: Cambridge University Press, 2020.

Garza, Andrew de la. *The Mughal Empire at War: Babur, Akbar and the Indian Military Revolution, 1500–1605*. New York: Routledge, 2016.

Gascoigne, John. "Introduction: Religion and Empire, an Historiographical Perspective." *Journal of Religious History* 32, no. 2 (2008): 159–79.

Geaves, Ron. *Islam and Britain: Muslim Mission in an Age of Empire*. London: Bloomsbury Academic, 2018.

Gecewicz, Claire. "'New Age' Beliefs Common among Both Religious and Nonreligious Americans." Pew Research Center. October 1, 2018. https://www.pewresearch.org/fact-tank/2018/10/01/new-age-beliefs-common-among-both-religious-and-nonreligious-americans/.

Geiger, Andrea. *Converging Empires: Citizens and Subjects in the North Pacific Borderlands, 1867–1945*. Chapel Hill: University of North Carolina Press, 2022.

George, Alain. *The Umayyad Mosque of Damascus: Art, Faith and Empire in Early Islam*. London: Gingko, 2021.

Geraci, Robert P., and Michael Khodarkovsky, eds. *Of Religion and Empire: Missions, Conversion, and Tolerance in Tsarist Russia*. Ithaca, N.Y.: Cornell University Press, 2001.

Gerbner, Katharine. *Christian Slavery: Conversion and Race in the Protestant Atlantic World*. Philadelphia: University of Pennsylvania Press, 2018.

Gertz, Jan Christian, Angelika Berlejung, Konrad Schmid, and Markus Witte. eds. *T&T Clark Handbook of the Old Testament: An Introduction to the Literature, Religion and History of the Old Testament*. London: T&T Clark, 2012.

Gheddo, Piero. *The Cross and the Bo-Tree: Catholics and Buddhists in Vietnam*. New York: Sheed and Ward, 1970.

Ghosh, Amitav. *The Nutmeg's Curse: Parables for a Planet in Crisis*. Chicago: University of Chicago Press, 2021.

Gildea, Robert. *Empires of the Mind: The Colonial Past and the Politics of the Present*. New York: Cambridge University Press, 2019.

Gilley, Sheridan, and Brian Stanley, eds. *World Christianities c.1815–c.1914*. Vol. 8 of *The Cambridge History of Christianity*. New York: Cambridge University Press, 2005.

Gillin, Edward J. *Entente Imperial: British and French Power in the Age of Empire*. Hill, UK: Amberley, 2022.

Giraldez, Arturo. *The Age of Trade: The Manila Galleons and the Dawn of the Global Economy*. Lanham, Md.: Rowman & Littlefield, 2015.

Goldsworthy, Adrian. *Pax Romana: War, Peace, and Conquest in the Roman World*. New Haven, Conn.: Yale University Press, 2016.

———. *Rome and Persia: The Seven Hundred Year Rivalry*. New York: Basic Books, 2023.

Goodhart, David. *The Road to Somewhere: The New Tribes Shaping British Politics*. London: Penguin, 2017.

Goodman, Martin. *A History of Judaism*. Princeton, N.J.: Princeton University Press, 2018.

Gopal, Priyamvada. *Insurgent Empire: Anticolonial Resistance and British Dissent*. London: Verso, 2019.

Gordon, Peter, and Juan José Morales. *The Silver Way: China, Spanish America and the Birth of Globalisation, 1565–1815*. Sydney: Penguin Australia, 2017.

Goss, Andrew, ed. *The Routledge Handbook of Science and Empire*. Abingdon, UK: Routledge, 2021.

Gott, Richard. *Britain's Empire: Resistance, Repression and Revolt*. London: Verso, 2011.

Gottschalk, Peter. *Religion, Science, and Empire: Classifying Hinduism and Islam in British India*. New York: Oxford University Press, 2013.

Goudie, Sean X. *Creole America: The West Indies and the Formation of Literature and Culture in the New Republic*. Philadelphia: University of Pennsylvania Press, 2006.

Graf, Tobias P. *The Sultan's Renegades: Christian-European Converts to Islam and the Making of the Ottoman Elite, 1575–1610*. New York: Oxford University Press, 2017.

Greatrex, Geoffrey, and Samuel N. C. Lieu. *The Roman Eastern Frontier and the Persian Wars AD 363–628*. Abingdon, UK: Routledge, 2005.

Green, Dominic. *The Religious Revolution: The Birth of Modern Spirituality, 1848–1898*. New York: Farrar, Straus and Giroux, 2022.

Green, Nile. *Afghanistan's Islam: From Conversion to the Taliban*. Oakland: University of California Press, 2017.

———. *How Asia Found Herself: A Story of Intercultural Understanding*. New Haven, Conn.: Yale University Press, 2023.

Greenhalgh, Michael. *Constantinople to Córdoba: Dismantling Ancient Architecture in the East, North Africa and Islamic Spain*. Leiden: Brill, 2012.

Greer, Allan. *Property and Dispossession: Natives, Empires and Land in Early Modern North America*. New York: Cambridge University Press, 2018.

Gregerson, Linda, and Susan Juster, eds. *Empires of God: Religious Encounters in the Early Modern Atlantic*. Philadelphia: University of Pennsylvania Press, 2011.

Gregory, Jeremy, ed. *Establishment and Empire, 1662–1829*. Vol. 2 of Strong, *The Oxford History of Anglicanism*. New York: Oxford University Press, 2017.

Grewal, J. S. *Guru Gobind Singh, 1666–1708: Master of the White Hawk*. New Delhi: Oxford University Press, 2020.

Griffith, Ruth Marie, and Barbara Dianne Savage, eds. *Women and Religion in the African Diaspora: Knowledge, Power, and Performance*. Baltimore: Johns Hopkins University Press, 2006.

Griffiths, John Charles. *Tea: The Drink That Changed the World*. London: Andre Deutsch, 2007.

Grijalvo, Elena Muñiz, Juan Manuel Cortés Copete, and Fernando Lozano Gómez, eds. *Empire and Religion: Religious Change in Greek Cities under Roman Rule*. Leiden: Brill, 2017.

Groen, Petra, Anita van Dissel, Mark Loderichs, Rémy Limpach, and Thijs Brocades Zaalberg. *Krijgsgeweld en kolonie: Opkomst en ondergang van Nederland als koloniale mogendheid 1816–2010*. Amsterdam: Boom, 2021.

Gruen, Erich S. *Diaspora: Jews amidst Greeks and Romans*. Cambridge, Mass.: Harvard University Press, 2002.

Gschwend, Annemarie Jordan, and K. J. P. Lowe, eds. *The Global City: On the Streets of Renaissance Lisbon*. Chicago: University of Chicago Press, 2016.

Guha-Thakurta, Tapati. *Monuments, Objects, Histories: Institutions of Art in Colonial and Postcolonial India*. New York: Columbia University Press, 2004.

Gusejnova, Dina. *European Elites and Ideas of Empire, 1917–1957*. New York: Cambridge University Press, 2016.

Habib, Irfan, and Vivekanand Jha. *Mauryan India*. New Delhi: Tulika Books, 2015.

Haefeli, Evan. *Accidental Pluralism: America and the Religious Politics of English Expansion*. Chicago: University of Chicago Press, 2021.

Hall, Kenneth R. *A History of Early Southeast Asia: Maritime Trade and Societal Development, 100–1500*. Lanham, Md.: Rowman & Littlefield, 2011.

Hallade, Madeleine. *Gandharan Art of North India*. New York: H. N. Abrams, 1968.

Halpern, Baruch. *From Gods to God*. Edited by M. J. Adams. Tübingen: Mohr Siebeck, 2009.

Hammel, Tanja. *Shaping Natural History and Settler Society: Mary Elizabeth Barber and the Nineteenth-Century Cape*. Cham, Switzerland: Springer International, 2019.

Hammond, Andrew. *Late Ottoman Origins of Modern Islamic Thought: Turkish and Egyptian Thinkers on the Disruption of Islamic Knowledge*. New York: Cambridge University Press, 2023.

Hanciles, Jehu. *Migration and the Making of Global Christianity*. Grand Rapids: Eerdmans, 2021.

Hannoum, Abdelmajid. *The Invention of the Maghreb: Between Africa and the Middle East*. Princeton, N.J.: Princeton University Press, 2021.

Hansen, Valerie. *The Silk Road: A New History*. New York: Oxford University Press, 2016.

Hanser, Jessica. *Mr. Smith Goes to China*. New Haven, Conn.: Yale University Press, 2019.

Harmatta, János, B. N. Puri, and G. F. Etemadi, eds. *History of Civilizations of Central Asia: The Development of Sedentary and Nomadic Civilizations; 700 B.C. to A.D. 250*. N.p.: UNESCO, 1994.

Harper, Marjory, and Stephen Constantine. *Migration and Empire*. Oxford History of the British Empire Companion Series. Oxford: Oxford University Press, 2014.

Harper, Tim. *Underground Asia: Global Revolutionaries and the Assault on Empire*. Cambridge, Mass.: Belknap Press of Harvard University Press, 2021.

Harris, Ruth. *Guru to the World: The Life and Legacy of Vivekananda*. Cambridge, Mass.: Belknap Press of Harvard University Press, 2022.

Harris, William. *Lebanon: A History, 600–2011*. New York: Oxford University Press, 2012.

Hart, Mitchell B., and Tony Michels, eds. *The Modern World, 1815–2000*. Vol. 8 of *The Cambridge History of Judaism*. New York: Cambridge University Press, 2017.

Hassett, Miranda K. *Anglican Communion in Crisis: How Episcopal Dissidents and Their African Allies Are Reshaping Anglicanism*. Princeton, N.J.: Princeton University Press, 2007.

Hatcher, Brian A. *Hinduism before Reform*. Cambridge, Mass.: Harvard University Press, 2020.

Hauben, Hans, and Alexander Meeus, eds. *The Age of the Successors and the Creation of the Hellenistic Kingdoms (323–276 B.C.)*. Leuven: Peeters, 2014.

Havea, Jione, ed. *Mission and Context*. Minneapolis: Fortress Academic, 2021.

Hazleton, Lesley. *After the Prophet: The Epic Story of the Shia-Sunni Split in Islam*. New York: Doubleday, 2009.

Heather, Peter. *Christendom: The Triumph of a Religion, AD 300–1300*. New York: Alfred A. Knopf, 2023.

———. *The Restoration of Rome: Barbarian Popes and Imperial Pretenders*. New York: Oxford University Press, 2014.

Heber, Bishop Reginald. "From Greenland's Icy Mountains." Victorian Web. https://victorianweb.org/religion/hymns/heber1.html.

Hefner, Robert W., ed. *Muslims and Modernity: Culture and Society since 1800*. Vol. 6 of Cook, *The New Cambridge History of Islam*.

Hegermann, Harald. "The Diaspora in the Hellenistic Age." In Davies and Finkelstein, *The Hellenistic Age*, 115–66.

Heitzman, James. *Gifts of Power: Lordship in an Early Indian State*. Delhi: Oxford University Press, 1997.

Hekster, Olivier. *Caesar Rules: The Emperor in the Changing Roman World (c.50 BC–AD 565)*. Cambridge: Cambridge University Press, 2023.

Hempton, David. *Methodism: Empire of the Spirit*. New Haven, Conn.: Yale University Press, 2005.

Herbert, George. "Religion Westward Bent." Bartleby. https://www.bartleby.com/400/poem/20.html.

Hevia, James. *The Imperial Security State: British Colonial Knowledge and Empire-Building in Asia*. New York: Cambridge University Press, 2012.

Higham, C. F. W., and Nam C. Kim, eds. *The Oxford Handbook of Early Southeast Asia*. New York: Oxford University Press, 2022.

Hill, A. C. *Christian Imperialism*. London: Hodder and Stoughton, 1917.

Hitchcock, Richard. *Mozarabs in Medieval and Early Modern Spain: Identities and Influences*. Burlington, Vt.: Ashgate, 2008.

Hobbes, Thomas. *Leviathan: With Selected Variants from the Latin Edition of 1668*. Edited by Edwin Curley. Indianapolis: Hackett, 1994.

Hodgkins, Christopher. *Reforming Empire: Protestant Colonialism and Conscience in British Literature*. Columbia: University of Missouri Press, 2002.

Hölbl, Günther. *A History of the Ptolemaic Empire*. New York: Routledge, 2001.

Hollinger, David A. *Protestants Abroad: How Missionaries Tried to Change the World but Changed America*. Princeton, N.J.: Princeton University Press, 2017.

Holloway, Steven W., ed. *Orientalism, Assyriology and the Bible*. Sheffield, UK: Sheffield Phoenix Press, 2007.

Holt, William H. *The Balkan Reconquista and Turkey's Forgotten Refugee Crisis*. Salt Lake City: University of Utah Press, 2019.

Hopkins, A. G. *American Empire: A Global History*. Princeton, N.J.: Princeton University Press, 2018.

Hopkins, Benjamin D. *Ruling the Savage Periphery: Frontier Governance and the Making of the Modern State*. Cambridge, Mass.: Harvard University Press, 2020.

Horace. *Epistles*. Edited by H. Rushton Fairclough. http://www.perseus.tufts.edu/hopper/text?doc=Hor.%20Ep.%202.1&lang=original.

Horbury, William, W. D. Davies, and John Sturdy, eds. *The Early Roman Period*. Vol. 3 of *The Cambridge History of Judaism*. New York: Cambridge University Press, 1999.

Horster, Marietta, and Nikolas Hächler. *The Impact of the Roman Empire on Landscapes: Proceedings of the Fourteenth Workshop of the International Network Impact of Empire (Mainz, June 12–15, 2019)*. Leiden: Brill, 2022.

Houlton, Thomas. *Monuments as Cultural and Critical Objects: From Mesolithic to Eco-queer*. New York: Routledge, 2022.

Houten, Pieter. *Urbanisation in Roman Spain and Portugal: Civitates Hispaniae in the Early Empire*. Abingdon, UK: Routledge, 2021.

Howard-Johnston, James. *The Last Great War of Antiquity*. New York: Oxford University Press, 2021.

Howe, Stephen. *Empire: A Very Short Introduction*. New York: Oxford University Press, 2002.

Hoyland, Robert G., ed. *The "History of the Kings of the Persians" in Three Arabic Chronicles: The Transmission of the Iranian Past from Late Antiquity to Early Islam*. Liverpool: Liverpool University Press, 2018.

Hsia, Ronnie Po-chia, ed. *A Companion to Early Modern Catholic Global Missions*. Leiden: Brill, 2018.

———, ed. *Reform and Expansion 1500–1660*. Vol. 6 of *The Cambridge History of Christianity*. New York: Cambridge University Press, 2007.

Huggan, Graham, ed. *The Oxford Handbook of Postcolonial Studies*. New York: Oxford University Press, 2013.

Hunt, Tristram. *Cities of Empire: The British Colonies and the Creation of the Urban World*. New York: Metropolitan Books, 2014.

Hunter, W. W. *The Indian Musalmans*. 3rd ed. London: Trübner, 1876.

Hyam, Ronald. *Britain's Declining Empire: The Road to Decolonisation, 1918–1968*. Cambridge: Cambridge University Press, 2006.

———. *Britain's Imperial Century, 1815–1914: A Study of Empire and Expansion*. 3rd ed. New York: Palgrave Macmillan, 2002.

———. *Empire and Sexuality: The British Experience*. Manchester: Manchester University Press, 1991.

———. *Understanding the British Empire*. Cambridge: Cambridge University Press, 2010.

Ibrahim, Ayman S. *Conversion to Islam: Competing Themes in Early Islamic Historiography*. New York: Oxford University Press, 2021.

Ibrahim, Farhana, and Tanuja Kothiyal, eds. *South Asian Borderlands: Mobility, History, Affect*. New York: Cambridge University Press, 2021.

Ibsen, Kristine. *Maximilian, Mexico, and the Invention of Empire*. Nashville, Tenn.: Vanderbilt University Press, 2010.

Immerwahr, Daniel. *How to Hide an Empire: A History of the Greater United States*. New York: Macmillan, 2019.

Ingram, Brannon D. *Revival from Below: The Deoband Movement and Global Islam*. Oakland: University of California Press, 2018.

Inikori, Joseph E., ed. *British Imperialism and Globalization, c. 1650–1960: Essays in Honour of Patrick O'Brien*. Woodbridge, UK: Boydell and Brewer, 2022.

Isayeva, Natalia. *Shankara and Indian Philosophy*. Albany: State University of New York Press, 1993.

Jackson, Peter. *The Mongols and the Islamic World: From Conquest to Conversion*. New Haven, Conn.: Yale University Press, 2017.

Jacobs, Janet Liebman. *Hidden Heritage: The Legacy of the Crypto-Jews*. Berkeley: University of California Press, 2002.

Jacobson, Abigail. *From Empire to Empire: Jerusalem between Ottoman and British Rule*. Syracuse, N.Y.: Syracuse University Press, 2011.

Jager, Sheila Miyoshi. *The Other Great Game: The Opening of Korea and the Birth of Modern East Asia*. Cambridge, Mass.: Harvard University Press, 2023.

Jaimoukha, Amjad. *The Circassians: A Handbook*. New York: Palgrave, 2001.

Jansen, Jan C., and Jürgen Osterhammel. *Decolonization: A Short History*. Princeton, N.J.: Princeton University Press, 2017.

Jayakar, Pupul. *Krishnamurti: A Biography*. San Francisco: Harper & Row, 1986.

Jenkins, Philip. *Climate, Catastrophe, and Faith: How Changes in Climate Drive Religious Upheaval*. New York: Oxford University Press, 2021.

———. *Crucible of Faith: The Ancient Revolution That Made Our Modern Religious World*. New York: Basic Books, 2017.

———. *Fertility and Faith: The Demographic Revolution That Is Transforming All the World's Religions*. Waco, Tex.: Baylor University Press, 2020.

———. *God's Continent: Christianity, Islam and Europe's Religious Crisis*. New York: Oxford University Press, 2007.

———. *The Great and Holy War: How World War I Became a Religious Crusade*. San Francisco: HarperOne, 2014.

———. "Infidels, Demons, Witches, and Quakers: The Affair of Colonel Bowen." *Fides et Historia* 49, no. 2 (2017): 1–15.

———. *Jesus Wars: How Four Patriarchs, Three Queens, and Two Emperors Decided What Christians Would Believe for the Next 1,500 Years*. San Francisco: HarperOne, 2010.

———. *The Lost History of Christianity: The Thousand-Year Golden Age of the Church in the Middle East, Africa, and Asia—and How It Died*. San Francisco: HarperOne, 2008.

———. *The Many Faces of Christ: The Thousand-Year Story of the Survival and Influence of the Lost Gospels*. New York: Basic Books, 2015.

———. *Mystics and Messiahs: Cults and New Religions in American History*. New York: Oxford University Press, 2000.

———. *The New Faces of Christianity: Believing the Bible in the Global South*. New York: Oxford University Press, 2006.

———. *The Next Christendom: The Rise of Global Christianity*. 3rd ed. New York: Oxford University Press, 2011.

———. *A Storm of Images: Iconoclasm and Religious Reformation in the Byzantine World*. Waco, Tex.: Baylor University Press, 2023.

Jensen, Lionel M. *Manufacturing Confucianism: Chinese Traditions and Universal Civilization*. Durham, N.C.: Duke University Press, 1998.

Jerónimo, Miguel Bandeira. *The "Civilising Mission" of Portuguese Colonialism, 1870–1930*. London: Palgrave Macmillan, 2015.

Johnston, Andrew C. *The Sons of Remus: Identity in Roman Gaul and Spain*. Cambridge, Mass.: Harvard University Press, 2017.

Johnston, Anna. *Missionary Writing and Empire, 1800–1860*. Cambridge: Cambridge University Press, 2003.

Jones, Justin. *Shi'a Islam in Colonial India: Religion, Community and Sectarianism*. New York: Cambridge University Press, 2012.

Judson, Pieter. *The Habsburg Empire: A New History*. Cambridge, Mass.: Belknap Press of Harvard University Press, 2016.

Juvenal. "Quis nescit, Volusi Bithynice, qualia demens / Aegyptos portenta colat?" *Satire* 15. Latin Library. https://www.thelatinlibrary.com/juvenal/15.shtml.

Kahler, Martin. *Schriften zur Christologie und Mission*. Munich: Christian Kaiser, 1971.

Kaim, Barbara, and Maja Kornacka. "Religious Landscape of the Ancient Merv Oasis." *Iran: Journal of the British Institute of Persian Studies* 54 (2016): 47–72.

Kaloyanides, Alexandra. *Baptizing Burma: Religious Change in the Last Buddhist Kingdom*. New York: Columbia University Press, 2023.

Kane, Eileen M. *Russian Hajj: Empire and the Pilgrimage to Mecca*. Ithaca, N.Y.: Cornell University Press, 2015.

Kanisetti, Anirudh. *Lords of the Deccan: Southern India from the Chalukyas to the Cholas*. New Delhi: Juggernaut, 2022.

Kappeler, Andreas. *The Russian Empire: A Multiethnic History*. New York: Routledge, 2001.

Karp, Jonathan, and Adam Sutcliffe, eds. *The Early Modern World, 1500–1815*. Vol. 7 of *The Cambridge History of Judaism*. New York: Cambridge University Press, 2017.

Karuka, Manu. *Empire's Tracks: Indigenous Nations, Chinese Workers, and the Transcontinental Railroad*. Berkeley: University of California Press, 2019.

Katz, Steven T., ed. *The Late Roman-Rabbinic Period*. Vol. 4 of *The Cambridge History of Judaism*. New York: Cambridge University Press, 2006.

Keay, John. *India Discovered*. New York: Harper Collins, 1988.

———. *The Spice Route: A History*. London: John Murray, 2005.

Kefeli, Agnès Nilüfer. *Becoming Muslim in Imperial Russia: Conversion, Apostasy, and Literacy*. Ithaca, N.Y.: Cornell University Press, 2014.

Keith, Charles. *Catholic Vietnam: A Church from Empire to Nation*. Berkeley: University of California Press, 2012.

Keller, Kathleen. *Colonial Suspects: Suspicion, Imperial Rule, and Colonial Society in Interwar French West Africa*. Lincoln: University of Nebraska Press, 2018.

Keller, Shoshana. *Russia and Central Asia: Coexistence, Conquest, Convergence*. Toronto: University of Toronto Press, 2019.

Kemper, Steven. *Rescued from the Nation: Anagarika Dharmapala and the Buddhist World*. Chicago: University of Chicago Press, 2015.

Kennedy, Hugh. *Caliphate: The History of an Idea*. New York: Basic Books, 2016.

———. *The Prophet and the Age of the Caliphates: The Islamic Near East from the Sixth to the Eleventh Century*. 4th ed. New York: Routledge, 2022.

Kersten, Carool. *A History of Islam in Indonesia: Unity in Diversity*. Edinburgh: Edinburgh University Press, 2017.

Ketelaar, James Edward. *Of Heretics and Martyrs in Meiji Japan: Buddhism and Its Persecution*. Princeton, N.J.: Princeton University Press, 1990.

Khafipour, Hani, ed. *The Empires of the Near East and India: Source Studies of the Safavid, Ottoman, and Mughal Literate Communities*. New York: Columbia University Press, 2019.

Kidd, Colin. *The Forging of Races: Race and Scripture in the Protestant Atlantic World, 1600–2000*. New York: Cambridge University Press, 2006.

Kidd, Thomas. *George Whitefield: America's Spiritual Founding Father*. New Haven, Conn.: Yale University Press, 2014.

Kim, Hyun Jin, Frederik Juliaan Vervaet, and Selim Ferruh Adali, eds. *Eurasian Empires in Antiquity and the Early Middle Ages: Contact and Exchange between the Graeco-Roman World, Inner Asia and China*. New York: Cambridge University Press, 2017.

King, Charles. *Odessa: Genius and Death in a City of Dreams*. New York: Norton, 2011.

King, Daniel, ed. *The Syriac World*. New York: Routledge, 2019.

Kipling, Rudyard. "Gallio's Song." *Poetry Lovers Page*. https://www.poetryloverspage.com/poets/kipling/gallios_song.html.

———. "Recessional." Poetry Foundation. https://www.poetryfoundation.org/poems/46780/recessional.

———. "The Church That Was at Antioch." In *Limits and Renewals*. London: Penguin Classics, 1987.

Kirchberger, Ulrike, and Brett M. Bennett, eds. *Environments of Empire: Networks and Agents of Ecological Change*. Chapel Hill: University of North Carolina Press, 2020.

Klokke, Marijke J., and Veronique Degroot, eds. *Materializing Southeast Asia's Past: Selected Papers from the 12th International Conference of the European Association of Southeast Asian Archaeologists*. Vol. 2. Singapore: NUS Press, 2013.

Knaap, Gerrit. "Islamic Resistance in the Dutch Colonial Empire." In Motadel, *Islam and the European Empires*, 213–30.

Knudsen, Britta Timm, John Oldfield, Elizabeth Buettner, and Elvan Zabunyan, eds. *Decolonizing Colonial Heritage: New Agendas, Actors and Practices in and beyond Europe*. Abingdon, UK: Routledge, 2022.

Kobayashi, Takeshi. *Nara Buddhist Art, Todai-ji*. New York: Weatherhill, 1975.

Kochhar, Rajesh. *Sanskrit and the British Empire*. New York: Routledge, 2021.

Koeppel, Dan. *Banana: The Fate of the Fruit that Changed the World*. New York: Penguin, 2008.

Kolb, Harold H., Jr. *Mark Twain: The Gift of Humor*. Lanham, Md.: University Press of America, 2014.

Koot, Christian J. *Empire at the Periphery: British Colonists, Anglo-Dutch Trade, and the Development of the British Atlantic, 1621–1713*. New York: New York University Press, 2011.

Kopf, David. *British Orientalism and the Bengal Renaissance: The Dynamics of Indian Modernization, 1773–1835*. Berkeley: University of California Press, 1969.

Korieh, Chima J., and Raphael Chijioke Njoku, eds. *Missions, States, and European Expansion in Africa*. New York: Routledge, 2007.

Kosmin, Paul J. *The Land of the Elephant Kings*. Cambridge, Mass.: Harvard University Press, 2014.

Ković, Miloš. *Disraeli and the Eastern Question*. New York: Oxford University Press, 2011.

Krahl, Regina, John Guy, Julian Raby, and J. Keith Wilson, eds. *Shipwrecked: Tang Treasures and Monsoon Winds*. Washington, D.C.: Arthur M. Sackler Gallery, Smithsonian Institution 2010.

Kulke, Hermann, and Bhairabi Prasad Sahu, eds. *The Routledge Handbook of the State in Premodern India*. New York: Routledge, 2022.

Kumar, Krishan. *Visions of Empire: How Five Imperial Regimes Shaped the World*. Princeton, N.J.: Princeton University Press, 2017.

Kumar, Pintu. *Buddhist Learning in South Asia: Education, Religion, and Culture at the Ancient Śrī Nālandā Mahāvihāra*. Lanham, Md.: Lexington Books, 2018.

Kundnani, Hans. *Eurowhiteness: Culture, Empire and Race in the European Project*. London: Hurst, 2023.

Kwarteng, Kwasi. *Ghosts of Empire: Britain's Legacies in the Modern World*. London: Public Affairs, 2012.

Lahiri, Nayanjot. *Ashoka in Ancient India*. Cambridge, Mass.: Harvard University Press, 2015.

Lai, Walton Look, and Tan Chee-Beng, eds. *The Chinese in Latin America and the Caribbean*. Leiden: Brill, 2010.

Laidlaw, Zoë. *Protecting the Empire's Humanity: Thomas Hodgkin and British Colonial Activism 1830–1870*. New York: Cambridge University Press, 2021.

Lake, Marilyn. *Drawing the Global Colour Line: White Men's Countries and the International Challenge of Racial Equality*. New York: Cambridge University Press, 2008.

Lalvani, Kartar. *The Making of India: The Untold Story of British Enterprise*. London: Bloomsbury, 2016.

Lambert, Andrew. *Seapower States: Maritime Culture, Continental Empires and the Conflict That Made the Modern World*. New Haven, Conn.: Yale University Press, 2018.

Lammerts, D. Christian, ed. *Buddhist Dynamics in Premodern and Early Modern Southeast Asia*. Singapore: ISEAS, 2015.

Lampe, John R,. and Ulf Brunnbauer, eds. *The Routledge Handbook of Balkan and Southeast European History*. Milton: Taylor & Francis, 2020.

Landon, Letitia. "Sarnat." In *The Cento: A Collection of Poetry, Original and Select*, 30. London: Mitchell, 1840.

Lane, Kris. *Potosí: The Silver City That Changed the World*. Berkeley: University of California Press, 2021.

Lanfranchi, Giovanni B., and Simo Parpola, eds. *Correspondence of Sargon II*. Winona Lake, Ind.: Eisenbrauns, 2014.

Lantigua, David M. *Infidels and Empires in a New World Order: Early Modern Spanish Contributions to International Legal Thought*. New York: Cambridge University Press, 2020.

Lara, Jaime. *Christian Texts for Aztecs: Art and Liturgy in Colonial Mexico*. Notre Dame, Ind.: University of Notre Dame Press, 2008.

Lartéguy, Jean. *The Centurions*. New York: Dutton, 1962.

———. *The Praetorians*. New York: Dutton, 1963.

Lauria, Valeria, and Corrado Fumagalli. "BRICS, The Southern Model, and the Evolving Landscape of Development Assistance: Toward a New Taxonomy." *Public Administration and Development* 39, nos. 4–5 (2019): 165–244.

Lavan, Myles, Richard E. Payne, and John Weisweiler, eds. *Cosmopolitanism and Empire: Universal Rulers, Local Elites, and Cultural Integration in the Ancient Near East and Mediterranean*. New York: Oxford University Press, 2016.

LeComte, Louis Daniel. *A Compleat History of the Empire of China: Being the Observations of Above Ten Years Travels Through That Country*. 2nd ed. London: James Hodges, 1739.

Ledger-Lomas, Michael. "Against Boiled Cabbage." *London Review of Books*, February 2, 2023.

Legge, James, ed. *A Record of Buddhistic Kingdoms: Being an Account by the Chinese Monk Fâ-Hien of His Travels in India and Ceylon (A.D. 399–414) in Search of the Buddhist Books of Discipline Translated and Annotated with a Corean Recension of the Chinese Text*. New York: Dover, 1991.

Le Maire, Bruno. *Le nouvel empire: L'Europe du vingt et unième siècle*. Paris: Éditions Gallimard, 2019.

Leow, Rachel. *Taming Babel: Language in the Making of Malaysia*. New York: Cambridge University Press, 2016.

Levine, Philippa, ed., *Gender and Empire*. New York: Oxford University Press, 2004.

Levy-Rubin, Milka. *Non-Muslims in the Early Islamic Empire: From Surrender to Coexistence*. New York: Cambridge University Press, 2011.

Lewis, Jori. *Slaves for Peanuts: A Story of Conquest, Liberation, and a Crop That Changed History*. New York: New Press, 2022.

Lieven, Dominic. *In the Shadow of the Gods: The Emperor in World History*. London: Allen Lane, 2022.

Lim, Timothy H. *The Formation of the Jewish Canon*. New Haven, Conn.: Yale University Press, 2013.

Lindenfeld, David. *World Christianity and Indigenous Experience: A Global History, 1500–2000*. New York: Cambridge University Press, 2021.

Lindner, Ulrike, and Dörte Lerp, eds. *New Perspectives on the History of Gender and Empire: Comparative and Global Approaches*. London: Bloomsbury Academic, 2018.

Liu, Lydia. *The Clash of Empires: The Invention of China in Modern World Making*. Cambridge, Mass.: Harvard University Press, 2004.

Liu, Xinru. *Early Buddhist Society: The World of Gautama Buddha*. Albany: SUNY Press, 2022.

———. *The Silk Road in World History*. New York: Oxford University Press, 2010.

Livesey, James. *Civil Society and Empire: Ireland and Scotland in the Eighteenth-Century Atlantic World*. New Haven, Conn.: Yale University Press, 2009.

Llewellyn-Jones, Lloyd. *Persians: The Age of the Great Kings*. New York: Basic Books, 2022.

Lopez, Donald S., Jr. *Prisoners of Shangri-La: Tibetan Buddhism and the West*. Chicago: University of Chicago Press, 1998.

Lorenzen, David N. *Who Invented Hinduism?* New Delhi: Yoda Press, 2006.

Louër, Laurence. *Sunnis and Shi'a: A Political History of Discord*. Princeton, N.J.: Princeton University Press, 2020.

Louis, William Roger, ed. *The Oxford History of the British Empire*. 5 vols. New York: Oxford University Press, 1998–1999.

Ludwig, Frieder, and J. Kwabena Asamoah-Gyadu. *African Christian Presence in the West: New Immigrant Congregations and Transnational Networks in North America and Europe*. Trenton, N.J.: Africa World Press, 2011.

Lugard, Flora Louise. "British Empire: Population." In *Encyclopædia Britannica*, vol. 4, edited by Hugh Chisholm. 11th ed. New York: Cambridge University Press, 1911.

Lynch, John. *New Worlds: A Religious History of Latin America*. New Haven, Conn.: Yale University Press, 2012.

MacCulloch, Diarmaid. *Christianity: The First Three Thousand Years*. New York: Viking, 2010.

MacInnes, Tom. *Oriental Occupation of British Columbia*. Vancouver: Sun, 1927.

MacKenzie, John. *A Cultural History of the British Empire*. New Haven, Conn.: Yale University Press, 2023.

MacMunn, George. *The Martial Races of India*. Quetta: Nisa Traders, 1977.

Madra, Amandeep Singh, and Parmjit Singh. *Warrior Saints: Three Centuries of the Sikh Military Tradition*. London: I. B. Tauris, 1999.

Mairs, Rachel. *The Hellenistic Far East*. Berkeley: University of California Press, 2014.

Mallampalli, Chandra. *A Muslim Conspiracy in British India? Politics and Paranoia in the Early Nineteenth-Century Deccan*. Cambridge: Cambridge University Press, 2017.

Malley, Shawn. *From Archaeology to Spectacle in Victorian Britain: The Case of Assyria, 1845–1854*. Burlington, Vt.: Ashgate, 2012.

Man, John. *Empire of Horses: The First Nomadic Civilization and the Making of China*. London: Pegasus Books, 2020.

Manjapra, Kris. *Colonialism in Global Perspective*. New York: Cambridge University Press, 2020.

Mankoff, Jeffrey. *Empires of Eurasia: How Imperial Legacies Shape International Security*. New Haven, Conn.: Yale University Press, 2022.

Mar, Tracey Banivanua. *Decolonisation and the Pacific: Indigenous Globalisation and the Ends of Empire*. New York: Cambridge University Press, 2016.

Marshall, P. J. *The British Discovery of Hinduism in the Eighteenth Century*. New York: Cambridge University Press, 1970.

Marshall, Ruth. *Political Spiritualities: The Pentecostal Revolution in Nigeria*. Chicago: University of Chicago Press, 2009.

Marsili, Filippo. *Heaven Is Empty: A Cross-Cultural Approach to "Religion" and Empire in Ancient China*. Albany: State University of New York Press, 2018.

Martínez-San Miguel, Yolanda, and Santa Arias, eds. *The Routledge Hispanic Studies Companion to Colonial Latin America and the Caribbean (1492–1898)*. New York: Routledge, 2021.

Masani, Zareer. "How the British Saved India's Classical History." *Spectator*, January 29, 2023.

Maskarinec, Maya. *City of Saints: Rebuilding Rome in the Early Middle Ages*. Philadelphia: University of Pennsylvania Press, 2022.

Masselos, Jim, ed., *The Great Empires of Asia*. Berkeley: University of California Press, 2010.

Masuzawa, Tomoko. *The Invention of World Religions; or, How European Universalism Was Preserved in the Language of Pluralism*. Chicago: University of Chicago Press, 2005

Matthee, Rudi, ed. *The Safavid World*. New York: Routledge, 2022.

Matthiesen, Toby. *The Caliph and the Imam: The Making of Sunnism and Shiism*. Oxford: Oxford University Press, 2023.

Maughan, Steven S. *Mighty England Do Good: Culture, Faith, Empire, and World in the Foreign Missions of the Church of England, 1850–1915*. Grand Rapids: Eerdmans, 2014.

Mazurek, Lindsey. *Isis in a Global Empire: Greek Identity through Egyptian Religion in Roman Greece*. Cambridge: Cambridge University Press, 2022.

McGrath, Ann, and Lynette Russell, eds. *The Routledge Companion to Global Indigenous History*. Abingdon, UK: Routledge, 2022.

McHale, Shawn Frederick. *Print and Power: Confucianism, Communism, and Buddhism in the Making of Modern Vietnam*. Honolulu: University of Hawai'i Press, 2004.

McIntyre, W. David. *Winding Up the British Empire in the Pacific Islands*. Oxford History of the British Empire Companion Series. Oxford: Oxford University Press, 2014.

McKitterick, Rosamond. *Rome and the Invention of the Papacy: The "Liber Pontificalis."* Cambridge: Cambridge University Press, 2020.

McLaughlin, Raoul. *The Roman Empire and the Silk Routes: The Ancient World Economy and the Empires of Parthia, Central Asia and Han China*. Barnsley, South Yorkshire: Pen & Sword History, 2016.

McLeod, Hugh, ed. *World Christianities c.1914–c.2000*. Vol. 9 of *The Cambridge History of Christianity*. New York: Cambridge University Press, 2006.

McLeod, John, ed. *The Routledge Companion to Postcolonial Studies*. Abingdon, UK: Routledge, 2007.

McNair, Amy. *Donors of Longmen: Faith, Politics, and Patronage in Medieval Chinese Buddhist Sculpture*. Honolulu: University of Hawai'i Press, 2007.

McShea, Bronwen. *Apostles of Empire: The Jesuits and New France*. Lincoln: University of Nebraska, 2019.

Meador, Betty De Shong, ed. *Inanna, Lady of Largest Heart: Poems of the Sumerian High Priestess Enheduanna*. Austin: University of Texas Press, 2000.

Mehta, Nitin. "A Nation Born Out of Sanskrit, and Still in Love with It." *Daily Guardian* (India), October 17, 2020.

Meijer, Roel, ed. *Global Salafism: Islam's New Religious Movement*. New York: Oxford University Press, 2013.

Mendelson, E. Michael. *Sangha and State in Burma*. Ithaca, N.Y.: Cornell University Press, 1975.

Merati, Simona E. *Muslims in Putin's Russia: Discourse on Identity, Politics, and Security*. Cham, Switzerland: Palgrave Macmillan, 2017.

Merdinger, J. E. *Rome and the African Church in the Time of Augustine*. New Haven, Conn.: Yale University Press, 1997.

Metcalf, Barbara Daly. *Islamic Revival in British India: Deoband, 1860–1900*. Princeton, N.J.: Princeton University Press, 1982.

Metcalf, Thomas R. *Imperial Connections: India in the Indian Ocean Arena, 1860–1920*. Berkeley: University of California Press, 2007.

Middelaar, Luuk van. *The Passage to Europe: How a Continent Became a Union*. New Haven, Conn.: Yale University Press, 2020.

Mikhail, Alan. *God's Shadow: Sultan Selim, His Ottoman Empire, and the Making of the Modern World*. New York: Liveright, 2020.

Miksic, John N., and Geok Yian Goh. *Ancient Southeast Asia*. London: Routledge, 2017.

Miller, Todd. *Empire of Borders: The Expansion of the US Border around the World*. London: Verso, 2019.

Milton, John. "On the Morning of Christ's Nativity." Poetry Foundation. https://www.poetryfoundation.org/poems/44735/on-the-morning-of-christs-nativity.

Minamiki, George. *The Chinese Rites Controversy: From Its Beginning to Modern Times*. Chicago: Loyola University Press, 1985.

Mishkova, Diana. *Rival Byzantiums: Empire and Identity in Southeastern Europe*. Cambridge: Cambridge University Press, 2023.

Mishra, Pankaj. *From the Ruins of Empire: The Intellectuals Who Remade Asia*. New York: Farrar, Straus and Giroux, 2012.

Mitchell, Donald W., and Sarah H. Jacoby. *Buddhism: Introducing the Buddhist Experience*. 3rd ed. New York: Oxford University Press, 2013.

Mitchell, Margaret M., and Frances M. Young, eds. *Origins to Constantine*. Vol. 1 of *The Cambridge History of Christianity*. New York: Cambridge University Press, 2006.

Moghissi, Haideh, Saeed Rahnema, and Mark J. Goodman. *Diaspora by Design: Muslims in Canada and Beyond*. Toronto: University of Toronto Press, 2009.

Montefiore, Simon Sebag. *The Romanovs: 1613–1918*. London: Weidenfeld & Nicolson, 2016.

Moore, Grace. *Dickens and Empire: Discourses of Class, Race and Colonialism in the Works of Charles Dickens*. Abingdon, UK: Routledge, 2004.

Morgan, David O., and Anthony Reid, eds. *The Eastern Islamic World, Eleventh to Eighteenth Centuries*. Vol 3. of Cook, *The New Cambridge History of Islam*.

Morris, Jan. *Pax Britannica: The Climax of an Empire*. New York: Harcourt, Brace & World, 1968.

Morrison, Alexander. *The Russian Conquest of Central Asia: A Study in Imperial Expansion, 1814–1914*. New York: Cambridge University Press, 2020.

Morrow, John Andrew. *The Covenants of the Prophet Muhammad with the Christians of the World*. Tacoma, Wash.: Angelico Press / Sophia Perennis, 2013.

Motadel, David, ed. *Islam and the European Empires*. New York: Oxford University Press, 2014.

Moya, José, ed. *Atlantic Crossroads: Webs of Migration, Culture and Politics between Europe, Africa, and the Americas, 1800–2020*. Abingdon, UK: Routledge, 2021.

Moyd, Michelle R. *Violent Intermediaries: African Soldiers, Conquest, and Everyday Colonialism in German East Africa*. Athens: Ohio University Press, 2014.

Mugane, John M. "The Story of How Swahili Became Africa's Most Spoken Language." *Conversation*, February 20, 2022. https://theconversation.com/the-story-of-how-swahili-became-africas-most-spoken-language-177259.

Mukherjee, Rila, and Radhika Seshan, eds. *Indian Ocean Histories: The Many Worlds of Michael Naylor Pearson*. New York: Routledge, 2020.

Münkler, Herfried. *Empires: The Logic of World Domination from Ancient Rome to the United States*. London: Polity, 2007.

Murphy, Tessa. *The Creole Archipelago: Race and Borders in the Colonial Caribbean*. Philadelphia: University of Pennsylvania Press, 2021.

Murray, Chris. *China from the Ruins of Athens and Rome: Classics, Sinology, and Romanticism, 1793–1938*. New York: Oxford University Press, 2020.

Murti, G. Srinivasa, and A. N. Krishna Aiyangar, eds. *Edicts of Aśoka (Priyadarśin) with English Translation*. 2nd ed. Adyar: Adyar Library, 1951.

Mutschler, Fritz-Heiner, and Achim Mittag, eds. *Conceiving the Empire: China and Rome Compared.* New York: Oxford University Press, 2008.

Naranch, Bradley, and Geoff Eley, eds. *German Colonialism in a Global Age.* Durham, N.C.: Duke University Press, 2014.

Nash, Elizabeth. *Seville, Córdoba, and Granada: A Cultural History.* New York: Oxford University Press, 2005.

Nath, Pratyay. *Climate of Conquest: War, Environment, and Empire in Mughal North India.* New York: Oxford University Press, 2019.

Nathan, Mark A. *From the Mountains to the Cities: A History of Buddhist Propagation in Modern Korea.* Honolulu: University of Hawai'i Press, 2018.

Natif, Mika. *Mughal Occidentalism: Artistic Encounters between Europe and Asia at the Courts of India, 1580–1630.* Leiden: Brill, 2018.

Nayar, Kamala Elizabeth. *The Punjabis in British Columbia: Location, Labour, First Nations, and Multiculturalism.* Montreal: McGill-Queen's University Press, 2012.

Nead, Lynda. "The Secret of England's Greatness." *Journal of Victorian Culture* 19 (2014): 161–82.

Nedostup, Rebecca. *Superstitious Regimes: Religion and the Politics of Chinese Modernity.* Cambridge, Mass.: Harvard University Press, 2009.

Neelis, Jason. *Early Buddhist Transmission and Trade Networks: Mobility and Exchange within and beyond the Northwestern Borderlands of South Asia.* Leiden: Brill, 2011.

Neill, Stephen. *Colonialism and Christian Missions.* New York: McGraw-Hill, 1966.

Newman, Andrew J. *Safavid Iran: Rebirth of a Persian Empire.* London: I. B. Tauris, 2006.

Ngai, Mae. *The Chinese Question: The Gold Rushes and Global Politics.* New York: Norton, 2021.

Nichols, Deborah L., and Enrique Rodríguez-Alegría, eds. *The Oxford Handbook of the Aztecs.* New York: Oxford University Press, 2017.

Noble, Thomas F. X., and Julia M. H. Smith, eds. *Early Medieval Christianities, c.600–c.1100.* Vol. 3 of *The Cambridge History of Christianity.* New York: Cambridge University Press, 2008.

Nongbri, Brent. *Before Religion: A History of a Modern Concept.* New Haven, Conn.: Yale University Press, 2013.

Noor, Farish A., and Peter Carey, eds. *Racial Difference and the Colonial Wars of 19th Century Southeast Asia.* Amsterdam: Amsterdam University Press, 2021.

Norman, Kenneth Roy. *Pali Literature.* Wiesbaden: Otto Harrassowitz, 1983.

Norton, Claire. *Conversion and Islam in the Early Modern Mediterranean: The Lure of the Other.* New York: Routledge, 2017.

Norwich, John Julius. *Venice: The Rise to Empire.* London: Allen Lane, 1977.

O'Neill, Kelly. *Claiming Crimea: A History of Catherine the Great's Southern Empire.* New Haven, Conn.: Yale University Press, 2017.

Ober, Douglas. *Dust on the Throne: The Search for Buddhism in Modern India.* Stanford, Calif.: Stanford University Press, 2023.

Obeyesekere, Gananath. *The Buddha in Sri Lanka: Histories and Stories.* London: Routledge, 2018.

———. *Cannibal Talk: The Man-Eating Myth and Human Sacrifice in the South Seas.* Berkeley: University of California Press, 2005.

Office for National Statistics. "Ethnic Group, England and Wales: Census 2021." https://www.ons.gov.uk/peoplepopulationandcommunity/culturalidentity/ethnicity/bulletins/ethnicgroupenglandandwales/census2021.

Office of International Religious Freedom. *2021 Report on International Religious Freedom: Guyana*. June 2, 2022. https://www.state.gov/reports/2021-report-on-international-religious-freedom/guyana/.

Oldfield, J. R. *Transatlantic Abolitionism in the Age of Revolution: An International History of Anti-slavery, c.1787–1820*. New York: Cambridge University Press, 2013.

Olivelle, Patrick, Janice Leoshko, and Himanshu Prabha Ray, eds. *Reimagining Aśoka: Memory and History*. New Delhi: Oxford University Press, 2012.

Olmos, Margarite Fernández, and Lizabeth Paravisini-Gebert. *Creole Religions of the Caribbean: An Introduction*. 3rd ed. New York: New York University Press, 2022.

Omissi, David. *The Sepoy and the Raj: The Indian Army, 1860–1940*. Studies in Military and Strategic History. Houndmills, UK: Macmillan, 1994.

Oonk, Gijsbert, ed. *Global Indian Diasporas: Exploring Trajectories of Migration and Theory*. Amsterdam: Amsterdam University Press, 2007.

Ostler, Nicholas. *Empires of the Word: A Language History of the World*. New York: Harper Collins, 2010.

Overy, Richard. *Blood and Ruins: The Great Imperial War 1931–1945*. London: Allen Lane, 2021.

———. *Blood and Ruins: The Last Imperial War 1931–1945*. New York: Viking, 2022.

Owens, Sarah E. *Nuns Navigating the Spanish Empire*. Albuquerque: University of New Mexico Press, 2017.

Oye, David Schimmelpenninck van der. *Russian Orientalism: Asia in the Russian Mind from Peter the Great to the Emigration*. New Haven, Conn.: Yale University Press, 2010.

Paine, Thomas. *Common Sense*. New York: P. Eckler, 1918.

Pankhurst, Reza. *The Inevitable Caliphate? A History of the Struggle for Global Islamic Union, 1924 to the Present*. London: Hurst, 2013.

Papaconstantinou, Arietta, Neil McLynn, and Daniel L. Schwartz, eds. *Conversion in Late Antiquity: Christianity, Islam, and Beyond; Papers from the Andrew W. Mellon Foundation Sawyer Seminar, University of Oxford, 2009–2010*. Burlington, Vt.: Ashgate, 2015.

Paquette, Gabriel. *The European Seaborne Empires: From the Thirty Years' War to the Age of Revolutions*. New Haven, Conn.: Yale University Press, 2019.

Parker, Charles H. *Global Calvinism: Conversion and Commerce in the Dutch Empire, 1600–1800*. New York: Oxford University Press, 2022.

Parker, Matthew. *One Fine Day: Britain's Empire on the Brink: September 29, 1923*. London: Public Affairs, 2023.

Parry, Jonathan. *Promised Lands: The British and the Ottoman Middle East*. Princeton, N.J.: Princeton University Press, 2022.

Paton, Diana. *The Cultural Politics of Obeah: Religion, Colonialism and Modernity in the Caribbean World*. New York: Cambridge University Press, 2015.

Patterson, Jessica. *Religion, Enlightenment and Empire: British Interpretations of Hinduism in the Eighteenth Century*. New York: Cambridge University Press, 2022.

Payne, Richard E. *A State of Mixture: Christians, Zoroastrians, and Iranian Political Culture in Late Antiquity*. Oakland: University of California Press, 2015.

Peacock, A. C. S., ed. *Islamisation: Comparative Perspectives from History*. Edinburgh: Edinburgh University Press, 2017.

Peacock, A. C. S., Bruno De Nicola, and Sara Nur Yıldız. *Islam and Christianity in Medieval Anatolia*. Burlington, Vt.: Ashgate, 2015.

Peacock, A. C. S., and Richard Piran McClary, eds. *Turkish History and Culture in India: Identity, Art and Transregional Connections*. Leiden: Brill, 2020.

Pellerin, Pascale, ed. *Les Lumières, l'esclavage et l'idéologie coloniale: XVIIIe–XXe siècles*. Paris: Classiques Garnier, 2020.

Penn, Michael Philip. *Envisioning Islam: Syriac Christianity and the Early Muslim World*. Philadelphia: University of Pennsylvania Press, 2015.

Perdue, Leo G., and Warren Carter. *Israel and Empire: A Postcolonial History of Israel and Early Judaism*. Edited by Coleman A. Baker. London: Bloomsbury T&T Clark, 2015.

Perdue, Peter. *China Marches West: The Qing Conquest of Central Eurasia*. Cambridge, Mass.: Belknap Press of Harvard University Press, 2005.

Perraudin, Michael, and Jürgen Zimmerer, with Katy Heady, eds. *German Colonialism and National Identity*. Abingdon, UK: Routledge, 2011.

Pestana, Carla. *Protestant Empire: Religion and the Making of the British Atlantic World*. Philadelphia: University of Pennsylvania Press, 2009.

Peterson, Joseph W. *Sacred Rivals: Catholic Missions and the Making of Islam in Nineteenth-Century France and Algeria*. New York: Oxford University Press, 2022.

Petkov, Kiril. *The Voices of Medieval Bulgaria, Seventh–Fifteenth Century: The Records of a Bygone Culture*. Leiden: Brill, 2008.

Petry, Carl F. *The Mamluk Sultanate: A History*. New York: Cambridge University Press, 2022.

Petry, Carl F., ed. *640–1517*. Vol. 1 of *The Cambridge History of Egypt*. New York: Cambridge University Press, 1998.

Phan, Peter C., ed. *Christianities in Asia*. Malden, Mass.: Wiley-Blackwell, 2011.

Phillips, Andrew. *How the East Was Won: Barbarian Conquerors, Universal Conquest and the Making of Modern Asia*. New York: Cambridge University Press, 2021.

Phillips, Andrew, and J. C. Sharman. *Outsourcing Empire: How Company-States Made the Modern World*. Princeton, N.J.: Princeton University Press, 2020.

Phillips, Mike, and Trevor Phillips. *Windrush: The Irresistible Rise of Multi-racial Britain*. London: HarperCollins, 1998.

Picard, Christophe. *Sea of the Caliphs: The Mediterranean in the Medieval Islamic World*. Cambridge, Mass.: Belknap Press of Harvard University Press, 2018.

Pine, Red. *The Heart Sutra: The Womb of Buddhas*. Washington, D.C.: Shoemaker & Hoard, 2004.

Pines, Yuri, Michal Biran, and Jörg Rüpke, eds. *The Limits of Universal Rule: Eurasian Empires Compared*. New York: Cambridge University Press, 2021.

Pittock, Murray. *Scotland: The Global History; 1603 to the Present*. New Haven, Conn.: Yale University Press, 2022.

Plokhy, Serhii. *The Russo-Ukrainian War: The Return of History*. New York: Norton, 2023.

Pohl, John M. D., and Claire L. Lyons, eds. *Altera Roma: Art and Empire from Mérida to México*. Los Angeles: Cotsen Institute of Archaeology Press, 2016.

Polk, William R. *Crusade and Jihad: The Thousand-Year War between the Muslim World and the Global North*. New Haven, Conn.: Yale University Press, 2018.

Pollard, Justin, and Howard Reid. *The Rise and Fall of Alexandria*. New York: Penguin Books, 2007.

Pongratz-Leisten, Beate. *Religion and Ideology in Assyria*. Berlin: De Gruyter, 2015.

Poo, Mu-chou, H. A. Drake, and Lisa Raphals, eds. *Old Society, New Belief: Religious Transformation of China and Rome, ca. 1st–6th Centuries*. New York: Oxford University Press, 2017.

Porter, Andrew. *Religion versus Empire? British Protestant Missionaries and Overseas Expansion, 1700–1914*. Manchester: Manchester University Press, 2004.

Porter, Andrew, ed. *The Imperial Horizons of British Protestant Missions, 1880–1914: The Interplay of Representation and Experience*. Grand Rapids: Eerdmans, 2003.

Porter, Andrew, and Alaine Low, eds. *The Nineteenth Century*. Vol. 3 of Louis, *Oxford History of the British Empire*.

Porter, Bernard. *British Imperial: What the Empire Wasn't*. London: I. B. Tauris, 2015.

———. *Empire Ways: Aspects of British Imperialism*. London: I. B. Tauris, 2020.

Potts, D. T. *Mesopotamia, Iran and Arabia from the Seleucids to the Sasanians*. Farnham: Ashgate Variorum, 2010.

Potts, D. T., ed. *The Oxford Handbook of Ancient Iran*. New York: Oxford University Press, 2013.

Powers, John. *The Buddha Party: How the People's Republic of China Works to Define and Control Tibetan Buddhism*. New York: Oxford University Press, 2016.

Prakash, Amit. *Empire on the Seine: The Policing of North Africans in Paris, 1925–1975*. New York: Oxford University Press, 2022.

Prasad, Birendra Nath. *Rethinking Bihar and Bengal: History, Culture and Religion*. Abingdon, UK: Routledge, 2021.

Price, Jonathan J., Margalit Finkelberg, and Yuval Shahar, eds. *Rome: An Empire of Many Nations; New Perspectives on Ethnic Diversity and Cultural Identity*. New York: Cambridge University Press, 2022.

Price, Richard. *Empire and Indigeneity: Histories and Legacies*. London: Routledge, 2021.

Priestley, Herbert Ingram. *France Overseas: A Study of Modern Imperialism*. London: Taylor and Francis, 2018.

Prinsep, James. *Essays on Indian Antiquities, Historic, Numismatic, and Palaeographic*. New Delhi: Asian Educational Services, 1995.

Quinn, Sholeh A. *Persian Historiography across Empires: The Ottomans, Safavids, and Mughals*. New York: Cambridge University Press, 2021.

Radner, Karen, and Eleanor Robson, eds. *The Oxford Handbook of Cuneiform Culture*. New York: Oxford University Press, 2011.

Raffield, Ben. "Broken Worlds: Towards an Archaeology of the Shatter Zone." *Journal of Archaeological Method and Theory* 28 (2021): 871–910.

Rainsford, Sarah. "Putin and Peter the Great: Russian Leader Likens Himself to 18th Century Tsar." BBC News. June 10, 2022. https://www.bbc.com/news/world-europe-61767191.

Ramachandran, R. *A History of Hinduism: The Past, Present, and Future*. New Delhi: Sage India, 2018.

Ranjan, Amit, ed. *Partition of India: Postcolonial Legacies*. Abingdon, UK: Routledge, 2019.

Rankin, F. Harrison. *The White Man's Grave: A Visit to Sierra Leone, in 1834*. London: Richard Bentley, 1836.

Raphael, Lois A. C. *The Cape-to-Cairo Dream: A Study in British Imperialism*. New York: Columbia University Press, 1936.

Ray, Himanshu Prabha. *Coastal Shrines and Transnational Maritime Networks across India and Southeast Asia*. New York: Routledge, 2021.

Rediker, Marcus, Titas Chakraborty, and Matthias van Rossum, eds. *A Global History of Runaways: Workers, Mobility, and Capitalism 1600–1850*. Oakland: University of California Press, 2019.

Regan-Lefebvre, Jennifer. *Imperial Wine: How the British Empire Made Wine's New World*. Berkeley: University of California Press, 2022.

Reid, Walter. *Empire of Sand: How Britain Made the Middle East*. Edinburgh: Birlinn, 2011.

Restall, Matthew, Amara Solari, John F. Chuchiak IV, and Traci Ardren. *The Friar and the Maya: Diego de Landa and the Account of the Things of Yucatan*. Denver: University Press of Colorado, 2023.

Reybrouck, David van. *Congo: The Epic History of a People*. New York: Ecco, 2014.

Reynolds, Michael A. "Muslim Mobilization in Imperial Russia's Caucasus." In Motadel, *Islam and the European Empires*, 187–212.

Rezakhani, Khodadad. *ReOrienting the Sasanians: East Iran in Late Antiquity*. Edinburgh: Edinburgh University Press, 2017.

Rhodes, Alexandre de. *Histoire du Royaume du Tonkin*. Edited by Jean-Pierre Duteil. Paris: Kimé, 1999.

Richards, John F. *The Mughal Empire*. New York: Cambridge University Press, 1993.

Rieber, Alfred J. *The Struggle for the Eurasian Borderlands from the Rise of Early Modern Empires to the End of the First World War*. New York: Cambridge University Press, 2014.

Riley, Charlotte Lydia. *Imperial Island: A History of Empire in Modern Britain*. London: Bodley Head, 2023.

Rizzo, Tracey, and Steven Gerontakis. *Intimate Empires: Body, Race, and Gender in the Modern World*. New York: Oxford University Press, 2016.

Robert, Dana L., ed. *Converting Colonialism: Visions and Realities in Mission History, 1706–1914*. Grand Rapids: Eerdmans, 2008.

Roberts, Alasdair. *Superstates: Empires of the 21st Century*. Cambridge: Polity, 2023.

Roberts, Sophie B. *Citizenship and Antisemitism in French Colonial Algeria, 1870–1962*. New York: Cambridge University Press, 2017.

Robinson, Chase F., ed. *The Formation of the Islamic World, Sixth to Eleventh Centuries*. Vol. 1 of Cook, *The New Cambridge History of Islam*.

Robinson, Francis, ed. *The Islamic World in the Age of Western Dominance*. Vol. 5 of Cook, *New Cambridge History of Islam*.

Robson, Eleanor. *Ancient Knowledge Networks: A Social Geography of Cuneiform Scholarship in First-Millennium Assyria and Babylonia*. London: University College London Press, 2019.

Robson, Kathryn, and Jennifer Yee, eds. *France and "Indochina": Cultural Representations*. Lanham, Md.: Lexington Books, 2005.

Roebuck, Valerie J., ed. *The Dhammapada*. London: Penguin Classics, 2010.

Römer, Thomas. *The Invention of God*. Cambridge, Mass.: Harvard University Press, 2015.

Rose, Jenny. *Zoroastrianism: An Introduction*. London: I. B. Tauris, 2011.

Rössler, Mechtild, and Sabine Schleiermacher, eds. *Der "Generalplan Ost": Hauptlinien der nationalsozialistischen Planungs- und Vernichtungspolitik*. Berlin: Akademie Verlag, 1993.

Rothermund, Dietmar, ed. *Memories of Post-imperial Nations: The Aftermath of Decolonization, 1945–2013*. Cambridge: Cambridge University Press, 2015.

Roy, Olivier. *Holy Ignorance: When Religion and Culture Part Ways*. New York: Columbia University Press, 2010.

Rozen, Minna, ed. *Homeland and Diasporas: Greeks, Jews and Their Migrations*. London: I. B. Tauris, 2008.

Rubin, Miri, and Walter P. Simons, eds. *Christianity in Western Europe, c.1100–c.1500*. Vol. 4 of *The Cambridge History of Christianity*. New York: Cambridge University Press, 2009.

Rudbøg, Tim, and Erik Reenberg, eds. *Imagining the East: The Early Theosophical Society*. New York: Oxford University Press, 2020.

Rupert, Linda M. *Creolization and Contraband: Curaçao in the Early Modern Atlantic World*. Athens: University of Georgia Press, 2012.

Ruthven, Malise. *Islam in the World*. 3rd ed. New York: Oxford University Press, 2006.

Ryad, Umar. "Anti-Imperialism and the Pan-Islamic Movement." In Motadel, *Islam and the European Empires*, 131–49.

Sachs, William L. *Global Anglicanism, c.1910–2000*. Vol. 5 of Strong, *The Oxford History of Anglicanism*. New York: Oxford University Press, 2018.

Saha, Jonathan. *Colonizing Animals: Interspecies Empire in Myanmar*. Cambridge: Cambridge University Press, 2021.

Said, Edward W. *Orientalism*. New York: Vintage Books, 2003.

Salisbury, Joyce E. *The Blood of Martyrs: The Impact and Memory of Ancient Violence*. London: Taylor & Francis, 2004.

Salt, Jeremy. *The Last Ottoman Wars: The Human Cost, 1877–1923*. Salt Lake City: University of Utah Press, 2019.

Samaroo, Brinsley, Primnath Gooptar, and Kumar Mahabir, eds. *Global Indian Diaspora: Charting New Frontiers*. Vol. 1. Abingdon: Routledge, 2022.

Sánchez, Joseph P. *Pueblos, Plains and Province: New Mexico in the Seventeenth Century*. Denver: University Press of Colorado, 2021.

Sanghera, Sathnam. *Empireland: How Imperialism Has Shaped Modern Britain*. London: Viking, 2021.

Sanneh, Lamin. *Disciples of All Nations: Pillars of World Christianity*. New York: Oxford University Press, 2007.

Sanneh, Lamin, and Michael J. McClymond, eds. *The Wiley Blackwell Companion to World Christianity*. Hoboken, N.J.: Wiley-Blackwell, 2016.

Sarreal, Julia J. S. *The Guaraní and Their Missions: A Socioeconomic History*. Stanford, Calif.: Stanford University Press, 2014.

Sassoon, Joseph. *The Sassoons: The Great Global Merchants and the Making of an Empire*. New York: Pantheon, 2022.

Satia, Priya. *Time's Monster: History, Conscience and Britain's Empire*. London: Allen Lane, 2020.

Sattin, Anthony. *Nomads: The Wanderers Who Shaped Our World*. London: John Murray, 2022.

Sauer, Eberhard W. ed. *Sasanian Persia: Between Rome and the Steppes of Eurasia*. Edinburgh: Edinburgh University Press, 2017.

Scanlan, Padraic X. *Slave Empire: How Slavery Built Modern Britain*. London: Robinson, 2022.

Schiebinger, Londa. *Plants and Empire: Colonial Bioprospecting in the Atlantic World*. Cambridge, Mass.: Harvard University Press. 2004.

———. *Secret Cures of Slaves: People, Plants, and Medicine in the Eighteenth-Century Atlantic World*. Stanford, Calif.: Stanford University Press, 2017.

Schields, Chelsea, and Dagmar Herzog, eds. *The Routledge Companion to Sexuality and Colonialism*. London: Routledge, 2021.

Schlenther, B. "Religious Faith and Commercial Empire." In *The Eighteenth Century*, edited by P. J. Marshall. Vol. 2 of Louis, *The Oxford History of the British Empire*.

Schreiner, Olive. *Trooper Peter Halket of Mashonaland*. London: T. Fisher Unwin, 1897.

Schwartz, Seth. *The Ancient Jews from Alexander to Muhammad*. New York: Cambridge University Press, 2014.

Scully, Richard, and Andrekos Varnava, eds. *Comic Empires: Imperialism in Cartoons, Caricatures, and Satirical Art*. Manchester: Manchester University Press, 2020.

Seager, Richard Hughes. *The World's Parliament of Religions: The East/West Encounter, Chicago, 1893*. Bloomington: Indiana University Press, 1995.

Sèbe, Berny, and Matthew G. Stanard, eds. *Decolonising Europe? Popular Responses to the End of Empire*. Abingdon, UK: Routledge, 2020.

Second Vatican Council, "Nostra Aetate: Declaration on the Relationship of the Church to Non-Christian Religions." October 28, 1965. https://www.bc.edu/content/dam/files/research_sites/cjl/texts/cjrelations/resources/documents/catholic/Nostra_Aetate.htm.

Secunda, Shai. *The Iranian Talmud: Reading the Bavli in Its Sasanian Context*. Philadelphia: University of Pennsylvania Press, 2014.

Seeley, J. R. *The Expansion of England*. 1883. Cambridge University Press, 2010.

———. *The Expansion of England: Two Courses of Lectures*. London: Macmillan, 1914.

Sen, Colleen Taylor. *Ashoka and the Maura Dynasty: The History and Legacy of Ancient India's Greatest Empire*. London: Reaktion Books, 2022.

Sen, Tansen. *Buddhism, Diplomacy, and Trade: The Realignment of India-China Relations, 600–1400*. Lanham, Md.: Rowman & Littlefield, 2015.

Sensbach, Jon F. *Rebecca's Revival*. Cambridge, Mass.: Harvard University Press, 2005.

Shaked, Shaul. *From Zoroastrian Iran to Islam: Studies in Religious History and Intercultural Contacts*. Brookfield, Vt.: Variorum, 1995.

———. "Iranian Influence on Judaism." In Davies and Finkelstein, *Introduction: The Persian Period*, 308–25.

Shanguhyia, Martin S., and Toyin Falola, eds. *The Palgrave Handbook of African Colonial and Postcolonial History*. 2 vols. London: Palgrave Macmillan, 2018.

Sharma, Arvind. *Modern Hindu Thought: The Essential Texts*. New York: Oxford University Press, 2002.

Shawcross, Edward. *The Last Emperor of Mexico: A Disaster in the New World*. London: Faber, 2022.

Shelley, Percy Bysshe. "Ozymandias." Poetry Foundation. https://www.poetryfoundation.org/poems/46565/ozymandias.

Shepherd, David J., and Christopher J. H. Wright. *Ezra and Nehemiah*. Grand Rapids: Eerdmans, 2018.

Shipley, Graham. *The Greek World after Alexander*. New York: Routledge, 2000.

Simmonds, Stuart, and Simon Digby, eds. *The Royal Asiatic Society: Its History and Treasures*. Leiden: Brill, 1979.

Singh, Pashaura, ed. *Sikhism in Global Context*. New Delhi: Oxford University Press, 2011.

Singh, Surinder. *Medieval Panjab in Transition: Authority, Resistance and Spirituality c.1500–c.1700*. New York: Routledge, 2022.

Sirriyeh, Elizabeth. *Sufis and Anti-Sufis: The Defense, Rethinking and Rejection of Sufism in the Modern World*. London: Curzon, 1999.

Sivasundaram, Sujit. *Nature and the Godly Empire: Science and Evangelical Mission in the Pacific, 1795–1850*. New York: Cambridge University Press, 2005.

———. *Waves across the South: A New History of Revolution and Empire*. Chicago: University of Chicago Press, 2020.

Slight, John. *The British Empire and the Hajj, 1865–1956*. Cambridge, Mass.: Harvard University Press, 2015.

Smith, Andrew F. *Sugar: A Global History*. London: Reaktion Books, 2015.

Smith, Andrew W. M., and Chris Jeppesen, eds. *Britain, France and the Decolonization of Africa: Future Imperfect?* London: University College London Press, 2017.

Smith, Douglas, ed. *Love and Conquest: Personal Correspondence of Catherine the Great and Prince Grigory Potemkin*. DeKalb: Northern Illinois University Press, 2004.

Smith, Graham. ed. *The Nationalities Question in the Soviet Union*. 2nd ed. London: Longman, 1995.

Smith, Haig Z. *Religion and Governance in England's Emerging Colonial Empire, 1601–1698*. London: Palgrave Macmillan, 2022.

Smith, Kyle. *Constantine and the Captive Christians of Persia: Martyrdom and Religious Identity in Late Antiquity*. Oakland: University of California Press, 2016.

Smith, Mark S. *The Early History of God: Yahweh and the Other Deities in Ancient Israel*. Grand Rapids: Eerdmans, 2002.

———. *The Origins of Biblical Monotheism: Israel's Polytheistic Background and the Ugaritic Texts*. New ed. New York: Oxford University Press, 2003.

Snow, Philip. *China and Russia: Four Centuries of Conflict and Concord*. New Haven, Conn.: Yale University Press, 2023.

Snyder, Timothy. *Bloodlands: Europe between Hitler and Stalin*. New York: Basic Books, 2012.

Sources for the History of the School of Nisibis. Translated by Adam H. Becker. Liverpool: Liverpool University Press, 2008.

Spink, Walter. *Ajanta: History and Development; Defining Features*. Leiden: Koninklijke Brill, 2014.

Sprengling, Martin. *Third Century Iran, Sapor and Kartir*. Chicago: Oriental Institute, 1953.

Stähle, Hanna. *Russian Church in the Digital Era: Mediatization of Orthodoxy*. New York: Routledge, 2021.

Stančo, Ladislav. *Greek Gods in the East: Hellenistic Iconographic Schemes in Central Asia*. Prague: Karolinum Press, 2012.

Stanley, Brian. *The Bible and the Flag: Protestant Missions and British Imperialism in the Nineteenth and Twentieth Centuries*. Leicester: Apollos, 1990.

———. *Christianity in the Twentieth Century: A World History*. Princeton, N.J.: Princeton University Press, 2018.

———. "Christian Missions, Antislavery and the Claims of Humanity, c.1813–1873." In Gilley and Stanley, *World Christianities c.1815–c.1914*, 443–57.

Starr, S. Frederick. *Lost Enlightenment: Central Asia's Golden Age from the Arab Conquest to Tamerlane*. Princeton, N.J.: Princeton University Press, 2013.

Stausberg, Michael, and Yuhan Sohrab-Dinshaw Vevaina, eds. *The Wiley Blackwell Companion to Zoroastrianism*. Hoboken, N.J.: John Wiley & Sons, 2015.

Stavrakopoulou, Francesca, and John Barton, eds. *Religious Diversity in Ancient Israel and Judah*. New York: Continuum, 2010.

Steiner, Benjamin. *Building the French Empire, 1600–1800: Colonialism and Material Culture*. Manchester: Manchester University Press, 2020.

Stern, Philip J. *Empire, Incorporated: The Corporations That Built British Colonialism*. Cambridge, Mass.: Harvard University Press, 2023.

Stökl, Jonathan, and Caroline Waerzeggers, eds. *Exile and Return*. Boston: De Gruyter, 2015.

Stone, Erin Woodruff. *Captives of Conquest: Slavery in the Early Modern Spanish Caribbean*. Philadelphia: University of Pennsylvania Press, 2021.

Stone, Jon R., ed. *The Essential Max Müller: On Language, Mythology, and Religion*. New York: Palgrave Macmillan, 2002.

Stoneman, Richard. *The Greek Experience of India: From Alexander to the Indo-Greeks*. Princeton, N.J.: Princeton University Press, 2019.

———. *Megasthenes' Indica: A New Translation of the Fragments with Commentary*. London: Routledge, 2021.

Storm, Jason Ananda Josephson. *The Invention of Religion in Japan*. Chicago: University of Chicago Press, 2012.

Story, Joanna. *Charlemagne and Rome: Alcuin and the Epitaph of Pope Hadrian I*. Oxford: Oxford University Press, 2023.

Stoyanov, Yuri. *The Other God: Dualist Religions from Antiquity to the Cathar Heresy*. New Haven, Conn.: Yale Nota Bene, 2000.

Streets-Salter, Heather. *Martial Races: The Military, Race, and Masculinity in British Imperial Culture, 1857–1914*. Manchester: Manchester University Press, 2004.

Streets-Salter, Heather, and Trevor R. Getz. *Empires and Colonies in the Modern World: A Global Perspective*. New York: Oxford University Press, 2015.

Streusand, Douglas E. *Islamic Gunpowder Empires: Ottomans, Safavids, and Mughals*. Boulder, Colo.: Westview Press, 2011.

Strong, John S. *The Buddha's Tooth: Western Tales of a Sri Lankan Relic*. Chicago: University of Chicago Press, 2021.

——. *Buddhisms: An Introduction*. London: Oneworld, 2015.

Strong, Rowan. *Anglicanism and the British Empire c. 1700–1850*. New York: Oxford University Press, 2007.

Strong, Rowan, ed. *Partisan Anglicanism and Its Global Expansion, 1829–c.1914*. Vol. 3 of Strong, *The Oxford History of Anglicanism*. New York: Oxford University Press, 2017.

Strong, Rowan, gen. ed. *The Oxford History of Anglicanism*. New York: Oxford University Press, 2017–.

Strootman, Rolf, Floris van den Eijnde, and Roy van Wijk, eds. *Empires of the Sea: Maritime Power Networks in World History*. Leiden: Brill, 2020.

Studdert-Kennedy, Gerald. *Providence and the Raj: Imperial Mission and Missionary Imperialism*. Walnut Creek, Calif.: Altamira, 1998.

Subin, Anna Della. *Accidental Gods: On Men Unwittingly Turned Divine*. New York: Macmillan, 2021.

Subrahmanyam, Sanjay. *Empires between Islam and Christianity, 1500–1800*. Albany: SUNY Press, 2019.

Sugirtharajah, R. S. *Jesus in Asia*. Cambridge, Mass.: Harvard University Press, 2018.

Sullivan, Brenton. *Building a Religious Empire: Tibetan Buddhism, Bureaucracy, and the Rise of the Gelukpa*. Philadelphia: University of Pennsylvania Press, 2020.

Suranyi, Anna. *Indentured Servitude: Unfree Labour and Citizenship in the British Colonies*. Montreal: McGill-Queen's University Press, 2021.

Tacitus, Cornelius. *De vita Iulii Agricolae*. Edited by Henry Furneaux. Oxford: Clarendon Press, 1900. http://www.perseus.tufts.edu/hopper/text?doc=Perseus%3Atext%3A1999.02.0084%3Achapter%3D30%3Asection%3D6.

Tagliacozzo, Eric. "The Dutch Empire and the Hajj." In Motadel, *Islam and the European Empires*, 73–89.

——. *In Asian Waters: Oceanic Worlds from Yemen to Yokohama*. Princeton, N.J.: Princeton University Press, 2022.

——. *The Longest Journey: Southeast Asians and the Pilgrimage to Mecca*. Oxford: Oxford University Press, 2013.

Tavarez, David, ed. *Words and Worlds Turned Around: Indigenous Christianities in Colonial Latin America*. Denver: University Press of Colorado, 2017.

Taylor, Philip Meadows. *Confessions of a Thug*. 1839; London: Richard Bentley, 1858.

Thapar, Romila. *Asoka and the Decline of the Mauryas*. 3rd ed. New York: Oxford University Press, 2012.

——. *Somanatha: The Many Voices of a History*. London: Verso, 2005.

Tharoor, Shashi. *Inglorious Empire: What the British Did to India*. London: Hurst, 2017.

Thomas, Hugh. *World without End: Spain, Philip II, and the First Global Empire*. New York: Random House, 2014.

Thomas, Martin, and Andrew Thompson, eds. *The Oxford Handbook of the Ends of Empire*. New York: Oxford University Press, 2018.

Thompson, Jon, and Sheila R. Canby, eds. *Hunt for Paradise: Court Arts of Safavid Iran, 1501–1576*. Milan: Skira; London: Thames & Hudson, 2003.

Thonemann, Peter. *The Hellenistic Age*. New York: Oxford University Press, 2016.

Thoreau, Henry David. *Walden*. New York: Oxford University Press, 1999.

Thorne, Susan. "Religion and Empire at Home." In *At Home with the Empire: Metropolitan Culture and the Imperial World*, edited by Catherine Hall and Sonya O. Rose, 143–65. New York: Cambridge University Press, 2006.

Thubron, Colin. *The Amur River: Between Russia and China*. New York: Harper, 2021.

Tiwary, Nishant. *Celebrating Bihar: The Heritage of Nalanda*. New Delhi: Oxford University Press, 2014.

Tritton, A. S. *The Caliphs and Their Non-Muslim Subjects: A Critical Study of the Covenant of 'Umar*. London: Routledge, 2008.

Truschke, Audrey. *Aurangzeb: The Life and Legacy of India's Most Controversial King*. Stanford, Calif.: Stanford University Press, 2017.

Tsetskhladze, Gocha R., ed. *Greek Colonisation: An Account of Greek Colonies and Other Settlements Overseas*. Leiden: Brill, 2006.

Tuna, Mustafa. *Imperial Russia's Muslims: Islam, Empire and European Modernity, 1788–1914*. New York: Cambridge University Press, 2015.

Turner, Alicia. *Saving Buddhism: The Impermanence of Religion in Colonial Burma*. Honolulu: University of Hawai'i Press, 2014.

Tyson, Craig W., and Virginia R. Herrmann, eds. *Imperial Peripheries in the Neo-Assyrian Period*. Louisville: University Press of Colorado, 2018.

Van Hove, Alphonse. "Diocese." *The Catholic Encyclopedia*. Vol. 5. New York: Robert Appleton Company, 1909. http://www.newadvent.org/cathen/05001a.htm.

Van Steenbergen, Jo. *A History of the Islamic World, 600–1800: Empire, Dynastic Formations, and Heterogeneities in Pre-modern Islamic West-Asia*. New York: Routledge, 2021.

Vanthemsche, Guy. *Belgium and the Congo, 1885–1980*. New York: Cambridge University Press, 2012.

Veevers, David. *The Great Defiance*. London: Ebury Press, 2023.

Vélez, Karin. *The Miraculous Flying House of Loreto: Spreading Catholicism in the Early Modern World*. Princeton, N.J.: Princeton University Press, 2018.

Veracini, Lorenzo. *Colonialism: A Global History*. New York: Routledge, 2023.

Vergil. *Bucolics, Aeneid, and Georgics of Vergil*. Edited by J. B. Greenough. Boston: Ginn, 1900. https://www.perseus.tufts.edu/hopper/text?doc=Perseus%3Atext%3A1999.02.0055%3Abook%3D6%3Acard%3D801.

Vidal, Cécile. *Caribbean New Orleans: Empire, Race, and the Making of a Slave Society*. Chapel Hill: University of North Carolina Press, 2019.

Vidas, Moulie. *Tradition and the Formation of the Talmud*. Princeton, N.J.: Princeton University Press, 2014.

Vikør, Knut S. "Religious Revolts in Colonial North Africa." In Motadel, *Islam and the European Empires*, 170–86.

Vilaça, Helena, Enzo Pace, Inger Furseth, and Per Pettersson, eds. *The Changing Soul of Europe: Religions and Migrations in Northern and Southern Europe*. Burlington, Vt.: Ashgate, 2014.

Vivekananda, Swami. Letter to Francis Leggett. July 6, 1896. https://www.swamivivekananda.guru/2017/06/20/6th-july-1896/.

Wagner, Kim A. *Thuggee: Banditry and the British in Early Nineteenth-Century India*. London: Palgrave Macmillan, 2007.

Wainwright, Geoffrey. *Lesslie Newbigin: A Theological Life*. New York: Oxford University Press, 2000.

Walbank, F. W., A. E. Astin, M. W. Fredriksen, and R. M. Ogilvie, eds. *The Hellenistic World*. 2nd ed. Vol. 7, pt. 1 of *The Cambridge Ancient History*. New York: Cambridge University Press, 1984.

Waldstein, Maxim, and Sanna Turoma, eds. *Empire De/Centered: New Spatial Histories of Russia and the Soviet Union*. Abingdon, UK: Routledge, 2013.

Wallace, Alfred. *The Malay Archipelago: The Land of the Orang-Utan and the Bird of Paradise*. Vol. 1. London: Macmillan, 1869.

Walls, Jerry L., ed. *The Oxford Handbook of Eschatology*. New York: Oxford University Press, 2008.

Walter, Michael. *Buddhism and Empire: The Political and Religious Culture of Early Tibet*. Leiden: Brill, 2009.

Walvin, James. *A World Transformed: Slavery in the Americas and the Origins of Global Power*. Oakland: University of California Press, 2022.

Wang, Dong. *China's Unequal Treaties: Narrating National History*. Lanham, Md.: Lexington Books, 2005.

Ward, Kevin. *A History of Global Anglicanism*. New York: Cambridge University Press, 2006.

Waterfield, Robin. *Taken at the Flood: The Roman Conquest of Greece*. New York: Oxford University Press, 2014.

Waters, Matt. *Ancient Persia: A Concise History of the Achaemenid Empire, 550–330 BCE*. New York: Cambridge University Press, 2014.

———. *King of the World: The Life of Cyrus the Great*. Oxford: Oxford University Press, 2022.

Welch, Stuart Cary. *A King's Book of Kings: The Shah-Nameh of Shah Tahmasp*. New York: Metropolitan Museum of Art, 1972.

Welsch, Christina. *The Company's Sword: The East India Company and the Politics of Militarism, 1644–1858*. New York: Cambridge University Press, 2022.

Wenger, Tisa, and Sylvester A. Johnson, eds. *Religion and US Empire: Critical New Histories*. New York: New York University Press, 2022.

Westerhoff, Jan. *The Golden Age of Indian Buddhist Philosophy*. New York: Oxford University Press, 2018.

Weston, Frank. *The Serfs of Great Britain*. London: W Knott, 1920.

Wheeler, Mortimer. *Civilizations of the Indus Valley and Beyond*. New York: McGraw-Hill, 1966.

White, Daniel E. *From Little London to Little Bengal: Religion, Print, and Modernity in Early British India, 1793–1835*. Baltimore: Johns Hopkins University Press, 2013.

White, Owen, and J. P. Daughton, eds. *In God's Empire*. New York: Oxford University Press, 2012.

Whitfield, Susan. *Life along the Silk Road*. 2nd ed. Oakland: University of California Press, 2015.

———. *Silk, Slaves, and Stupas: Material Culture of the Silk Road*. Oakland: University of California Press, 2018.

Wickham, Chris. *Framing the Early Middle Ages: Europe and the Mediterranean 400–800*. Oxford: Oxford University Press, 2005.

Wilkinson, Callie. *Empire of Influence: The East India Company and the Making of Indirect Rule*. Cambridge: Cambridge University Press, 2023.

Williams, Brian Glyn. *The Crimean Tatars: From Soviet Genocide to Putin's Conquest*. New York: Oxford University Press, 2016.
Wilson, Jon. *India Conquered: Britain's Raj and the Chaos of Empire*. New York: Simon and Schuster, 2016.
Wilson, Thomas M., and Hastings Donnan, eds. *A Companion to Border Studies*. Malden, Mass: Wiley-Blackwell, 2012.
Wimbush, Vincent L. *White Men's Magic: Scripturalization as Slavery*. New York: Oxford University Press, 2012.
Wolff, Larry. *The Idea of Galicia: History and Fantasy in Habsburg Political Culture*. Stanford, Calif.: Stanford University Press, 2010.
Wolters, O. W. *The Fall of Śrīvijaya in Malay History*. Ithaca, N.Y.: Cornell University Press, 1970.
Wong, Dorothy C., and Gustav Heldt, eds. *China and beyond in the Mediaeval Period: Cultural Crossings and Inter-regional Connections*. New Delhi: Manohar; Amherst, N.Y.: Cambria Press, 2014.
Wootton, Janet, ed. *Women in Christianity in the Age of Empire (1800–1920)*. London: Routledge, 2022.
Worthington, Ian. *Ptolemy I: King and Pharaoh of Egypt*. New York: Oxford University Press, 2016.
Wriggins, Sally Hovey. *Xuanzang: A Buddhist Pilgrim on the Silk Road*. Boulder, Colo.: Westview Press, 1996.
Wright, Louis B. *Religion and Empire: The Alliance between Piety and Commerce in English Expansion, 1558–1625*. 1943; New York: Octagon Books, 1965.
Wright-Carr, David Charles, and Francisco Marco Simón, eds. *From Ancient Rome to Colonial Mexico: Religious Globalization in the Context of Empire*. Denver: University Press of Colorado, 2023.
Wu, Lan. *Common Ground: Tibetan Buddhist Expansion and Qing China's Inner Asia*. New York: Columbia University Press, 2022.
Yarshater, Ehsan, ed. *The Seleucid, Parthian and Sasanid Periods*. Vol. 3, 2 pts. (numbered consecutively) of *The Cambridge History of Iran*. New York: Cambridge University Press, 1983.
Yavuz, M. Hakan. *Erdoğan: The Making of an Autocrat*. Edinburgh: Edinburgh University Press, 2021.
Yee, Jennifer. *The Colonial Comedy: Imperialism in the French Realist Novel*. New York: Oxford University Press, 2016.
———. *Exotic Subversions in Nineteenth-Century French Fiction*. Leeds, England: Legenda, 2008.
Yian, Goh Geok, John N. Miksic, and Michael Aung-Thwin, eds. *Bagan and the World: Early Myanmar and Its Global Connections*. Singapore: ISEAS—Yusof Ishak Institute, 2018.
Yonglin, Jiang. *The Mandate of Heaven and the Great Ming Code*. Seattle: University of Washington Press, 2011.
Yumiko, Ishihama, and Alex McKay, eds. *The Early 20th Century Resurgence of the Tibetan Buddhist World: Studies in Central Asian Buddhism*. Amsterdam: Amsterdam University Press, 2021.
Yürekli, Zeynep. *Architecture and Hagiography in the Ottoman Empire: The Politics of Bektashi Shrines in the Classical Age*. Burlington, Vt.: Ashgate, 2012.

Zaalberg, Thijs Brocades, and Bart Luttikhuis, eds. *Empire's Violent End: Comparing Dutch, British, and French Wars of Decolonization, 1945–1962*. Ithaca, N.Y.: Cornell University Press, 2022.

Zaborowski, Jason R. *The Coptic Martyrdom of John of Phanijōit: Assimilation and Conversion to Islam in Thirteenth-Century Egypt*. Leiden: Brill, 2005.

Zarakol, Ayşe. *Before the West: The Rise and Fall of Eastern World Orders*. New York: Cambridge University Press, 2022.

Zoellner, Tom. *Island on Fire: The Revolt That Ended Slavery in the British Empire*. Cambridge, Mass.: Harvard University Press, 2020.

Zurlo, Gina A. *Global Christianity: A Guide to the World's Largest Religion from Afghanistan to Zimbabwe*. Grand Rapids: Zondervan, 2022.

Index